To Mary and Clare
with all our love.

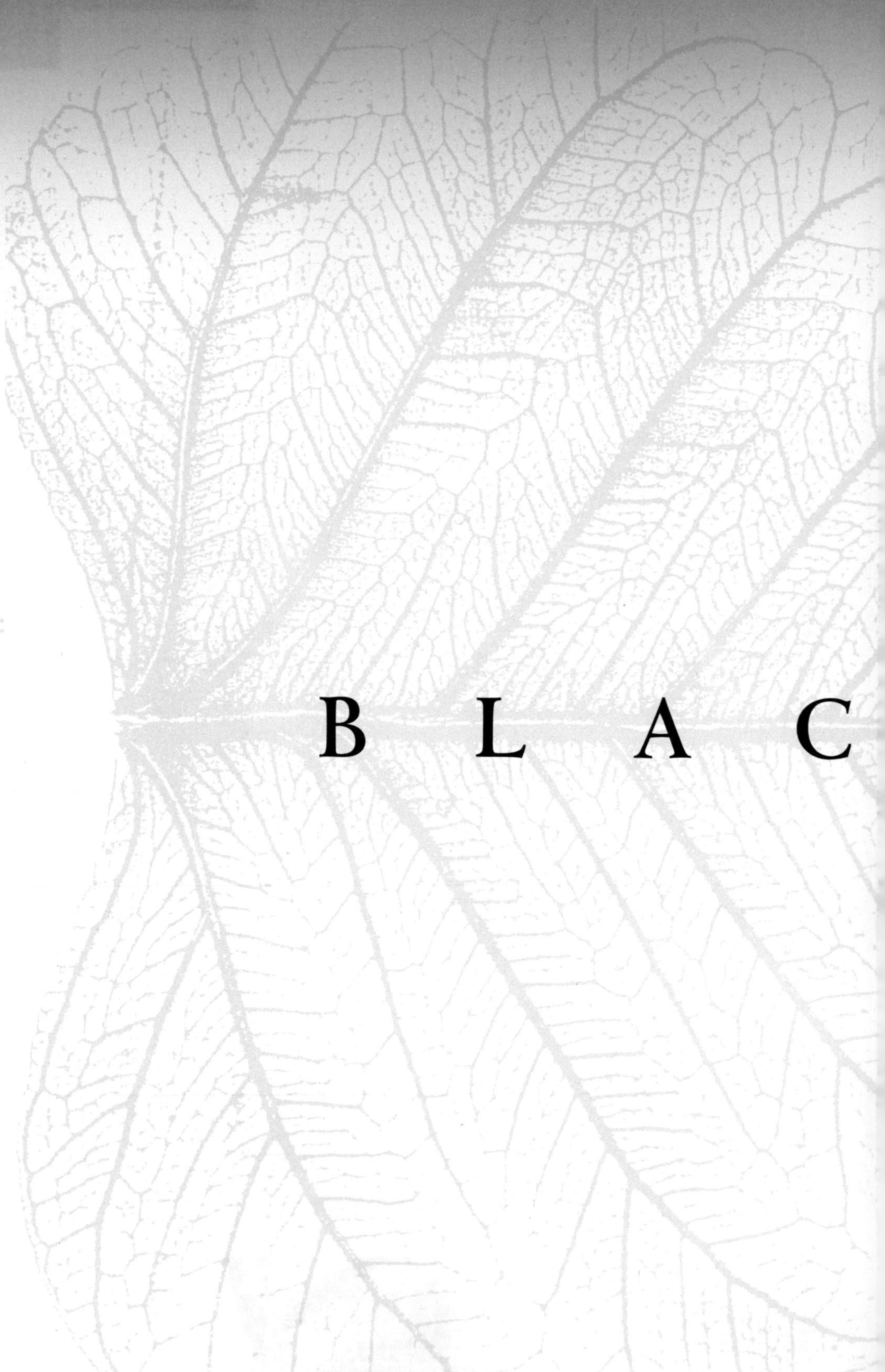

B L A C

KORCHID

Written by **NEIL GAIMAN**

Illustrated by **DAVE McKEAN**

Lettered by **TODD KLEIN**

KAREN BERGER *Editor – Original Series*
JEB WOODARD *Group Editor – Collected Editions*
ALEX GALER, SCOTT NYBAKKEN *Editors – Collected Edition*
STEVE COOK *Design Director – Books*
JOHN J. HILL *Publication Design*
ERIN VANOVER *Publication Production*

BOB HARRAS *Senior VP – Editor-in-Chief, DC Comics*
MARK DOYLE *Executive Editor, Vertigo & Black Label*

DAN DiDIO *Publisher*
JIM LEE *Publisher & Chief Creative Officer*
BOBBIE CHASE *VP – New Publishing Initiatives & Talent Development*
DON FALLETTI *VP – Manufacturing Operations & Workflow Management*
LAWRENCE GANEM *VP – Talent Services*
ALISON GILL *Senior VP – Manufacturing and Operations*
HANK KANALZ *Senior VP – Publishing Strategy & Support Services*
DAN MIRON *VP – Publishing Operations*
NICK J. NAPOLITANO *VP – Manufacturing Administration & Design*
NANCY SPEARS *VP – Sales*
MICHELE R. WELLS *VP & Executive Editor, Young Reader*

PEFC Certified
This product is from
sustainably managed
forests and controlled
sources
PEFC/29-31-337   www.pefc.org

INTRODUCTION

Like so many of the tales that make up our complex webwork of modern myths and contemporary entertainment, the tale you are about to read begins in violence. A woman — a super-hero crime-fighter known as Black Orchid — is tripped up by a crew of sophisticated crime-lords, just as she is about to penetrate their most closely guarded secrets. So far, so predictable. In the comics world, super-heroes are always discovered and threatened at crucial moments; indeed, it is how the hero overcomes his or her nemesis that too often imbues a comic book tale with not only its sense of plot or suspense, but also with its sense of mortal risk and moral triumph.

But in this tale, something unanticipated happens. The man who has caught Black Orchid stands before her and says: "Hey, you know something? I've read the comics... I'm not going to lock you up in the basement before interrogating you... then leave you alone to escape. That stuff is so dumb. But you know what I am going to do? I'm going to kill you. *Now.*" And then he does just what he has promised: He kills her — the woman who is the namesake of this book — in a brutal and unflinching manner. It is a startling moment, and not just for its suddenness and matter-of-factness. It is also startling because, in those moments when the killer tells Black Orchid that he understands how the rules of the super-hero genre work, he isn't merely addressing an endangered heroine of a comic book drama; he is also addressing the readers of that genre in ways that we have rarely been addressed before. In effect, in this one moment the killer is a stand-in voice for the writer of this tale, Neil Gaiman, and he is informing us that all the familiar rules of comic book storytelling — all those rules that insure the hard-earned triumph and inevitability of justice — will not apply in this narrative. Enter this story, the author is saying, and you enter a place where all the accepted customs of the genre's mythology have been suspended, and a new mythology — much closer to the dark dreams and darker realities of modern-day life — is about to be constructed. In other words, we are not only at the beginning of a new story, we are at the beginning of a new *way* of telling such a story. It isn't just the Black Orchid who is killed in these opening pages; it is also the ethos of the super-hero genre that is being set up for its long overdue death.

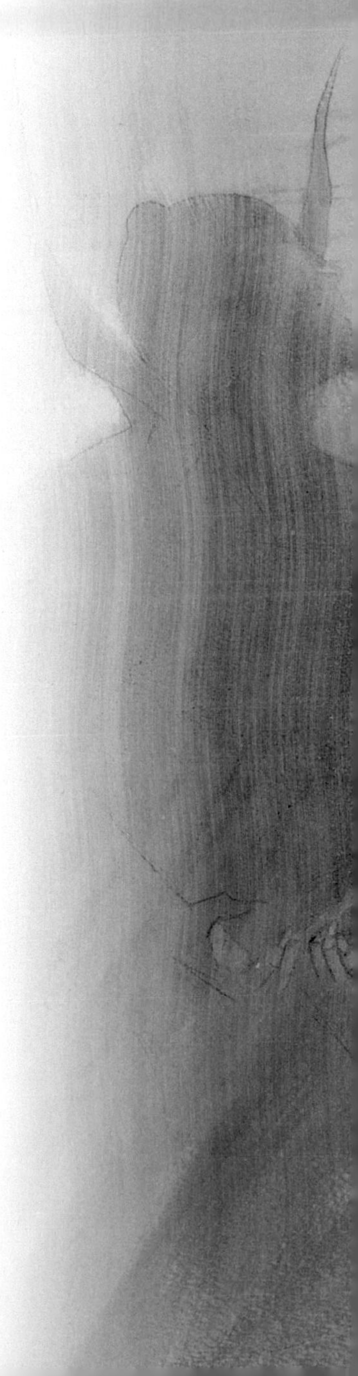

This may sound like a grisly promise, but some 140-or-so pages later, BLACK ORCHID comes to a redemptive conclusion that simply cannot be predicted. Indeed, back in 1988, when this work first appeared in comic book specialty stores in three installments, there were numerous readers who failed to accept that the story truly ended where and how it ended, and who kept waiting for a fourth volume that might finish the tale on more familiar ground. After all, in the world of comic books — as in the worlds of film, literature and global politics — any story that begins in violence must necessarily also end in violence (after all, there are few tactics that settle a fight more effectively than killing your enemy). Plus, violence has come to enjoy a certain aesthetic cachet in comics. At times it's almost as if the medium had been designed to invite contemplation of brutal action and physical conflict. On a comics page, you can freeze an act just as it is happening or before it happens; you can study its details, its logic and its art, and perhaps in doing so you can divine the mysteries of violence — that is, understand not only how it is happening, but *why* it happens. Maybe if we study those moments long enough, we can figure a way of stopping such moments in the world around us — or maybe we'll simply find depictions of those acts so repellent that real-life violence will hold a little less intrigue for us. Or maybe it's just the opposite: Maybe by freezing a violent moment on the page we're simply looking for a better way to enjoy the violence, to pore over its minutiae and nuances at length and at leisure.

Either way, BLACK ORCHID works against all these conventions of violence: It begins in the horror of reality and it works its way towards a lovely dreamlike end that is no less powerful or hard-hitting for all its fable-style grace. As a result, BLACK ORCHID is the first major work of comic book literature that uses violence as a critique of the uses of violence — that is, as a critique of not only how violence figures into our actions and our psychology, but also how it figures into our myths and our art. Reviewing this work now, it is clear that BLACK ORCHID — like Frank Miller's *Daredevil* and THE DARK KNIGHT RETURNS and Alan Moore's *Miracleman*, SWAMP THING and WATCHMEN — is one of those books that has helped break modern comics history in two and signalled the rise of a new courage and a new spirit of aspiration within the medium. But in a way, BLACK ORCHID attempts to go even further than these other breakthrough works by making plain that, no matter how bold or smart or hip the new comics may be, most of them still end up resorting to hackneyed moral and narrative customs: violent me save the world through violent choices or violent bravery. In this book something altogether different occurs. As a result, BLACK ORCHID is a pivotal work in comic books: It is an act of imagination and hope that tries to take a much undervalued form of literature into places where it has never gone before.

But BLACK ORCHID is also something more: It is also the work that brought its British creative team, author Neil Gaiman and artist Dave McKean, to the attention of the mainstream comics audience. Though the pair had collaborated on a couple of earlier projects (chiefly, a strange and haunting volume entitled *Violent Cases*), it was with BLACK ORCHID that McKean arrived at the matchless blend of photolike realism and dreamlike expressionism that would characterize his later work on BATMAN: ARKHAM ASYLUM (as well as on his current self-authored *Cages* series), and it was also here that Neil Gaiman first demonstrated his flair for transmogrifying mythologies and making them hit home with a rare emotional force. With THE SANDMAN in particular, Gaiman has taken the themes of hope and horror, reality and dream, that run throughout BLACK ORCHID and turned them into the meat and matter of what is clearly the finest mainstream comic book being published today. "I know that some people regard this sort of writing as escapist fiction," says Gaiman, "but I think that tales of myth and horror are probably the easiest and most effective way to talk about the real world. It's like they are the lies that tell the truth about our lives. At the same time, I think of books like SANDMAN and BLACK ORCHID as optimistic works: Sometimes, bad things happen to the wrong people in my stories, and that leaves my characters realizing that they have to change or die. That choice gives you the chance to remake not just yourself, but sometimes the world around you as well."

In BLACK ORCHID, all of Gaiman's major characters, in one fashion or another, come to the place where they must make that choice: They have to decide what to do in the face of violence. Some of them choose right and die anyway, and some choose wrong and survive, but that isn't the point. What matters is that the book itself also makes a clear choice, and in doing so it has given comics literature a new lease on creativity. We could use more works like BLACK ORCHID: a work that struggles to move from a place of horrible ruin to a stance of brave refusal and indomitable faith and compassion.

— **Mikal Gilmore**
1991

Mikal Gilmore is a contributing editor for Rolling Stone.

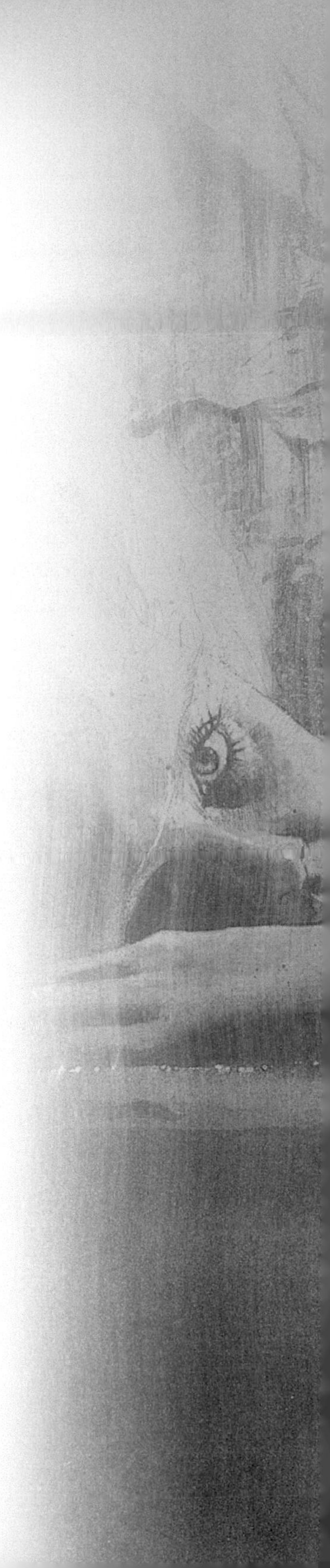

CHAPTER 1

One thing is certain...

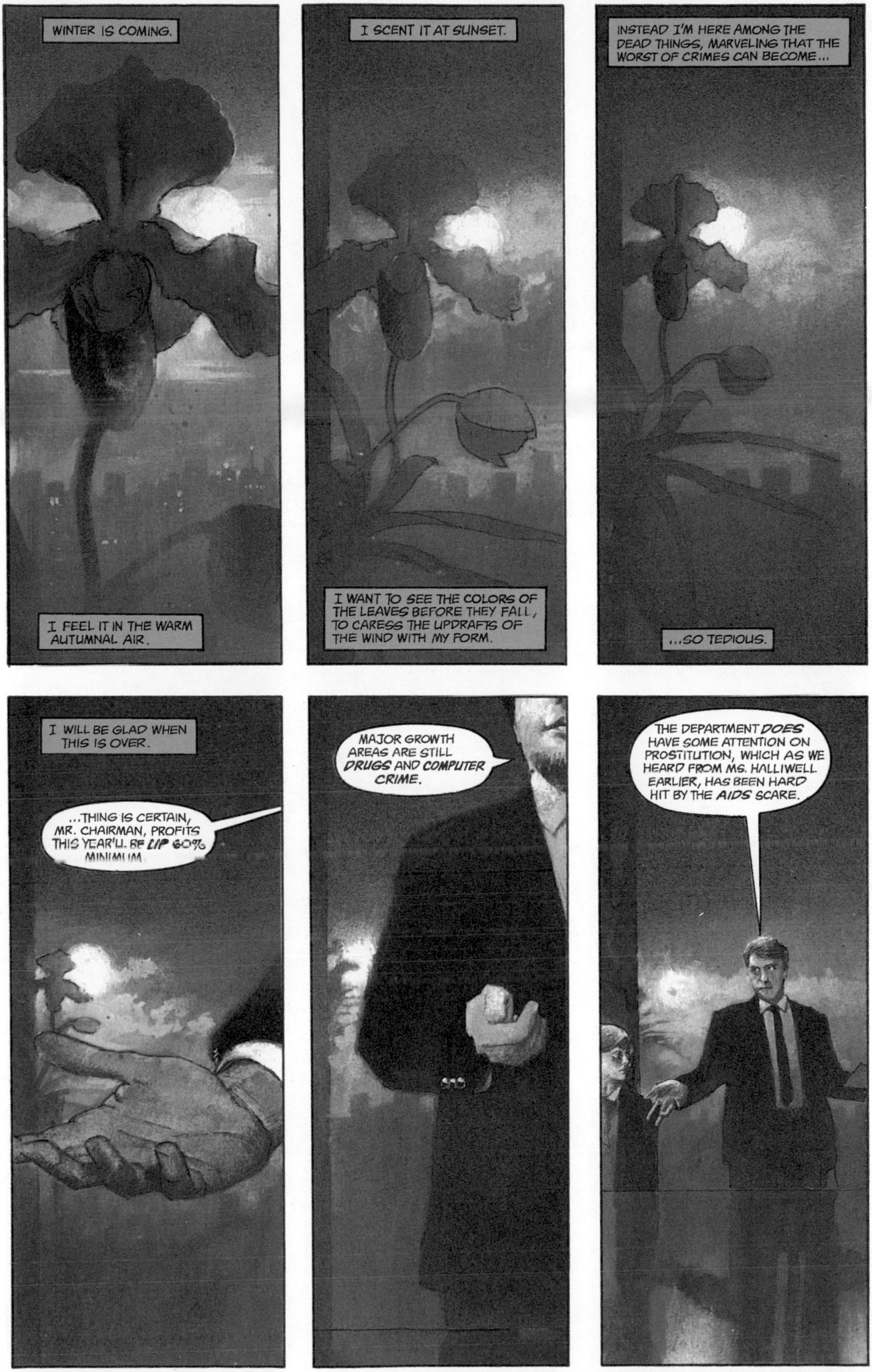
WINTER IS COMING.
I FEEL IT IN THE WARM AUTUMNAL AIR.
I SCENT IT AT SUNSET.
I WANT TO SEE THE COLORS OF THE LEAVES BEFORE THEY FALL, TO CARESS THE UPDRAFTS OF THE WIND WITH MY FORM.
INSTEAD I'M HERE AMONG THE DEAD THINGS, MARVELING THAT THE WORST OF CRIMES CAN BECOME...
...SO TEDIOUS.
I WILL BE GLAD WHEN THIS IS OVER.
...THING IS CERTAIN, MR. CHAIRMAN, PROFITS THIS YEAR'LL BE UP 60% MINIMUM.
MAJOR GROWTH AREAS ARE STILL DRUGS AND COMPUTER CRIME.
THE DEPARTMENT DOES HAVE SOME ATTENTION ON PROSTITUTION, WHICH AS WE HEARD FROM MS. HALLIWELL EARLIER, HAS BEEN HARD HIT BY THE AIDS SCARE.

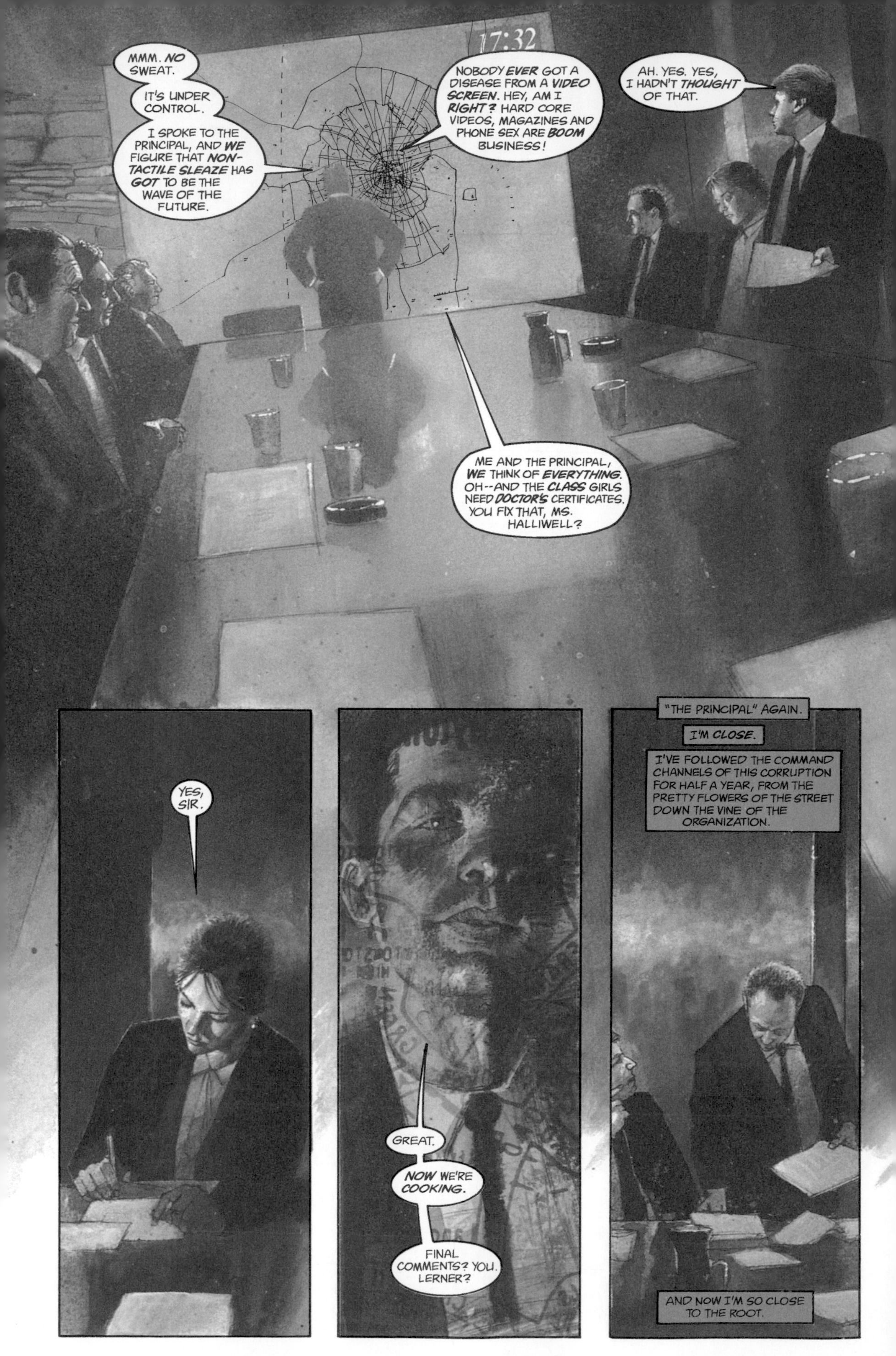
17:32
MMM. NO SWEAT.
IT'S UNDER CONTROL.
I SPOKE TO THE PRINCIPAL, AND WE FIGURE THAT NON-TACTILE SLEAZE HAS GOT TO BE THE WAVE OF THE FUTURE.
NOBODY EVER GOT A DISEASE FROM A VIDEO SCREEN. HEY, AM I RIGHT? HARD CORE VIDEOS, MAGAZINES AND PHONE SEX ARE BOOM BUSINESS!
AH. YES. YES, I HADN'T THOUGHT OF THAT.
ME AND THE PRINCIPAL, WE THINK OF EVERYTHING. OH--AND THE CLASS GIRLS NEED DOCTOR'S CERTIFICATES. YOU FIX THAT, MS. HALLIWELL?
YES, SIR.
GREAT.
NOW WE'RE COOKING.
FINAL COMMENTS? YOU. LERNER?
"THE PRINCIPAL" AGAIN.
I'M CLOSE.
I'VE FOLLOWED THE COMMAND CHANNELS OF THIS CORRUPTION FOR HALF A YEAR, FROM THE PRETTY FLOWERS OF THE STREET DOWN THE VINE OF THE ORGANIZATION.
AND NOW I'M SO CLOSE TO THE ROOT.

SO CLOSE...

...PAYOFFS TO THE POLICE ARE APPROACHING THE MAXIMUM SET ASIDES. I PROPOSE WE UP THE BASIC WEEKLY SLUSH FUND ANOTHER FIFTY GRAND, WITH AN EXTRA HUNDRED THOU FOR RESERVES.

UH-HUH. I'D NEED A *FULL* PROPOSAL, WITH EXPENDITURE BREAKDOWNS.

YES, SIR.

I THOUGHT IT WAS *YOU,* BUT I WAS WRONG. YOU'RE A *FRONT.* A COVER FOR THE BIG MAN.

THE *PRINCIPAL.* THE *HEART* OF THE *ROT.*

FABULOUS. WELL, *THAT* CONCLUDES THIS MONTH'S BUSINESS. YOU'RE ALL DOING A GREAT JOB. Y'KNOW? TERR*IF*IC.

I *REALLY* MEAN IT.

KEEP IT UP, HUH?

YES, SIR.

YES, MR. CHAIRMAN.

UH-HUH.

YESSIR.

--OHH, I NEARLY FOR*GOT!*

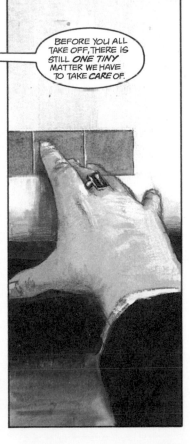

BEFORE YOU ALL TAKE OFF, THERE IS STILL *ONE TINY* MATTER WE HAVE TO TAKE *CARE* OF.

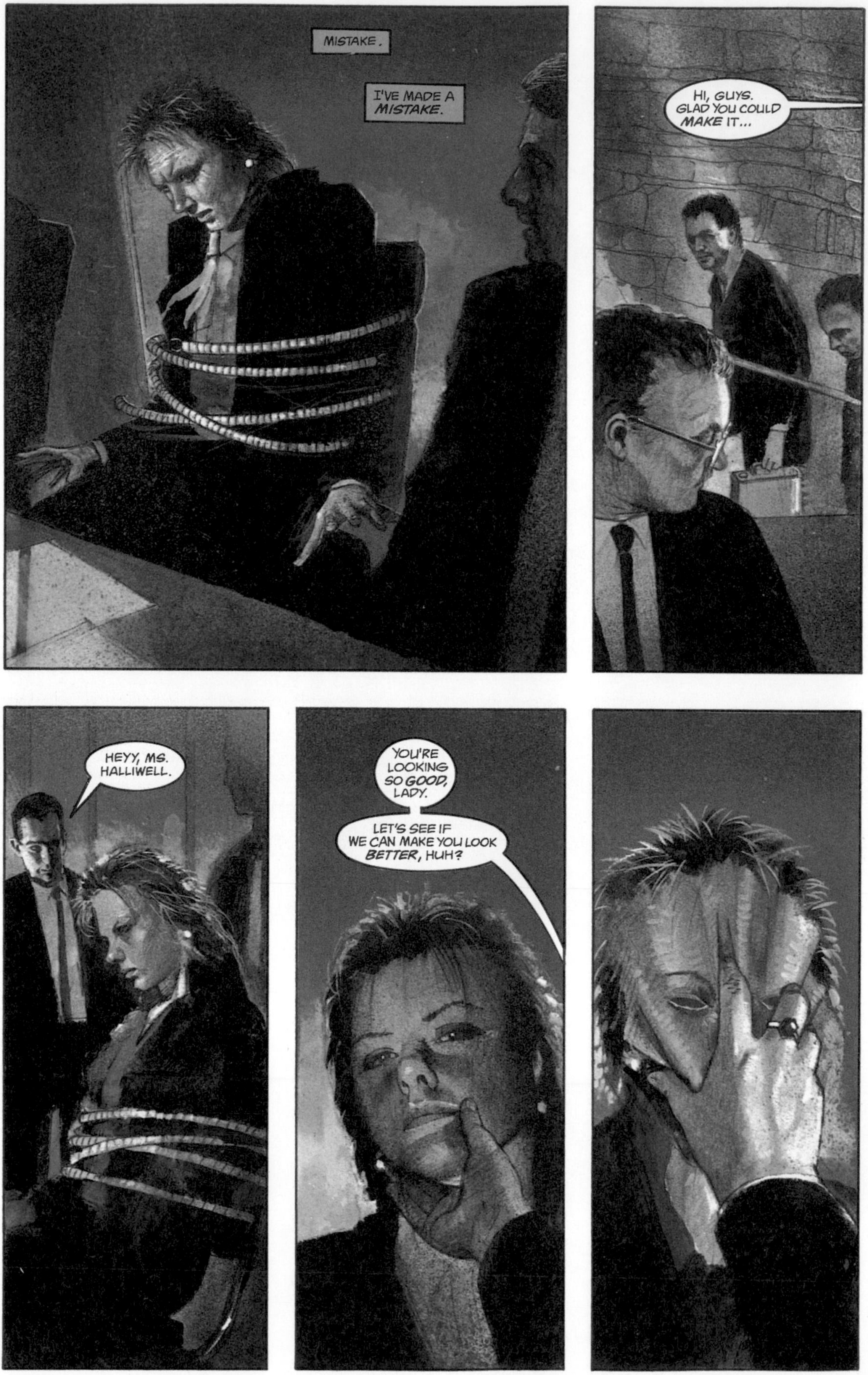
MISTAKE.
I'VE MADE A MISTAKE.
HI, GUYS. GLAD YOU COULD MAKE IT...
HEYY, MS. HALLIWELL.
YOU'RE LOOKING SO GOOD, LADY.
LET'S SEE IF WE CAN MAKE YOU LOOK BETTER, HUH?

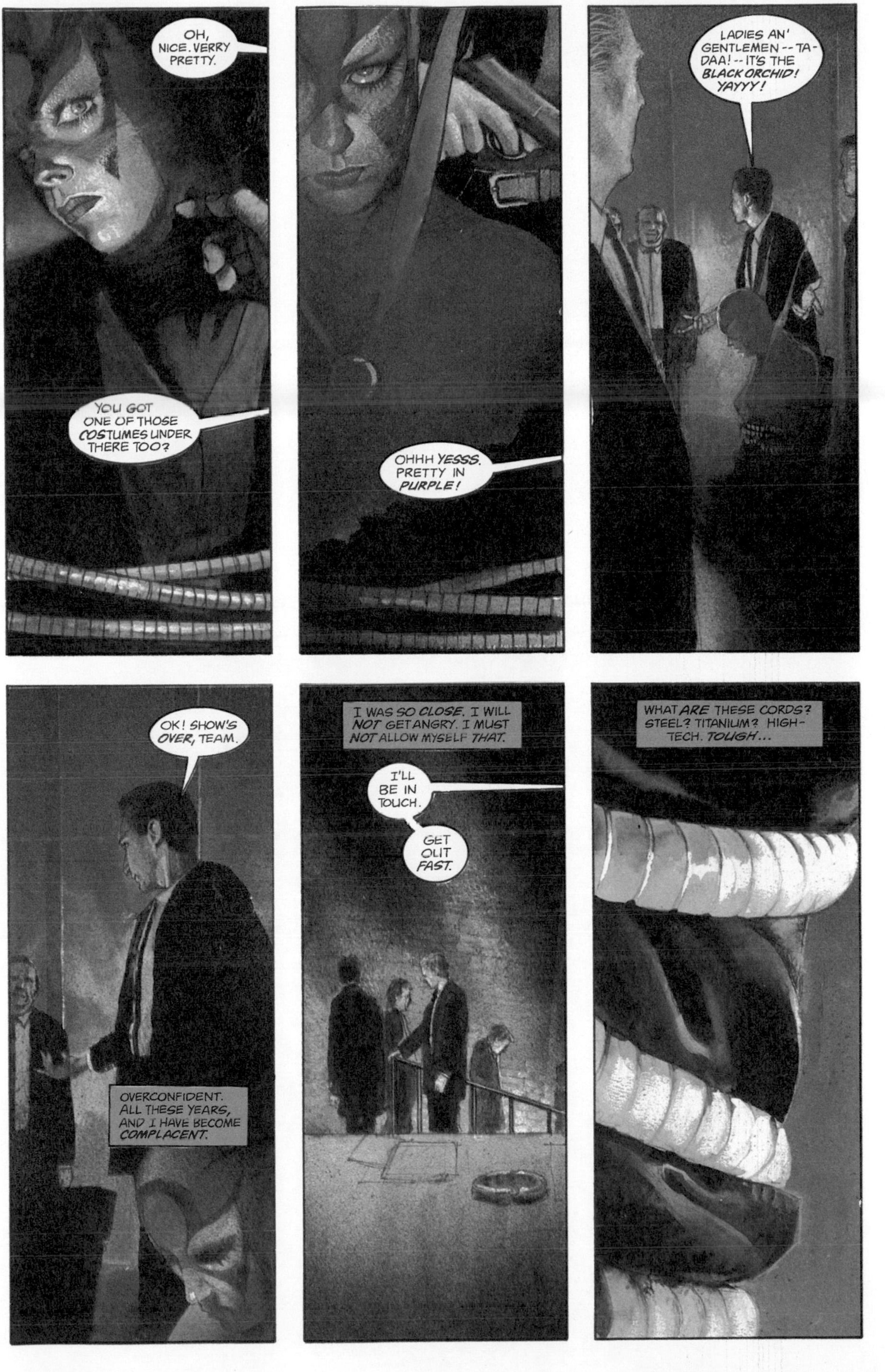
OH, NICE. VERRY PRETTY.
YOU GOT ONE OF THOSE COSTUMES UNDER THERE TOO?
OHHH YESSS. PRETTY IN PURPLE!
LADIES AN' GENTLEMEN -- TA-DAA! -- IT'S THE BLACK ORCHID! YAYYY!
OK! SHOW'S OVER, TEAM.
OVERCONFIDENT. ALL THESE YEARS, AND I HAVE BECOME COMPLACENT.
I WAS SO CLOSE. I WILL NOT GET ANGRY. I MUST NOT ALLOW MYSELF THAT.
I'LL BE IN TOUCH.
GET OUT FAST.
WHAT ARE THESE CORDS? STEEL? TITANIUM? HIGH-TECH. TOUGH...

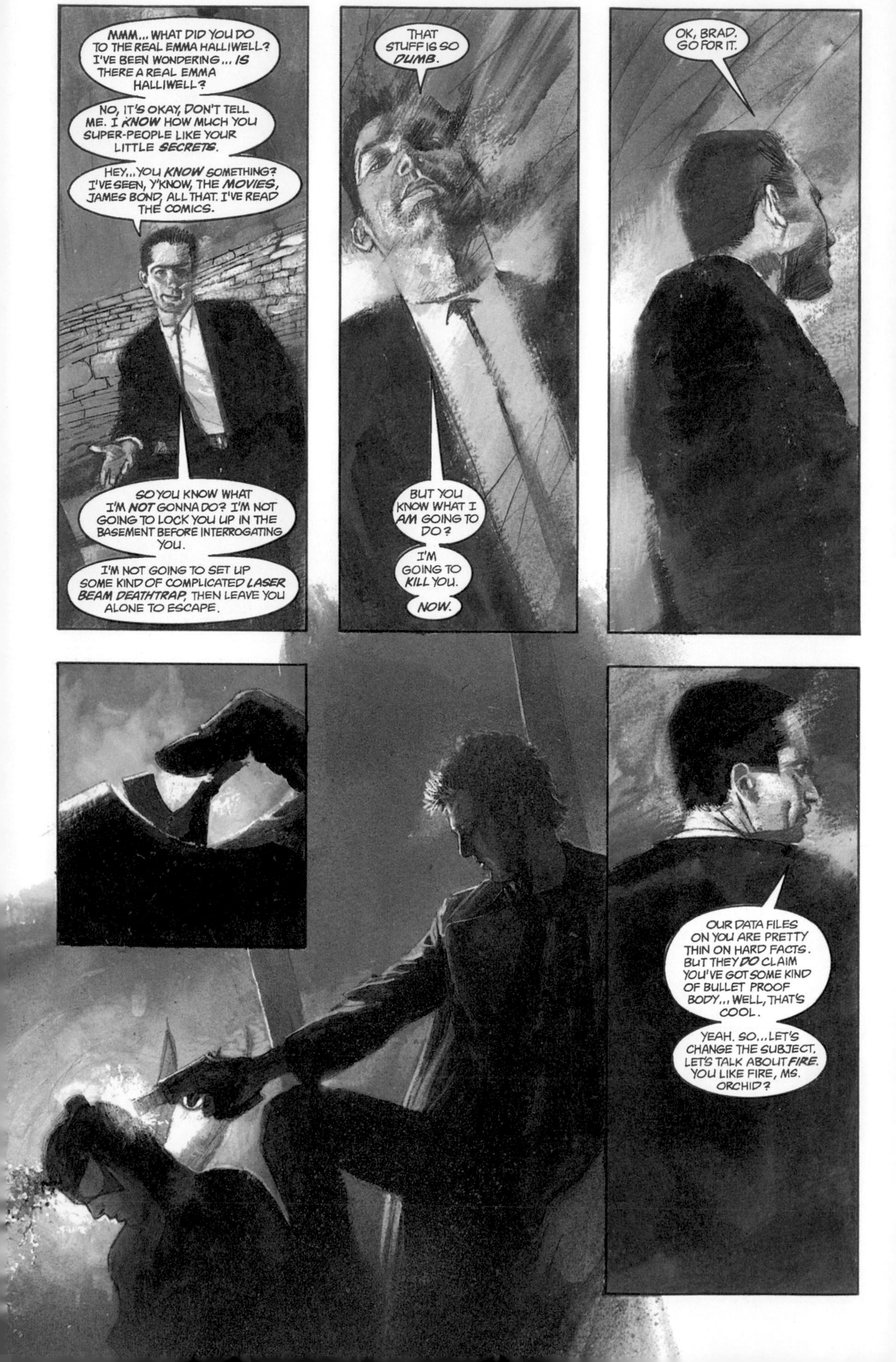
MMM... WHAT DID YOU DO TO THE REAL EMMA HALLIWELL? I'VE BEEN WONDERING... IS THERE A REAL EMMA HALLIWELL?
NO, IT'S OKAY, DON'T TELL ME. I KNOW HOW MUCH YOU SUPER-PEOPLE LIKE YOUR LITTLE SECRETS.
HEY... YOU KNOW SOMETHING? I'VE SEEN, Y'KNOW, THE MOVIES, JAMES BOND, ALL THAT. I'VE READ THE COMICS.
SO YOU KNOW WHAT I'M NOT GONNA DO? I'M NOT GOING TO LOCK YOU UP IN THE BASEMENT BEFORE INTERROGATING YOU.
I'M NOT GOING TO SET UP SOME KIND OF COMPLICATED LASER BEAM DEATHTRAP, THEN LEAVE YOU ALONE TO ESCAPE.
THAT STUFF IS SO DUMB.
BUT YOU KNOW WHAT I AM GOING TO DO?
I'M GOING TO KILL YOU.
NOW.
OK, BRAD. GO FOR IT.
OUR DATA FILES ON YOU ARE PRETTY THIN ON HARD FACTS. BUT THEY DO CLAIM YOU'VE GOT SOME KIND OF BULLET PROOF BODY... WELL, THAT'S COOL.
YEAH. SO... LET'S CHANGE THE SUBJECT. LET'S TALK ABOUT FIRE. YOU LIKE FIRE, MS. ORCHID?

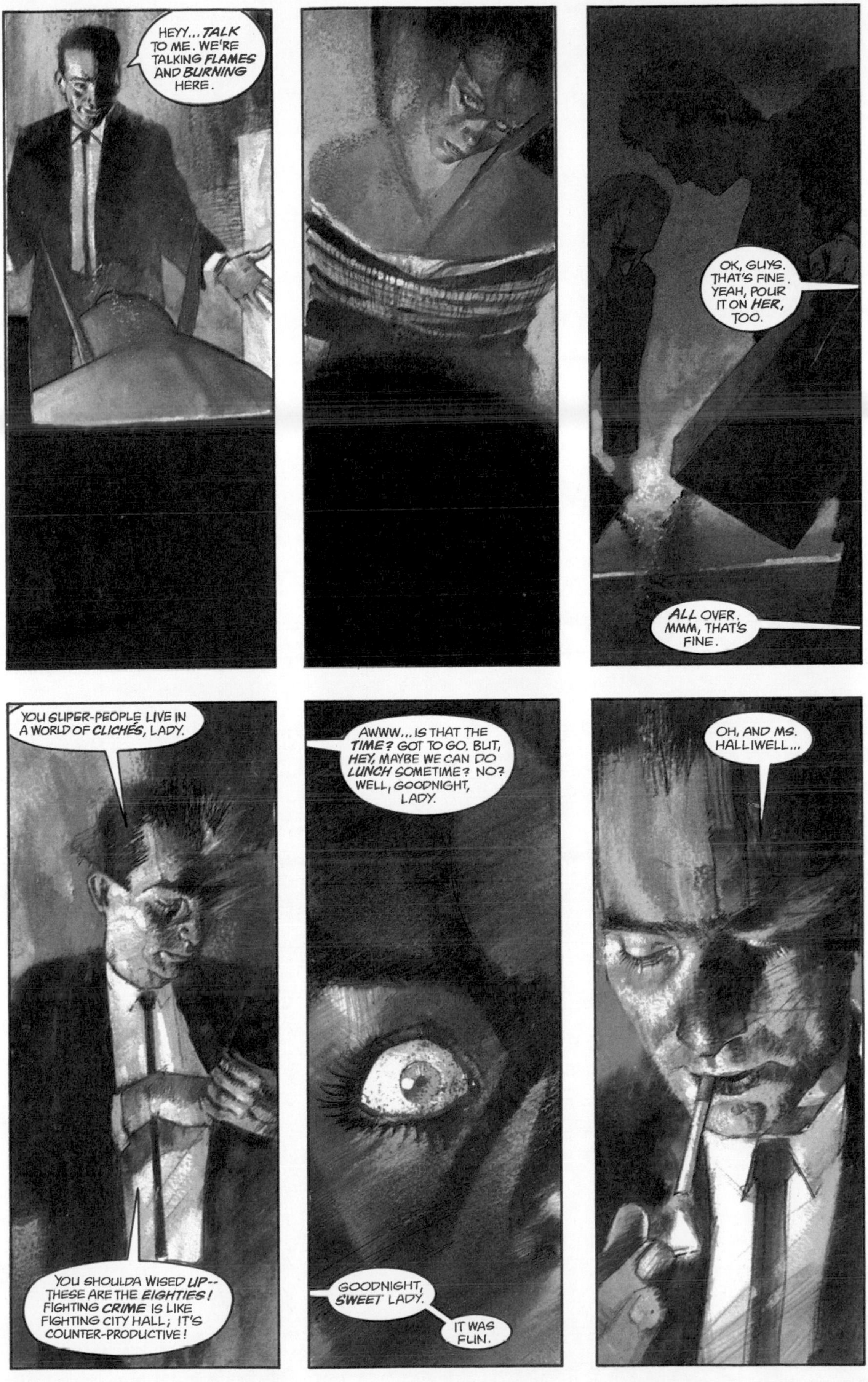
HEYY... TALK TO ME. WE'RE TALKING FLAMES AND BURNING HERE.
OK, GUYS. THAT'S FINE. YEAH, POUR IT ON HER, TOO.
ALL OVER. MMM, THAT'S FINE.
YOU SUPER-PEOPLE LIVE IN A WORLD OF CLICHÉS, LADY.
YOU SHOULDA WISED UP-- THESE ARE THE EIGHTIES! FIGHTING CRIME IS LIKE FIGHTING CITY HALL; IT'S COUNTER-PRODUCTIVE!
AWWW... IS THAT THE TIME? GOT TO GO. BUT, HEY, MAYBE WE CAN DO LUNCH SOMETIME? NO? WELL, GOODNIGHT, LADY.
GOODNIGHT, SWEET LADY.
IT WAS FUN.
OH, AND MS. HALLIWELL...

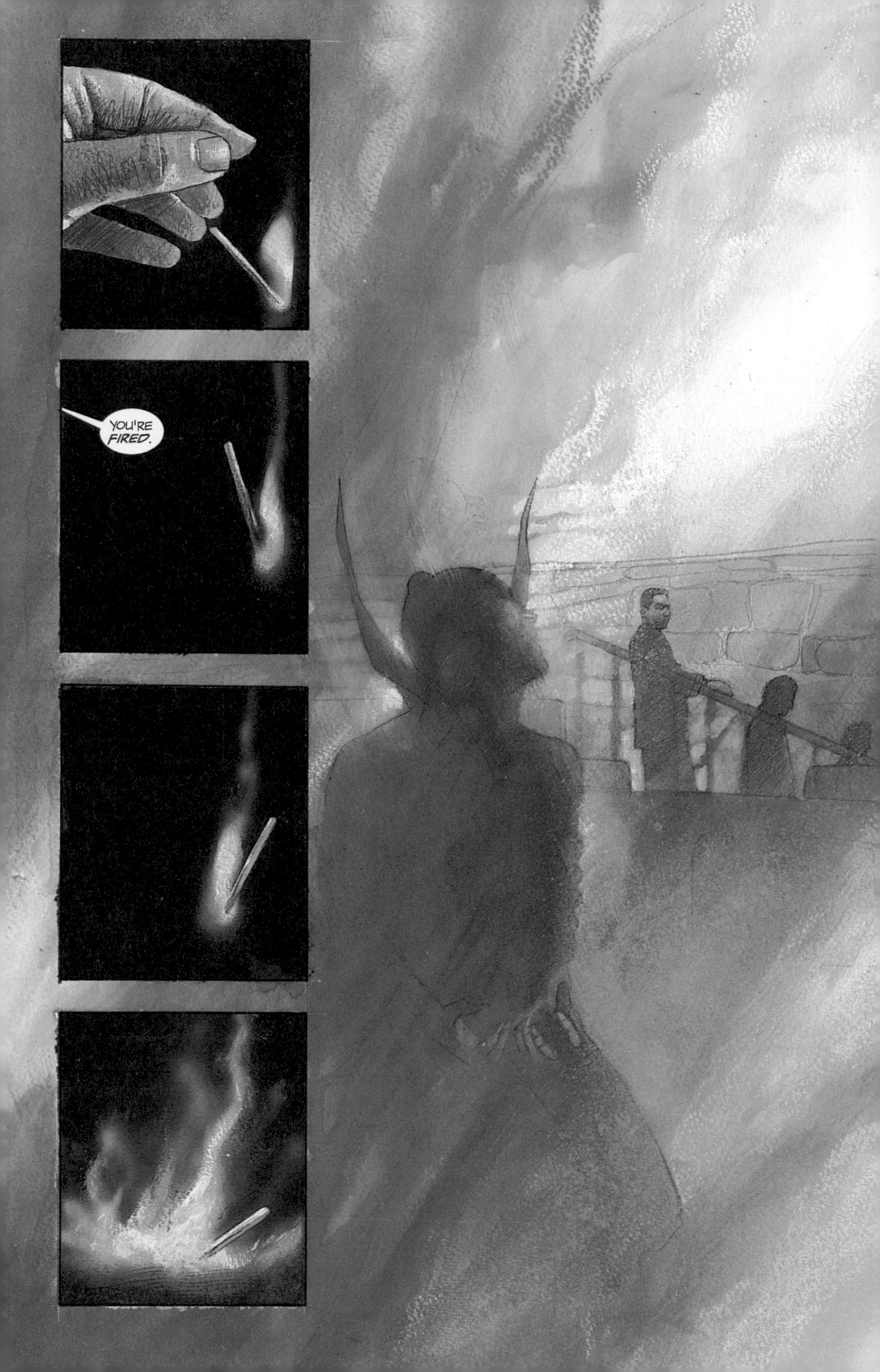
YOU'RE FIRED.

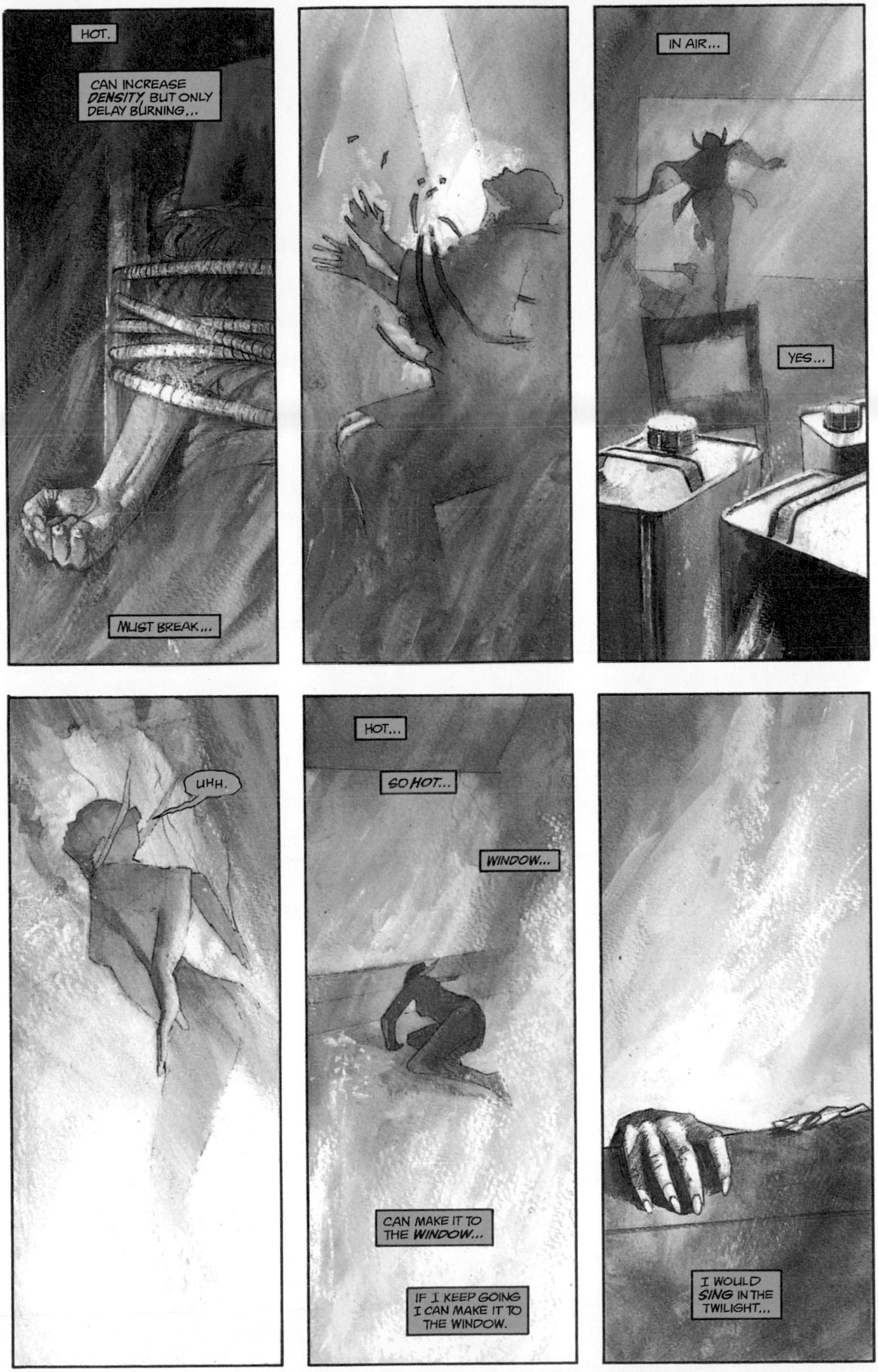
HOT.
CAN INCREASE DENSITY, BUT ONLY DELAY BURNING...
MUST BREAK...
IN AIR...
YES...
UHH.
HOT...
SO HOT...
WINDOW...
CAN MAKE IT TO THE WINDOW...
IF I KEEP GOING I CAN MAKE IT TO THE WINDOW.
I WOULD SING IN THE TWILIGHT...

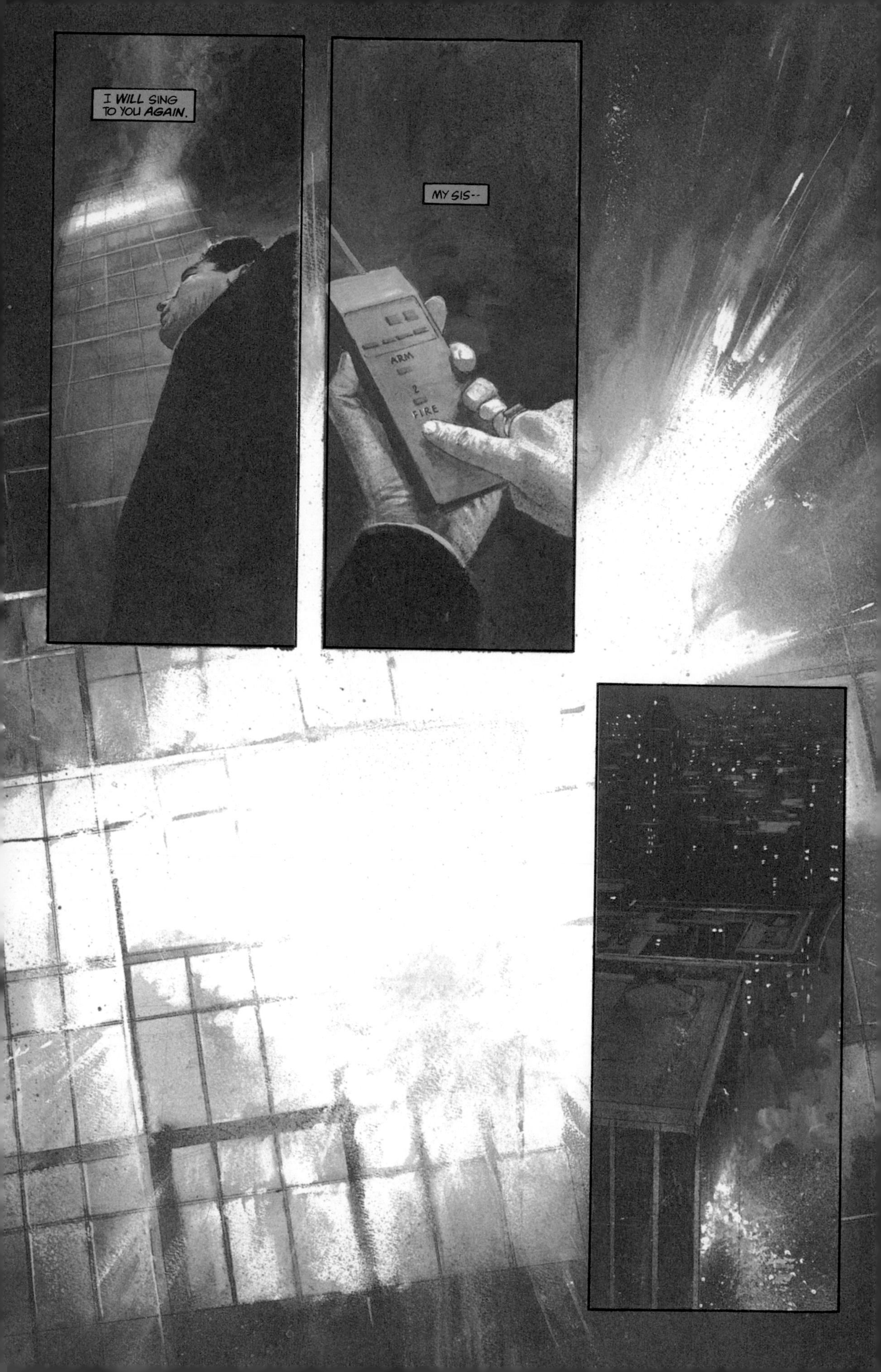
I WILL SING TO YOU AGAIN.
MY SIS--
ARM
2
FIRE

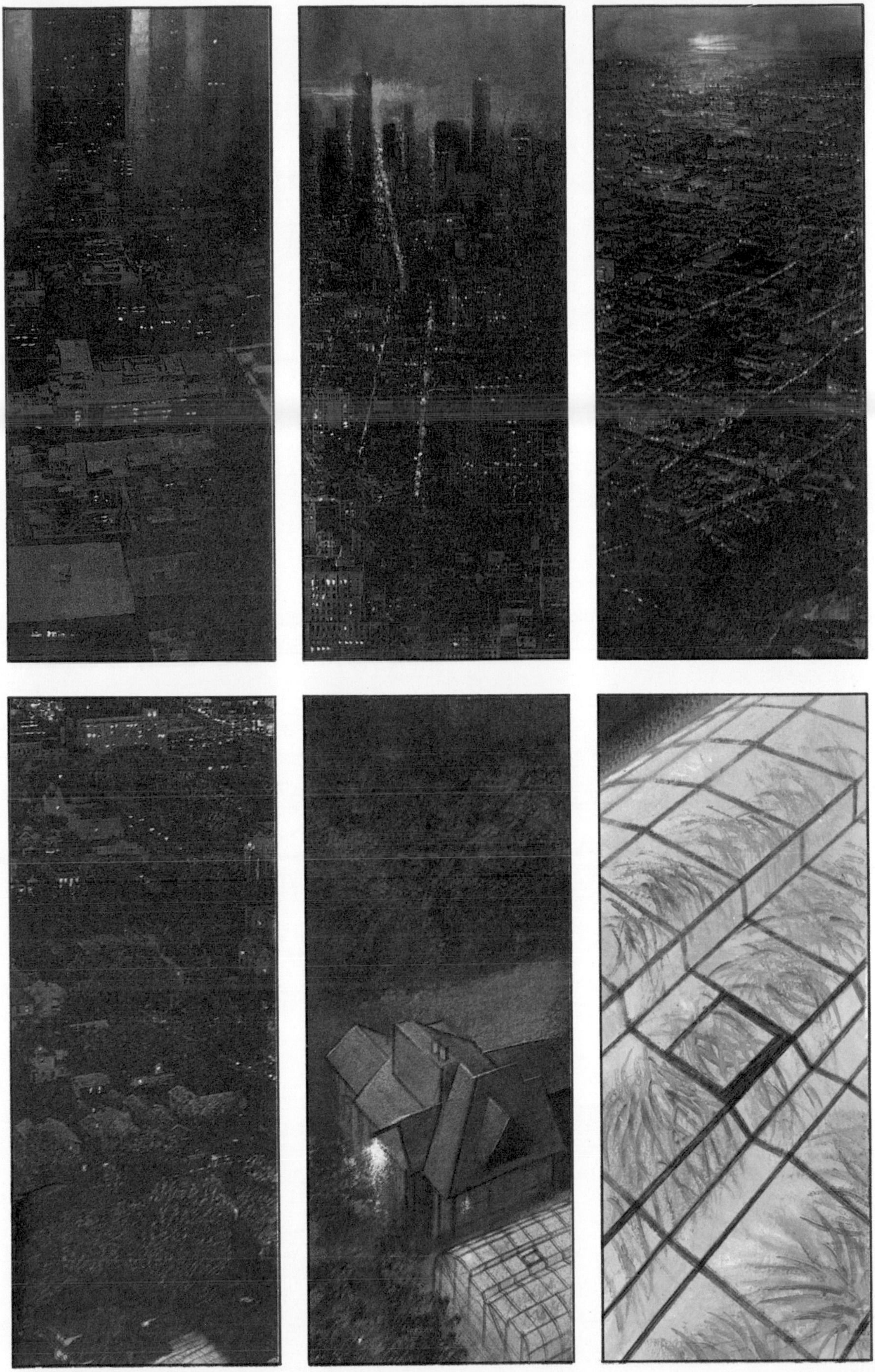

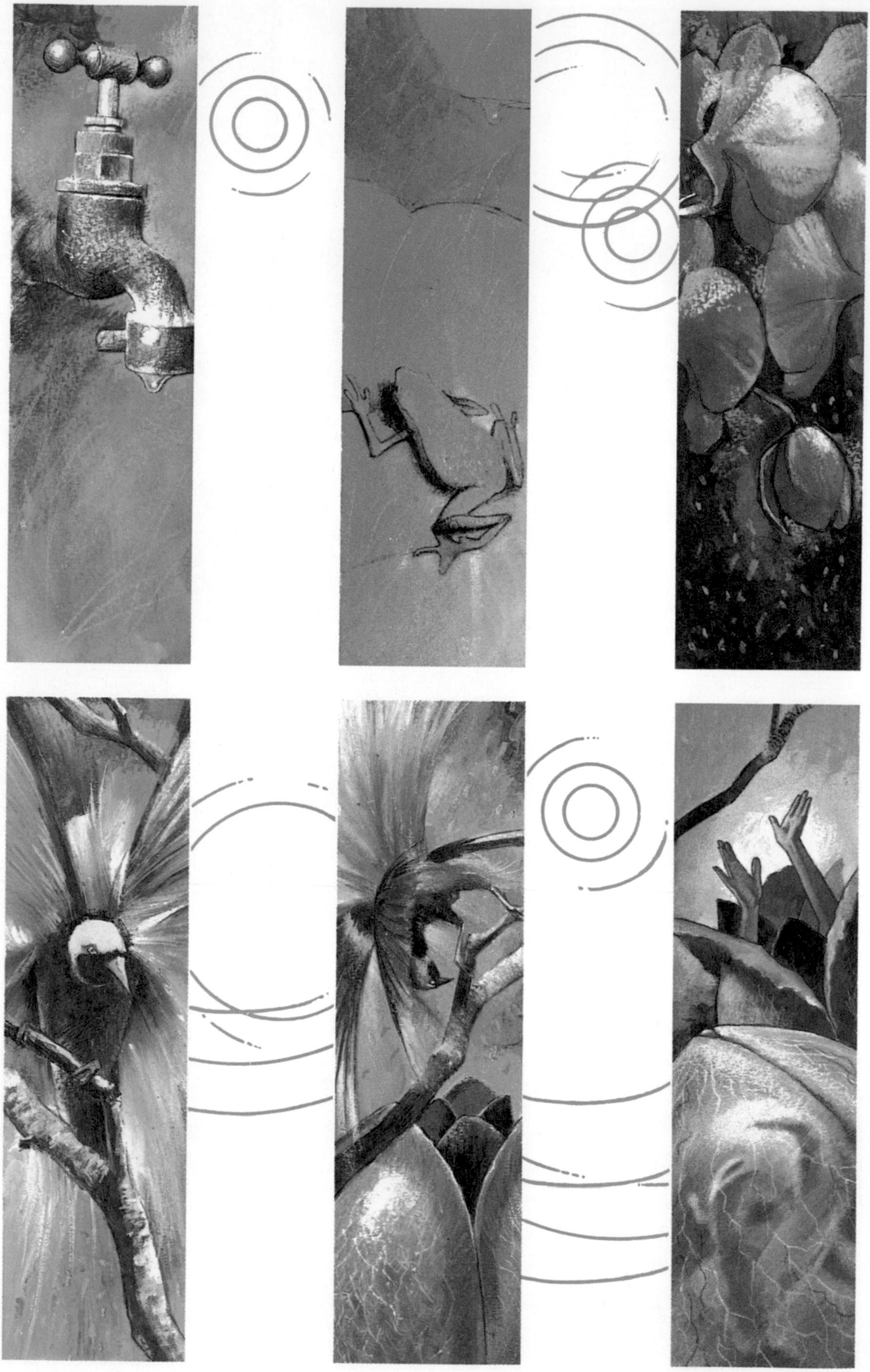

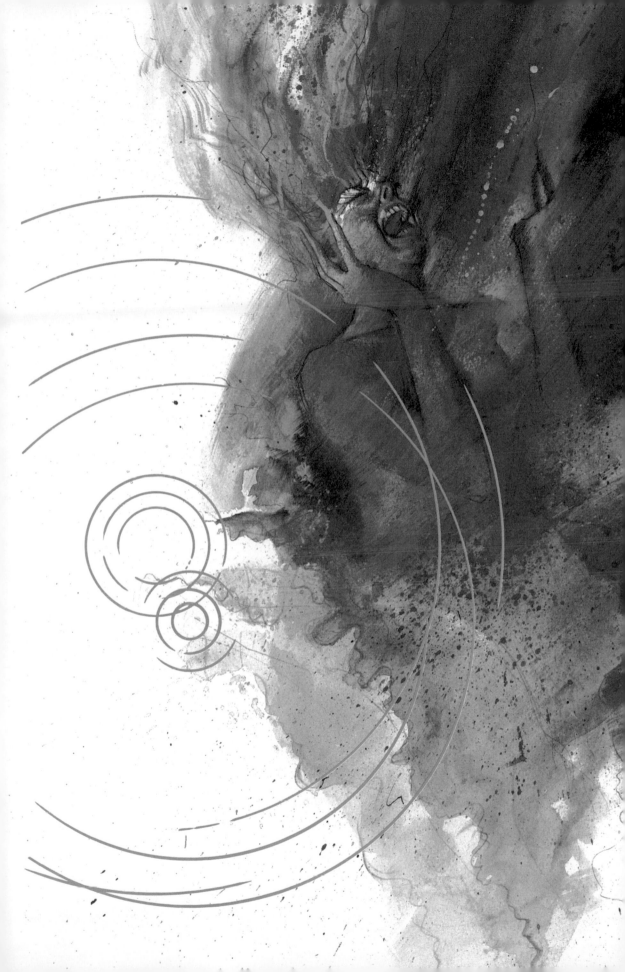

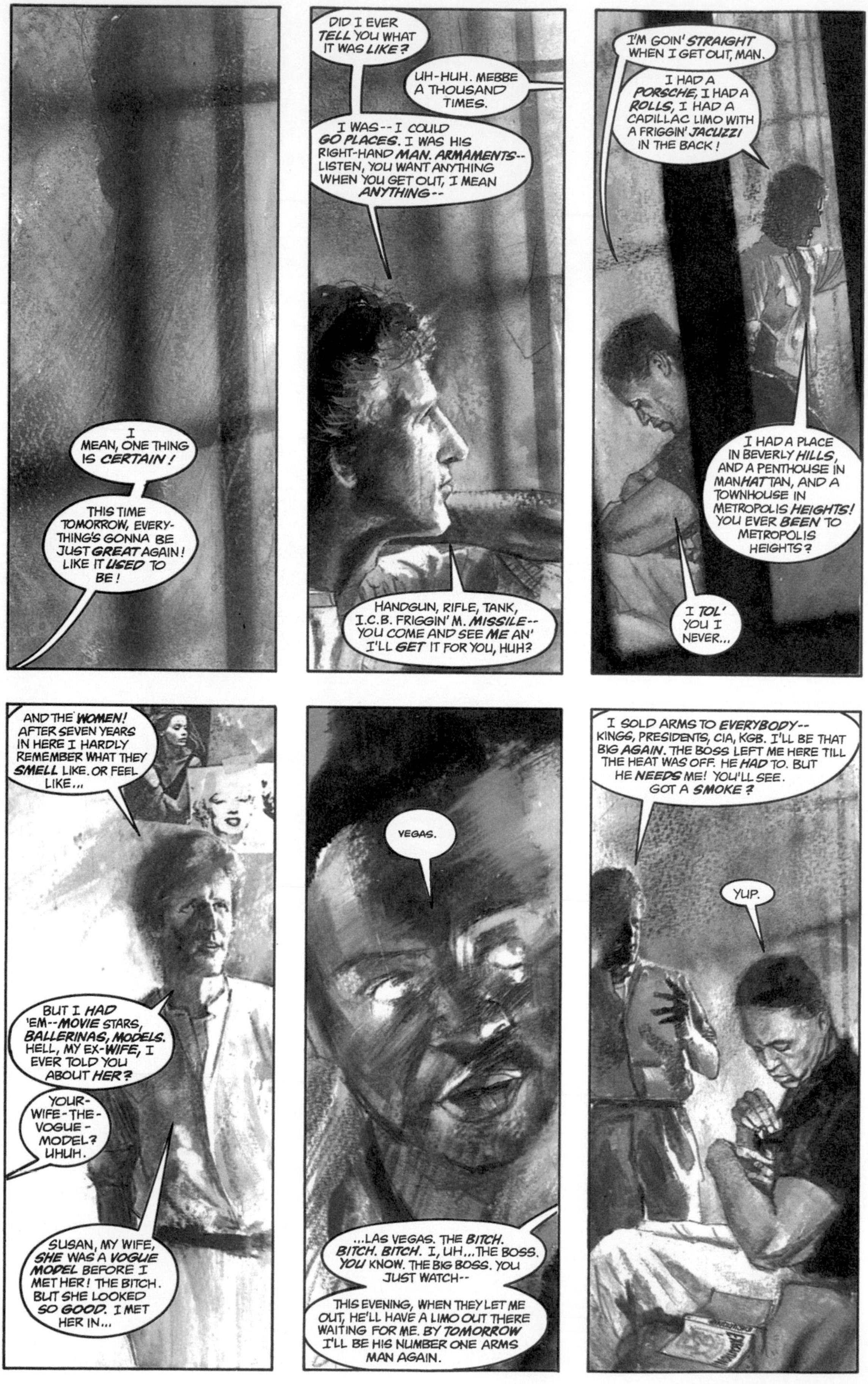
I MEAN, ONE THING IS CERTAIN!
THIS TIME TOMORROW, EVERYTHING'S GONNA BE JUST GREAT AGAIN! LIKE IT USED TO BE!
DID I EVER TELL YOU WHAT IT WAS LIKE?
UH-HUH. MEBBE A THOUSAND TIMES.
I WAS-- I COULD GO PLACES. I WAS HIS RIGHT-HAND MAN. ARMAMENTS-- LISTEN, YOU WANT ANYTHING WHEN YOU GET OUT, I MEAN ANYTHING--
HANDGUN, RIFLE, TANK, I.C.B. FRIGGIN' M. MISSILE-- YOU COME AND SEE ME AN' I'LL GET IT FOR YOU, HUH?
I'M GOIN' STRAIGHT WHEN I GET OUT, MAN.
I HAD A PORSCHE, I HAD A ROLLS, I HAD A CADILLAC LIMO WITH A FRIGGIN' JACUZZI IN THE BACK!
I HAD A PLACE IN BEVERLY HILLS, AND A PENTHOUSE IN MANHATTAN, AND A TOWNHOUSE IN METROPOLIS HEIGHTS! YOU EVER BEEN TO METROPOLIS HEIGHTS?
I TOL' YOU I NEVER...
AND THE WOMEN! AFTER SEVEN YEARS IN HERE I HARDLY REMEMBER WHAT THEY SMELL LIKE. OR FEEL LIKE...
BUT I HAD 'EM--MOVIE STARS, BALLERINAS, MODELS. HELL, MY EX-WIFE, I EVER TOLD YOU ABOUT HER?
YOUR-WIFE-THE-VOGUE-MODEL? UHUH.
SUSAN, MY WIFE, SHE WAS A VOGUE MODEL BEFORE I MET HER! THE BITCH. BUT SHE LOOKED SO GOOD. I MET HER IN...
VEGAS.
...LAS VEGAS. THE BITCH. BITCH. BITCH. I, UH... THE BOSS. YOU KNOW. THE BIG BOSS. YOU JUST WATCH--
THIS EVENING, WHEN THEY LET ME OUT, HE'LL HAVE A LIMO OUT THERE WAITING FOR ME. BY TOMORROW I'LL BE HIS NUMBER ONE ARMS MAN AGAIN.
I SOLD ARMS TO EVERYBODY-- KINGS, PRESIDENTS, CIA, KGB. I'LL BE THAT BIG AGAIN. THE BOSS LEFT ME HERE TILL THE HEAT WAS OFF. HE HAD TO. BUT HE NEEDS ME! YOU'LL SEE. GOT A SMOKE?
YUP.

THANKS, MAN. I TELL YOU, WHEN I'M OUT OF HERE, YOU *NAME* IT AND I'LL SEND IT IN TO YOU. CAVIAR, CIGARS, COKE...

JUST TWO HOURS...

YOU JUST TELL ME WHAT YOU WANT. YOU GOT A LIGHT?

...BARS.

HUH?

WHAT I *WANT.* I MISS JUS' HANGIN' AROUN' IN *BARS.* YOU *DO* THAT FOR ME? GO TO SOME BAR, HAVE A *BEER* OR TWO, SOME *PRETZELS.* *TALK* TO THE *BARTENDER.* YOU *DO* THAT?

UH... *SURE.* SURE, PAL.

THAT'S WHAT I *MISS* IN JAIL.

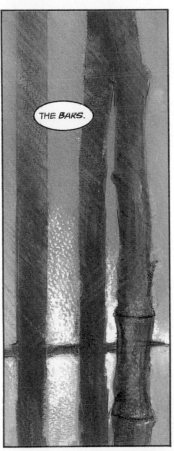

THE *BARS.*

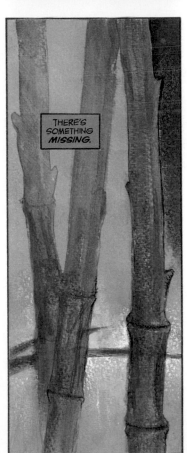

THERE'S SOMETHING *MISSING.*

THIS IS THE GARDEN, STILL AND GREEN.

THERE IS A HUMMING SOMEWHERE.

SOMEONE WAS *BURNING*.

SOMEONE HAS *GONE*.

I FELT IT.

A DREAM?

PERHAPS...

PERFUME?

WARM.

WHAT WAS I DOING IN HERE?

I MUST HAVE FALLEN ASLEEP...

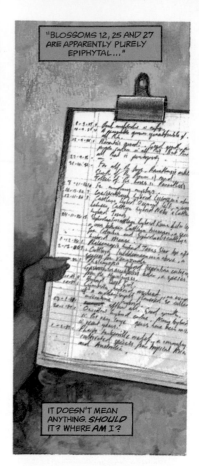

"BLOSSOMS 12, 25 AND 27 ARE APPARENTLY PURELY EPIPHYTAL..."

IT DOESN'T MEAN ANYTHING. *SHOULD* IT? WHERE *AM* I?

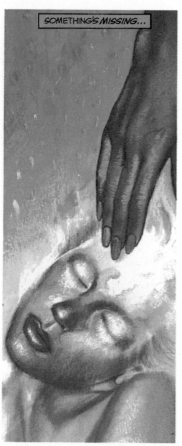

SOMETHING'S *MISSING*...

FLOWERS HALF STARE FROM COOL, FAMILIAR FACES. A SLOW DEEP PLACE, THE *GARDEN*.

THIS IS WHERE I *COME* FROM...

WHERE DO I *GO*?

COOLER OUT HERE.

IT WASN'T TIME TO *AWAKE*.

I DIDN'T WANT TO LEAVE THE *GREEN DREAM* UNTIL THE *END*...

BUT THE *RED*... THE *FLAMES*...

SOMETHING ABOUT *SINGING?*

THERE WAS FAR *MUSIC* IN THE PAIN...

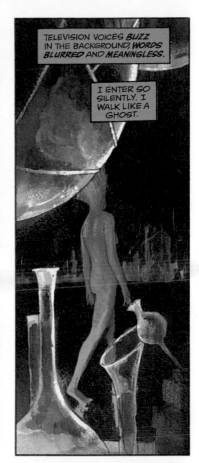

TELEVISION VOICES *BUZZ* IN THE BACKGROUND; WORDS *BLURRED* AND *MEANINGLESS*.

I ENTER SO *SILENTLY*. I WALK LIKE A *GHOST*.

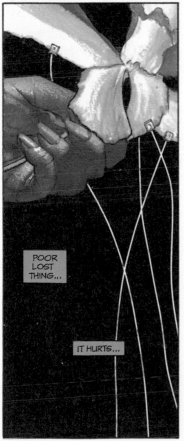

POOR LOST THING...

IT HURTS...

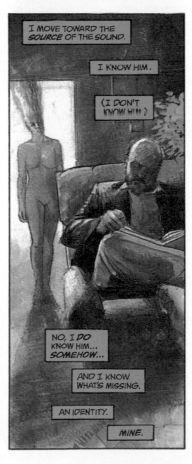

I MOVE TOWARD THE *SOURCE* OF THE SOUND.

I KNOW HIM.

(I DON'T KNOW HIM.)

NO, I *DO* KNOW HIM... *SOMEHOW*...

AND I KNOW WHAT'S MISSING.

AN IDENTITY.

MINE.

WHO AM I?

UH --

-- WHO *ARE* YOU? YOU REALLY DON'T *KNOW?* THAT'S *STRANGE*...

"THE *OTHER* ONE KNEW *IMMEDIATELY.*"

YOUR TEAM WAS VERY *PROMPT,* CAPTAIN. I'M *IMPRESSED.* NO, *REALLY.* I'M *PERSONALLY* GOING TO MAKE SURE THE *MAYOR* HEARS ABOUT THIS!

THANK *YOU,* MR. *STERLING.* WE'VE GOT A *BACKUP* FIRE TRUCK COMING DOWN FROM *METROPOLIS* AS WELL... SHOULD BE ANOTHER *FIFTEEN* MINUTES MAYBE...

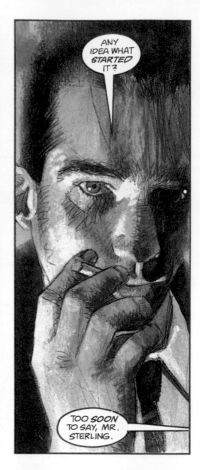

ANY IDEA WHAT *STARTED* IT?

TOO *SOON* TO SAY, MR. STERLING.

THIS IS FOR YOU AND YOUR MEN, CHIEF.

I APPRECIATE WHAT YOU'RE DOING.

IF YOU *NEED* ME I'LL BE IN THE *BAR* ACROSS THE STREET.

GOT TO PHONE HOME.

AND...UH... DON'T PUT IT OUT *TOO* FAST. KNOW WHAT I'M SAYING?

WHAT? OH... YEAH. RIGHT. FOR *CERTAIN.*

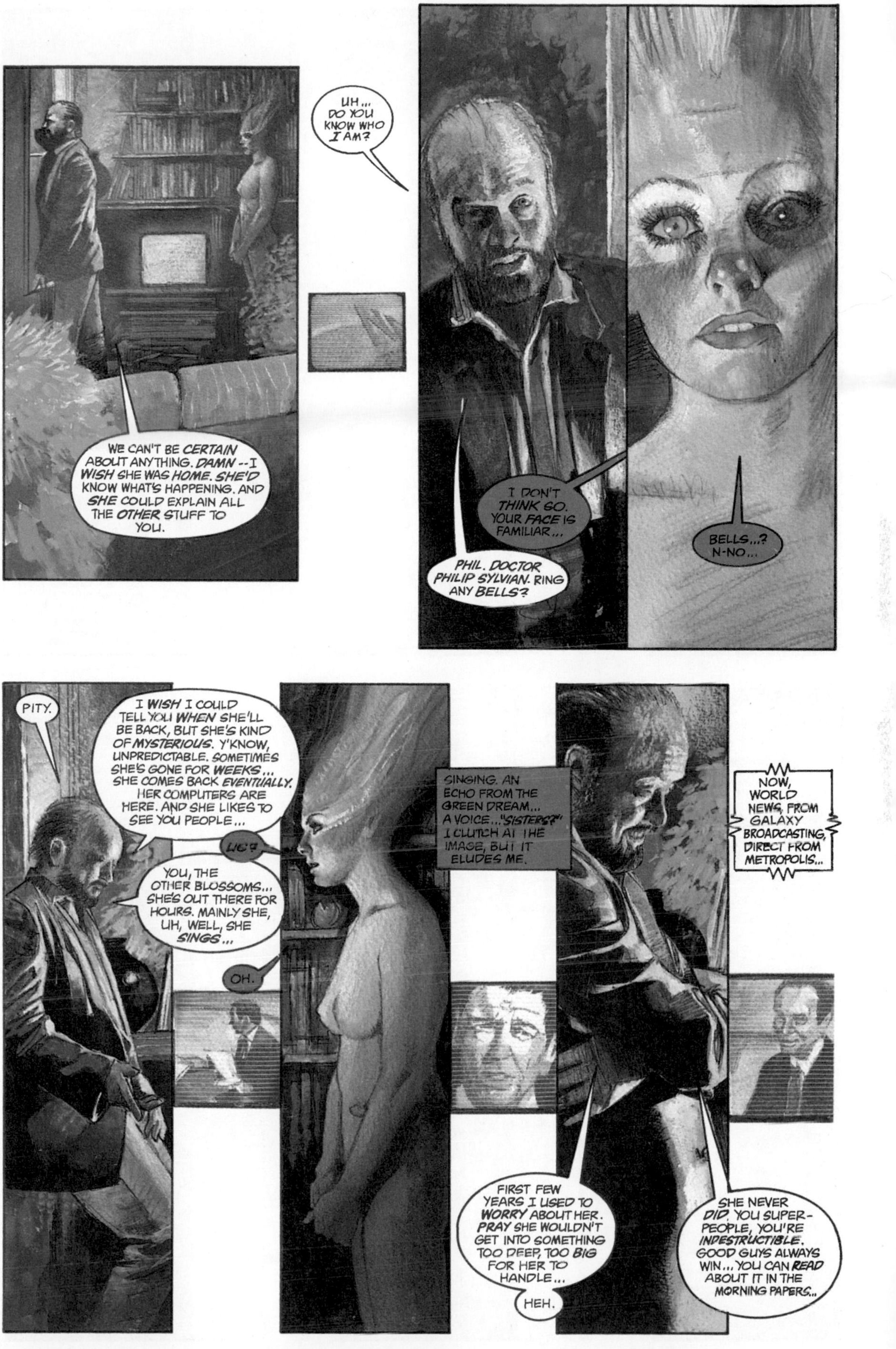
WE CAN'T BE CERTAIN ABOUT ANYTHING. DAMN -- I WISH SHE WAS HOME. SHE'D KNOW WHAT'S HAPPENING. AND SHE COULD EXPLAIN ALL THE OTHER STUFF TO YOU.
UH... DO YOU KNOW WHO I AM?
I DON'T THINK SO. YOUR FACE IS FAMILIAR...
PHIL. DOCTOR PHILIP SYLVIAN. RING ANY BELLS?
BELLS...? N-NO...
PITY.
I WISH I COULD TELL YOU WHEN SHE'LL BE BACK, BUT SHE'S KIND OF MYSTERIOUS. Y'KNOW, UNPREDICTABLE. SOMETIMES SHE'S GONE FOR WEEKS... SHE COMES BACK EVENTUALLY. HER COMPUTERS ARE HERE. AND SHE LIKES TO SEE YOU PEOPLE...
UH?
YOU, THE OTHER BLOSSOMS... SHE'S OUT THERE FOR HOURS. MAINLY SHE, UH, WELL, SHE SINGS...
OH.
SINGING. AN ECHO FROM THE GREEN DREAM... A VOICE... "SISTERS?" I CLUTCH AT THE IMAGE, BUT IT ELUDES ME.
NOW, WORLD NEWS, FROM GALAXY BROADCASTING, DIRECT FROM METROPOLIS...
FIRST FEW YEARS I USED TO WORRY ABOUT HER. PRAY SHE WOULDN'T GET INTO SOMETHING TOO DEEP, TOO BIG FOR HER TO HANDLE...
HEH.
SHE NEVER DID. YOU SUPER-PEOPLE, YOU'RE INDESTRUCTIBLE. GOOD GUYS ALWAYS WIN... YOU CAN READ ABOUT IT IN THE MORNING PAPERS...

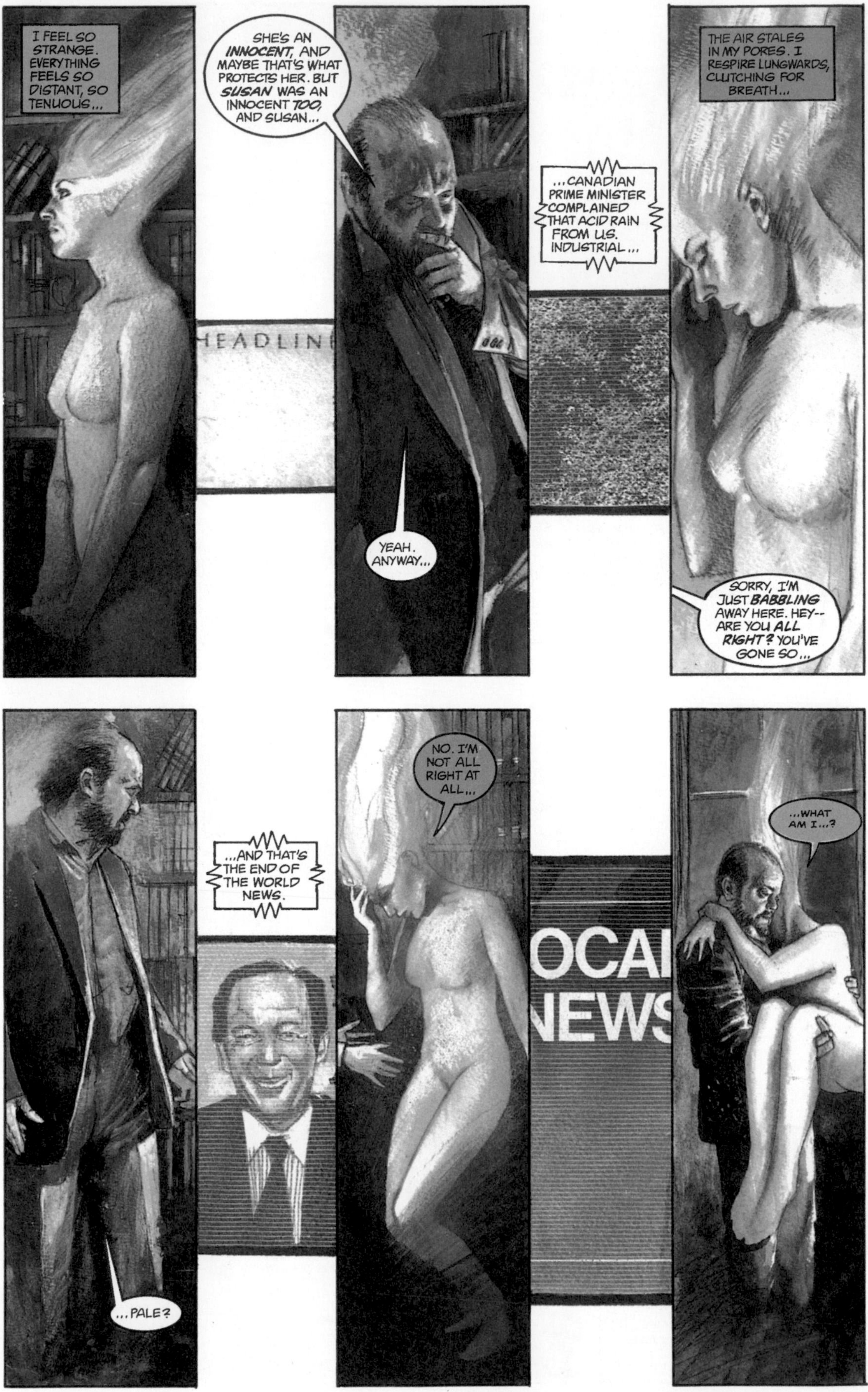
I FEEL SO STRANGE. EVERYTHING FEELS SO DISTANT, SO TENUOUS...
SHE'S AN INNOCENT, AND MAYBE THAT'S WHAT PROTECTS HER. BUT SUSAN WAS AN INNOCENT TOO, AND SUSAN...
HEADLIN
YEAH. ANYWAY...
...CANADIAN PRIME MINISTER COMPLAINED THAT ACID RAIN FROM U.S. INDUSTRIAL...
THE AIR STALES IN MY PORES. I RESPIRE LUNGWARDS, CLUTCHING FOR BREATH...
SORRY, I'M JUST BABBLING AWAY HERE. HEY-- ARE YOU ALL RIGHT? YOU'VE GONE SO...
...PALE?
...AND THAT'S THE END OF THE WORLD NEWS.
NO. I'M NOT ALL RIGHT AT ALL...
OCAL NEWS
...WHAT AM I...?

...RAGES IN A DOWNTOWN OFFICE BUILDING EVEN AS I SPEAK.

FILM TAKEN BY AN AMATEUR CAMERAMAN SHOWS AT LEAST ONE WOMAN LOST HER LIFE IN THE BLAZING INFERNO...

AMATEUR VIDE

OH GOD.

TH-THAT'S ALL I N-NEED...

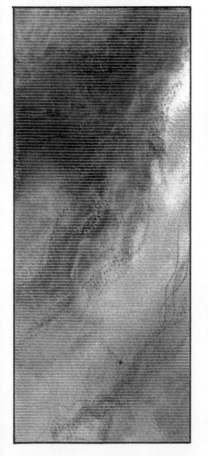

THAT ALL YOU NEED, SIR?

I'D LIKE TO USE YOUR *PHONE*, IF I MAY.

SURE THING. PHONE'S OVER THERE.

HELLO, SIR.

AH, MR. CHAIRMAN. YOU HAVE *NEWS* FOR ME...?

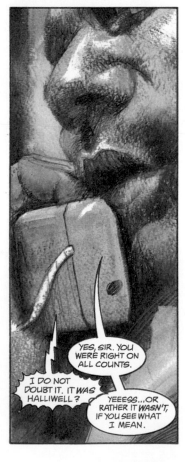

YES, SIR. YOU WERE RIGHT ON ALL COUNTS.

I DO NOT DOUBT IT. IT *WAS* HALLIWELL?

YEEESS...OR RATHER IT *WASN'T*, IF YOU SEE WHAT I MEAN.

VERY DROLL. AND SHE HAS BEEN SUCCESSFULLY *DISPOSED OF*? IN THE *MANNER* I *SUGGESTED*?

OH, SURE. I TOOK CARE OF IT *PERSONALLY*.

HEH... "NO *FLOWERS BY REQUEST*"..

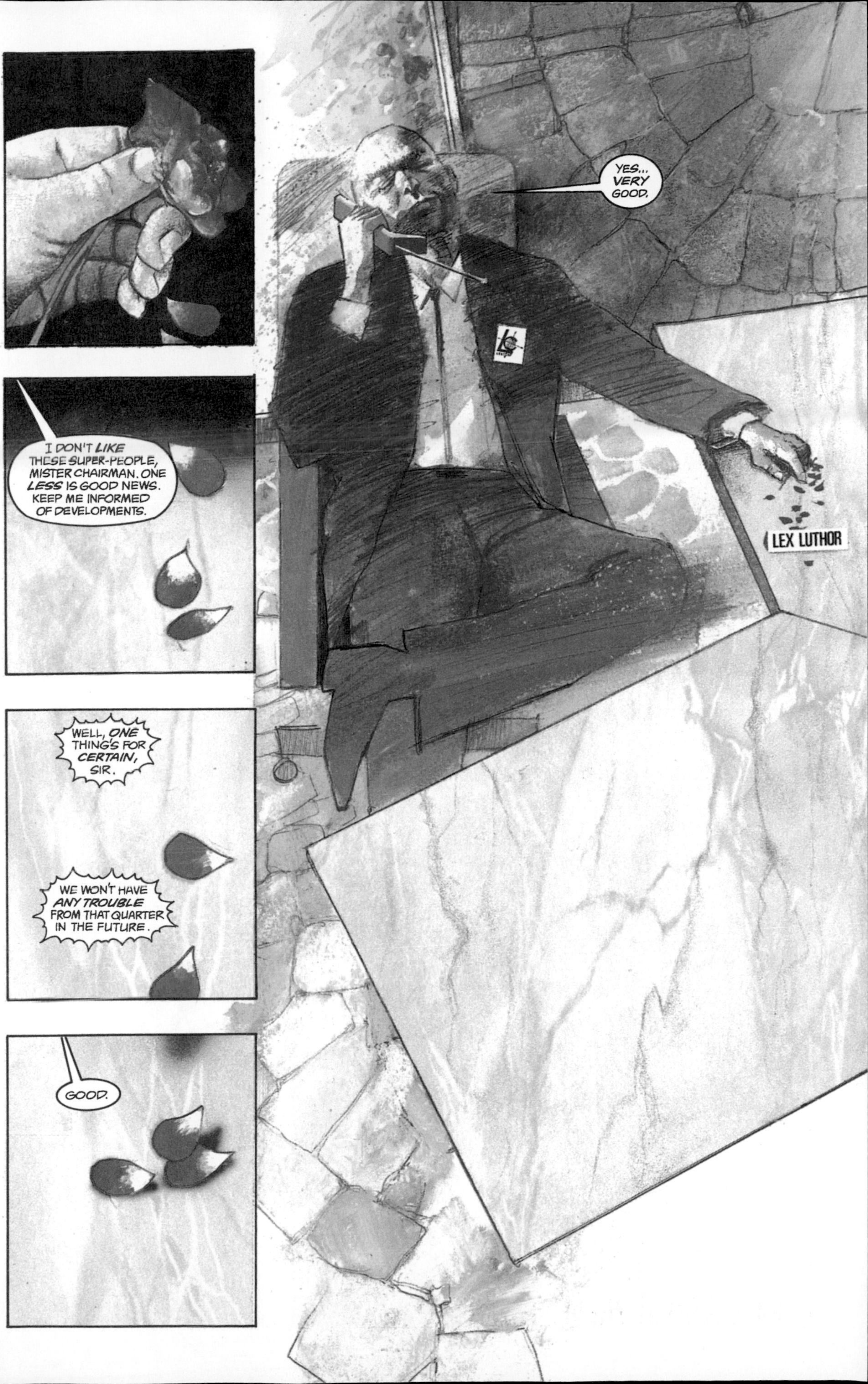
YES... VERY GOOD.
I DON'T LIKE THESE SUPER-PEOPLE, MISTER CHAIRMAN. ONE LESS IS GOOD NEWS. KEEP ME INFORMED OF DEVELOPMENTS.
LEX LUTHOR
WELL, ONE THING'S FOR CERTAIN, SIR.
WE WON'T HAVE ANY TROUBLE FROM THAT QUARTER IN THE FUTURE.
GOOD.

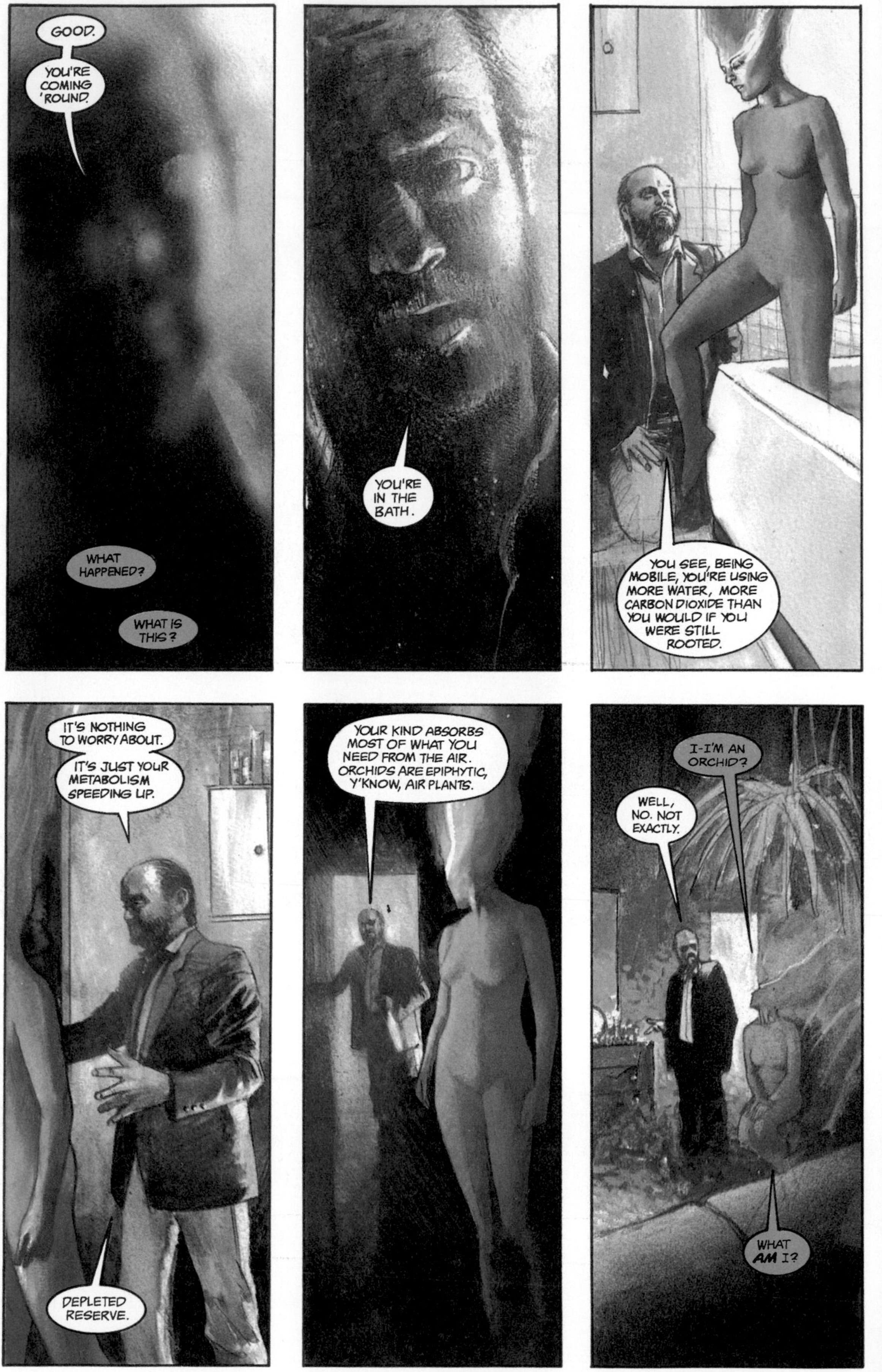
GOOD.
YOU'RE COMING 'ROUND.
WHAT HAPPENED?
WHAT IS THIS?
YOU'RE IN THE BATH.
YOU SEE, BEING MOBILE, YOU'RE USING MORE WATER, MORE CARBON DIOXIDE THAN YOU WOULD IF YOU WERE STILL ROOTED.
IT'S NOTHING TO WORRY ABOUT.
IT'S JUST YOUR METABOLISM SPEEDING UP.
DEPLETED RESERVE.
YOUR KIND ABSORBS MOST OF WHAT YOU NEED FROM THE AIR. ORCHIDS ARE EPIPHYTIC, Y'KNOW, AIR PLANTS.
I-I'M AN ORCHID?
WELL, NO. NOT EXACTLY.
WHAT AM I?

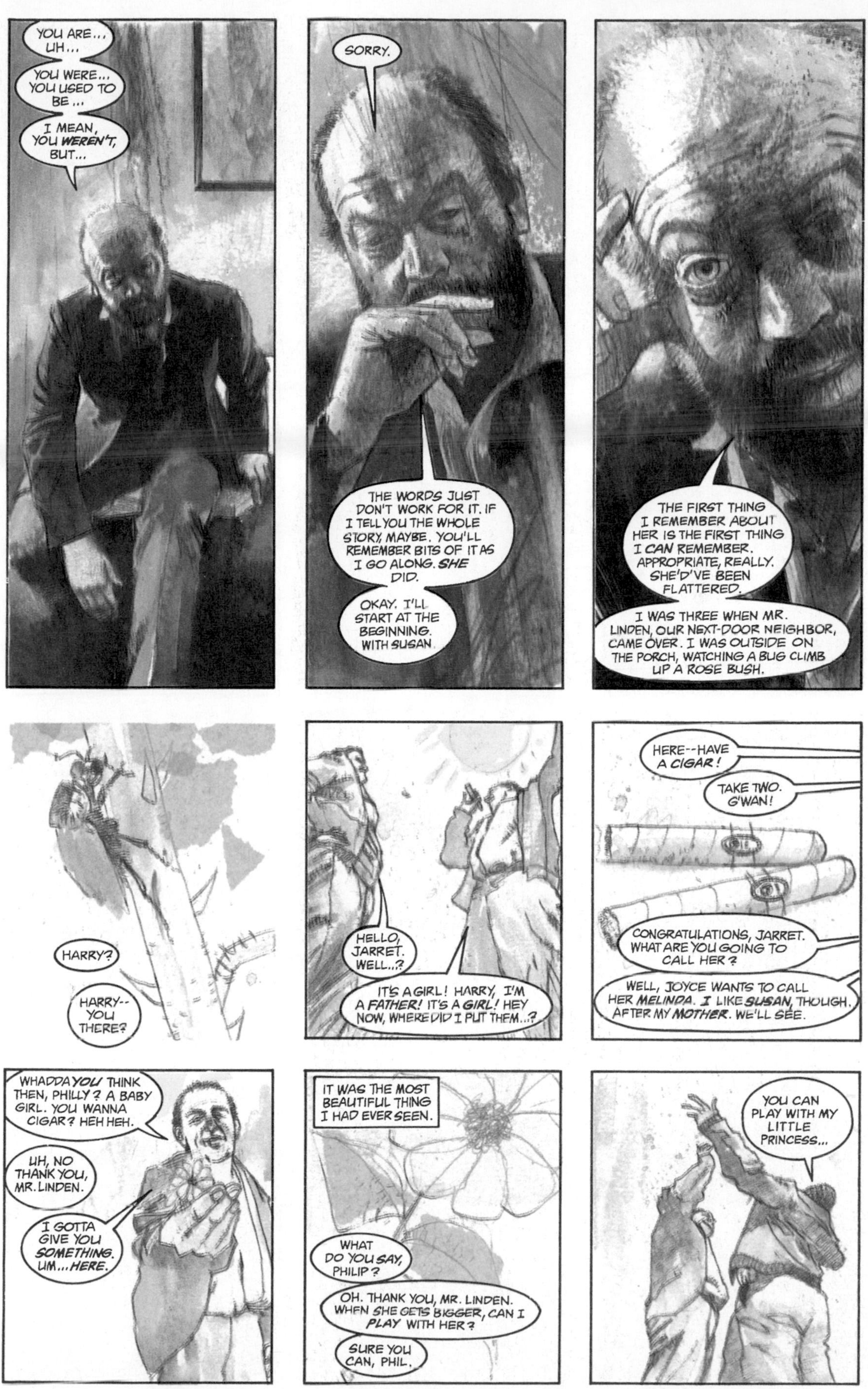

YOU ARE... UH...
YOU WERE... YOU USED TO BE...
I MEAN, YOU WEREN'T, BUT...
SORRY.
THE WORDS JUST DON'T WORK FOR IT. IF I TELL YOU THE WHOLE STORY, MAYBE. YOU'LL REMEMBER BITS OF IT AS I GO ALONG. SHE DID.
OKAY. I'LL START AT THE BEGINNING. WITH SUSAN.
THE FIRST THING I REMEMBER ABOUT HER IS THE FIRST THING I CAN REMEMBER. APPROPRIATE, REALLY. SHE'D'VE BEEN FLATTERED.
I WAS THREE WHEN MR. LINDEN, OUR NEXT-DOOR NEIGHBOR, CAME OVER. I WAS OUTSIDE ON THE PORCH, WATCHING A BUG CLIMB UP A ROSE BUSH.
HARRY?
HARRY-- YOU THERE?
HELLO, JARRET. WELL...?
IT'S A GIRL! HARRY, I'M A FATHER! IT'S A GIRL! HEY NOW, WHERE DID I PUT THEM...?
HERE--HAVE A CIGAR!
TAKE TWO. G'WAN!
CONGRATULATIONS, JARRET. WHAT ARE YOU GOING TO CALL HER?
WELL, JOYCE WANTS TO CALL HER MELINDA. I LIKE SUSAN, THOUGH. AFTER MY MOTHER. WE'LL SEE.
WHADDA YOU THINK THEN, PHILLY? A BABY GIRL. YOU WANNA CIGAR? HEH HEH.
UH, NO THANK YOU, MR. LINDEN.
I GOTTA GIVE YOU SOMETHING. UM... HERE.
IT WAS THE MOST BEAUTIFUL THING I HAD EVER SEEN.
WHAT DO YOU SAY, PHILIP?
OH. THANK YOU, MR. LINDEN. WHEN SHE GETS BIGGER, CAN I PLAY WITH HER?
SURE YOU CAN, PHIL.
YOU CAN PLAY WITH MY LITTLE PRINCESS...

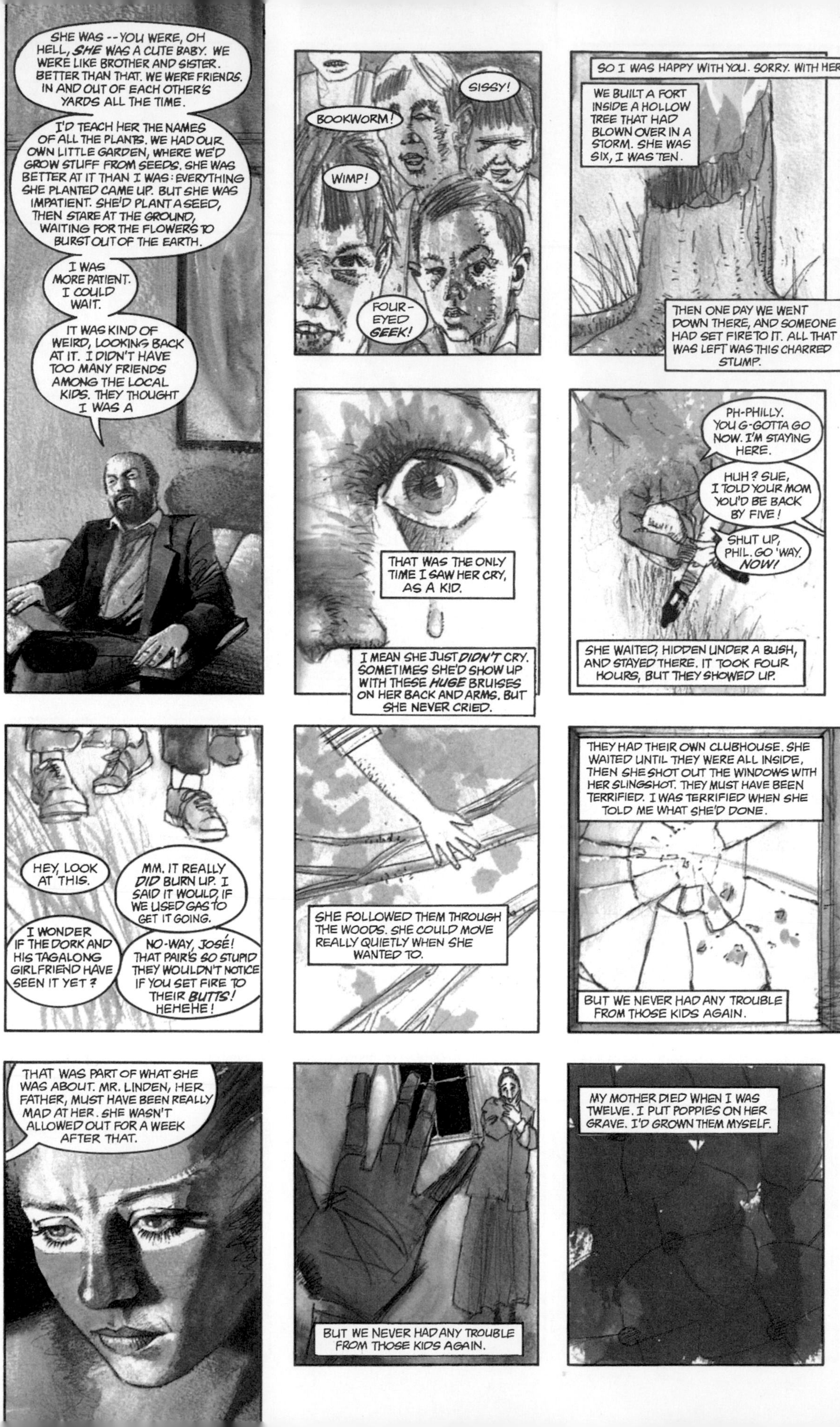
SHE WAS --YOU WERE, OH HELL, SHE WAS A CUTE BABY. WE WERE LIKE BROTHER AND SISTER. BETTER THAN THAT. WE WERE FRIENDS. IN AND OUT OF EACH OTHER'S YARDS ALL THE TIME.
I'D TEACH HER THE NAMES OF ALL THE PLANTS. WE HAD OUR OWN LITTLE GARDEN, WHERE WE'D GROW STUFF FROM SEEDS. SHE WAS BETTER AT IT THAN I WAS: EVERYTHING SHE PLANTED CAME UP. BUT SHE WAS IMPATIENT. SHE'D PLANT A SEED, THEN STARE AT THE GROUND, WAITING FOR THE FLOWERS TO BURST OUT OF THE EARTH.
I WAS MORE PATIENT. I COULD WAIT.
IT WAS KIND OF WEIRD, LOOKING BACK AT IT. I DIDN'T HAVE TOO MANY FRIENDS AMONG THE LOCAL KIDS. THEY THOUGHT I WAS A
SISSY!
BOOKWORM!
WIMP!
FOUR-EYED GEEK!
SO I WAS HAPPY WITH YOU. SORRY. WITH HER.
WE BUILT A FORT INSIDE A HOLLOW TREE THAT HAD BLOWN OVER IN A STORM. SHE WAS SIX, I WAS TEN.
THEN ONE DAY WE WENT DOWN THERE, AND SOMEONE HAD SET FIRE TO IT. ALL THAT WAS LEFT WAS THIS CHARRED STUMP.
THAT WAS THE ONLY TIME I SAW HER CRY, AS A KID.
I MEAN SHE JUST DIDN'T CRY. SOMETIMES SHE'D SHOW UP WITH THESE HUGE BRUISES ON HER BACK AND ARMS. BUT SHE NEVER CRIED.
PH-PHILLY. YOU G-GOTTA GO NOW. I'M STAYING HERE.
HUH? SUE, I TOLD YOUR MOM YOU'D BE BACK BY FIVE!
SHUT UP, PHIL. GO 'WAY. NOW!
SHE WAITED, HIDDEN UNDER A BUSH, AND STAYED THERE. IT TOOK FOUR HOURS, BUT THEY SHOWED UP.
HEY, LOOK AT THIS.
MM. IT REALLY DID BURN UP. I SAID IT WOULD, IF WE USED GAS TO GET IT GOING.
I WONDER IF THE DORK AND HIS TAGALONG GIRLFRIEND HAVE SEEN IT YET?
NO-WAY, JOSÉ! THAT PAIR'S SO STUPID THEY WOULDN'T NOTICE IF YOU SET FIRE TO THEIR BUTTS! HEHEHE!
SHE FOLLOWED THEM THROUGH THE WOODS. SHE COULD MOVE REALLY QUIETLY WHEN SHE WANTED TO.
THEY HAD THEIR OWN CLUBHOUSE. SHE WAITED UNTIL THEY WERE ALL INSIDE, THEN SHE SHOT OUT THE WINDOWS WITH HER SLINGSHOT. THEY MUST HAVE BEEN TERRIFIED. I WAS TERRIFIED WHEN SHE TOLD ME WHAT SHE'D DONE.
BUT WE NEVER HAD ANY TROUBLE FROM THOSE KIDS AGAIN.
THAT WAS PART OF WHAT SHE WAS ABOUT. MR. LINDEN, HER FATHER, MUST HAVE BEEN REALLY MAD AT HER. SHE WASN'T ALLOWED OUT FOR A WEEK AFTER THAT.
BUT WE NEVER HAD ANY TROUBLE FROM THOSE KIDS AGAIN.
MY MOTHER DIED WHEN I WAS TWELVE. I PUT POPPIES ON HER GRAVE. I'D GROWN THEM MYSELF.

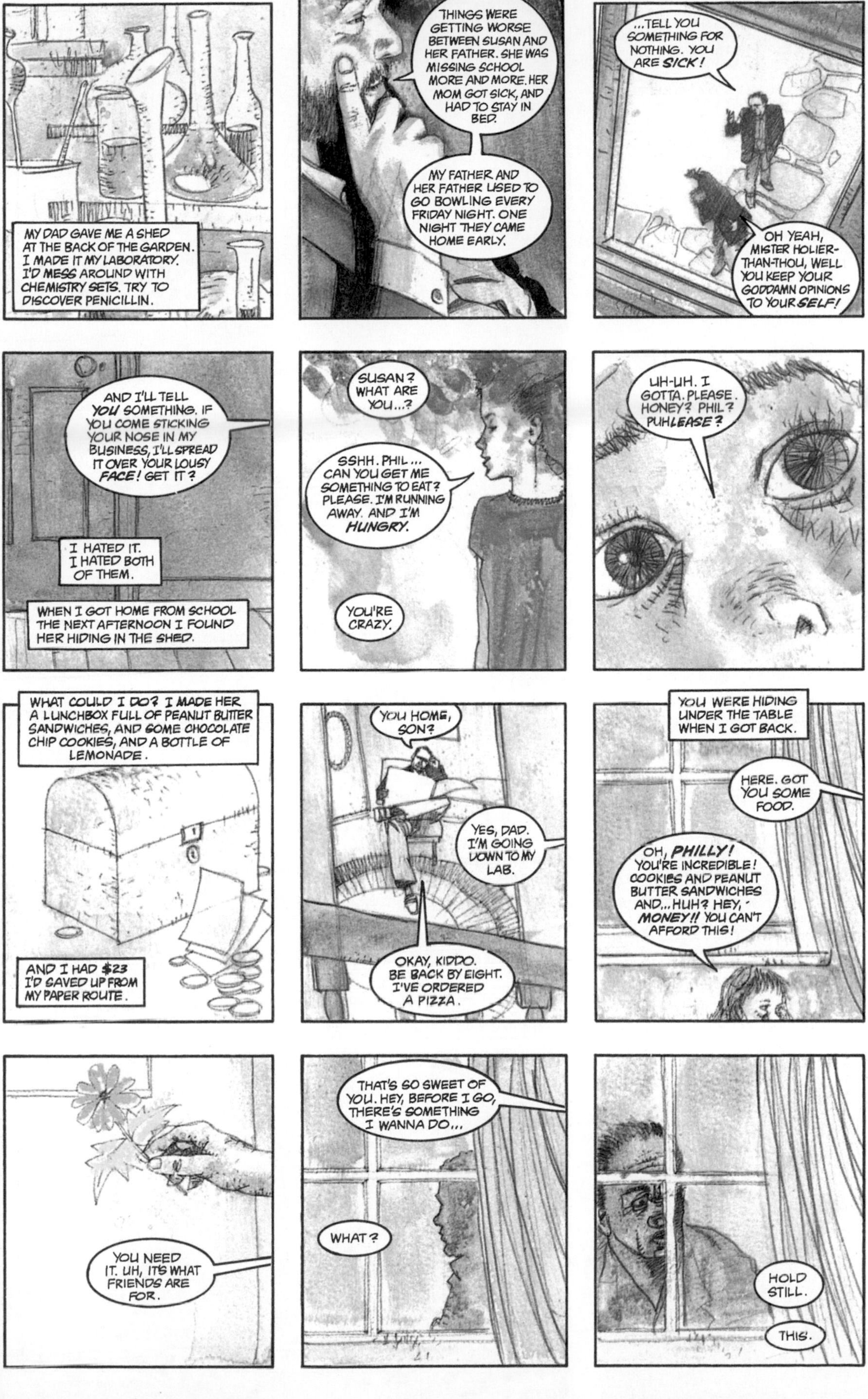
MY DAD GAVE ME A SHED AT THE BACK OF THE GARDEN. I MADE IT MY LABORATORY. I'D MESS AROUND WITH CHEMISTRY SETS. TRY TO DISCOVER PENICILLIN.
THINGS WERE GETTING WORSE BETWEEN SUSAN AND HER FATHER. SHE WAS MISSING SCHOOL MORE AND MORE. HER MOM GOT SICK, AND HAD TO STAY IN BED.
MY FATHER AND HER FATHER USED TO GO BOWLING EVERY FRIDAY NIGHT. ONE NIGHT THEY CAME HOME EARLY.
...TELL YOU SOMETHING FOR NOTHING. YOU ARE SICK!
OH YEAH, MISTER HOLIER-THAN-THOU, WELL YOU KEEP YOUR GODDAMN OPINIONS TO YOUR SELF!
AND I'LL TELL YOU SOMETHING. IF YOU COME STICKING YOUR NOSE IN MY BUSINESS, I'LL SPREAD IT OVER YOUR LOUSY FACE! GET IT?
I HATED IT. I HATED BOTH OF THEM.
WHEN I GOT HOME FROM SCHOOL THE NEXT AFTERNOON I FOUND HER HIDING IN THE SHED.
SUSAN? WHAT ARE YOU...?
SSHH. PHIL... CAN YOU GET ME SOMETHING TO EAT? PLEASE. I'M RUNNING AWAY. AND I'M HUNGRY.
YOU'RE CRAZY.
UH-UH. I GOTTA. PLEASE. HONEY? PHIL? PUHLEASE?
WHAT COULD I DO? I MADE HER A LUNCHBOX FULL OF PEANUT BUTTER SANDWICHES, AND SOME CHOCOLATE CHIP COOKIES, AND A BOTTLE OF LEMONADE.
AND I HAD $23 I'D SAVED UP FROM MY PAPER ROUTE.
YOU HOME, SON?
YES, DAD. I'M GOING DOWN TO MY LAB.
OKAY, KIDDO. BE BACK BY EIGHT. I'VE ORDERED A PIZZA.
YOU WERE HIDING UNDER THE TABLE WHEN I GOT BACK.
HERE. GOT YOU SOME FOOD.
OH, PHILLY! YOU'RE INCREDIBLE! COOKIES AND PEANUT BUTTER SANDWICHES AND... HUH? HEY, MONEY!! YOU CAN'T AFFORD THIS!
YOU NEED IT. UH, IT'S WHAT FRIENDS ARE FOR.
THAT'S SO SWEET OF YOU. HEY, BEFORE I GO, THERE'S SOMETHING I WANNA DO...
WHAT?
HOLD STILL.
THIS.

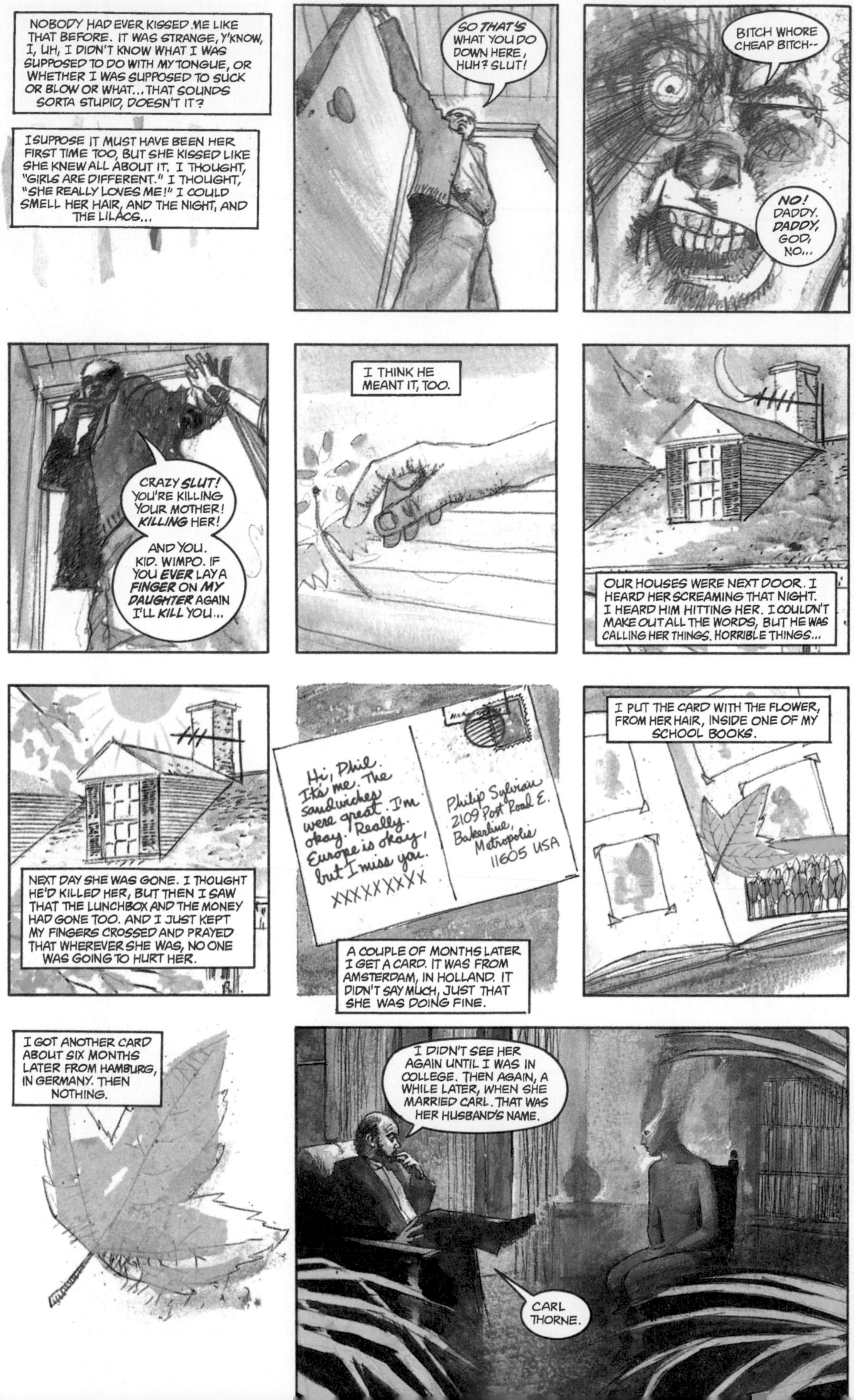
NOBODY HAD EVER KISSED ME LIKE THAT BEFORE. IT WAS STRANGE, Y'KNOW, I, UH, I DIDN'T KNOW WHAT I WAS SUPPOSED TO DO WITH MY TONGUE, OR WHETHER I WAS SUPPOSED TO SUCK OR BLOW OR WHAT... THAT SOUNDS SORTA STUPID, DOESN'T IT?
I SUPPOSE IT MUST HAVE BEEN HER FIRST TIME TOO, BUT SHE KISSED LIKE SHE KNEW ALL ABOUT IT. I THOUGHT, "GIRLS ARE DIFFERENT." I THOUGHT, "SHE REALLY LOVES ME!" I COULD SMELL HER HAIR, AND THE NIGHT, AND THE LILACS...
SO THAT'S WHAT YOU DO DOWN HERE, HUH? SLUT!
BITCH WHORE CHEAP BITCH--
NO! DADDY. DADDY, GOD, NO...
CRAZY SLUT! YOU'RE KILLING YOUR MOTHER! KILLING HER!
AND YOU. KID. WIMPO. IF YOU EVER LAY A FINGER ON MY DAUGHTER AGAIN I'LL KILL YOU...
I THINK HE MEANT IT, TOO.
OUR HOUSES WERE NEXT DOOR. I HEARD HER SCREAMING THAT NIGHT. I HEARD HIM HITTING HER. I COULDN'T MAKE OUT ALL THE WORDS, BUT HE WAS CALLING HER THINGS. HORRIBLE THINGS...
NEXT DAY SHE WAS GONE. I THOUGHT HE'D KILLED HER, BUT THEN I SAW THAT THE LUNCHBOX AND THE MONEY HAD GONE TOO. AND I JUST KEPT MY FINGERS CROSSED AND PRAYED THAT WHEREVER SHE WAS, NO ONE WAS GOING TO HURT HER.
Hi, Phil. It's me. The sandwiches were great. I'm okay. Really. Europe is okay, but I miss you. XXXXXXXX
Philip Sylvian 2109 Post Road E. Bakerline, Metropolis 11605 USA
A COUPLE OF MONTHS LATER I GET A CARD. IT WAS FROM AMSTERDAM, IN HOLLAND. IT DIDN'T SAY MUCH, JUST THAT SHE WAS DOING FINE.
I PUT THE CARD WITH THE FLOWER, FROM HER HAIR, INSIDE ONE OF MY SCHOOL BOOKS.
I GOT ANOTHER CARD ABOUT SIX MONTHS LATER FROM HAMBURG, IN GERMANY. THEN NOTHING.
I DIDN'T SEE HER AGAIN UNTIL I WAS IN COLLEGE. THEN AGAIN, A WHILE LATER, WHEN SHE MARRIED CARL. THAT WAS HER HUSBAND'S NAME.
CARL THORNE.

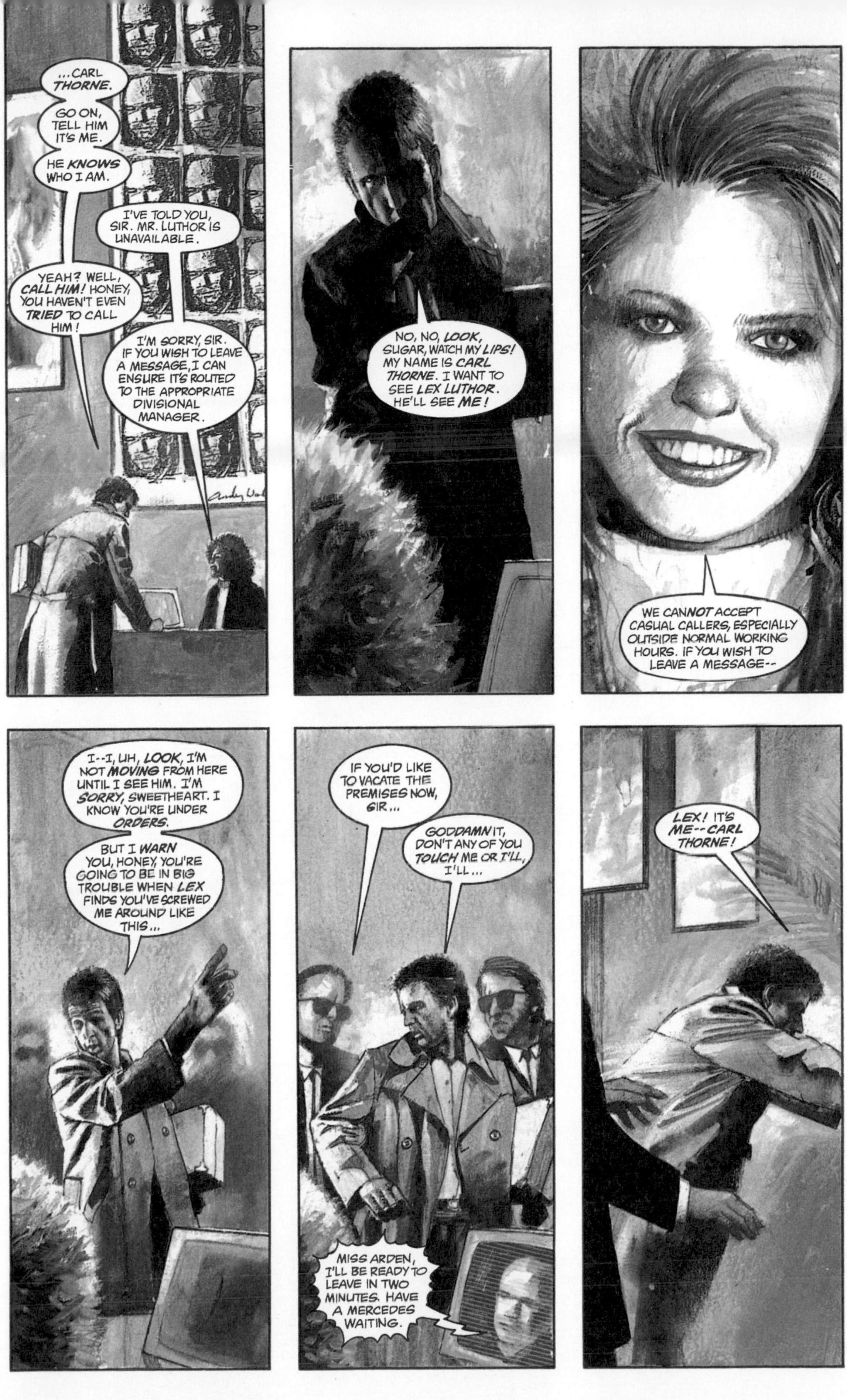
...CARL THORNE.
GO ON, TELL HIM IT'S ME.
HE KNOWS WHO I AM.
I'VE TOLD YOU, SIR. MR. LUTHOR IS UNAVAILABLE.
YEAH? WELL, CALL HIM! HONEY, YOU HAVEN'T EVEN TRIED TO CALL HIM!
I'M SORRY, SIR. IF YOU WISH TO LEAVE A MESSAGE, I CAN ENSURE IT'S ROUTED TO THE APPROPRIATE DIVISIONAL MANAGER.
NO, NO, LOOK, SUGAR, WATCH MY LIPS! MY NAME IS CARL THORNE. I WANT TO SEE LEX LUTHOR. HE'LL SEE ME!
WE CANNOT ACCEPT CASUAL CALLERS, ESPECIALLY OUTSIDE NORMAL WORKING HOURS. IF YOU WISH TO LEAVE A MESSAGE--
I--I, UH, LOOK, I'M NOT MOVING FROM HERE UNTIL I SEE HIM. I'M SORRY, SWEETHEART. I KNOW YOU'RE UNDER ORDERS.
BUT I WARN YOU, HONEY, YOU'RE GOING TO BE IN BIG TROUBLE WHEN LEX FINDS YOU'VE SCREWED ME AROUND LIKE THIS...
IF YOU'D LIKE TO VACATE THE PREMISES NOW, SIR...
GODDAMN IT, DON'T ANY OF YOU TOUCH ME OR I'LL, I'LL...
MISS ARDEN, I'LL BE READY TO LEAVE IN TWO MINUTES. HAVE A MERCEDES WAITING.
LEX! IT'S ME--CARL THORNE!

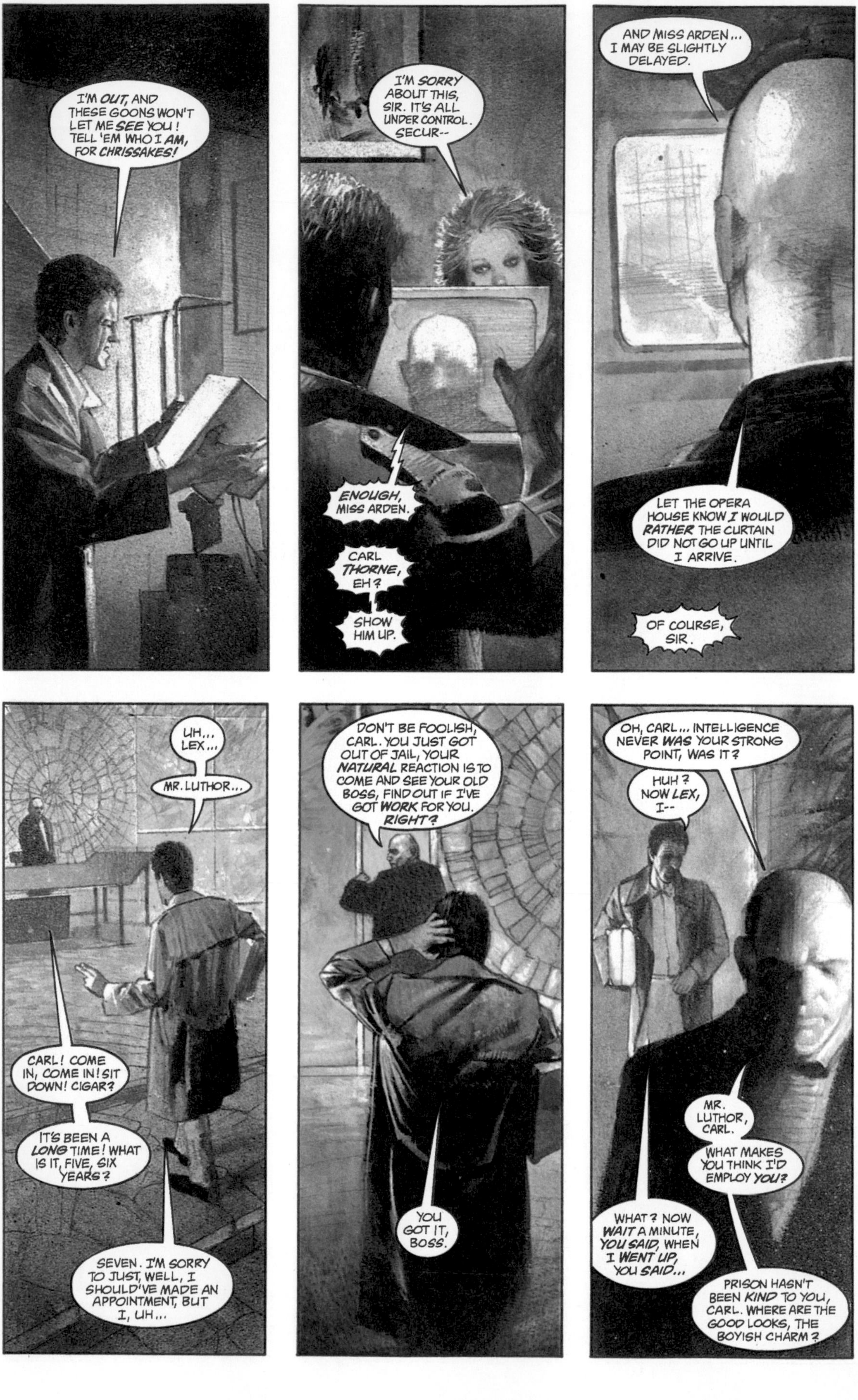
I'M OUT, AND THESE GOONS WON'T LET ME SEE YOU! TELL 'EM WHO I AM, FOR CHRISSAKES!
I'M SORRY ABOUT THIS, SIR. IT'S ALL UNDER CONTROL. SECUR--
ENOUGH, MISS ARDEN.
CARL THORNE, EH?
SHOW HIM UP.
AND MISS ARDEN... I MAY BE SLIGHTLY DELAYED.
LET THE OPERA HOUSE KNOW I WOULD RATHER THE CURTAIN DID NOT GO UP UNTIL I ARRIVE.
OF COURSE, SIR.
UH... LEX...
MR. LUTHOR...
CARL! COME IN, COME IN! SIT DOWN! CIGAR?
IT'S BEEN A LONG TIME! WHAT IS IT, FIVE, SIX YEARS?
SEVEN. I'M SORRY TO JUST, WELL, I SHOULD'VE MADE AN APPOINTMENT, BUT I, UH...
DON'T BE FOOLISH, CARL. YOU JUST GOT OUT OF JAIL, YOUR NATURAL REACTION IS TO COME AND SEE YOUR OLD BOSS, FIND OUT IF I'VE GOT WORK FOR YOU. RIGHT?
YOU GOT IT, BOSS.
OH, CARL... INTELLIGENCE NEVER WAS YOUR STRONG POINT, WAS IT?
HUH? NOW LEX, I--
MR. LUTHOR, CARL.
WHAT MAKES YOU THINK I'D EMPLOY YOU?
WHAT? NOW WAIT A MINUTE, YOU SAID, WHEN I WENT UP, YOU SAID...
PRISON HASN'T BEEN KIND TO YOU, CARL. WHERE ARE THE GOOD LOOKS, THE BOYISH CHARM?

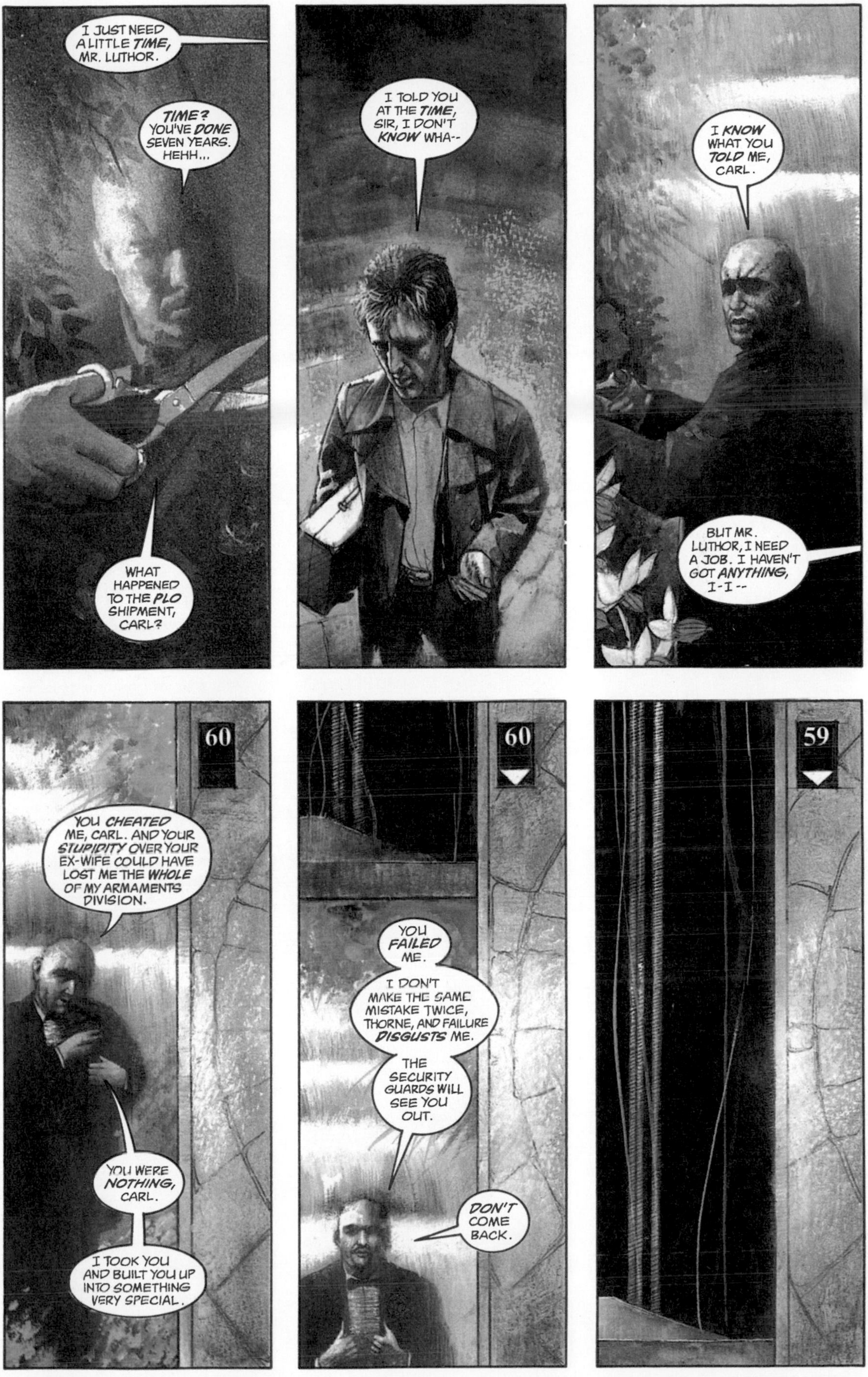
I JUST NEED A LITTLE TIME, MR. LUTHOR.
TIME? YOU'VE DONE SEVEN YEARS. HEHH...
WHAT HAPPENED TO THE PLO SHIPMENT, CARL?
I TOLD YOU AT THE TIME, SIR, I DON'T KNOW WHA--
I KNOW WHAT YOU TOLD ME, CARL.
BUT MR. LUTHOR, I NEED A JOB. I HAVEN'T GOT ANYTHING, I-I--
60
YOU CHEATED ME, CARL. AND YOUR STUPIDITY OVER YOUR EX-WIFE COULD HAVE LOST ME THE WHOLE OF MY ARMAMENTS DIVISION.
YOU WERE NOTHING, CARL.
I TOOK YOU AND BUILT YOU UP INTO SOMETHING VERY SPECIAL.
60
YOU FAILED ME.
I DON'T MAKE THE SAME MISTAKE TWICE, THORNE, AND FAILURE DISGUSTS ME.
THE SECURITY GUARDS WILL SEE YOU OUT.
DON'T COME BACK.
59

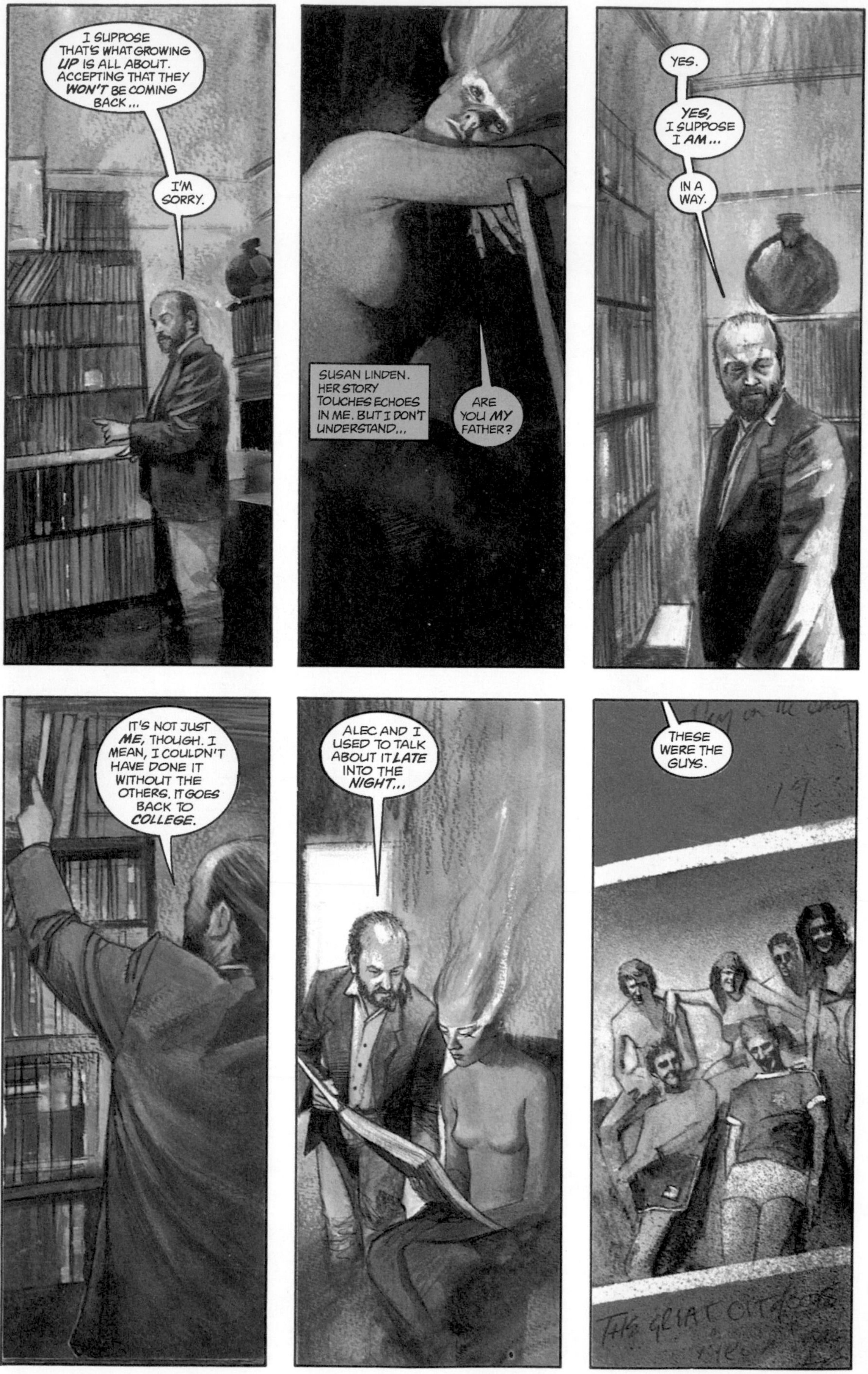
I SUPPOSE THAT'S WHAT GROWING UP IS ALL ABOUT. ACCEPTING THAT THEY WON'T BE COMING BACK...
I'M SORRY.
SUSAN LINDEN. HER STORY TOUCHES ECHOES IN ME. BUT I DON'T UNDERSTAND...
ARE YOU MY FATHER?
YES.
YES, I SUPPOSE I AM...
IN A WAY.
IT'S NOT JUST ME, THOUGH. I MEAN, I COULDN'T HAVE DONE IT WITHOUT THE OTHERS. IT GOES BACK TO COLLEGE.
ALEC AND I USED TO TALK ABOUT IT LATE INTO THE NIGHT...
THESE WERE THE GUYS.

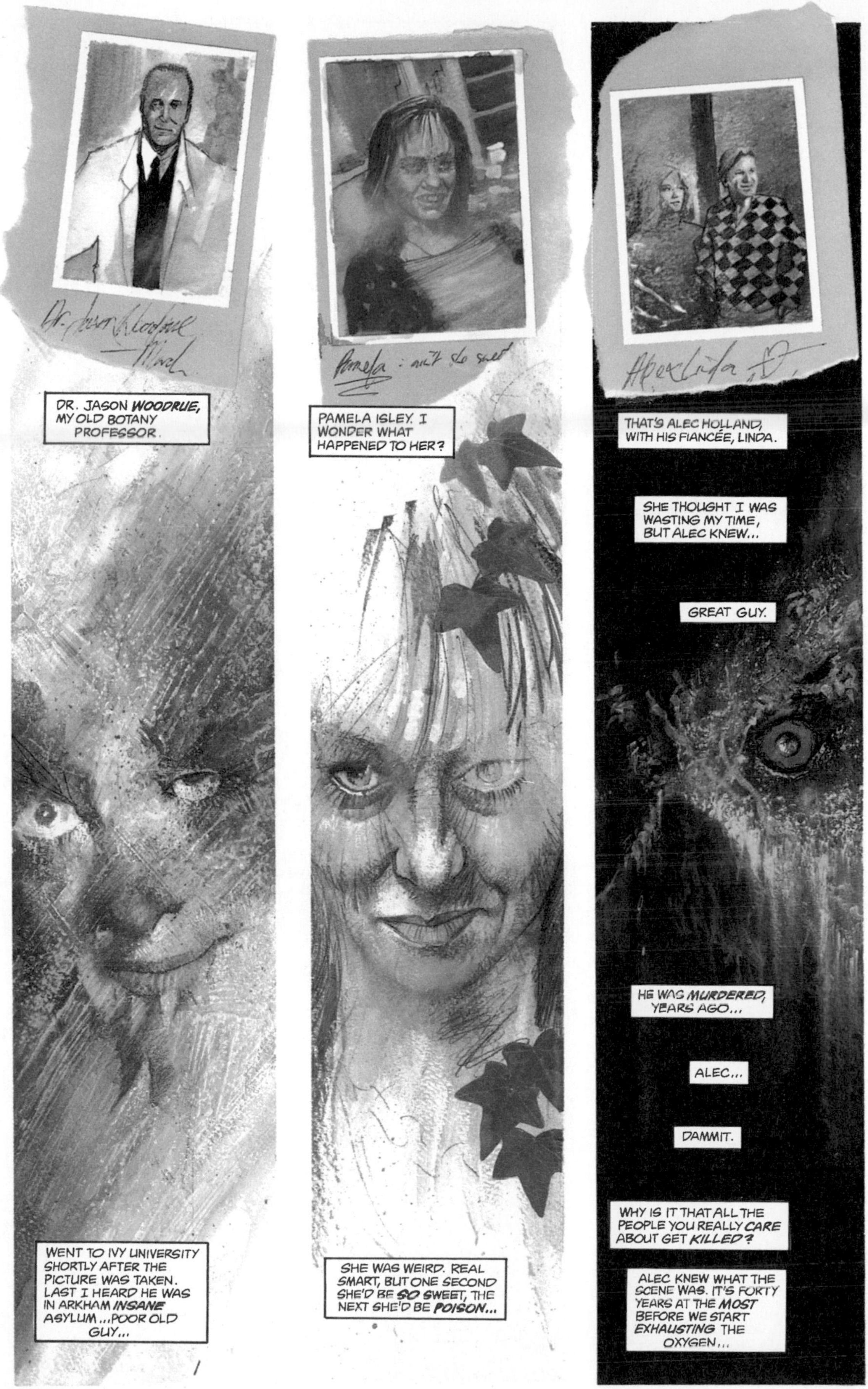
DR. JASON WOODRUE, MY OLD BOTANY PROFESSOR.
WENT TO IVY UNIVERSITY SHORTLY AFTER THE PICTURE WAS TAKEN. LAST I HEARD HE WAS IN ARKHAM INSANE ASYLUM ...POOR OLD GUY...
PAMELA ISLEY. I WONDER WHAT HAPPENED TO HER?
SHE WAS WEIRD. REAL SMART, BUT ONE SECOND SHE'D BE SO SWEET, THE NEXT SHE'D BE POISON...
THAT'S ALEC HOLLAND, WITH HIS FIANCÉE, LINDA.
SHE THOUGHT I WAS WASTING MY TIME, BUT ALEC KNEW...
GREAT GUY.
HE WAS MURDERED, YEARS AGO...
ALEC...
DAMMIT.
WHY IS IT THAT ALL THE PEOPLE YOU REALLY CARE ABOUT GET KILLED?
ALEC KNEW WHAT THE SCENE WAS. IT'S FORTY YEARS AT THE MOST BEFORE WE START EXHAUSTING THE OXYGEN...

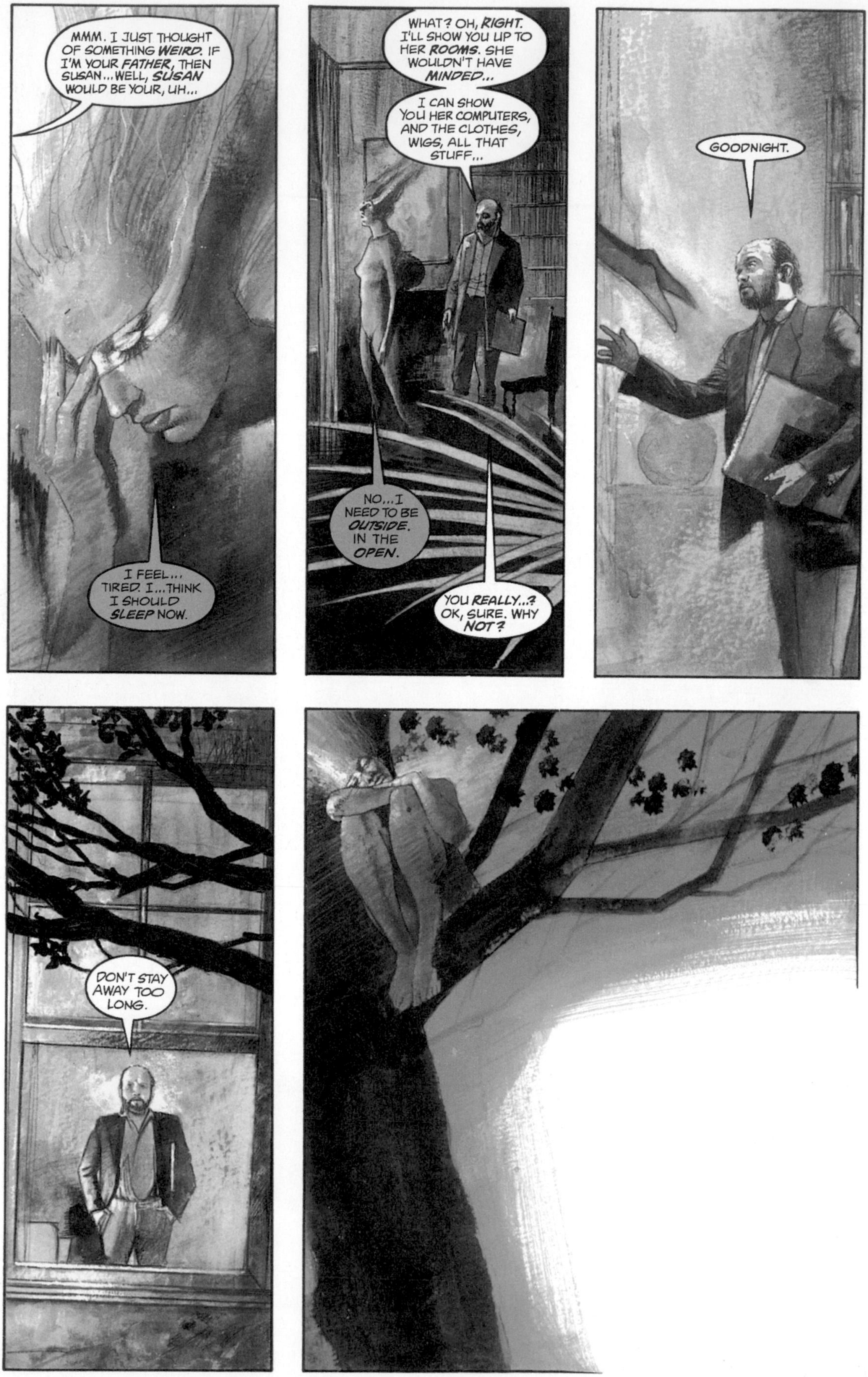
MMM. I JUST THOUGHT OF SOMETHING WEIRD. IF I'M YOUR FATHER, THEN SUSAN...WELL, SUSAN WOULD BE YOUR, UH...
I FEEL... TIRED. I...THINK I SHOULD SLEEP NOW.
WHAT? OH, RIGHT. I'LL SHOW YOU UP TO HER ROOMS. SHE WOULDN'T HAVE MINDED...
I CAN SHOW YOU HER COMPUTERS, AND THE CLOTHES, WIGS, ALL THAT STUFF...
NO...I NEED TO BE OUTSIDE. IN THE OPEN.
YOU REALLY...? OK, SURE. WHY NOT?
GOODNIGHT.
DON'T STAY AWAY TOO LONG.

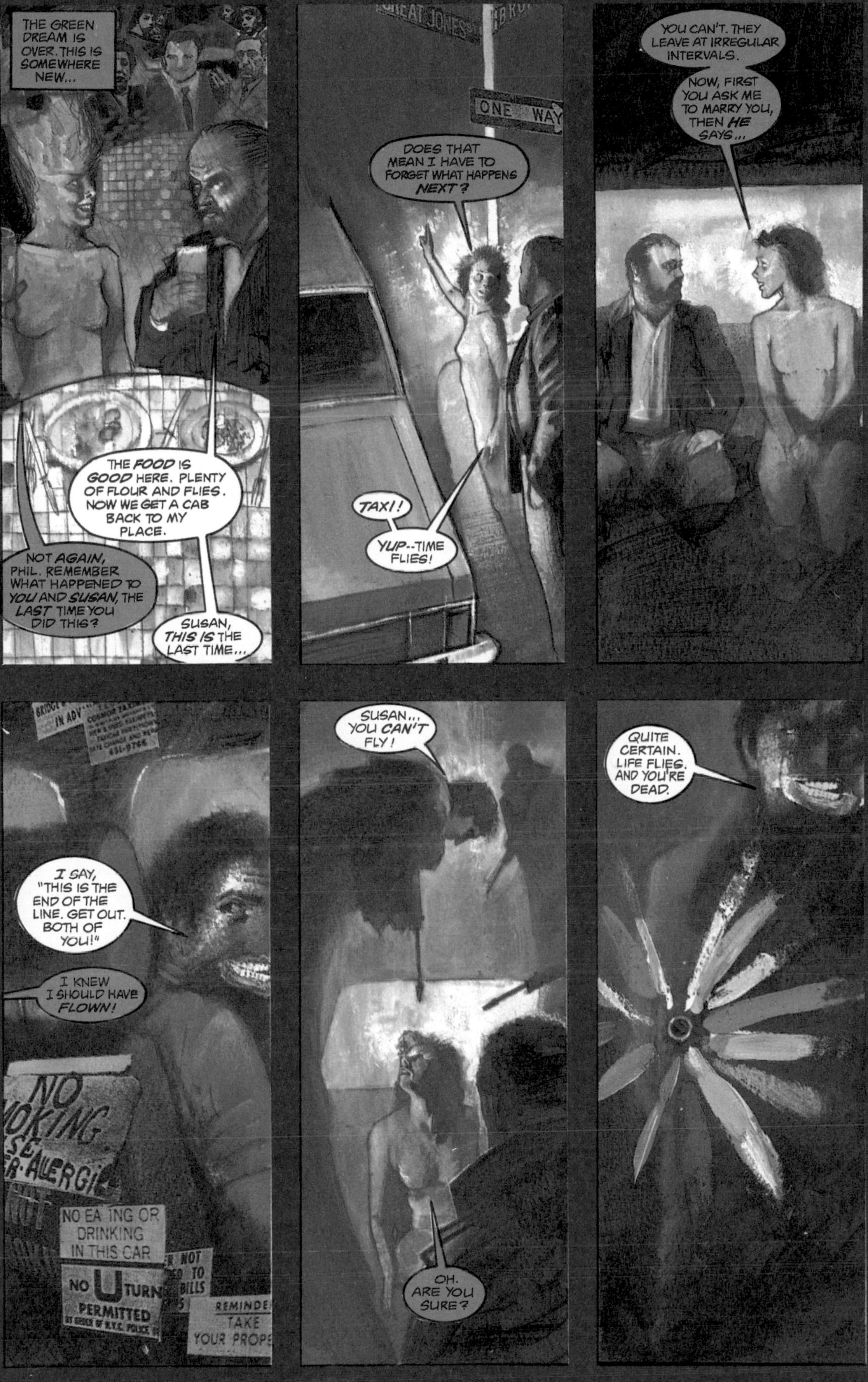
THE GREEN DREAM IS OVER. THIS IS SOMEWHERE NEW...
THE *FOOD* IS *GOOD* HERE. PLENTY OF FLOUR AND FLIES. NOW WE GET A CAB BACK TO MY PLACE.
NOT *AGAIN*, PHIL. REMEMBER WHAT HAPPENED TO *YOU* AND *SUSAN*, THE *LAST* TIME YOU DID THIS?
SUSAN, *THIS IS* THE LAST TIME...
ONE WAY
DOES THAT MEAN I HAVE TO FORGET WHAT HAPPENS *NEXT?*
TAXI!
YUP--TIME FLIES!
YOU CAN'T. THEY LEAVE AT IRREGULAR INTERVALS.
NOW, FIRST YOU ASK ME TO MARRY YOU, THEN *HE* SAYS...
I SAY, "THIS IS THE END OF THE LINE. GET OUT. BOTH OF YOU!"
I KNEW I SHOULD HAVE *FLOWN!*
NO EA ING OR DRINKING IN THIS CAR
NO U TURN PERMITTED
SUSAN... YOU *CAN'T* FLY!
OH. ARE YOU SURE?
QUITE CERTAIN. LIFE FLIES. AND YOU'RE DEAD.

...ONE THING IS CERTAIN.

I MEAN,

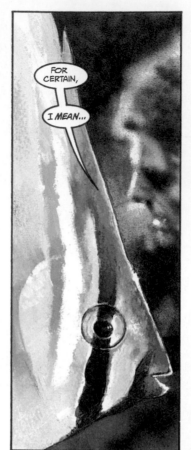

FOR CERTAIN,

I MEAN...

...WHAT WAS I SAYING?

YOU WOULDN'T TREAT NOBODY LIKE THAT.

RIGHT.

YEAH.

I WOULDN'T.

I MEAN, IT'S ALL ABOUT, YOU KNOW, BEING NICE TO PEOPLE. THAT'S WHAT IT'S ABOUT...

UH-HUH.

ANOTHER BEER?

SURE.

HEY! YOU! SAME AGAIN OVER HERE!

ound

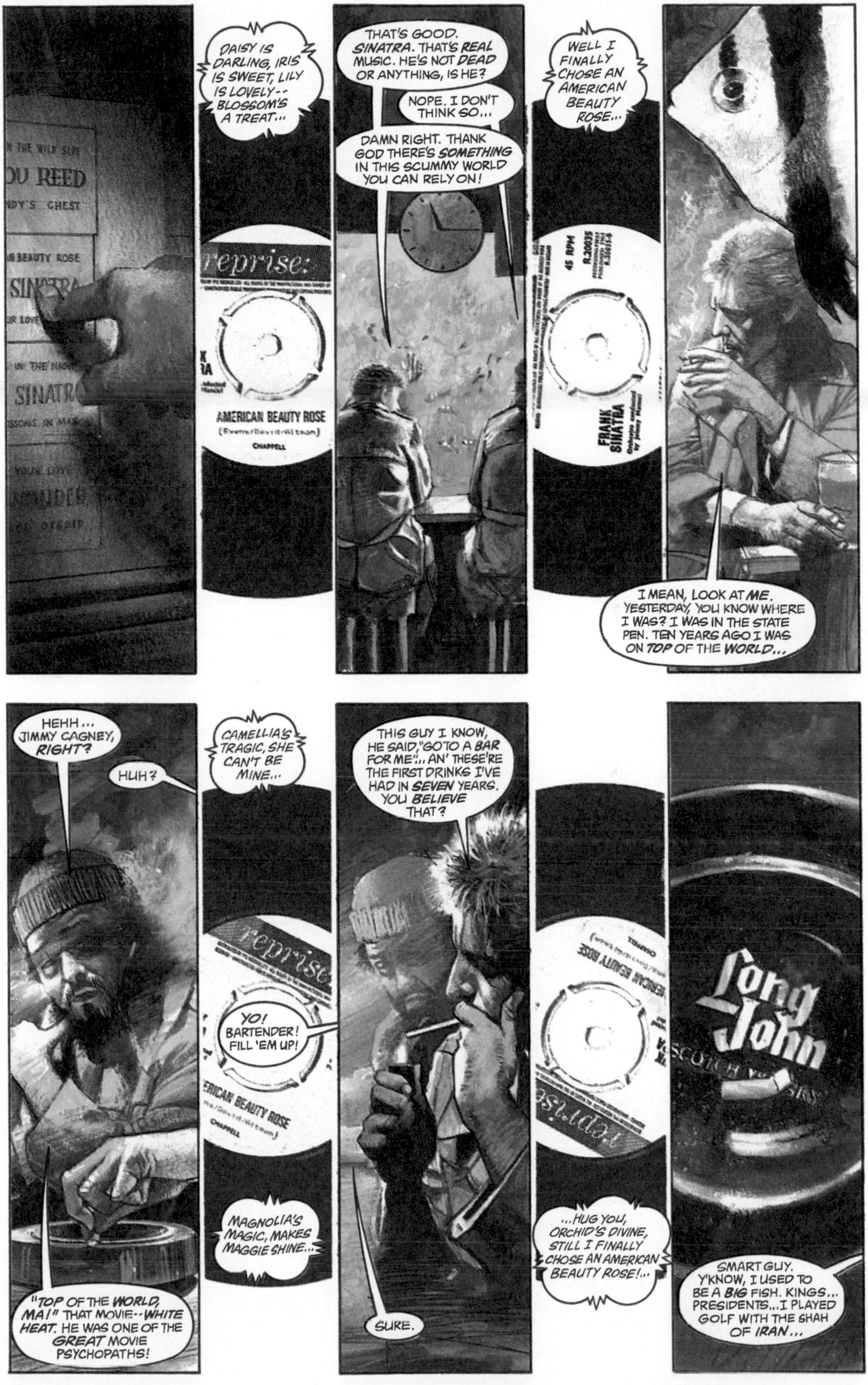
DAISY IS DARLING, IRIS IS SWEET, LILY IS LOVELY-- BLOSSOM'S A TREAT...
reprise:
AMERICAN BEAUTY ROSE
CHAPPELL
THAT'S GOOD. SINATRA. THAT'S REAL MUSIC. HE'S NOT DEAD OR ANYTHING, IS HE?
NOPE. I DON'T THINK SO...
DAMN RIGHT. THANK GOD THERE'S SOMETHING IN THIS SCUMMY WORLD YOU CAN RELY ON!
WELL I FINALLY CHOSE AN AMERICAN BEAUTY ROSE...
45 RPM
FRANK SINATRA
I MEAN, LOOK AT ME. YESTERDAY, YOU KNOW WHERE I WAS? I WAS IN THE STATE PEN. TEN YEARS AGO I WAS ON TOP OF THE WORLD...
HEHH... JIMMY CAGNEY, RIGHT?
HUH?
"TOP OF THE WORLD, MA!" THAT MOVIE--WHITE HEAT. HE WAS ONE OF THE GREAT MOVIE PSYCHOPATHS!
CAMELLIA'S TRAGIC, SHE CAN'T BE MINE...
YO! BARTENDER! FILL 'EM UP!
MAGNOLIA'S MAGIC, MAKES MAGGIE SHINE...
THIS GUY I KNOW, HE SAID, "GO TO A BAR FOR ME"... AN' THESE'RE THE FIRST DRINKS I'VE HAD IN SEVEN YEARS. YOU BELIEVE THAT?
SURE.
...HUG YOU, ORCHID'S DIVINE, STILL I FINALLY CHOSE AN AMERICAN BEAUTY ROSE!...
Long John
SMART GUY. Y'KNOW, I USED TO BE A BIG FISH. KINGS... PRESIDENTS... I PLAYED GOLF WITH THE SHAH OF IRAN...

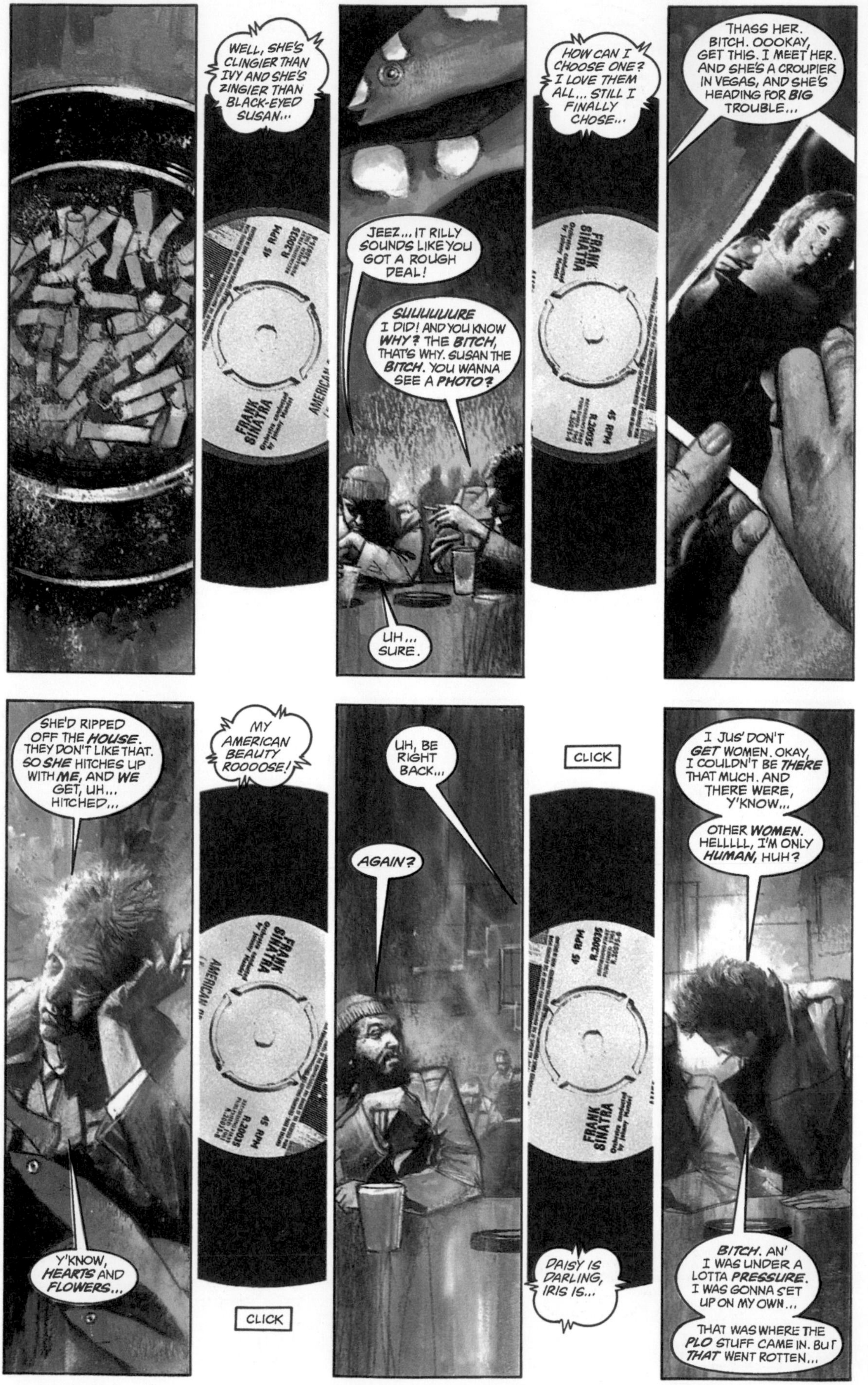
WELL, SHE'S CLINGIER THAN IVY AND SHE'S ZINGIER THAN BLACK-EYED SUSAN...
FRANK SINATRA
AMERICAN
JEEZ... IT RILLY SOUNDS LIKE YOU GOT A ROUGH DEAL!
SUUUUUURE I DID! AND YOU KNOW WHY? THE BITCH, THAT'S WHY. SUSAN THE BITCH. YOU WANNA SEE A PHOTO?
UH... SURE.
HOW CAN I CHOOSE ONE? I LOVE THEM ALL... STILL I FINALLY CHOSE...
FRANK SINATRA
45 RPM
THASS HER. BITCH. OOOKAY, GET THIS. I MEET HER. AND SHE'S A CROUPIER IN VEGAS, AND SHE'S HEADING FOR BIG TROUBLE...
SHE'D RIPPED OFF THE HOUSE. THEY DON'T LIKE THAT. SO SHE HITCHES UP WITH ME, AND WE GET, UH... HITCHED...
Y'KNOW, HEARTS AND FLOWERS...
MY AMERICAN BEAUTY ROOOOSE!
FRANK SINATRA
45 RPM
CLICK
UH, BE RIGHT BACK...
AGAIN?
CLICK
FRANK SINATRA
45 RPM
DAISY IS DARLING, IRIS IS...
I JUS' DON'T GET WOMEN. OKAY, I COULDN'T BE THERE THAT MUCH. AND THERE WERE, Y'KNOW...
OTHER WOMEN. HELLLLL, I'M ONLY HUMAN, HUH?
BITCH. AN' I WAS UNDER A LOTTA PRESSURE. I WAS GONNA SET UP ON MY OWN...
THAT WAS WHERE THE PLO STUFF CAME IN. BUT THAT WENT ROTTEN...

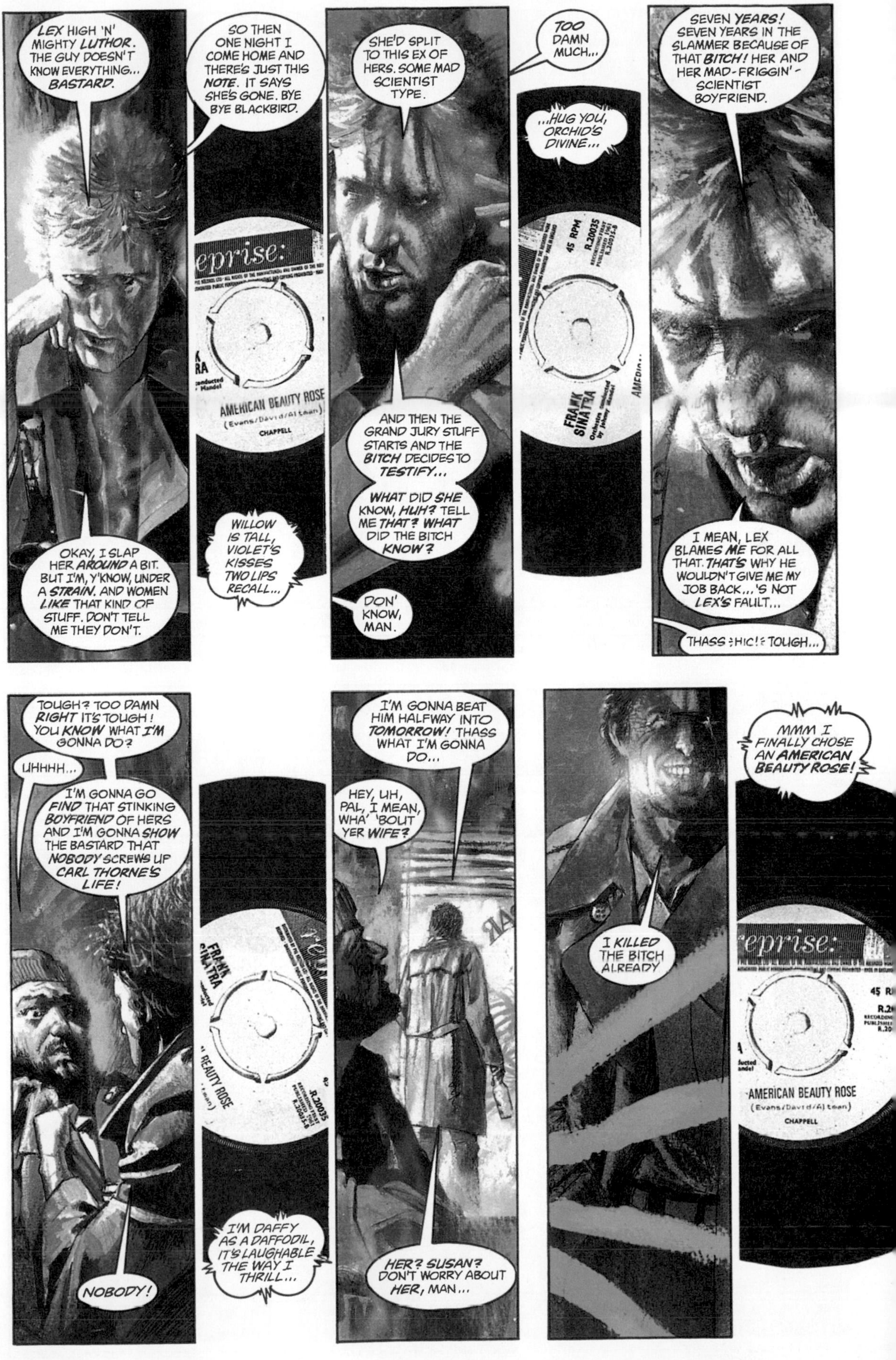

LEX HIGH 'N' MIGHTY *LUTHOR*. THE GUY DOESN'T KNOW EVERYTHING... *BASTARD*.
OKAY, I SLAP HER *AROUND* A BIT. BUT I'M, Y'KNOW, UNDER A *STRAIN*. AND WOMEN *LIKE* THAT KIND OF STUFF. DON'T TELL ME THEY DON'T.
SO THEN ONE NIGHT I COME HOME AND THERE'S JUST THIS *NOTE*. IT SAYS SHE'S GONE. BYE BYE BLACKBIRD.
eprise:
AMERICAN BEAUTY ROSE
(Evans/David/Altman)
CHAPPELL
WILLOW IS TALL, VIOLET'S KISSES TWO LIPS RECALL...
SHE'D SPLIT TO THIS EX OF HERS. SOME MAD SCIENTIST TYPE.
AND THEN THE GRAND JURY STUFF STARTS AND THE *BITCH* DECIDES TO *TESTIFY...*
WHAT DID *SHE* KNOW, *HUH?* TELL ME *THAT? WHAT* DID THE BITCH *KNOW?*
DON' KNOW, MAN.
TOO DAMN MUCH...
...HUG YOU, ORCHID'S DIVINE...
45 RPM
R.20035
FRANK SINATRA
SEVEN *YEARS!* SEVEN YEARS IN THE SLAMMER BECAUSE OF THAT *BITCH!* HER AND HER MAD-FRIGGIN'-SCIENTIST BOYFRIEND.
I MEAN, LEX BLAMES *ME* FOR ALL THAT. *THAT'S* WHY HE WOULDN'T GIVE ME MY JOB BACK... 'S NOT *LEX'S* FAULT...
THASS ÷HIC!÷ TOUGH...
TOUGH? TOO DAMN *RIGHT* IT'S TOUGH! YOU *KNOW* WHAT *I'M* GONNA DO?
UHHHH...
I'M GONNA GO *FIND* THAT STINKING *BOYFRIEND* OF HERS AND I'M GONNA *SHOW* THE BASTARD THAT *NOBODY* SCREWS UP *CARL THORNE'S LIFE!*
NOBODY!
FRANK SINATRA
BEAUTY ROSE
R.20035
I'M DAFFY AS A DAFFODIL, IT'S LAUGHABLE THE WAY I THRILL...
I'M GONNA BEAT HIM HALFWAY INTO *TOMORROW!* THASS WHAT I'M GONNA DO...
HEY, UH, PAL, I MEAN, WHA' 'BOUT YER *WIFE?*
HER? SUSAN? DON'T WORRY ABOUT *HER*, MAN...
I *KILLED* THE BITCH ALREADY
MMM I FINALLY CHOSE AN AMERICAN BEAUTY ROSE!
eprise:
AMERICAN BEAUTY ROSE
(Evans/David/Altman)
CHAPPELL

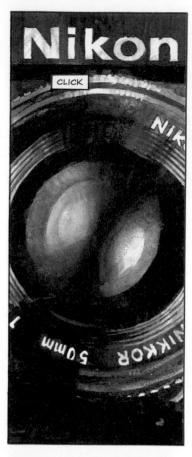

Nikon
CLICK
NIKON
NIKKOR 50mm
I ASSUMED YOU'D WANT TO SEE THIS, MR. STERLING.
Nikon
SIR.
I DON'T WANT THIS TOUCHED.

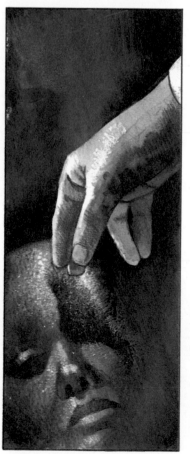

HEY, ROXY? YEAH. I GOT A PICKUP FOR YOU... UH-HUH...CORNER OF MAIN STREET AND ELM.

WELL, I'D SAY IT'S SORTA *BODY*-SIZED... YOU GOT IT... I'LL BE HERE. OK.

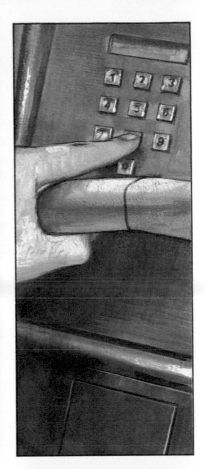

SIR, YOU SAID YOU WANTED TO BE KEPT INFORMED...

YEAH. WELL, I JUST SAW THE BODY, AND... SHE *WASN'T* HUMAN. NO, SIR, I'M *CERTAIN*.

I DON'T KNOW. MAYBE SOME KIND OF *PLANT*...?

MM-HM. TAKEN CARE OF. YOU GOT IT.

YOU NEVER FOUND THAT BODY.

WHAT BODY?

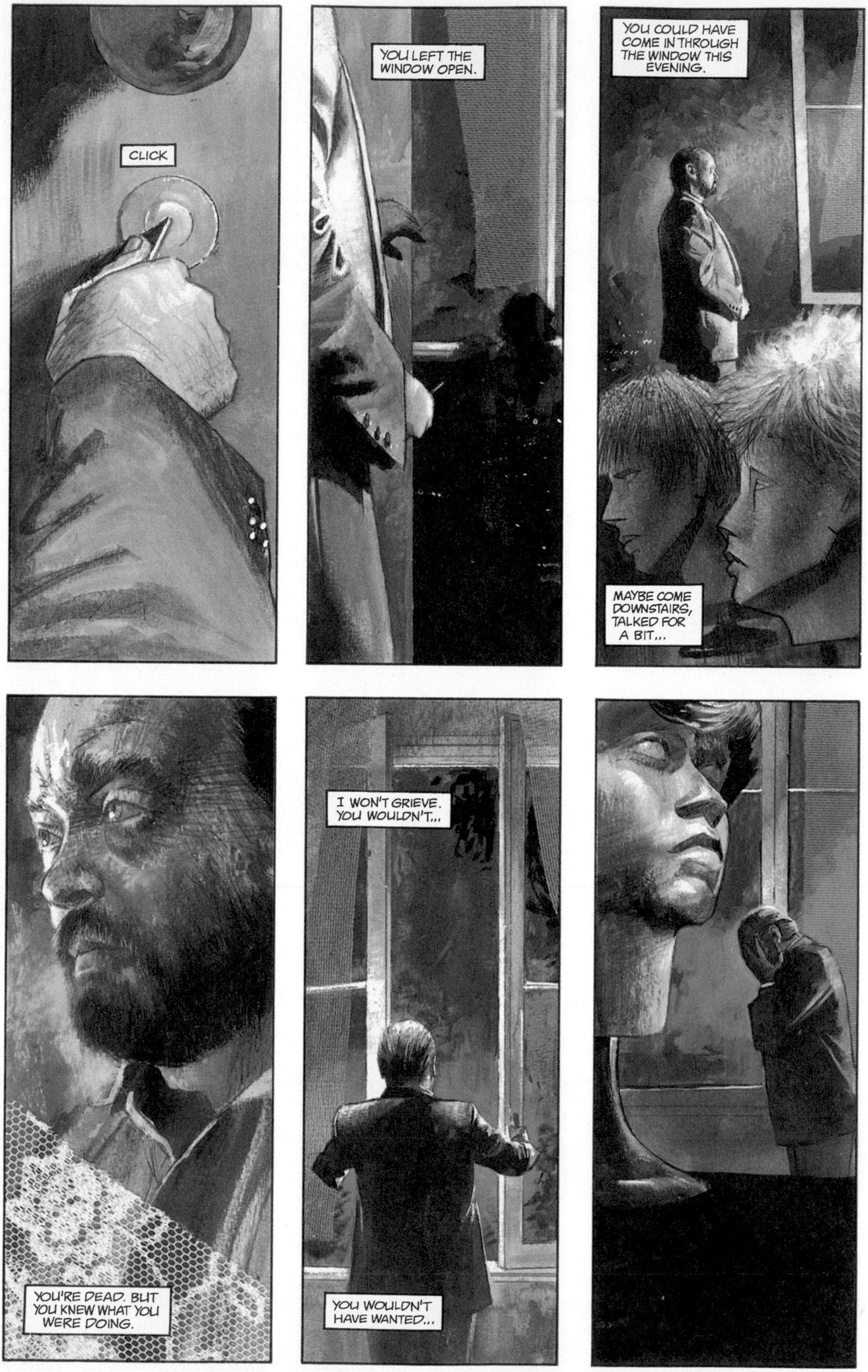
CLICK
YOU LEFT THE WINDOW OPEN.
YOU COULD HAVE COME IN THROUGH THE WINDOW THIS EVENING.
MAYBE COME DOWNSTAIRS, TALKED FOR A BIT...
YOU'RE DEAD. BUT YOU KNEW WHAT YOU WERE DOING.
I WON'T GRIEVE. YOU WOULDN'T...
YOU WOULDN'T HAVE WANTED...

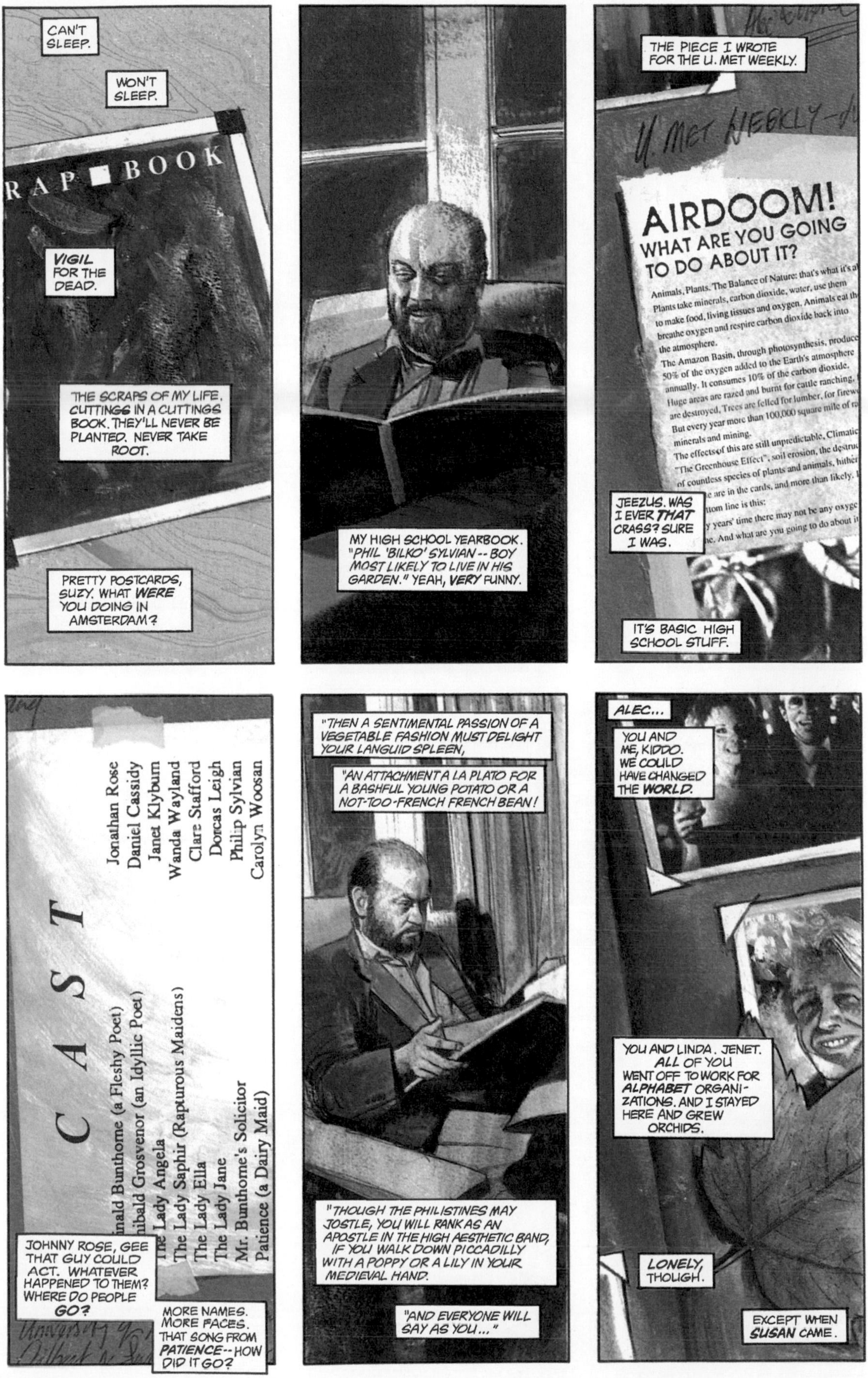
CAN'T SLEEP.
WON'T SLEEP.
RAP BOOK
VIGIL FOR THE DEAD.
THE SCRAPS OF MY LIFE. CUTTINGS IN A CUTTINGS BOOK. THEY'LL NEVER BE PLANTED. NEVER TAKE ROOT.
PRETTY POSTCARDS, SUZY. WHAT WERE YOU DOING IN AMSTERDAM?
MY HIGH SCHOOL YEARBOOK. "PHIL 'BILKO' SYLVIAN -- BOY MOST LIKELY TO LIVE IN HIS GARDEN." YEAH, VERY FUNNY.
THE PIECE I WROTE FOR THE U. MET WEEKLY.
U. MET WEEKLY
AIRDOOM! WHAT ARE YOU GOING TO DO ABOUT IT?
Animals, Plants. The Balance of Nature: that's what it's a
Plants take minerals, carbon dioxide, water, use them to make food, living tissues and oxygen. Animals eat th breathe oxygen and respire carbon dioxide back into the atmosphere.
The Amazon Basin, through photosynthesis, produce 50% of the oxygen added to the Earth's atmosphere annually. It consumes 10% of the carbon dioxide. Huge areas are razed and burnt for cattle ranching, are destroyed. Trees are felled for lumber, for firew But every year more than 100,000 square mile of ra minerals and mining.
The effects of this are still unpredictable. Climatic "The Greenhouse Effect", soil erosion, the destruc of countless species of plants and animals, hither e are in the cards, and more than likely. ttom line is this: y years' time there may not be any oxyge ne. And what are you going to do about it
JEEZUS. WAS I EVER THAT CRASS? SURE I WAS.
IT'S BASIC HIGH SCHOOL STUFF.
CAST
nald Bunthorne (a Fleshy Poet) Jonathan Rose
nibald Grosvenor (an Idyllic Poet) Daniel Cassidy
The Lady Angela Janet Klyburn
The Lady Saphir (Rapturous Maidens) Wanda Wayland
The Lady Ella Clare Stafford
The Lady Jane Dorcas Leigh
Mr. Bunthorne's Solicitor Philip Sylvian
Patience (a Dairy Maid) Carolyn Woosan
JOHNNY ROSE, GEE THAT GUY COULD ACT. WHATEVER HAPPENED TO THEM? WHERE DO PEOPLE GO?
MORE NAMES. MORE FACES. THAT SONG FROM PATIENCE -- HOW DID IT GO?
"THEN A SENTIMENTAL PASSION OF A VEGETABLE FASHION MUST DELIGHT YOUR LANGUID SPLEEN,
"AN ATTACHMENT A LA PLATO FOR A BASHFUL YOUNG POTATO OR A NOT-TOO-FRENCH FRENCH BEAN!
"THOUGH THE PHILISTINES MAY JOSTLE, YOU WILL RANK AS AN APOSTLE IN THE HIGH AESTHETIC BAND, IF YOU WALK DOWN PICCADILLY WITH A POPPY OR A LILY IN YOUR MEDIEVAL HAND.
"AND EVERYONE WILL SAY AS YOU..."
ALEC...
YOU AND ME, KIDDO. WE COULD HAVE CHANGED THE WORLD.
YOU AND LINDA. JENET. ALL OF YOU WENT OFF TO WORK FOR ALPHABET ORGANIZATIONS. AND I STAYED HERE AND GREW ORCHIDS.
LONELY, THOUGH.
EXCEPT WHEN SUSAN CAME.

2:00 AM.

READ SOMEWHERE THAT MOST *DEATHS* OCCUR AT 2:00 AM.

RIP BLACK ORCHID.

RIP SUSAN.

COMING BACK FROM THE RESTAURANT. THE CAB PULLED OVER IN SOME WASTELAND. AND SUSAN WAS WASTED.

HORRIBLE PHRASE. BUT ACCURATE.

ONE HUMAN LIFE, *WASTED.*

AND...

AND THE MAN IN THE BLACK MASK SHOT SUSAN.

BANG

BANG

BANG

AND HE SHOT SUSAN.

BANG

BANG

BANG

AND HE SHOT.

UH?

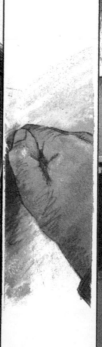

OKAY, OKAY! I'M COMING!

"AND EVERYONE WILL SAY AS YOU WALK YOUR FLOWERY WAY, IF..."

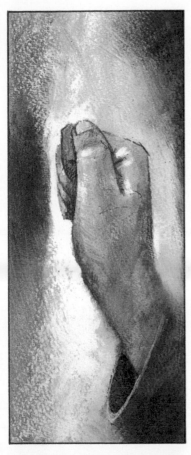

I DON'T BELIEVE IT. DO YOU KNOW WHAT *TIME* IT IS?

OKAY. I *HEARD* YOU!

WHO *IS* IT?

"...HE'S CONTENT WITH A VEGETABLE LOVE WHICH WOULD CERTAINLY NOT SUIT ME..."

DOCTOR SYLVIAN? I GOT A *MESSAGE* FOR YA.

AT *THIS* TIME OF NIGHT?

"WHY, WHAT A MOST PARTICULARLY PURE YOUNG MAN..."

SURE, I KNOW HOW IT SOUNDS. THIS CHICK, SHE GAVE ME TEN BUCKS TO GIVE YOU A *PACKAGE.*

SAID HER NAME WAS *SUE.* SUSAN *LINDEN.*

HUH? SUE'S... HANG ON.

"THIS PURE YOUNG MAN MUST..."

UH, THIS *WOMAN.* YOU'RE *CERTAIN* SHE SAID --

SO I LIED.

SUE ME.

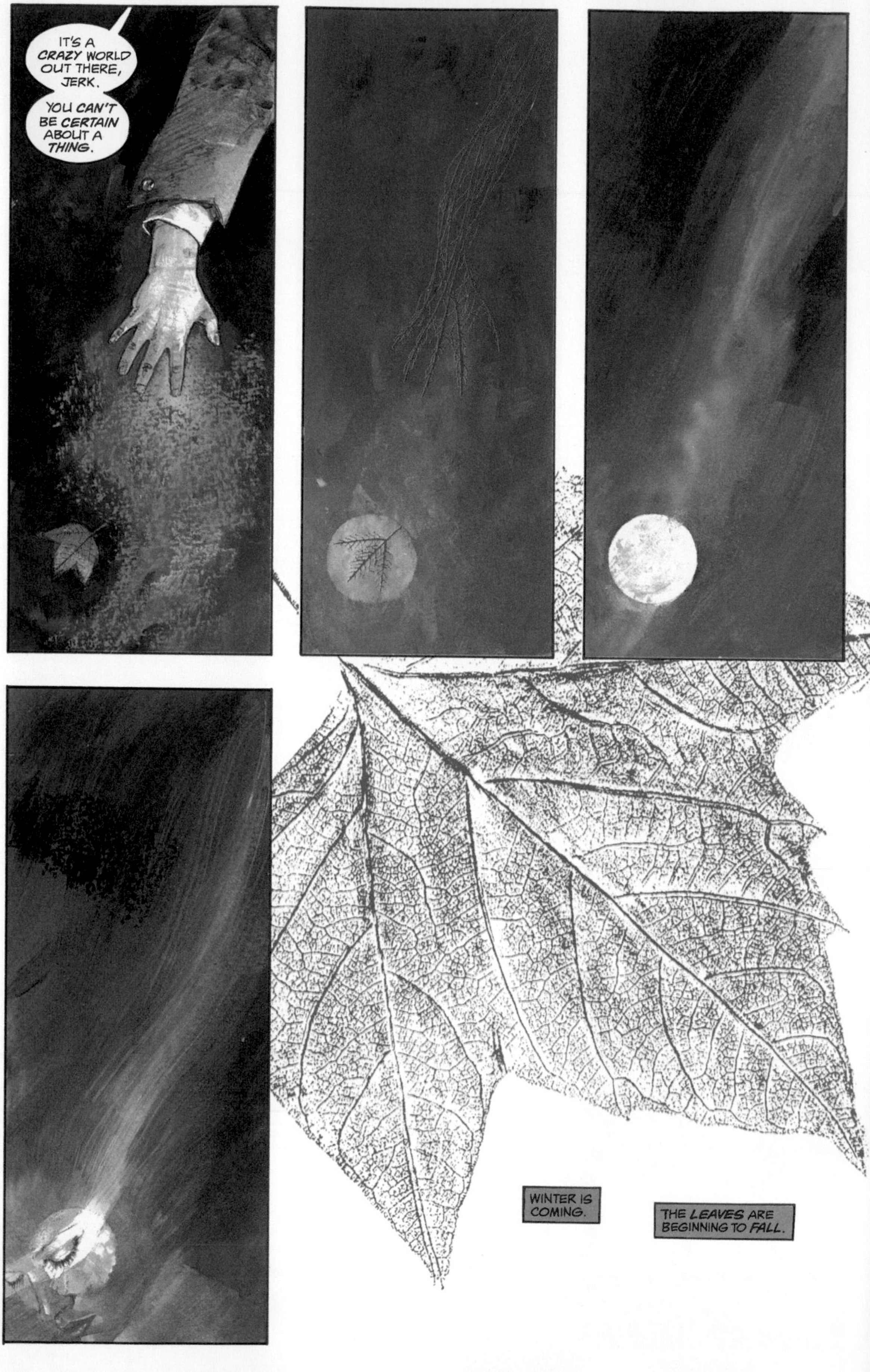
IT'S A CRAZY WORLD OUT THERE, JERK.
YOU CAN'T BE CERTAIN ABOUT A THING.
WINTER IS COMING.
THE LEAVES ARE BEGINNING TO FALL.

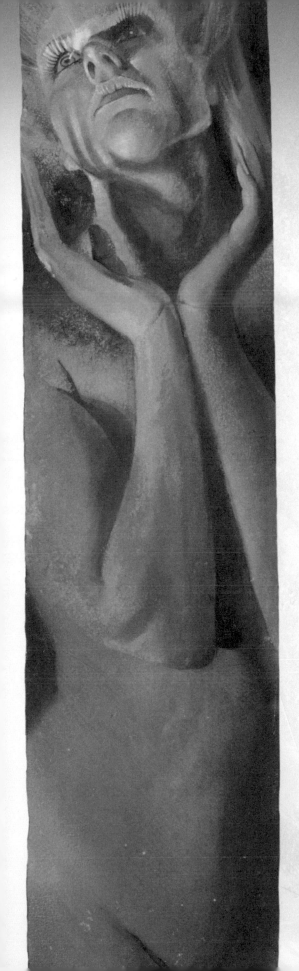

Oh, come with me to old

Khayyam and leave the Wise

To talk; **one thing is certain**, that *Life flies;*

One thing is certain, and the Rest is Lies;

The Flower that once has blown forever dies.

Rubaiyat of Omar Khayyam: Quatrain 26

CHAPTER 2

Going down...

GOING DOWN.

GOING BACK.

FALLING.

IN DREAMS WE FIND ONLY CONTRADICTIONS.

I TUMBLE INTO THE PAST, AWASH IN ANOTHER'S MEMORIES.

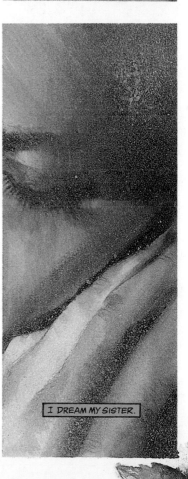

I DREAM MY SISTER.

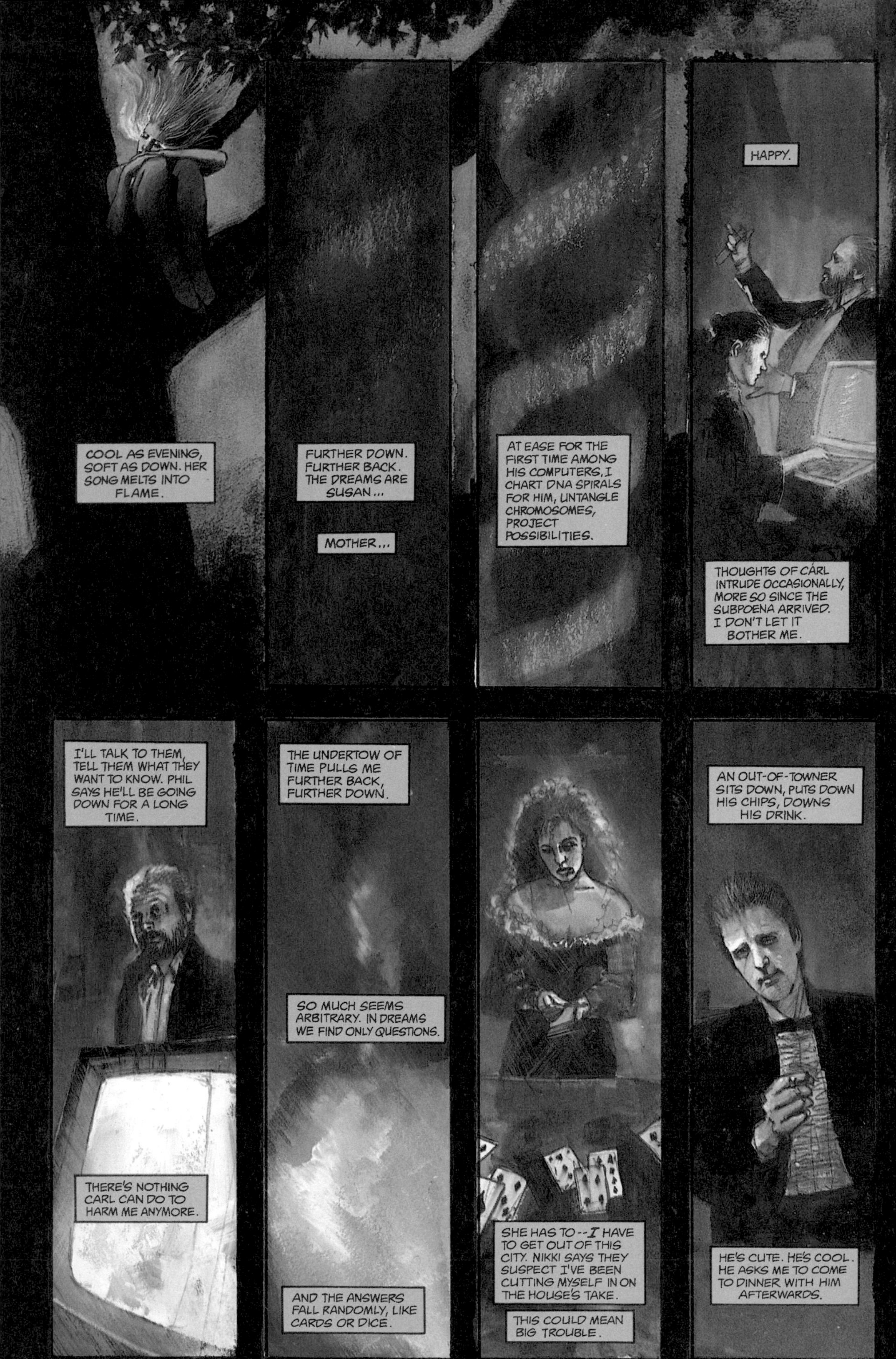
COOL AS EVENING, SOFT AS DOWN. HER SONG MELTS INTO FLAME.
FURTHER DOWN. FURTHER BACK. THE DREAMS ARE SUSAN...
MOTHER...
AT EASE FOR THE FIRST TIME AMONG HIS COMPUTERS, I CHART DNA SPIRALS FOR HIM, UNTANGLE CHROMOSOMES, PROJECT POSSIBILITIES.
HAPPY.
THOUGHTS OF CARL INTRUDE OCCASIONALLY, MORE SO SINCE THE SUBPOENA ARRIVED. I DON'T LET IT BOTHER ME.
I'LL TALK TO THEM, TELL THEM WHAT THEY WANT TO KNOW. PHIL SAYS HE'LL BE GOING DOWN FOR A LONG TIME.
THERE'S NOTHING CARL CAN DO TO HARM ME ANYMORE.
THE UNDERTOW OF TIME PULLS ME FURTHER BACK, FURTHER DOWN.
SO MUCH SEEMS ARBITRARY. IN DREAMS WE FIND ONLY QUESTIONS.
AND THE ANSWERS FALL RANDOMLY, LIKE CARDS OR DICE.
SHE HAS TO -- I HAVE TO GET OUT OF THIS CITY. NIKKI SAYS THEY SUSPECT I'VE BEEN CUTTING MYSELF IN ON THE HOUSE'S TAKE.
THIS COULD MEAN BIG TROUBLE.
AN OUT-OF-TOWNER SITS DOWN, PUTS DOWN HIS CHIPS, DOWNS HIS DRINK.
HE'S CUTE. HE'S COOL. HE ASKS ME TO COME TO DINNER WITH HIM AFTERWARDS.

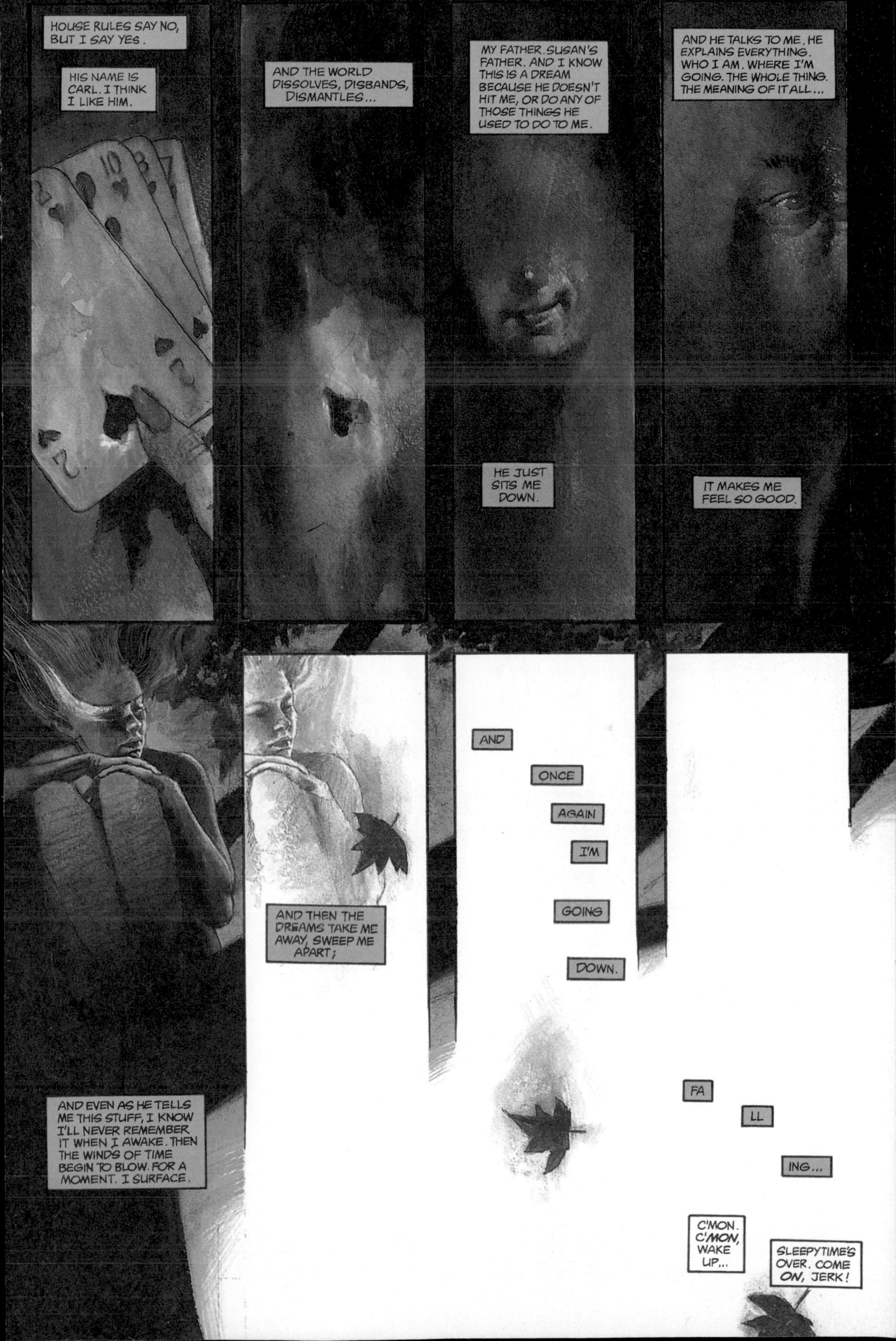
HOUSE RULES SAY NO, BUT I SAY YES.
HIS NAME IS CARL. I THINK I LIKE HIM.
AND THE WORLD DISSOLVES, DISBANDS, DISMANTLES...
MY FATHER. SUSAN'S FATHER. AND I KNOW THIS IS A DREAM BECAUSE HE DOESN'T HIT ME, OR DO ANY OF THOSE THINGS HE USED TO DO TO ME.
HE JUST SITS ME DOWN.
AND HE TALKS TO ME. HE EXPLAINS EVERYTHING. WHO I AM. WHERE I'M GOING. THE WHOLE THING. THE MEANING OF IT ALL...
IT MAKES ME FEEL SO GOOD.
AND EVEN AS HE TELLS ME THIS STUFF, I KNOW I'LL NEVER REMEMBER IT WHEN I AWAKE. THEN THE WINDS OF TIME BEGIN TO BLOW. FOR A MOMENT. I SURFACE.
AND THEN THE DREAMS TAKE ME AWAY, SWEEP ME APART;
AND
ONCE
AGAIN
I'M
GOING
DOWN.
FA
LL
ING...
C'MON. C'MON, WAKE UP...
SLEEPYTIME'S OVER. COME ON, JERK!

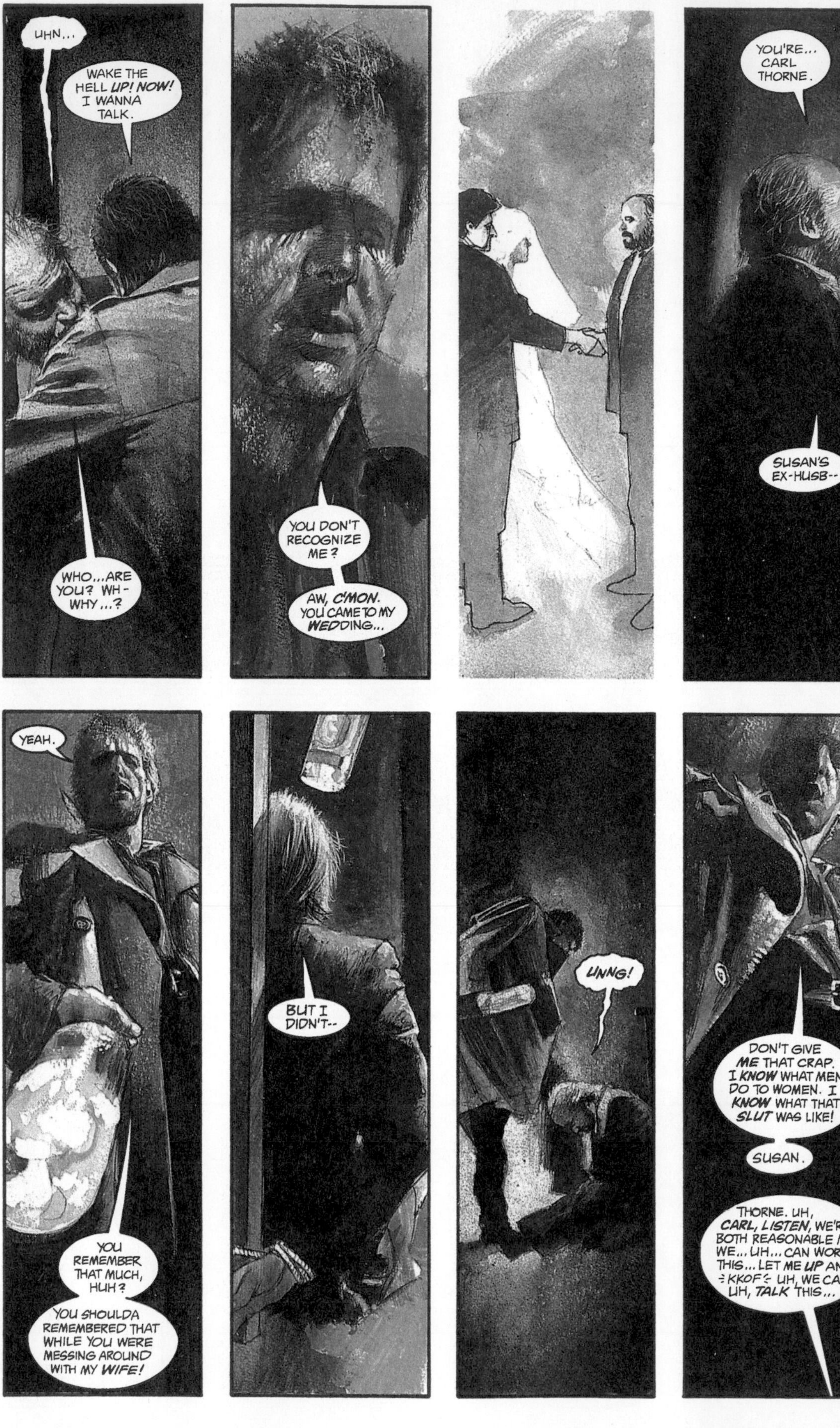
UHN...
WAKE THE HELL UP! NOW! I WANNA TALK.
WHO...ARE YOU? WH- WHY...?
YOU DON'T RECOGNIZE ME?
AW, C'MON. YOU CAME TO MY WEDDING...
YOU'RE... CARL THORNE.
SUSAN'S EX-HUSB--
YEAH.
YOU REMEMBER THAT MUCH, HUH?
YOU SHOULDA REMEMBERED THAT WHILE YOU WERE MESSING AROUND WITH MY WIFE!
BUT I DIDN'T--
UNNG!
DON'T GIVE ME THAT CRAP. I KNOW WHAT MEN DO TO WOMEN. I KNOW WHAT THAT SLUT WAS LIKE!
SUSAN.
THORNE. UH, CARL, LISTEN, WE'RE BOTH REASONABLE MEN, WE... UH... CAN WORK THIS... LET ME UP AND =KKOF= UH, WE CAN, UH, TALK THIS...

SHE COULDA HAD *ME!* DAMMIT, SHE *DID* HAVE *ME!* AND SHE *WENT* TO *YOU?*

JUST THE *THOUGHT* IS ENOUGH TO MAKE ME SICK TO MY *GODDAMN STOMACH.*

I MEAN, I *LOVED* HER, Y'KNOW? I REALLY *DID.*

≈SNF≈

I

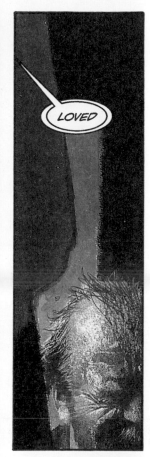

LOVED

HER...

UNH...

SHE'S *DEAD,* CARL. THIS WON'T BRING HER *BACK.*

OF *COURSE* SHE'S DEAD.

WHO THE *HELL* DID YOU THINK IT WAS THAT *KILLED* HER?

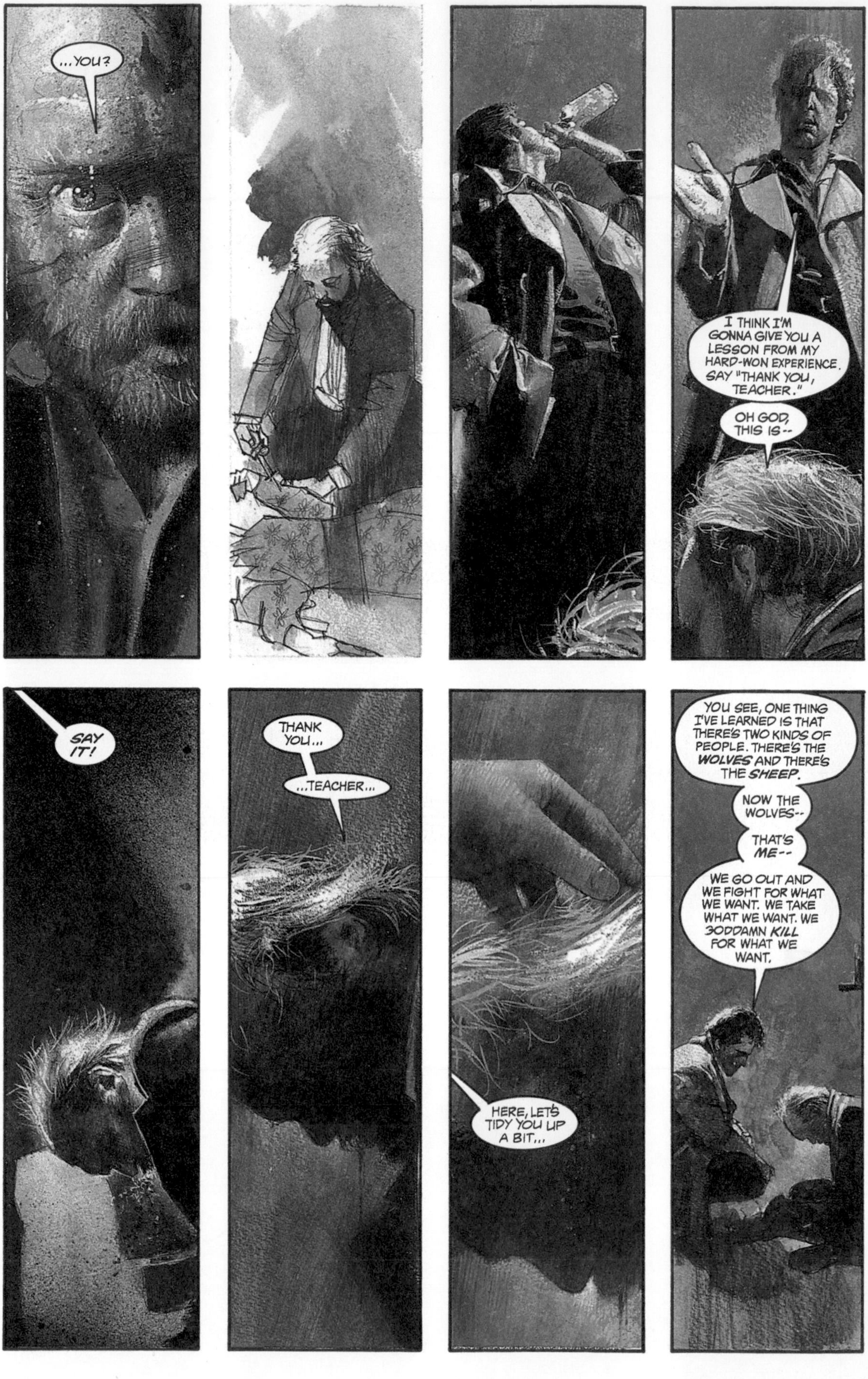
...YOU?
I THINK I'M GONNA GIVE YOU A LESSON FROM MY HARD-WON EXPERIENCE. SAY "THANK YOU, TEACHER."
OH GOD, THIS IS--
SAY IT!
THANK YOU...
...TEACHER...
HERE, LET'S TIDY YOU UP A BIT...
YOU SEE, ONE THING I'VE LEARNED IS THAT THERE'S TWO KINDS OF PEOPLE. THERE'S THE WOLVES AND THERE'S THE SHEEP.
NOW THE WOLVES--
THAT'S ME--
WE GO OUT AND WE FIGHT FOR WHAT WE WANT. WE TAKE WHAT WE WANT. WE GODDAMN KILL FOR WHAT WE WANT.

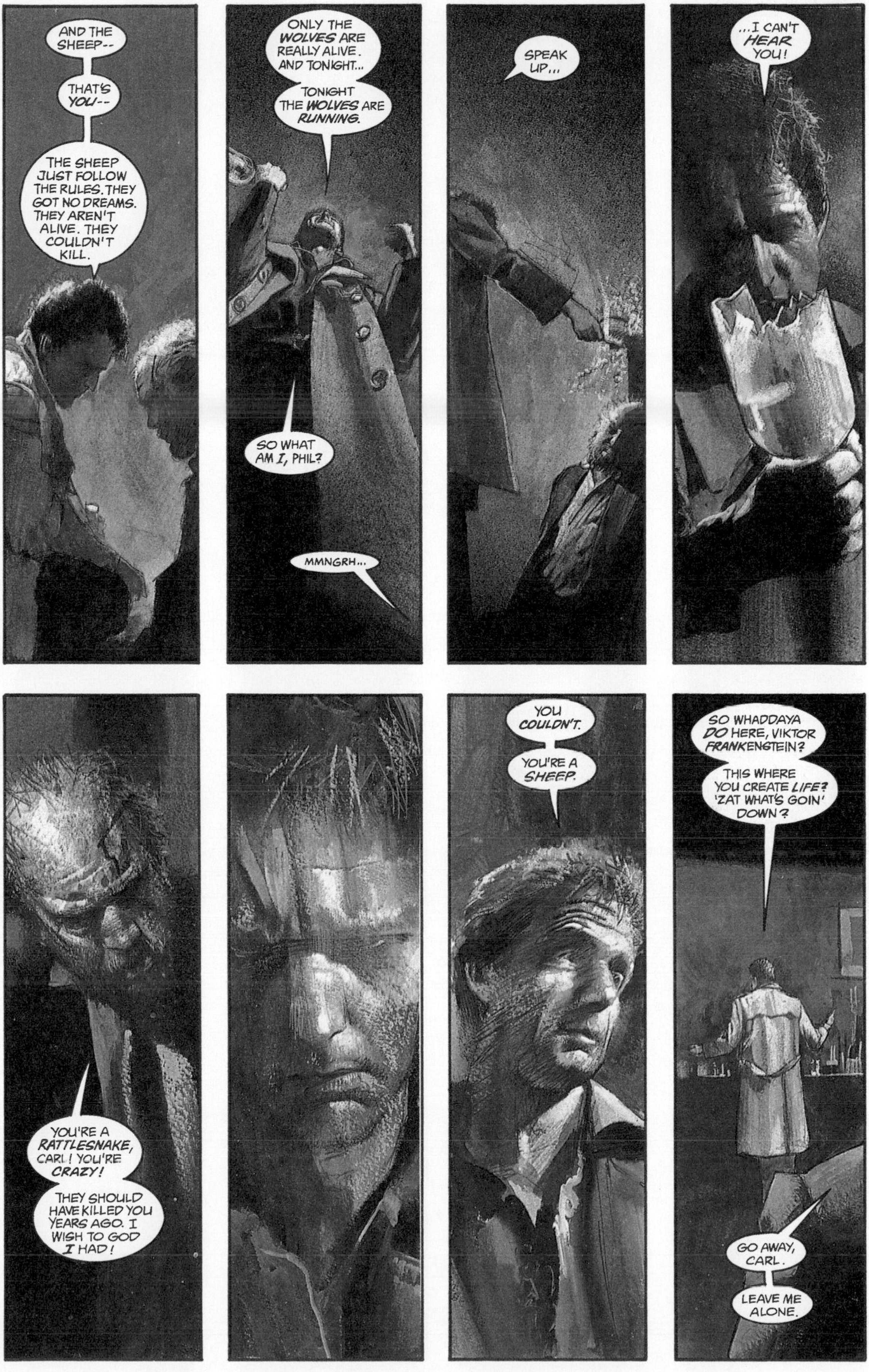
AND THE SHEEP--
THAT'S YOU--
THE SHEEP JUST FOLLOW THE RULES. THEY GOT NO DREAMS. THEY AREN'T ALIVE. THEY COULDN'T KILL.
ONLY THE WOLVES ARE REALLY ALIVE. AND TONIGHT...
TONIGHT THE WOLVES ARE RUNNING.
SO WHAT AM I, PHIL?
MMNGRH...
SPEAK UP...
...I CAN'T HEAR YOU!
YOU'RE A RATTLESNAKE, CARL! YOU'RE CRAZY!
THEY SHOULD HAVE KILLED YOU YEARS AGO. I WISH TO GOD I HAD!
YOU COULDN'T.
YOU'RE A SHEEP.
SO WHADDAYA DO HERE, VIKTOR FRANKENSTEIN?
THIS WHERE YOU CREATE LIFE? 'ZAT WHAT'S GOIN' DOWN?
GO AWAY, CARL.
LEAVE ME ALONE.

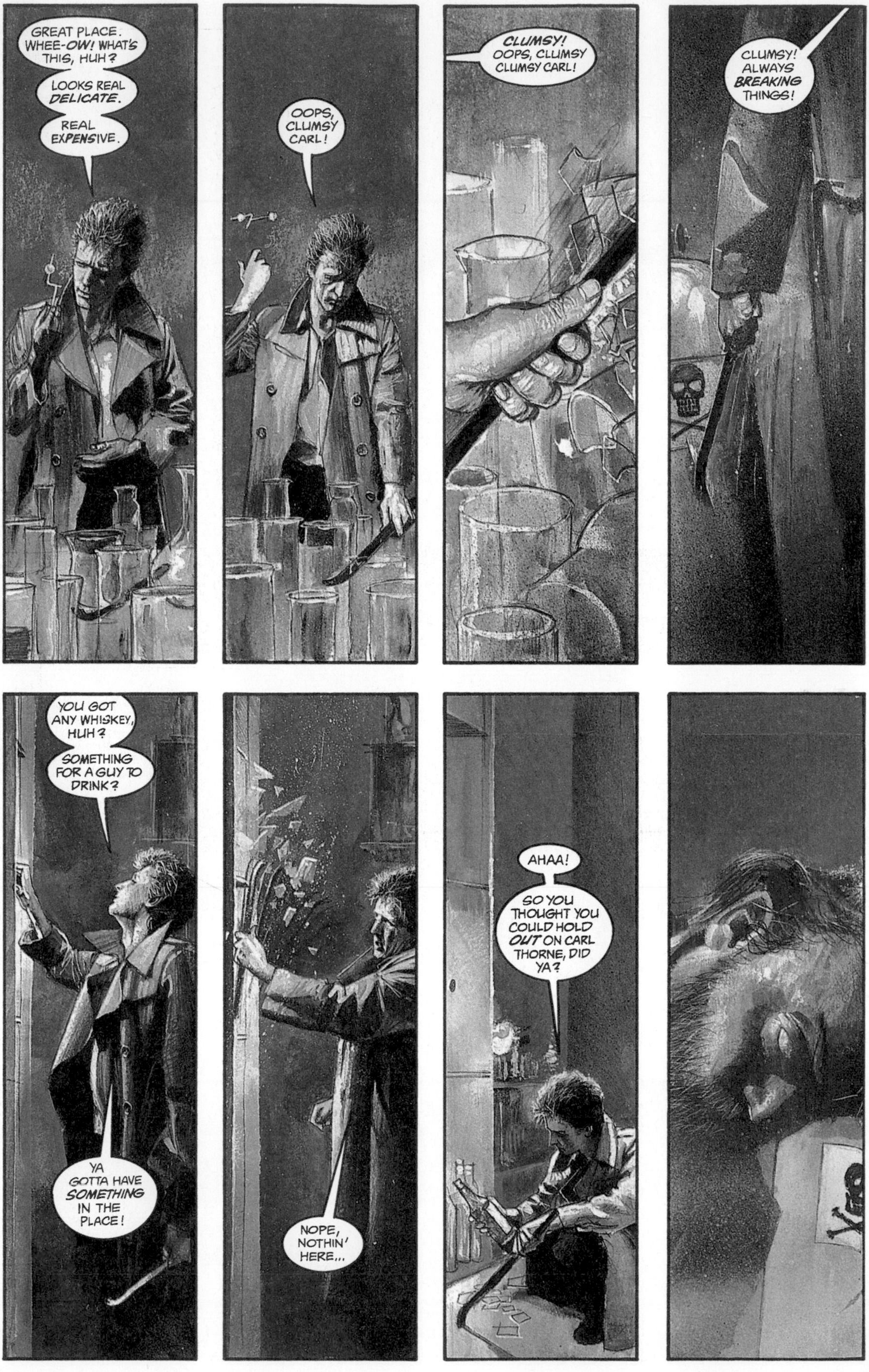
GREAT PLACE. WHEE-OW! WHAT'S THIS, HUH?
LOOKS REAL DELICATE.
REAL EXPENSIVE.
OOPS, CLUMSY CARL!
CLUMSY! OOPS, CLUMSY CLUMSY CARL!
CLUMSY! ALWAYS BREAKING THINGS!
YOU GOT ANY WHISKEY, HUH?
SOMETHING FOR A GUY TO DRINK?
YA GOTTA HAVE SOMETHING IN THE PLACE!
NOPE, NOTHIN' HERE...
AHAA!
SO YOU THOUGHT YOU COULD HOLD OUT ON CARL THORNE, DID YA?

I SAID, "SO YOU THOUGHT YOU COULD HOLD OUT ON ME?"
SCUM.
SHA DOO-BE DOODO DOO-DOOBY DO DOO
DOO DOOBY DOODOO DA-DOOBY DADOOOO
DOO DOO DADOO DOO DOOBY DA DOOOOO
THAT'S WHY THE LAY-DEE IZZA TRAMP!

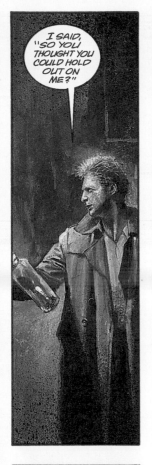

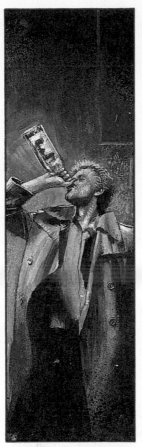

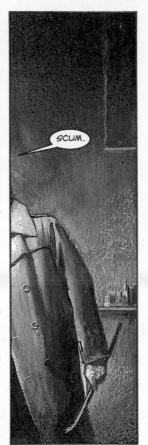

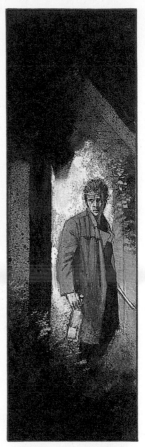

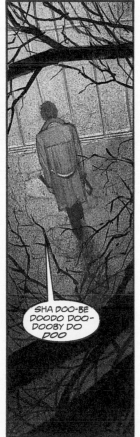

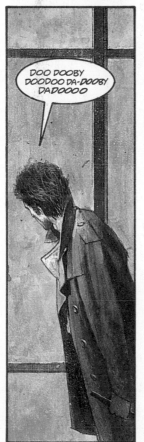

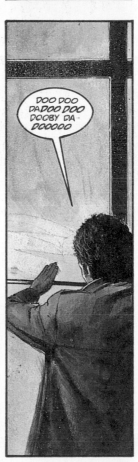

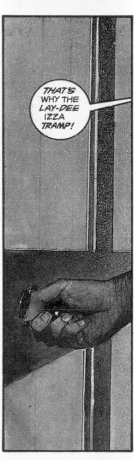

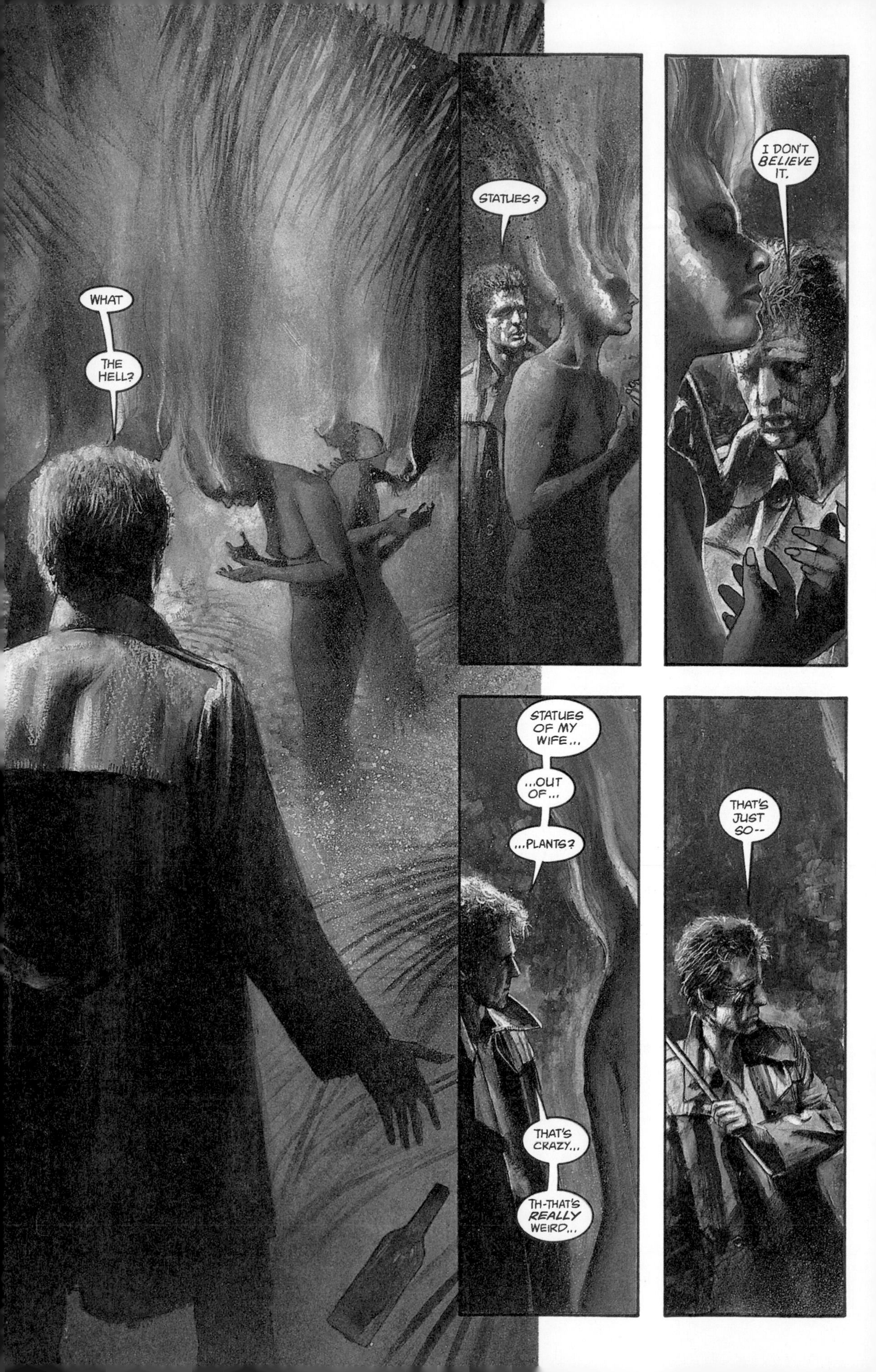
WHAT
THE HELL?
STATUES?
I DON'T *BELIEVE* IT.
STATUES OF MY WIFE...
...OUT OF...
...PLANTS?
THAT'S CRAZY...
TH-THAT'S *REALLY* WEIRD...
THAT'S JUST SO--

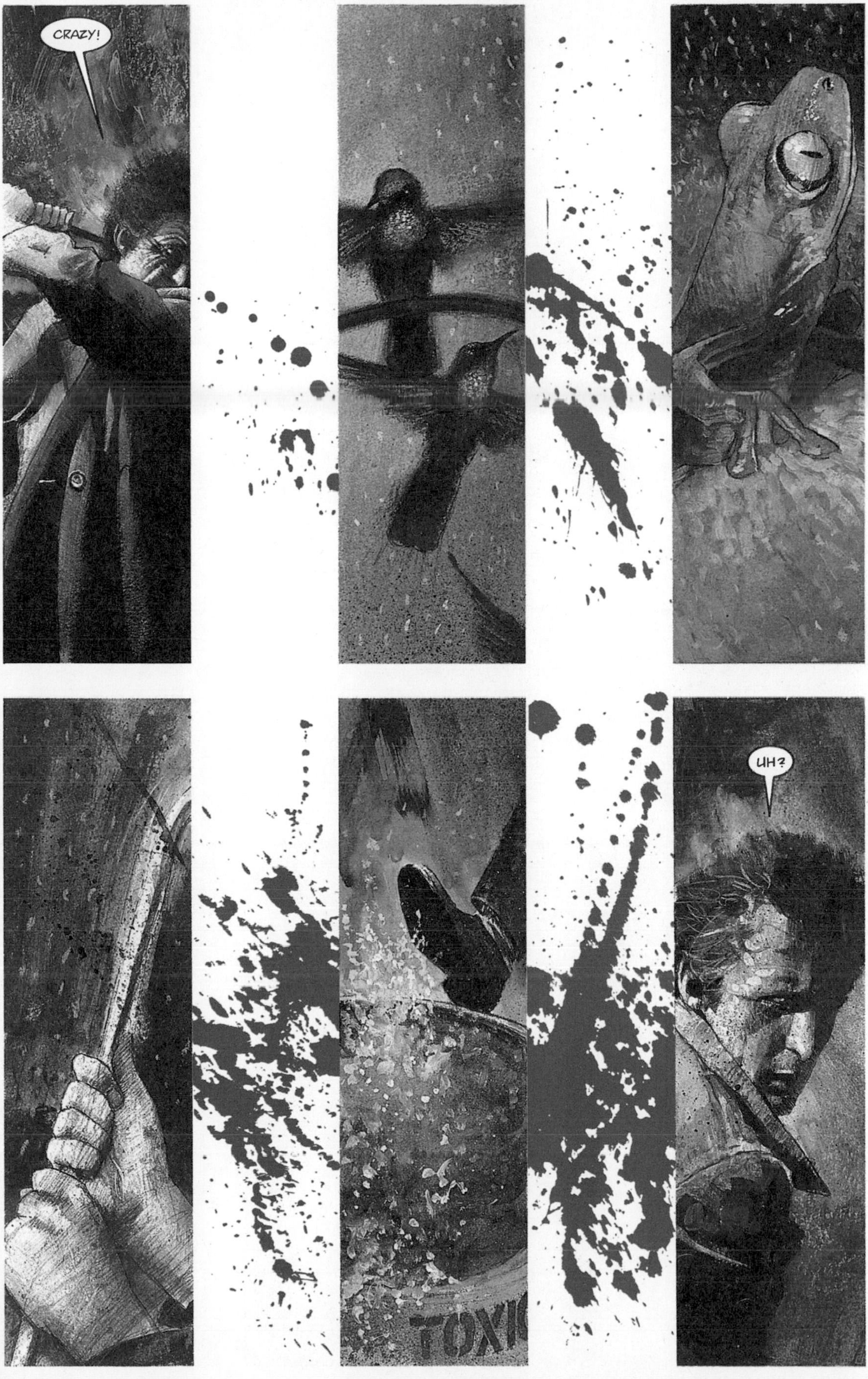
CRAZY!
UH?
TOXIC

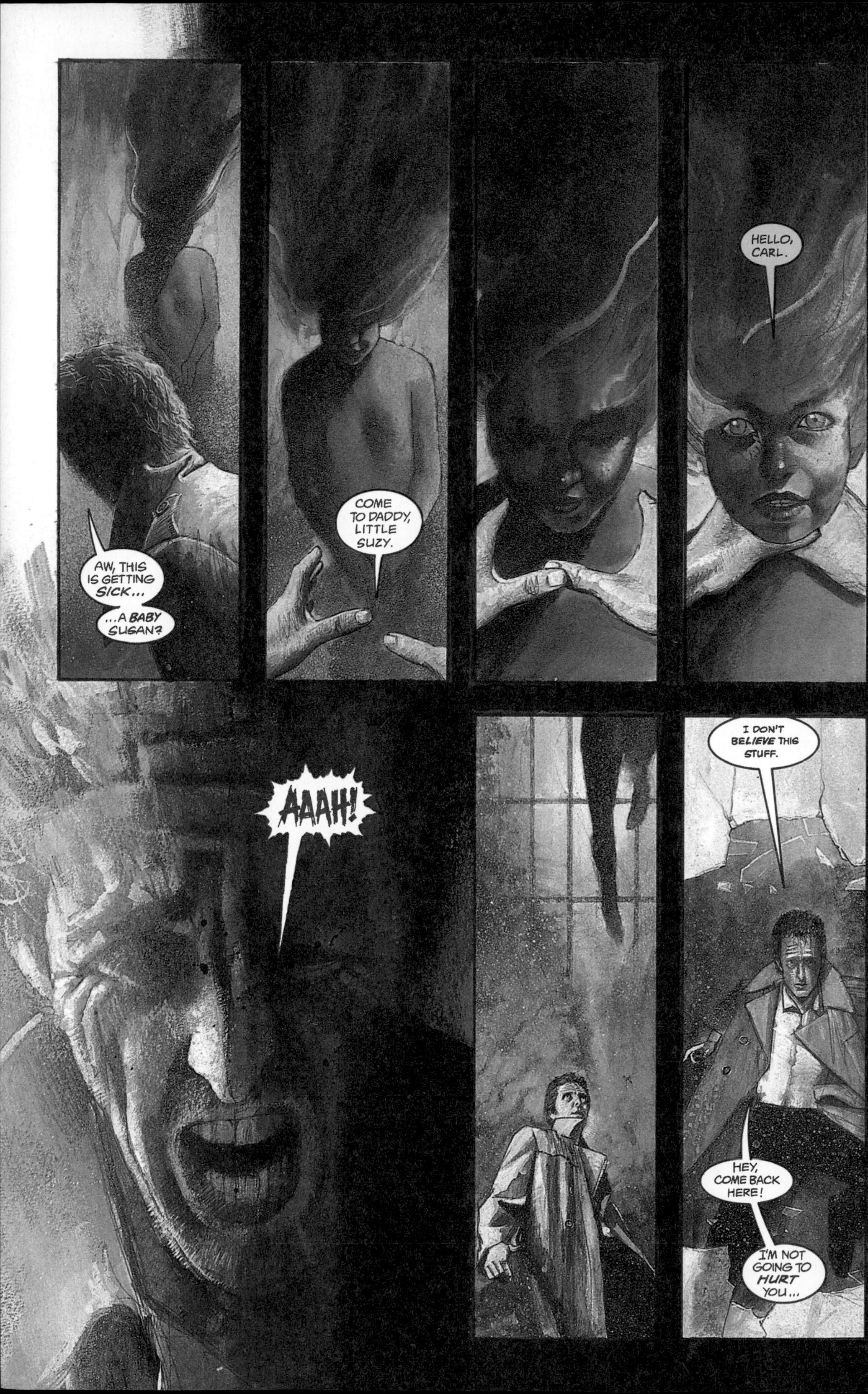
AW, THIS IS GETTING SICK...
...A BABY SUSAN?
COME TO DADDY, LITTLE SUZY.
HELLO, CARL.
AAAH!
I DON'T BELIEVE THIS STUFF.
HEY, COME BACK HERE!
I'M NOT GOING TO HURT YOU...

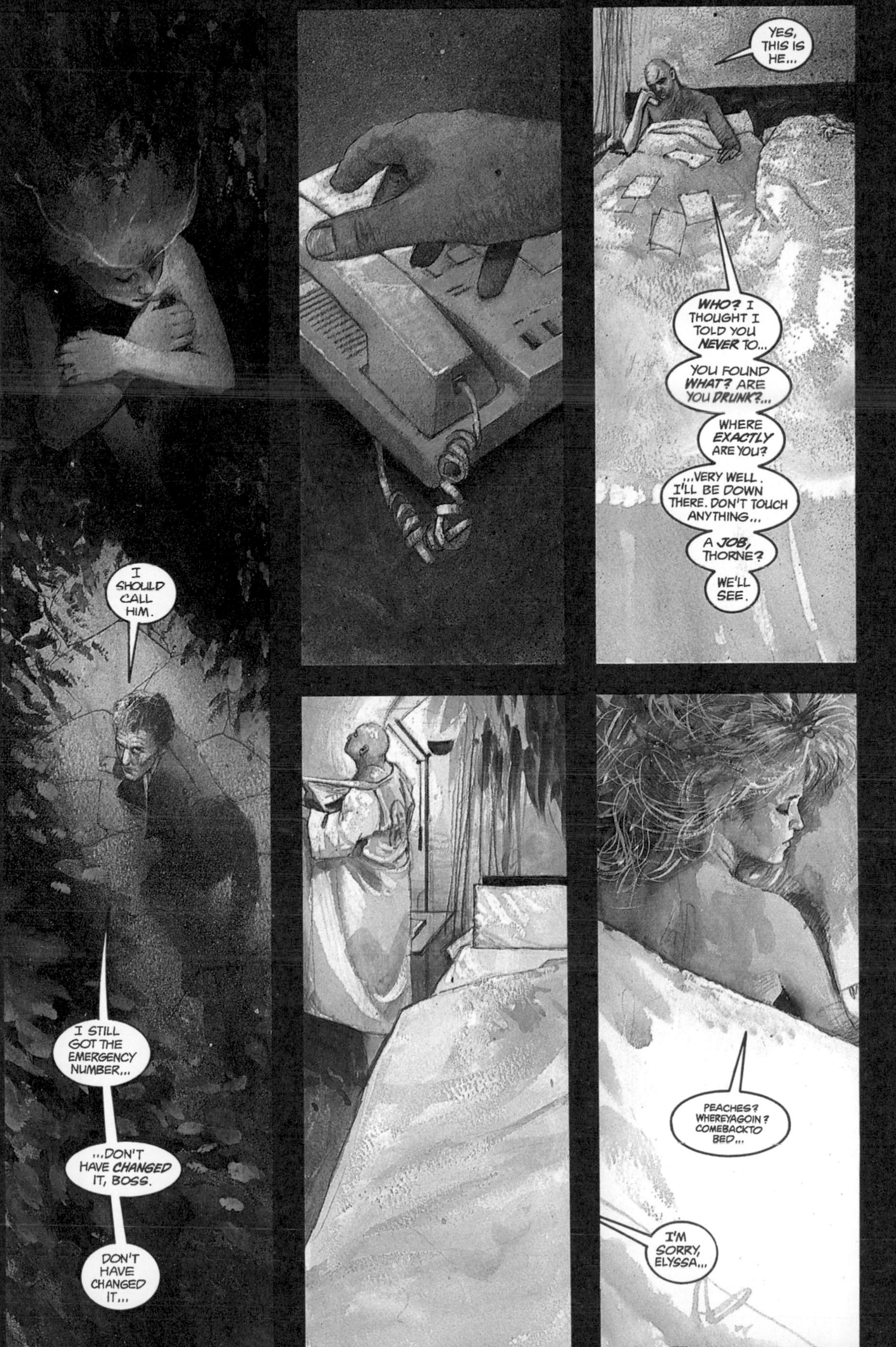
I SHOULD CALL HIM.
I STILL GOT THE EMERGENCY NUMBER...
...DON'T HAVE CHANGED IT, BOSS.
DON'T HAVE CHANGED IT...
YES, THIS IS HE...
WHO? I THOUGHT I TOLD YOU NEVER TO...
YOU FOUND WHAT? ARE YOU DRUNK?...
WHERE EXACTLY ARE YOU?
...VERY WELL. I'LL BE DOWN THERE. DON'T TOUCH ANYTHING...
A JOB, THORNE?
WE'LL SEE.
PEACHES? WHEREYAGOIN? COMEBACKTO BED...
I'M SORRY, ELYSSA...

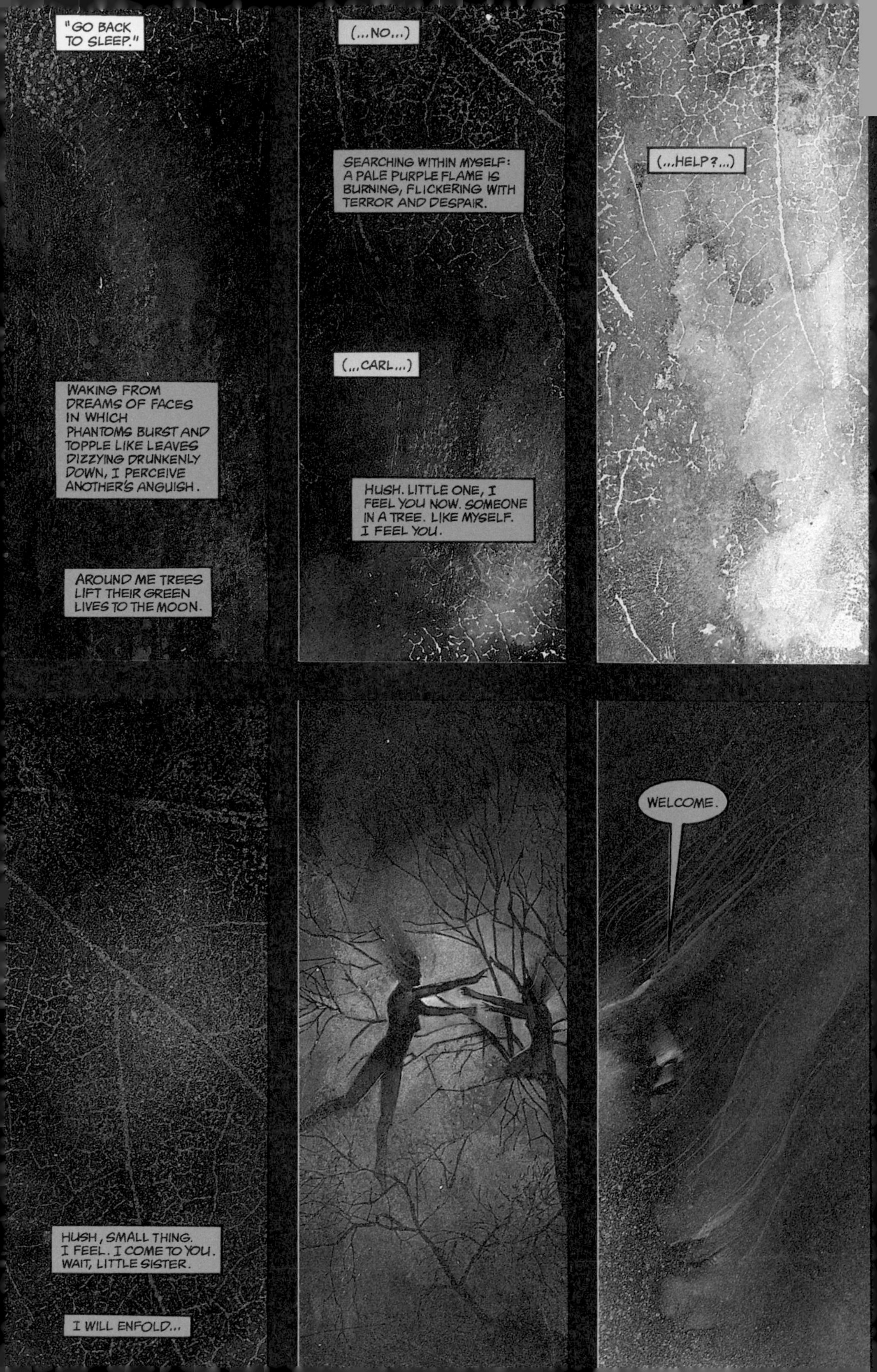
"GO BACK TO SLEEP."
WAKING FROM DREAMS OF FACES IN WHICH PHANTOMS BURST AND TOPPLE LIKE LEAVES DIZZYING DRUNKENLY DOWN, I PERCEIVE ANOTHER'S ANGUISH.
AROUND ME TREES LIFT THEIR GREEN LIVES TO THE MOON.
(...NO...)
SEARCHING WITHIN MYSELF: A PALE PURPLE FLAME IS BURNING, FLICKERING WITH TERROR AND DESPAIR.
(...CARL...)
HUSH. LITTLE ONE, I FEEL YOU NOW. SOMEONE IN A TREE. LIKE MYSELF. I FEEL YOU.
(...HELP?...)
HUSH, SMALL THING. I FEEL. I COME TO YOU. WAIT, LITTLE SISTER.
I WILL ENFOLD...
WELCOME.

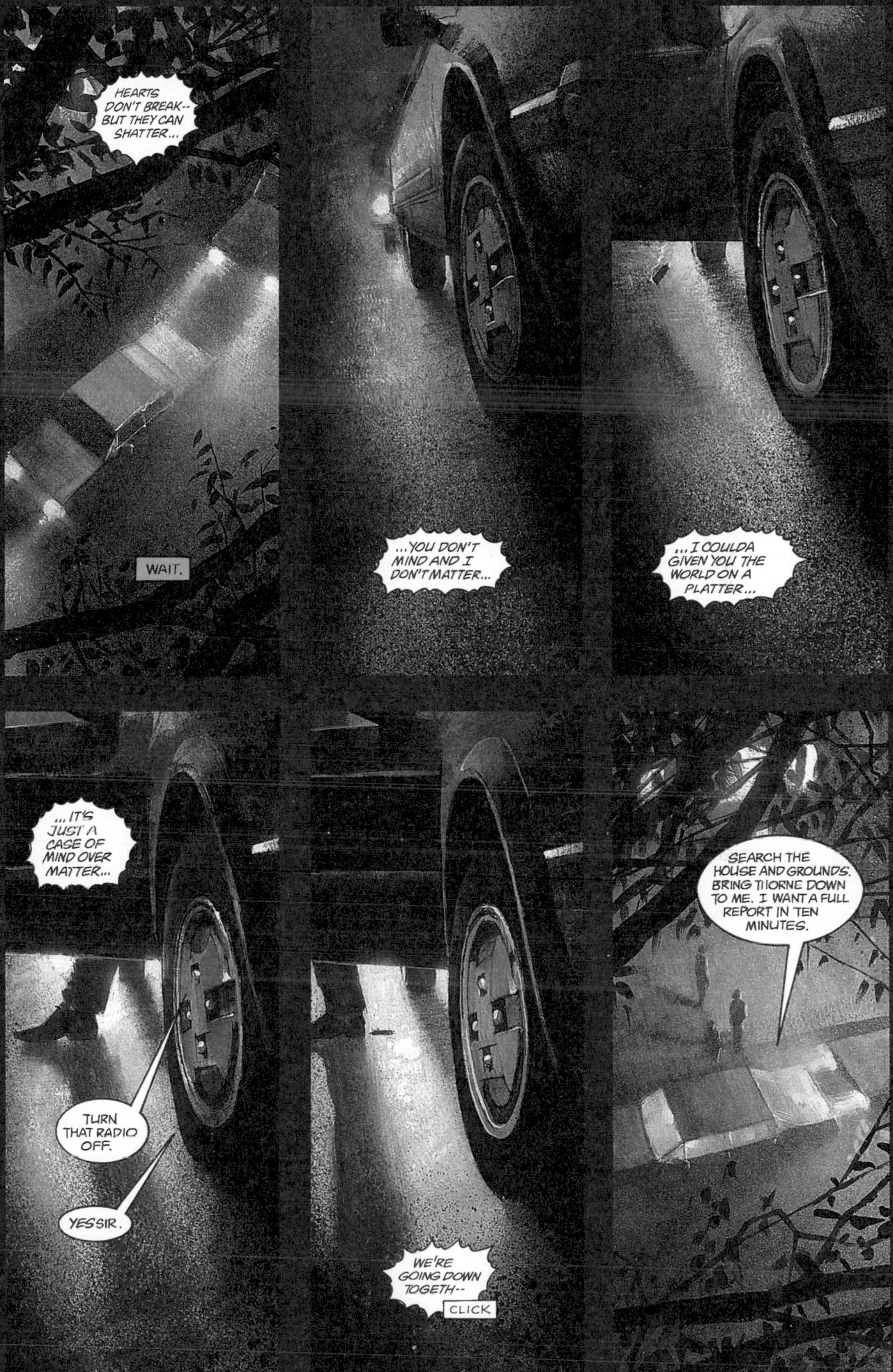
HEARTS DON'T BREAK-- BUT THEY CAN SHATTER...
WAIT.
...YOU DON'T MIND AND I DON'T MATTER...
...I COULDA GIVEN YOU THE WORLD ON A PLATTER...
...IT'S JUST A CASE OF MIND OVER MATTER...
TURN THAT RADIO OFF.
YES'SIR.
WE'RE GOING DOWN TOGETH--
CLICK
SEARCH THE HOUSE AND GROUNDS. BRING THORNE DOWN TO ME. I WANT A FULL REPORT IN TEN MINUTES.

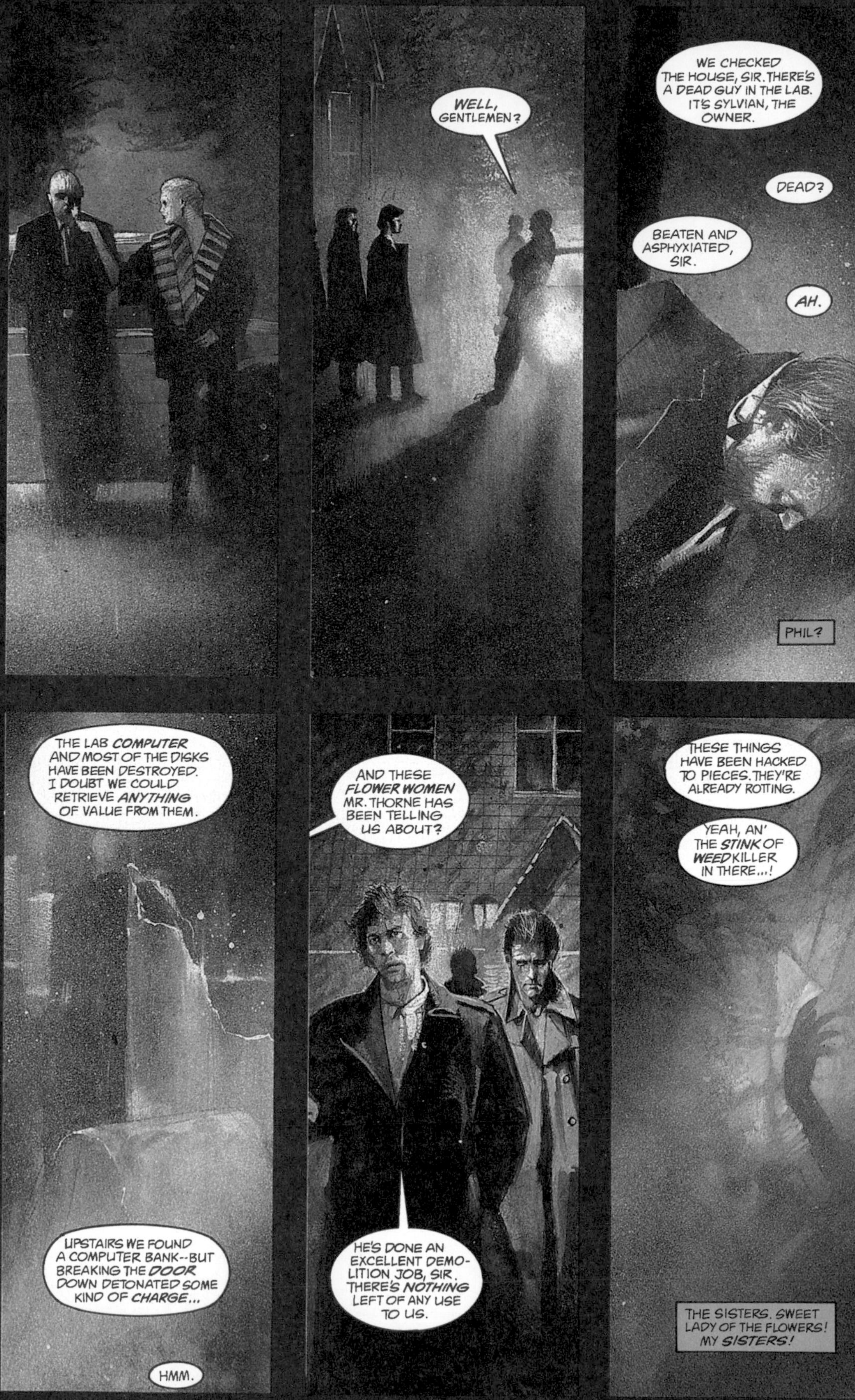
WELL, GENTLEMEN?
WE CHECKED THE HOUSE, SIR. THERE'S A DEAD GUY IN THE LAB. IT'S SYLVIAN, THE OWNER.
DEAD?
BEATEN AND ASPHYXIATED, SIR.
AH.
PHIL?
THE LAB COMPUTER AND MOST OF THE DISKS HAVE BEEN DESTROYED. I DOUBT WE COULD RETRIEVE ANYTHING OF VALUE FROM THEM.
UPSTAIRS WE FOUND A COMPUTER BANK--BUT BREAKING THE DOOR DOWN DETONATED SOME KIND OF CHARGE...
HMM.
AND THESE FLOWER WOMEN MR. THORNE HAS BEEN TELLING US ABOUT?
HE'S DONE AN EXCELLENT DEMOLITION JOB, SIR. THERE'S NOTHING LEFT OF ANY USE TO US.
THESE THINGS HAVE BEEN HACKED TO PIECES. THEY'RE ALREADY ROTTING.
YEAH, AN' THE STINK OF WEED KILLER IN THERE...!
THE SISTERS. SWEET LADY OF THE FLOWERS! MY SISTERS!

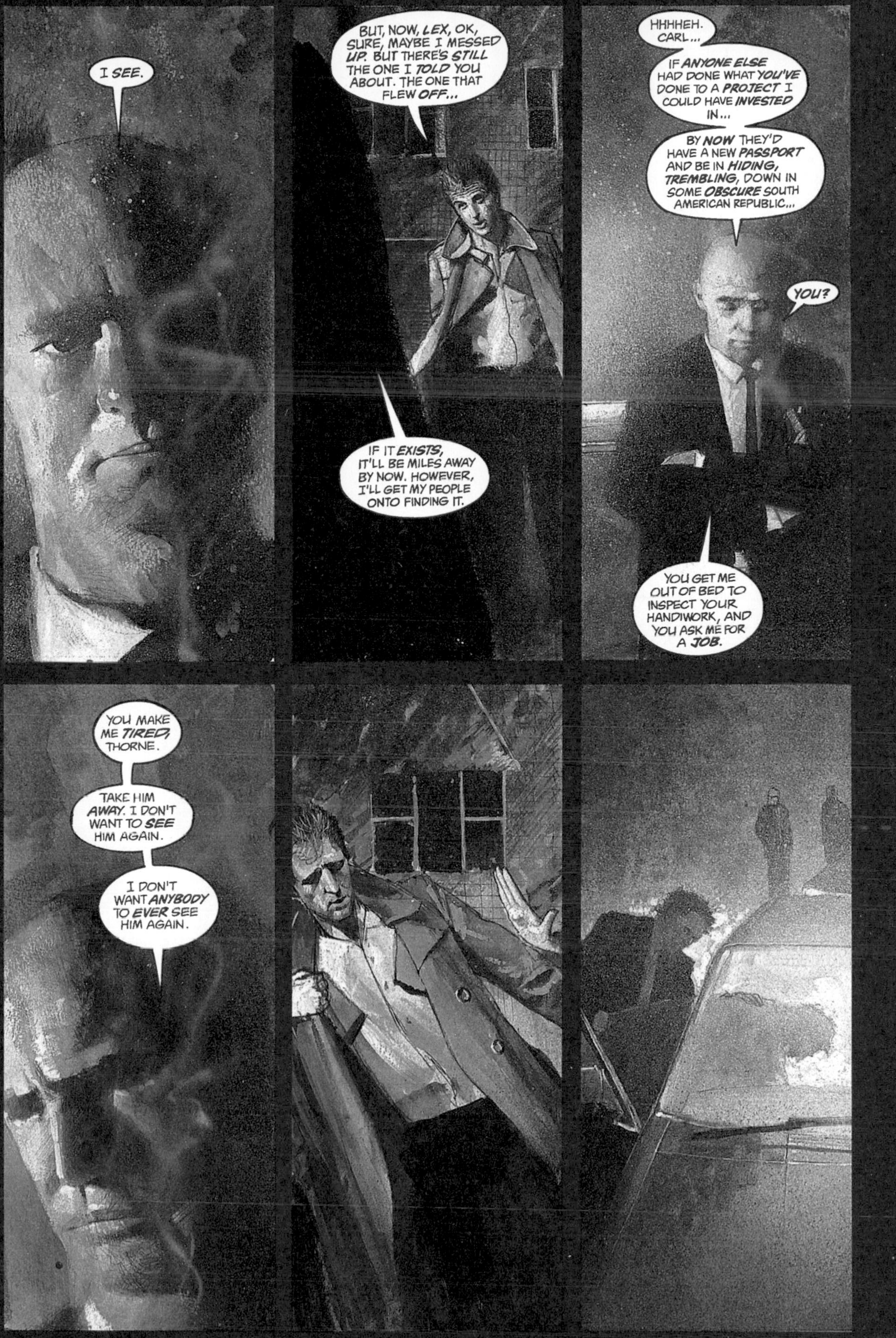
I SEE.
BUT, NOW, LEX, OK, SURE, MAYBE I MESSED UP. BUT THERE'S STILL THE ONE I TOLD YOU ABOUT. THE ONE THAT FLEW OFF...
IF IT EXISTS, IT'LL BE MILES AWAY BY NOW. HOWEVER, I'LL GET MY PEOPLE ONTO FINDING IT.
HHHHEH. CARL...
IF ANYONE ELSE HAD DONE WHAT YOU'VE DONE TO A PROJECT I COULD HAVE INVESTED IN...
BY NOW THEY'D HAVE A NEW PASSPORT AND BE IN HIDING, TREMBLING, DOWN IN SOME OBSCURE SOUTH AMERICAN REPUBLIC...
YOU?
YOU GET ME OUT OF BED TO INSPECT YOUR HANDIWORK, AND YOU ASK ME FOR A JOB.
YOU MAKE ME TIRED, THORNE.
TAKE HIM AWAY. I DON'T WANT TO SEE HIM AGAIN.
I DON'T WANT ANYBODY TO EVER SEE HIM AGAIN.

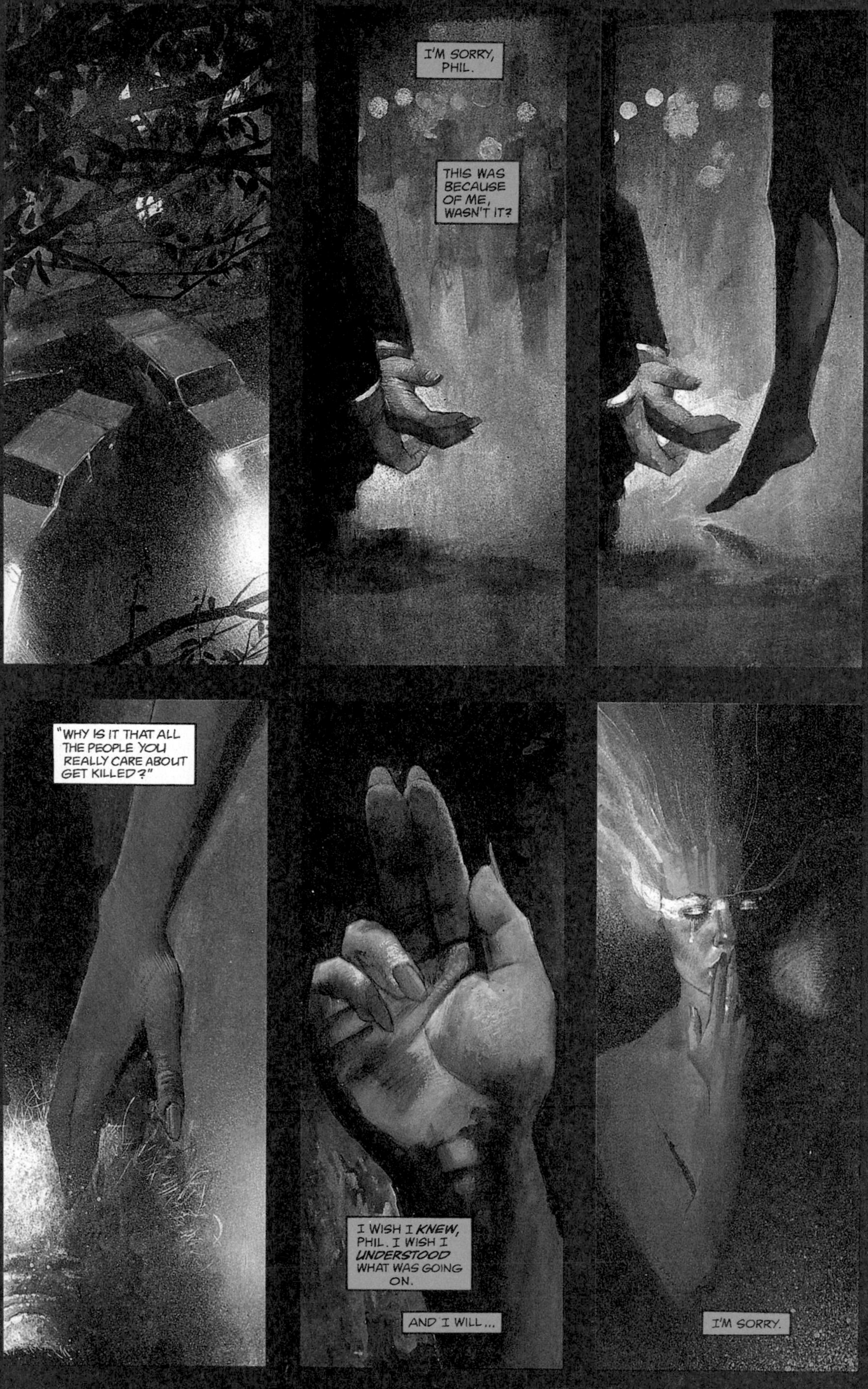
I'M SORRY, PHIL.
THIS WAS BECAUSE OF ME, WASN'T IT?
"WHY IS IT THAT ALL THE PEOPLE YOU REALLY CARE ABOUT GET KILLED?"
I WISH I *KNEW*, PHIL. I WISH I *UNDERSTOOD* WHAT WAS GOING ON.
AND I WILL...
I'M SORRY.

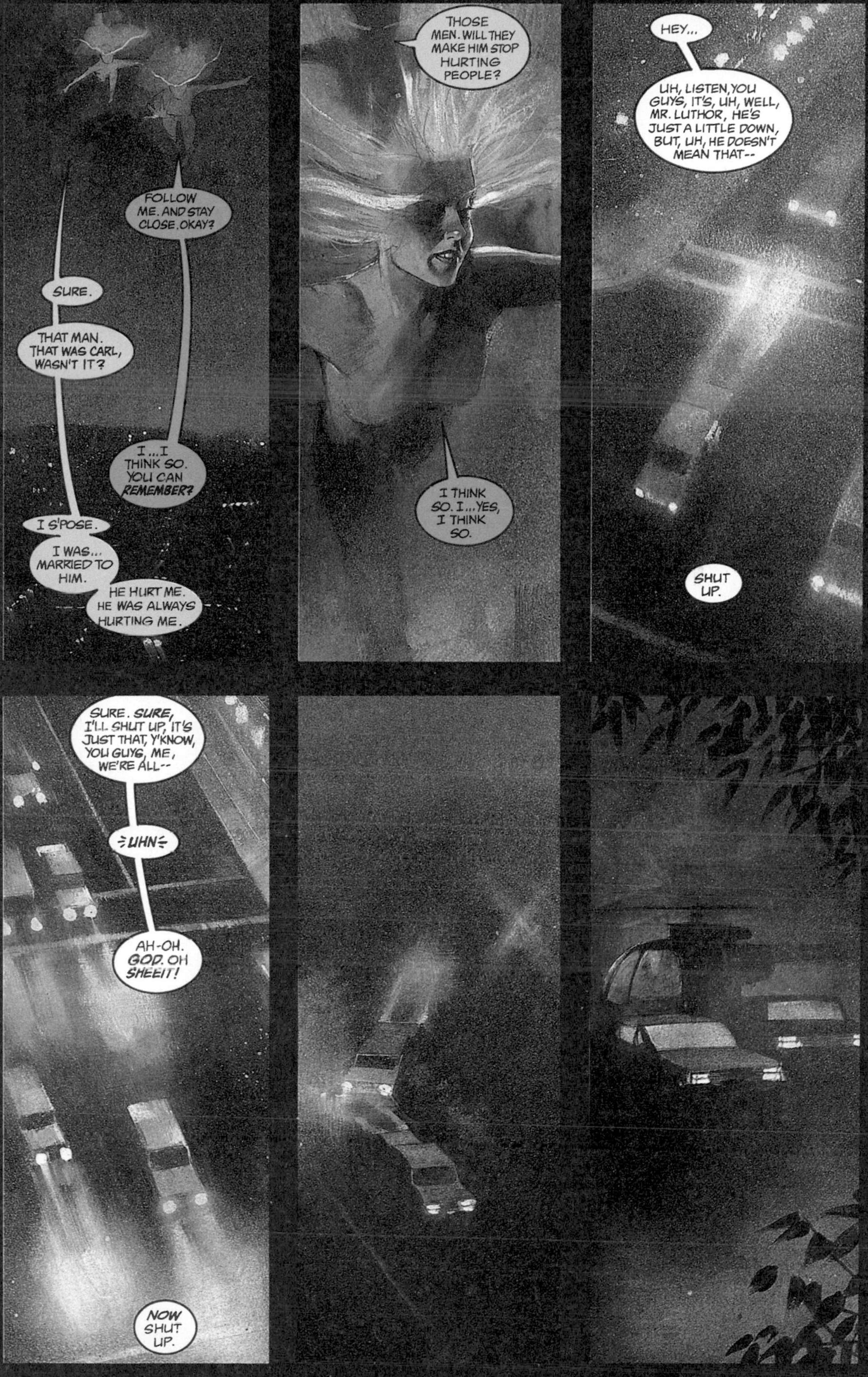
FOLLOW ME. AND STAY CLOSE. OKAY?
SURE.
THAT MAN. THAT WAS CARL, WASN'T IT?
I...I THINK SO. YOU CAN REMEMBER?
I S'POSE.
I WAS... MARRIED TO HIM.
HE HURT ME. HE WAS ALWAYS HURTING ME.
THOSE MEN. WILL THEY MAKE HIM STOP HURTING PEOPLE?
I THINK SO. I...YES, I THINK SO.
HEY...
UH, LISTEN, YOU GUYS, IT'S, UH, WELL, MR. LUTHOR, HE'S JUST A LITTLE DOWN, BUT, UH, HE DOESN'T MEAN THAT--
SHUT UP.
SURE. SURE, I'LL SHUT UP, IT'S JUST THAT, Y'KNOW, YOU GUYS, ME, WE'RE ALL--
UHN
AH-OH. GOD. OH SHEEIT!
NOW SHUT UP.

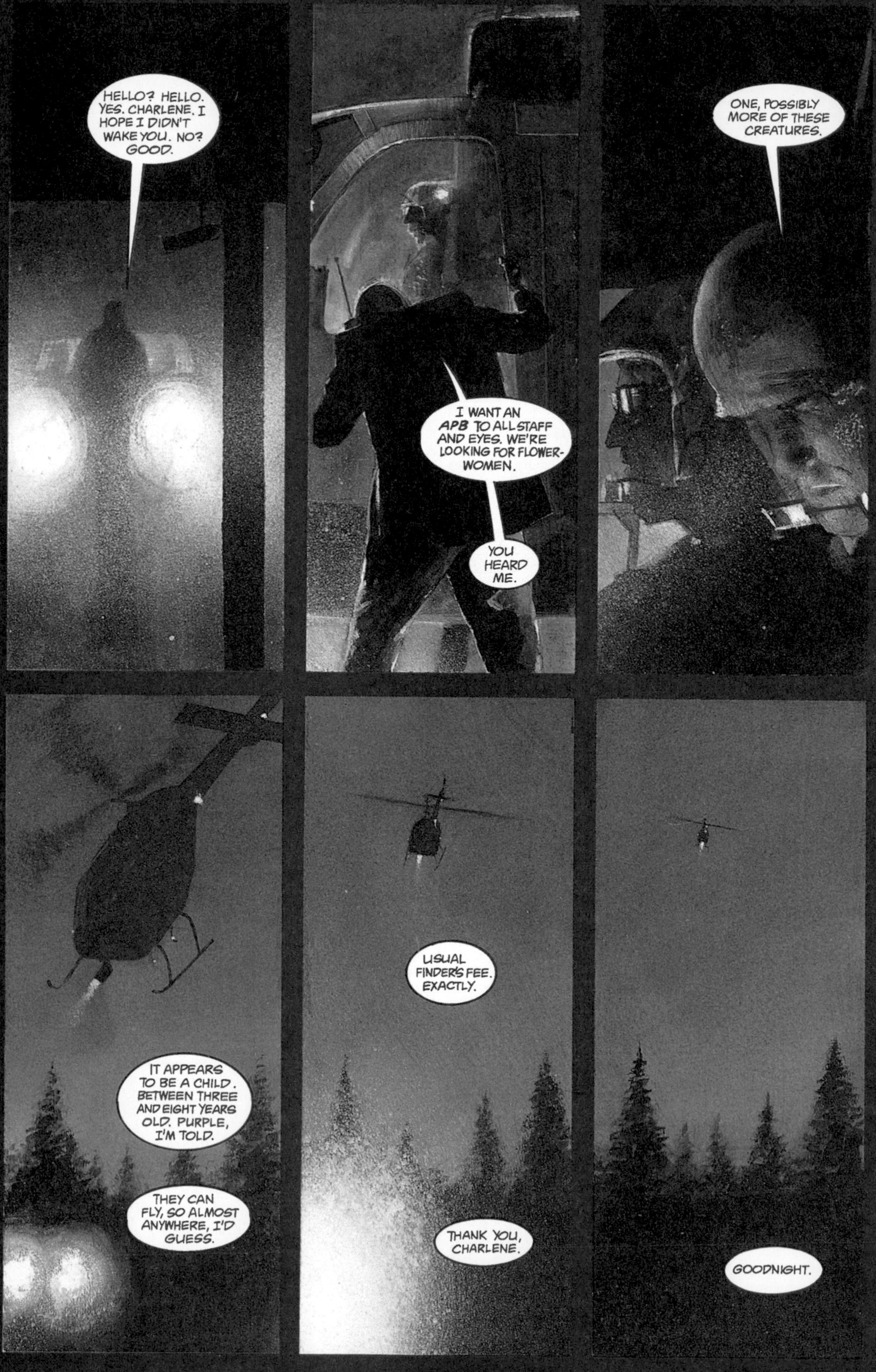
HELLO? HELLO. YES. CHARLENE. I HOPE I DIDN'T WAKE YOU. NO? GOOD.
I WANT AN APB TO ALL STAFF AND EYES. WE'RE LOOKING FOR FLOWER-WOMEN.
YOU HEARD ME.
ONE, POSSIBLY MORE OF THESE CREATURES.
IT APPEARS TO BE A CHILD. BETWEEN THREE AND EIGHT YEARS OLD. PURPLE, I'M TOLD.
THEY CAN FLY, SO ALMOST ANYWHERE, I'D GUESS.
USUAL FINDER'S FEE. EXACTLY.
THANK YOU, CHARLENE.
GOODNIGHT.

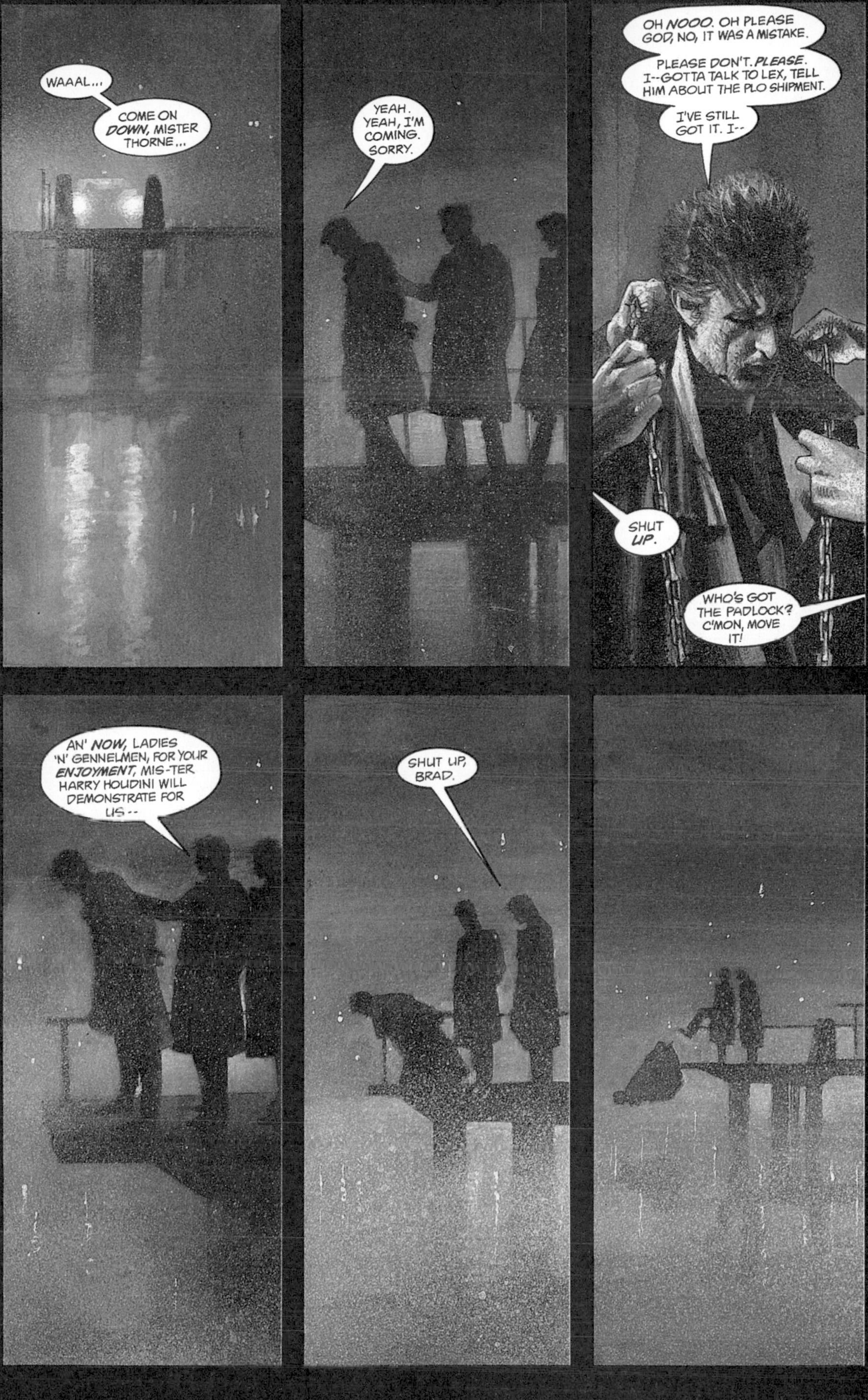
WAAAL...
COME ON DOWN, MISTER THORNE...
YEAH. YEAH, I'M COMING. SORRY.
OH NOOO. OH PLEASE GOD, NO, IT WAS A MISTAKE.
PLEASE DON'T. PLEASE. I--GOTTA TALK TO LEX, TELL HIM ABOUT THE PLO SHIPMENT.
I'VE STILL GOT IT. I--
SHUT UP.
WHO'S GOT THE PADLOCK? C'MON, MOVE IT!
AN' NOW, LADIES 'N' GENNELMEN, FOR YOUR ENJOYMENT, MIS-TER HARRY HOUDINI WILL DEMONSTRATE FOR US--
SHUT UP, BRAD.

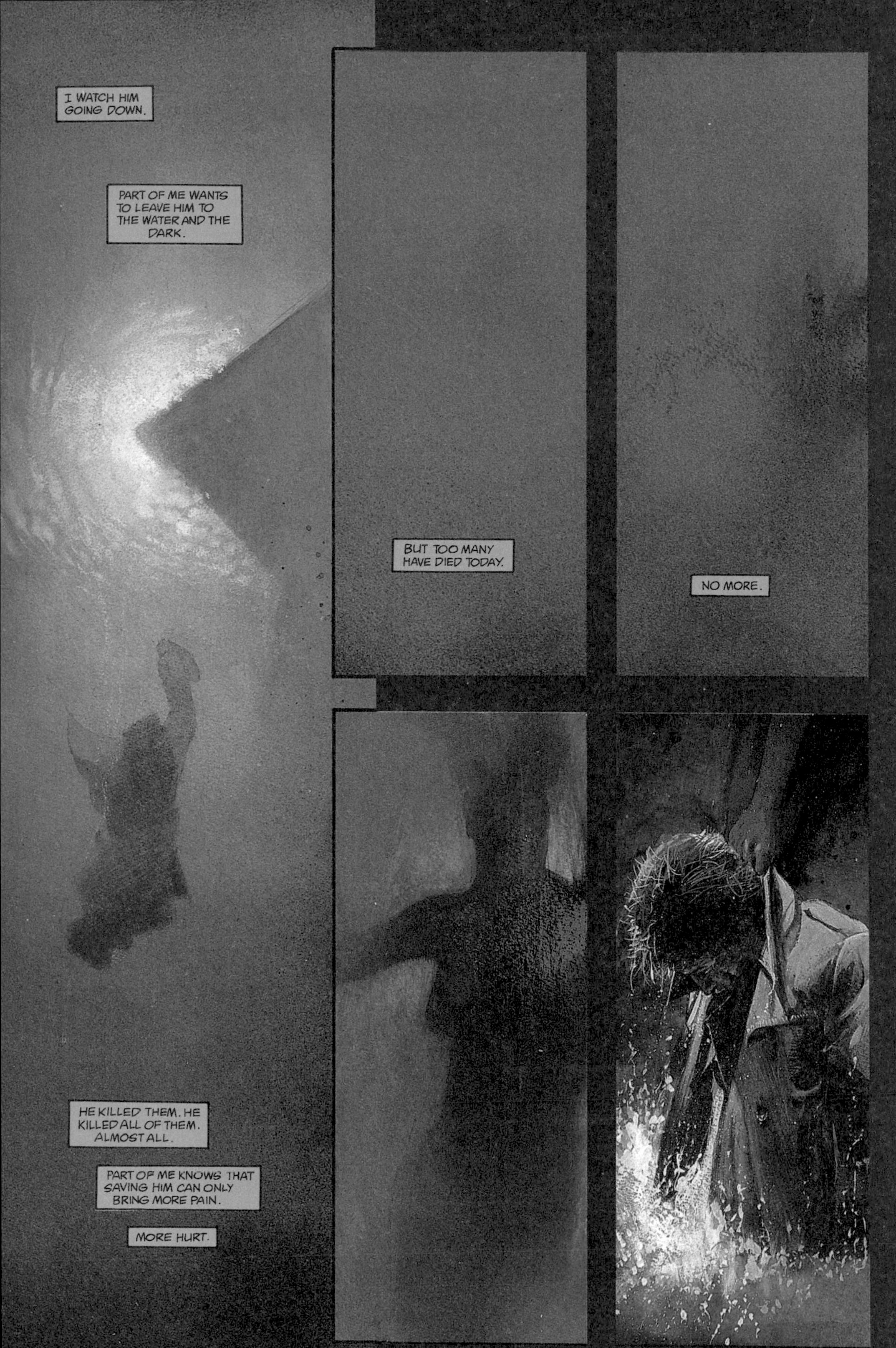
I WATCH HIM GOING DOWN.
PART OF ME WANTS TO LEAVE HIM TO THE WATER AND THE DARK.
HE KILLED THEM. HE KILLED ALL OF THEM. ALMOST ALL.
PART OF ME KNOWS THAT SAVING HIM CAN ONLY BRING MORE PAIN.
MORE HURT.
BUT TOO MANY HAVE DIED TODAY.
NO MORE.

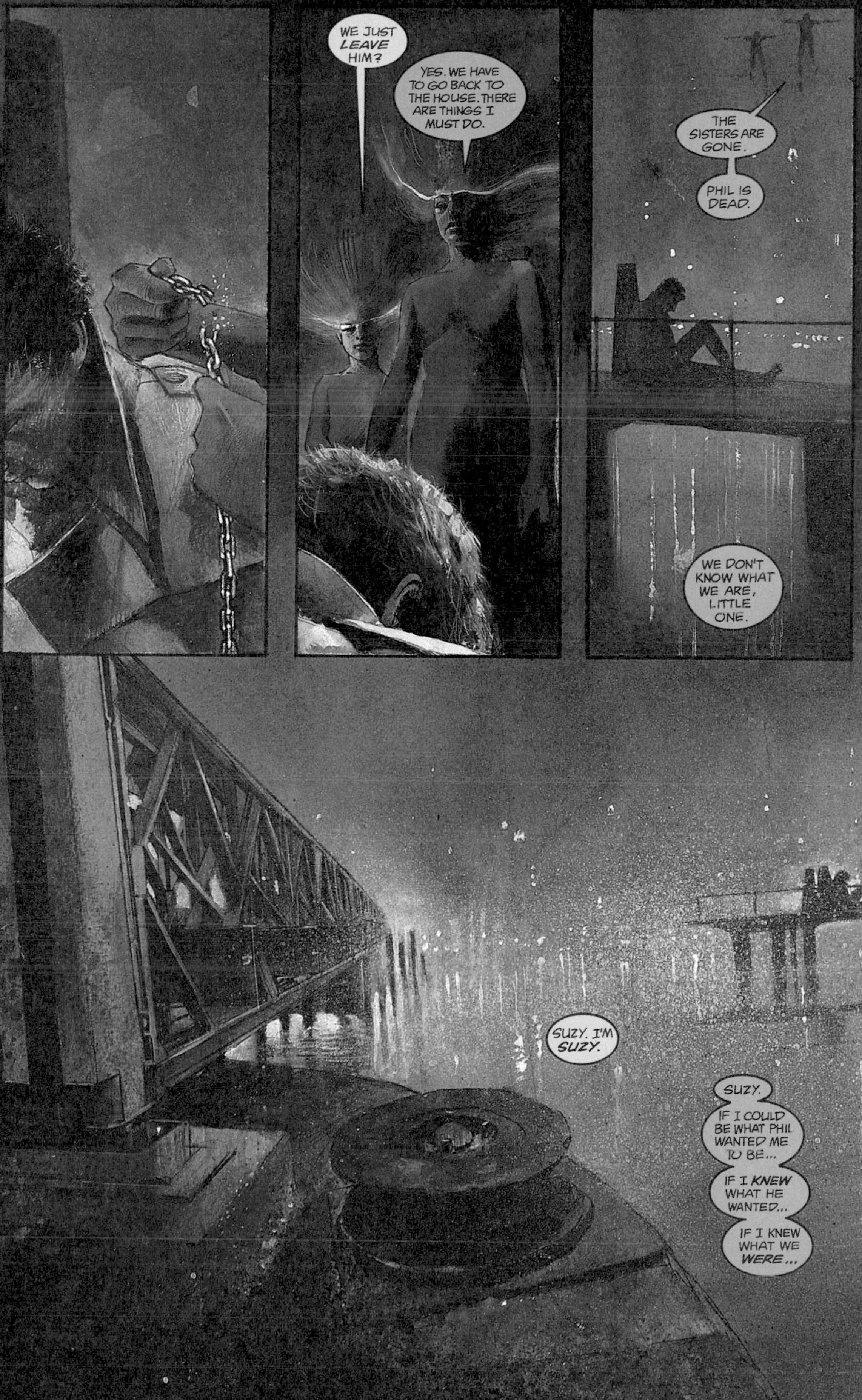
WE JUST LEAVE HIM?
YES. WE HAVE TO GO BACK TO THE HOUSE. THERE ARE THINGS I MUST DO.
THE SISTERS ARE GONE.
PHIL IS DEAD.
WE DON'T KNOW WHAT WE ARE, LITTLE ONE.
SUZY. I'M SUZY.
SUZY.
IF I COULD BE WHAT PHIL WANTED ME TO BE...
IF I KNEW WHAT HE WANTED...
IF I KNEW WHAT WE WERE...

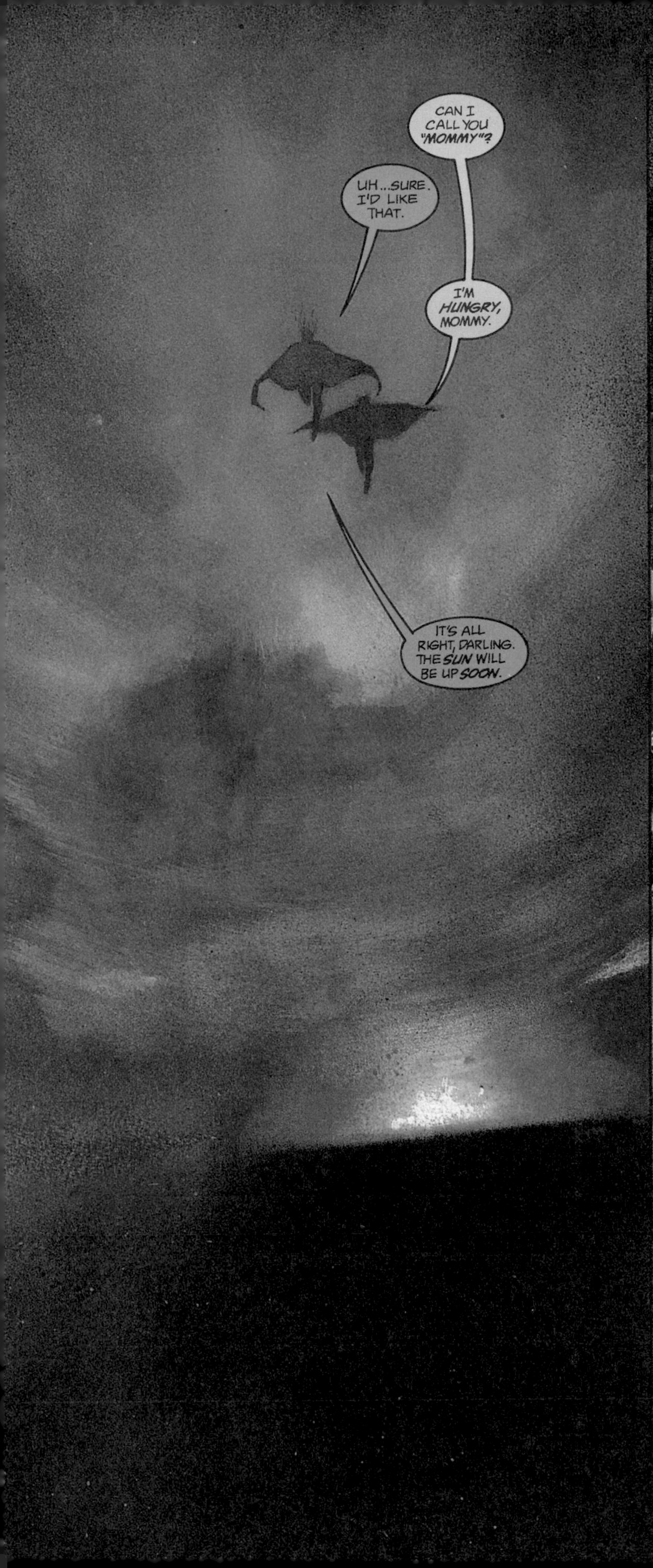
CAN I CALL YOU "MOMMY"?
UH...SURE. I'D LIKE THAT.
I'M HUNGRY, MOMMY.
IT'S ALL RIGHT, DARLING. THE SUN WILL BE UP SOON.

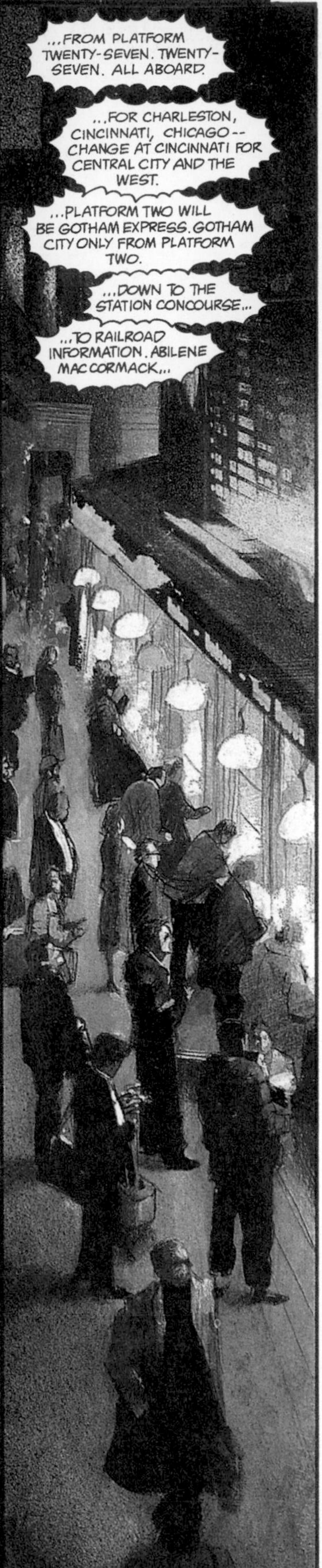
...FROM PLATFORM TWENTY-SEVEN. TWENTY-SEVEN. ALL ABOARD.
...FOR CHARLESTON, CINCINNATI, CHICAGO--CHANGE AT CINCINNATI FOR CENTRAL CITY AND THE WEST.
...PLATFORM TWO WILL BE GOTHAM EXPRESS. GOTHAM CITY ONLY FROM PLATFORM TWO.
...DOWN TO THE STATION CONCOURSE...
...TO RAILROAD INFORMATION. ABILENE MACCORMACK...

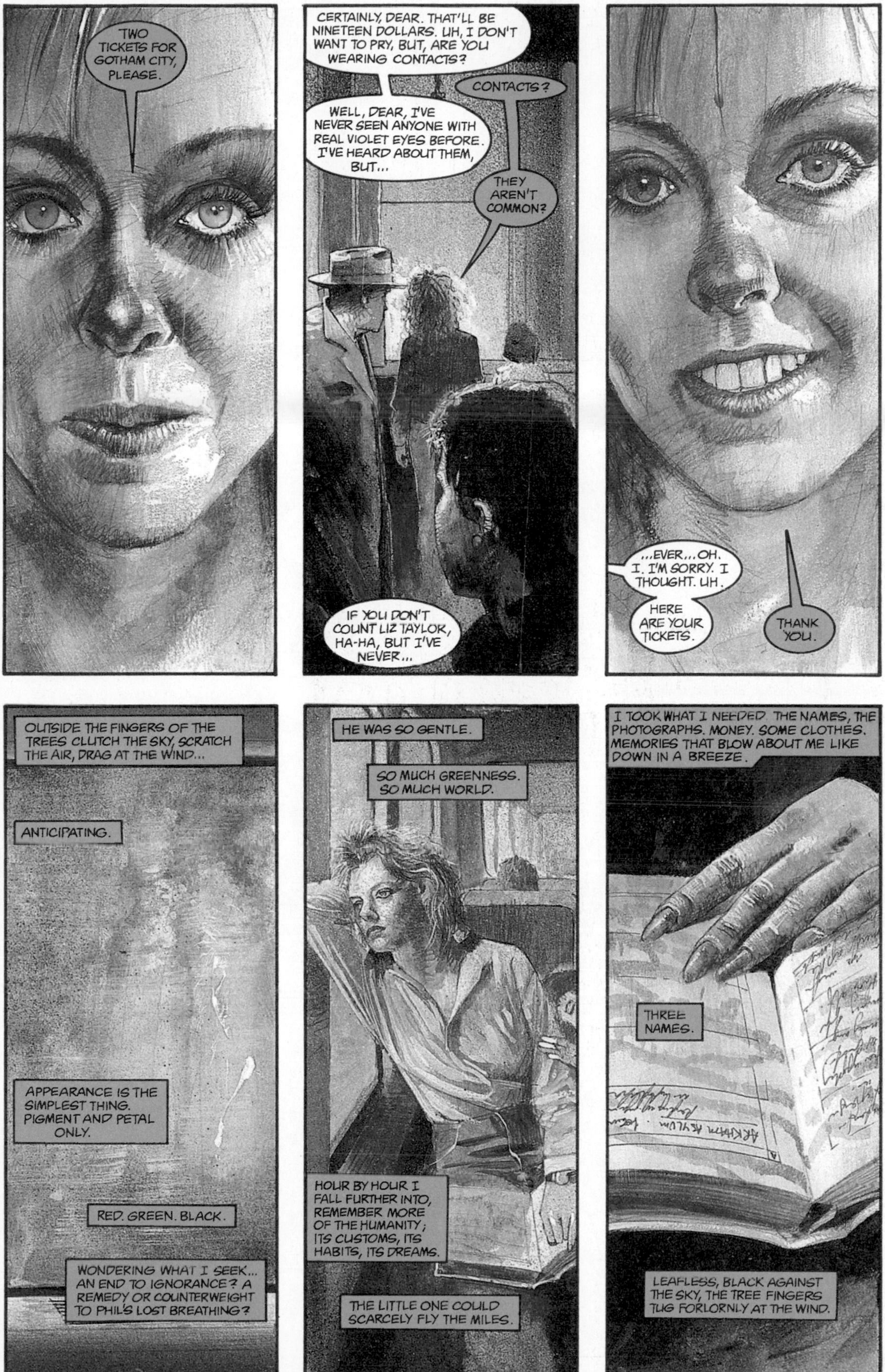
TWO TICKETS FOR GOTHAM CITY, PLEASE.
CERTAINLY, DEAR. THAT'LL BE NINETEEN DOLLARS. UH, I DON'T WANT TO PRY, BUT, ARE YOU WEARING CONTACTS?
CONTACTS?
WELL, DEAR, I'VE NEVER SEEN ANYONE WITH REAL VIOLET EYES BEFORE. I'VE HEARD ABOUT THEM, BUT...
THEY AREN'T COMMON?
IF YOU DON'T COUNT LIZ TAYLOR, HA-HA, BUT I'VE NEVER...
...EVER... OH. I. I'M SORRY. I THOUGHT. UH.
HERE ARE YOUR TICKETS.
THANK YOU.
OUTSIDE THE FINGERS OF THE TREES CLUTCH THE SKY, SCRATCH THE AIR, DRAG AT THE WIND...
ANTICIPATING.
APPEARANCE IS THE SIMPLEST THING. PIGMENT AND PETAL ONLY.
RED. GREEN. BLACK.
WONDERING WHAT I SEEK... AN END TO IGNORANCE? A REMEDY OR COUNTERWEIGHT TO PHIL'S LOST BREATHING?
HE WAS SO GENTLE.
SO MUCH GREENNESS. SO MUCH WORLD.
HOUR BY HOUR I FALL FURTHER INTO, REMEMBER MORE OF THE HUMANITY; ITS CUSTOMS, ITS HABITS, ITS DREAMS.
THE LITTLE ONE COULD SCARCELY FLY THE MILES.
I TOOK WHAT I NEEDED. THE NAMES, THE PHOTOGRAPHS. MONEY. SOME CLOTHES. MEMORIES THAT BLOW ABOUT ME LIKE DOWN IN A BREEZE.
THREE NAMES.
LEAFLESS, BLACK AGAINST THE SKY, THE TREE FINGERS TUG FORLORNLY AT THE WIND.

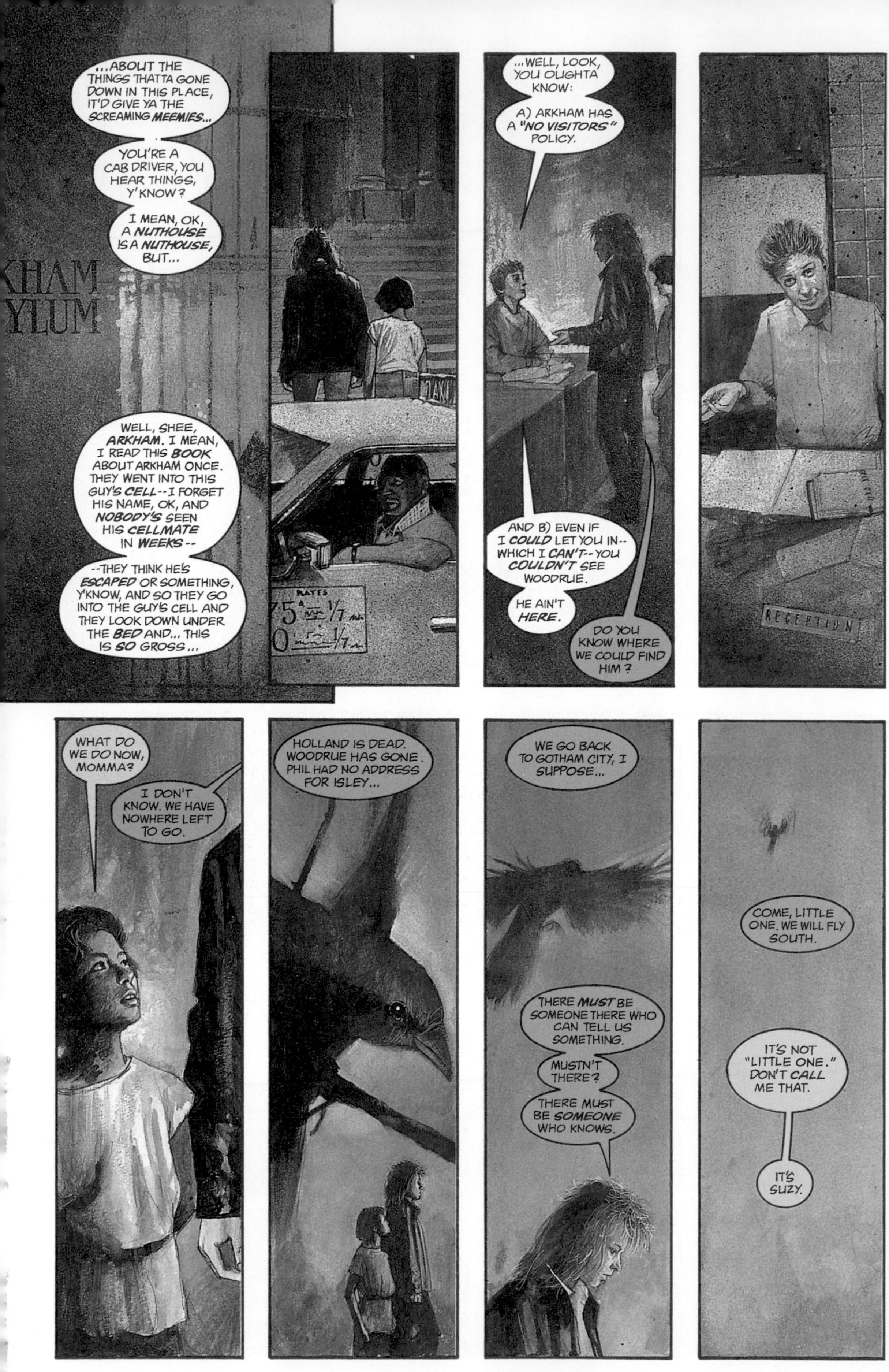
...ABOUT THE THINGS THATTA GONE DOWN IN THIS PLACE, IT'D GIVE YA THE SCREAMING MEEMIES...
YOU'RE A CAB DRIVER, YOU HEAR THINGS, Y'KNOW?
I MEAN, OK, A NUTHOUSE IS A NUTHOUSE, BUT...
KHAM
YLUM
WELL, SHEE, ARKHAM. I MEAN, I READ THIS BOOK ABOUT ARKHAM ONCE. THEY WENT INTO THIS GUY'S CELL--I FORGET HIS NAME, OK, AND NOBODY'S SEEN HIS CELLMATE IN WEEKS--
--THEY THINK HE'S ESCAPED OR SOMETHING, Y'KNOW, AND SO THEY GO INTO THE GUY'S CELL AND THEY LOOK DOWN UNDER THE BED AND... THIS IS SO GROSS...
TAXI
RATES
...WELL, LOOK, YOU OUGHTA KNOW:
A) ARKHAM HAS A "NO VISITORS" POLICY.
AND B) EVEN IF I COULD LET YOU IN--WHICH I CAN'T--YOU COULDN'T SEE WOODRUE.
HE AIN'T HERE.
DO YOU KNOW WHERE WE COULD FIND HIM?
RECEPTION
WHAT DO WE DO NOW, MOMMA?
I DON'T KNOW. WE HAVE NOWHERE LEFT TO GO.
HOLLAND IS DEAD. WOODRUE HAS GONE. PHIL HAD NO ADDRESS FOR ISLEY...
WE GO BACK TO GOTHAM CITY, I SUPPOSE...
THERE MUST BE SOMEONE THERE WHO CAN TELL US SOMETHING.
MUSTN'T THERE?
THERE MUST BE SOMEONE WHO KNOWS.
COME, LITTLE ONE. WE WILL FLY SOUTH.
IT'S NOT "LITTLE ONE." DON'T CALL ME THAT.
IT'S SUZY.

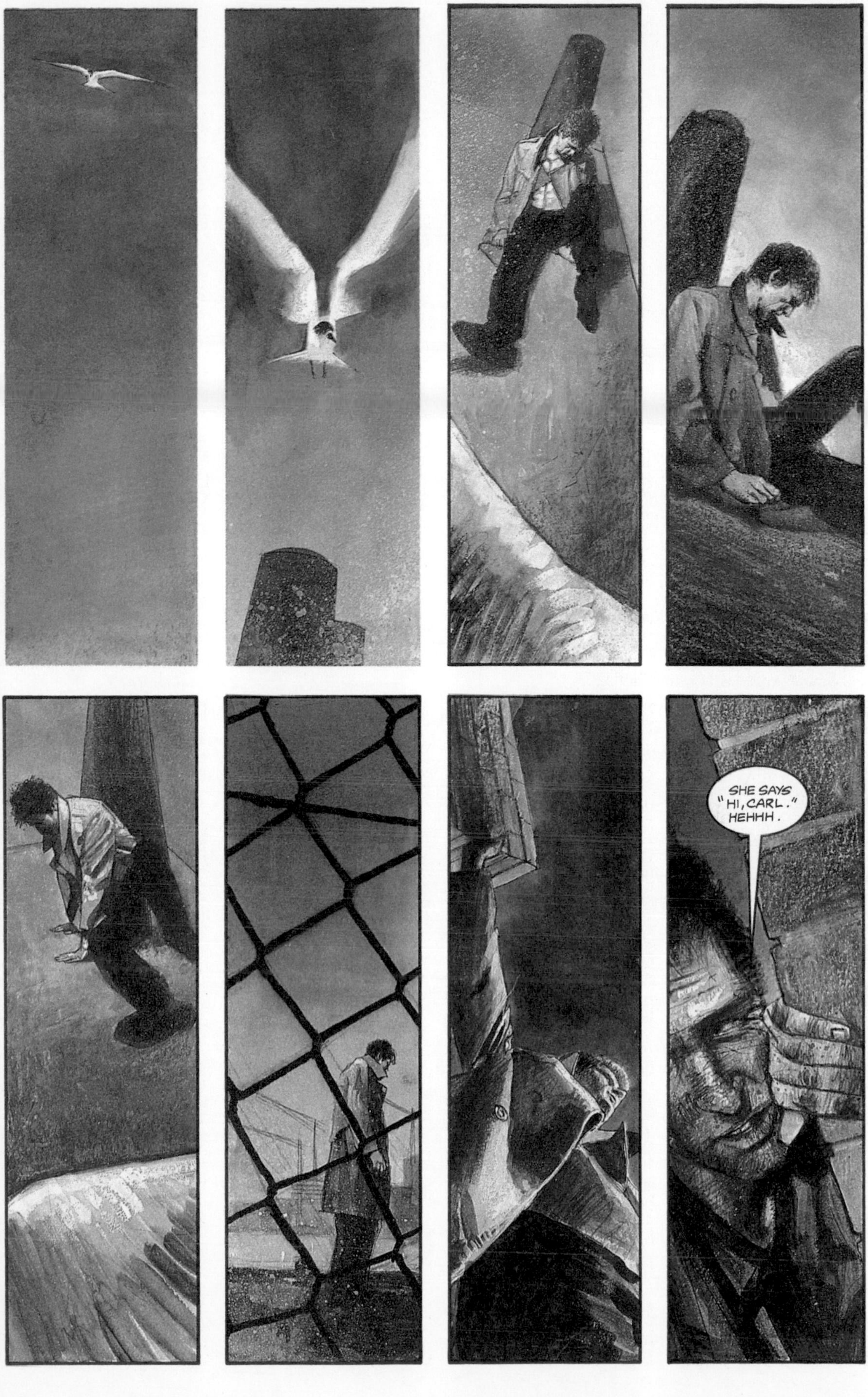
SHE SAYS "HI, CARL." HEHHH.

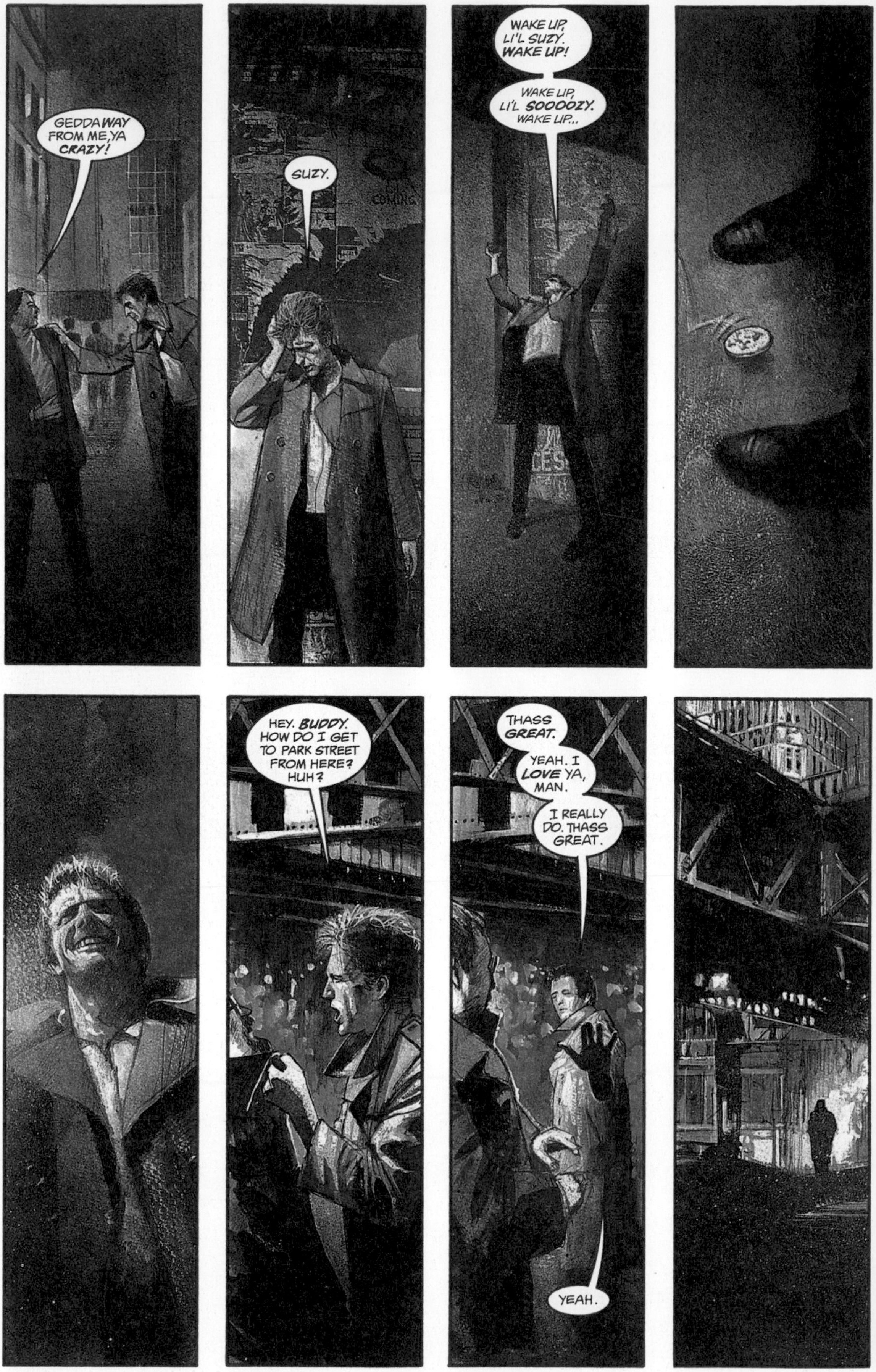
GEDDAWAY FROM ME, YA CRAZY!
SUZY.
WAKE UP, LI'L SUZY. WAKE UP!
WAKE UP, LI'L SOOOOZY. WAKE UP...
HEY. BUDDY. HOW DO I GET TO PARK STREET FROM HERE? HUH?
THASS GREAT.
YEAH. I LOVE YA, MAN.
I REALLY DO. THASS GREAT.
YEAH.

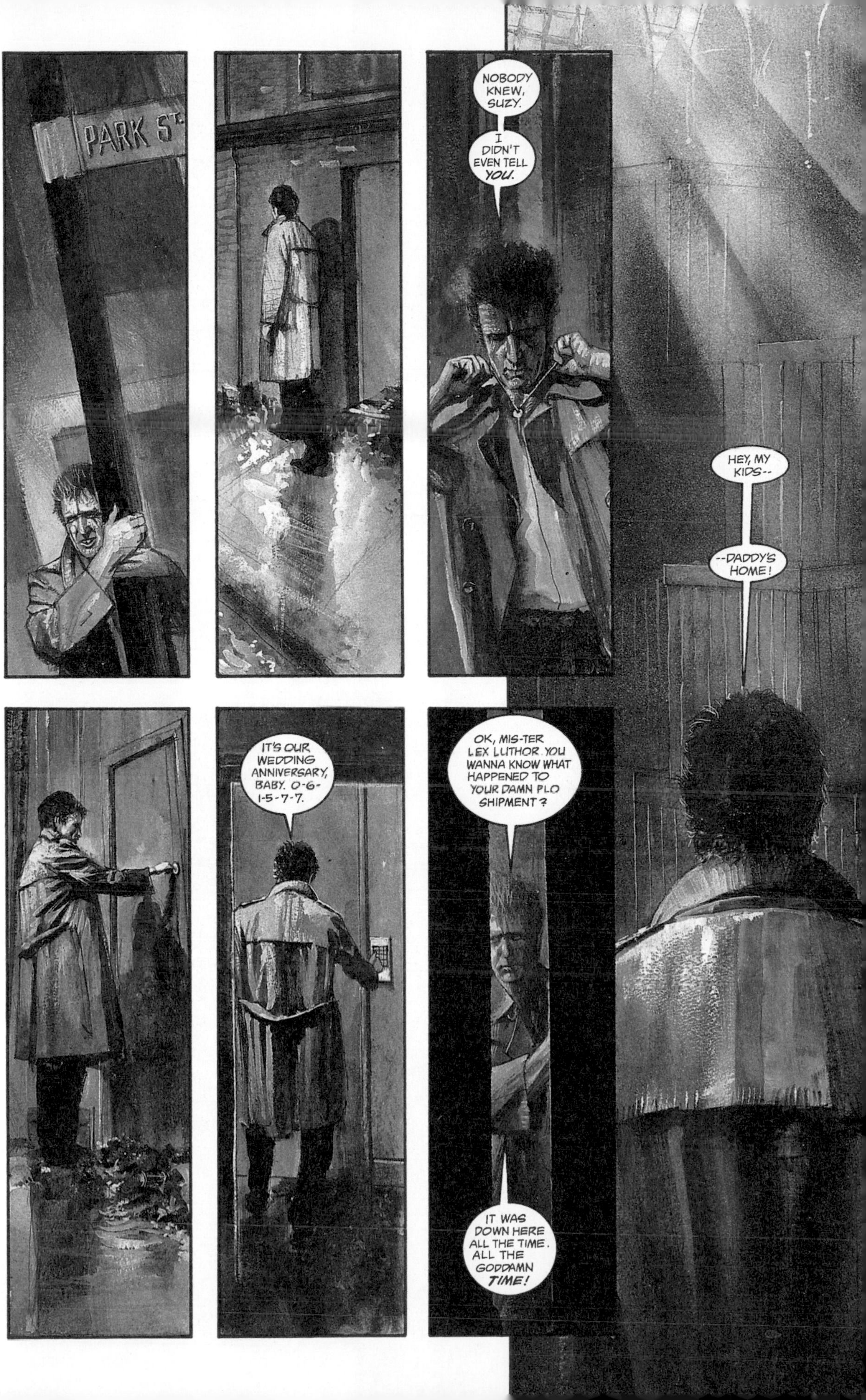
PARK St.
NOBODY KNEW, SUZY.
I DIDN'T EVEN TELL YOU.
IT'S OUR WEDDING ANNIVERSARY, BABY. 0-6-1-5-7-7.
OK, MIS-TER LEX LUTHOR. YOU WANNA KNOW WHAT HAPPENED TO YOUR DAMN PLO SHIPMENT?
IT WAS DOWN HERE ALL THE TIME. ALL THE GODDAMN TIME!
HEY, MY KIDS--
--DADDY'S HOME!

YOU STAY UP HERE, SUZY. DON'T COME DOWN.

I'LL TRY NOT TO BE AWAY TOO LONG... BUT JUST WAIT FOR ME.

OKAY?

SWAM

SHE'S CHANGED SO MUCH IN THESE FEW HOURS. AT FIRST SHE SEEMED SO MUCH OLDER, SO MUCH WISER...

SHE REMEMBERED SO MUCH MORE THAN I DID...

AND NOW SHE'S A CHILD.

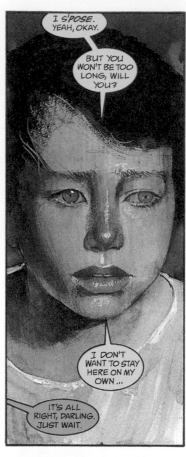

I S'POSE. YEAH, OKAY.

BUT YOU WON'T BE TOO LONG, WILL YOU?

I DON'T WANT TO STAY HERE ON MY OWN ...

IT'S ALL RIGHT, DARLING. JUST WAIT.

I PRAY TO WHATEVER GREEN GODDESSES THERE MAY BE THAT SHE ISN'T HURT FURTHER...

...AND THAT MY SEARCH BEARS FRUIT.

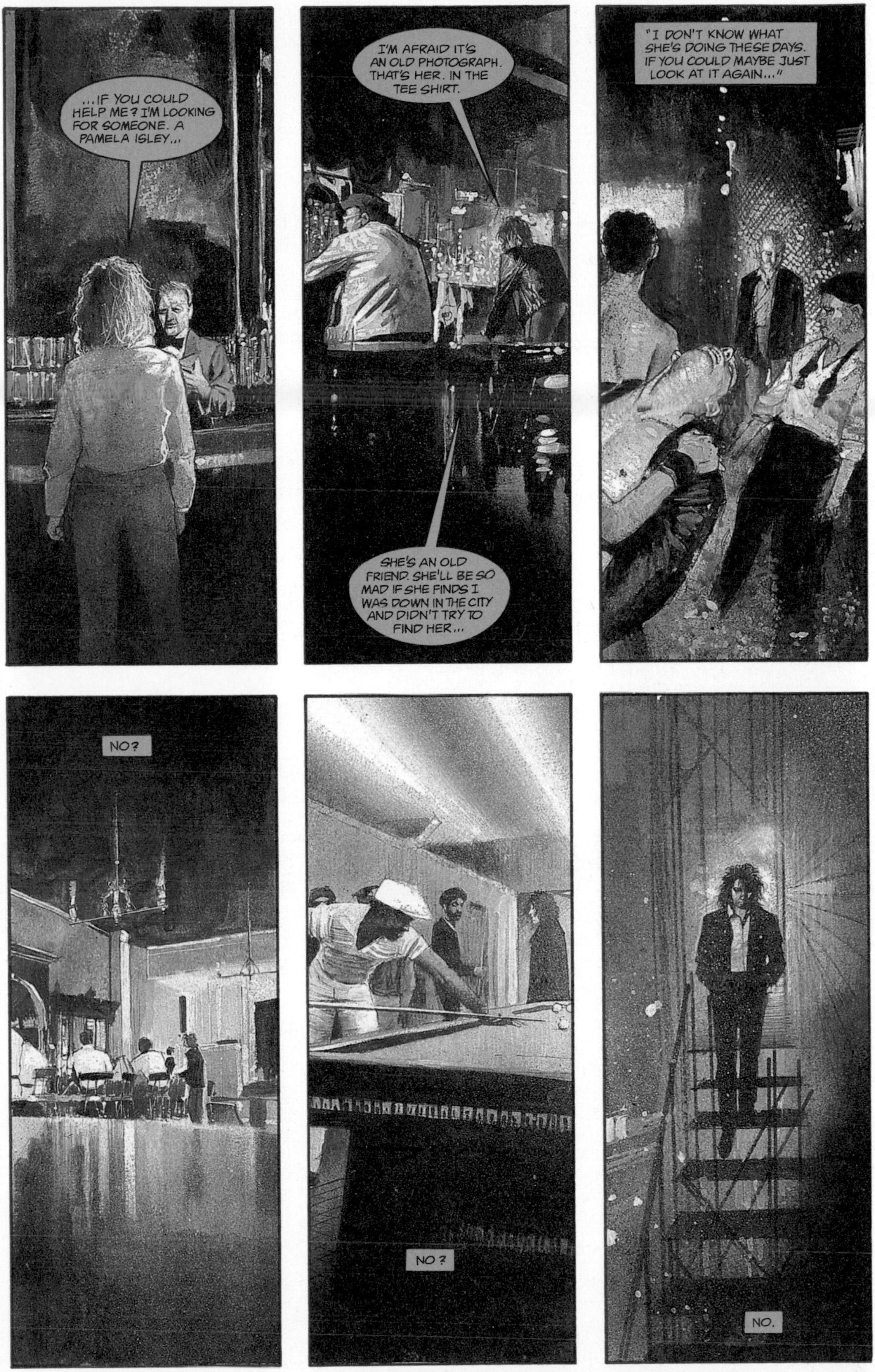
...IF YOU COULD HELP ME? I'M LOOKING FOR SOMEONE. A PAMELA ISLEY...
I'M AFRAID IT'S AN OLD PHOTOGRAPH. THAT'S HER. IN THE TEE SHIRT.
SHE'S AN OLD FRIEND. SHE'LL BE SO MAD IF SHE FINDS I WAS DOWN IN THE CITY AND DIDN'T TRY TO FIND HER...
"I DON'T KNOW WHAT SHE'S DOING THESE DAYS. IF YOU COULD MAYBE JUST LOOK AT IT AGAIN..."
NO?
NO?
NO.

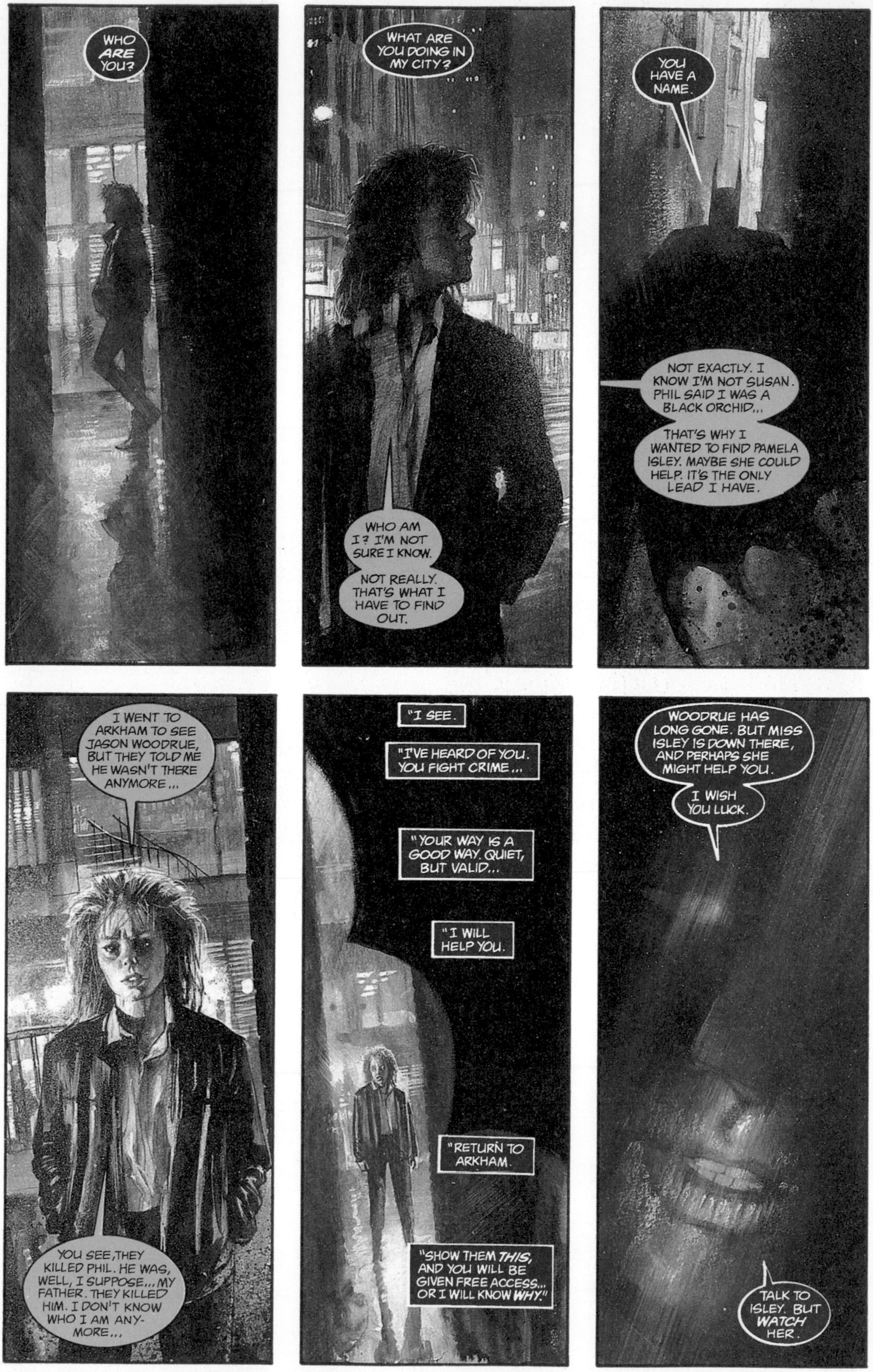
WHO ARE YOU?
WHAT ARE YOU DOING IN MY CITY?
WHO AM I? I'M NOT SURE I KNOW.
NOT REALLY. THAT'S WHAT I HAVE TO FIND OUT.
YOU HAVE A NAME.
NOT EXACTLY. I KNOW I'M NOT SUSAN. PHIL SAID I WAS A BLACK ORCHID...
THAT'S WHY I WANTED TO FIND PAMELA ISLEY. MAYBE SHE COULD HELP. IT'S THE ONLY LEAD I HAVE.
I WENT TO ARKHAM TO SEE JASON WOODRUE, BUT THEY TOLD ME HE WASN'T THERE ANYMORE...
YOU SEE, THEY KILLED PHIL. HE WAS, WELL, I SUPPOSE... MY FATHER. THEY KILLED HIM. I DON'T KNOW WHO I AM ANYMORE...
"I SEE.
"I'VE HEARD OF YOU. YOU FIGHT CRIME...
"YOUR WAY IS A GOOD WAY. QUIET, BUT VALID...
"I WILL HELP YOU.
"RETURN TO ARKHAM.
"SHOW THEM THIS, AND YOU WILL BE GIVEN FREE ACCESS... OR I WILL KNOW WHY."
WOODRUE HAS LONG GONE. BUT MISS ISLEY IS DOWN THERE, AND PERHAPS SHE MIGHT HELP YOU.
I WISH YOU LUCK.
TALK TO ISLEY. BUT WATCH HER.

"SHE'S POISON."

HELLO. WHAT'S YOUR NAME?

MOSTLY THEY CALL ME DAN, LITTLE LADY. WHAT'S YOUR NAME?

AN' HOW THE HECK DID YOU CLIMB UP THAT TREE?

I FLEW UP, SILLY...

I'LL BE BLOWED! WHAT DID YOU SAY YOUR NAME WAS?

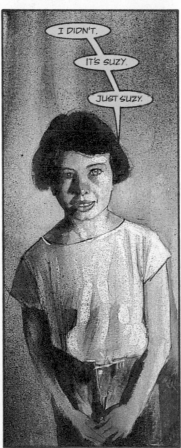

I DIDN'T.

IT'S SUZY.

JUST SUZY.

WELL, JUST-SUZY, YOU WANT TO COME ALONG WITH ME AND SEE SOME KITTENS? PURTIEST LITTLE THINGS YOU EVER DID SEE. SOFT AS DOWN AND CUTER'N BUTTONS.

I CAN'T BE AWAY TOO LONG, THOUGH

TRUST ME, HONEY. YOUR MOM WILL NEVER EVEN NOTICE YOU'VE GONE.

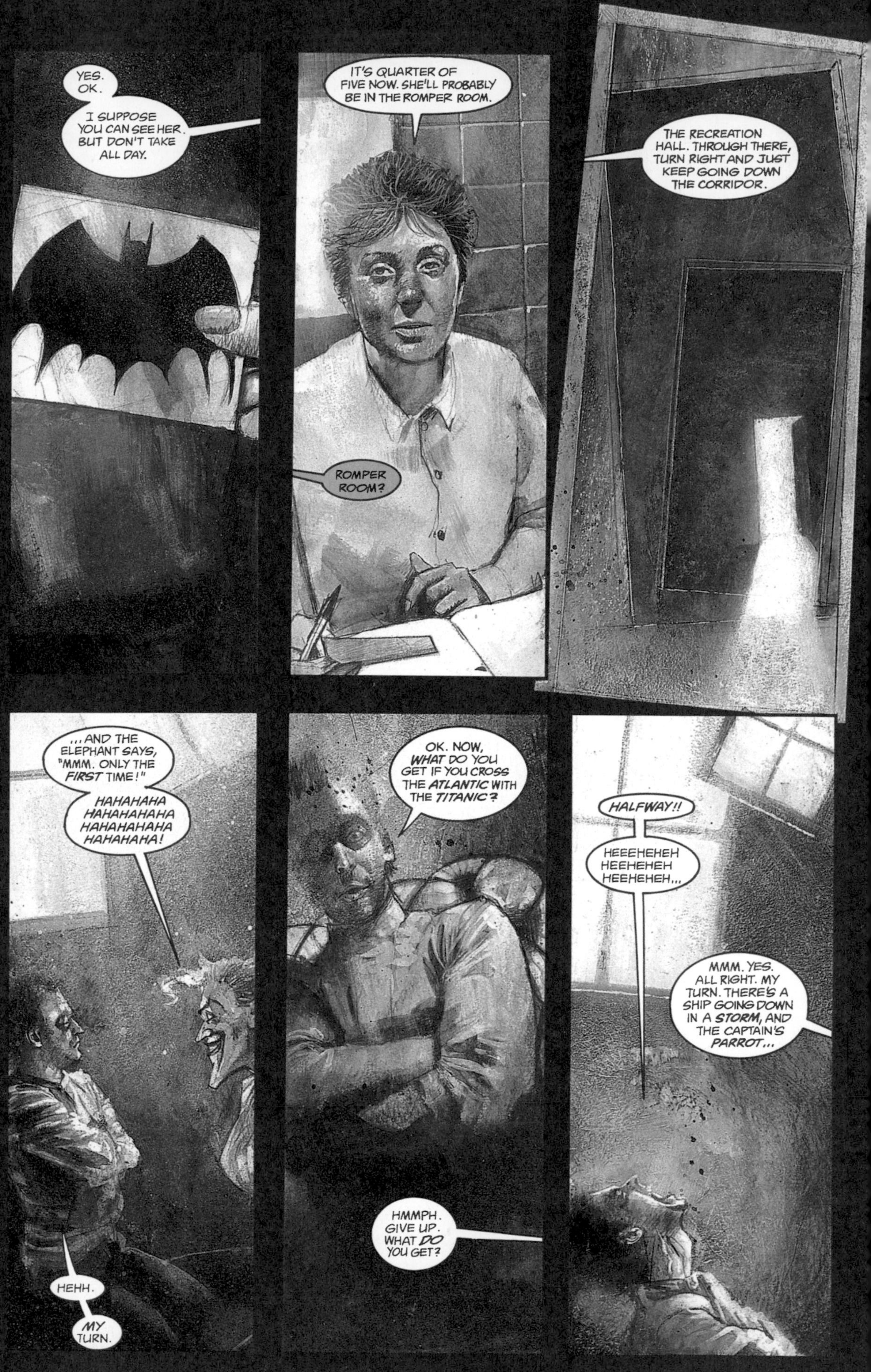
YES. OK.
I SUPPOSE YOU CAN SEE HER. BUT DON'T TAKE ALL DAY.
IT'S QUARTER OF FIVE NOW. SHE'LL PROBABLY BE IN THE ROMPER ROOM.
ROMPER ROOM?
THE RECREATION HALL. THROUGH THERE, TURN RIGHT AND JUST KEEP GOING DOWN THE CORRIDOR.
...AND THE ELEPHANT SAYS, "MMM. ONLY THE FIRST TIME!"
HAHAHAHA HAHAHAHAHA HAHAHAHAHA HAHAHAHA!
HEHH.
MY TURN.
OK. NOW, WHAT DO YOU GET IF YOU CROSS THE ATLANTIC WITH THE TITANIC?
HMMPH. GIVE UP. WHAT DO YOU GET?
HALFWAY!!
HEEEHEHEH HEEHEHEH HEEHEHEH...
MMM. YES. ALL RIGHT. MY TURN. THERE'S A SHIP GOING DOWN IN A STORM, AND THE CAPTAIN'S PARROT...

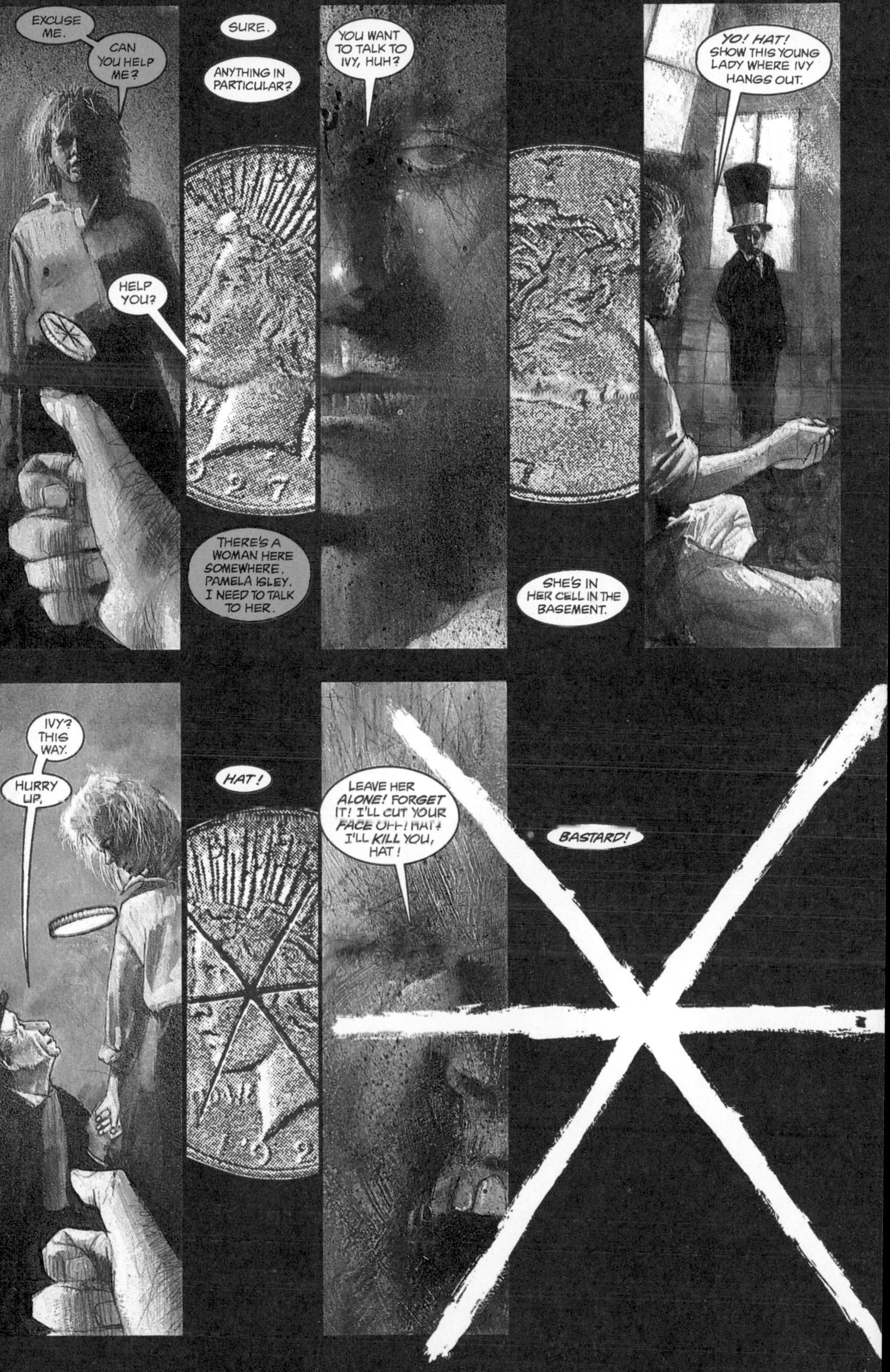
EXCUSE ME.
CAN YOU HELP ME?
SURE.
ANYTHING IN PARTICULAR?
YOU WANT TO TALK TO IVY, HUH?
YO! HAT! SHOW THIS YOUNG LADY WHERE IVY HANGS OUT.
HELP YOU?
THERE'S A WOMAN HERE SOMEWHERE. PAMELA ISLEY. I NEED TO TALK TO HER.
SHE'S IN HER CELL IN THE BASEMENT.
IVY? THIS WAY.
HURRY UP.
HAT!
LEAVE HER ALONE! FORGET IT! I'LL CUT YOUR FACE OFF! HAT! I'LL KILL YOU, HAT!
BASTARD!

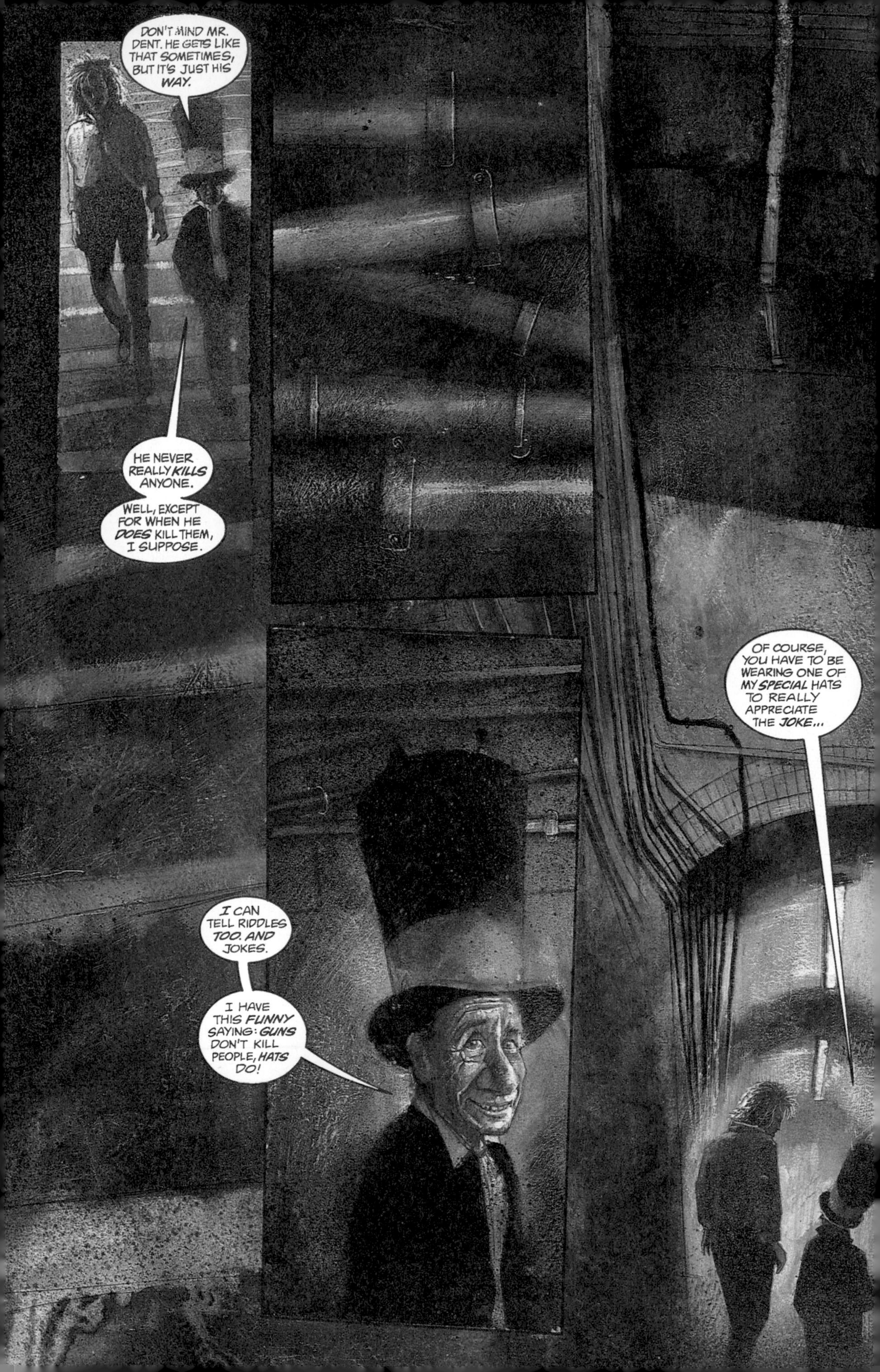
DON'T MIND MR. DENT. HE GETS LIKE THAT SOMETIMES, BUT IT'S JUST HIS *WAY.*
HE NEVER REALLY *KILLS* ANYONE.
WELL, EXCEPT FOR WHEN HE *DOES* KILL THEM, I SUPPOSE.
I CAN TELL RIDDLES *TOO.* AND JOKES.
I HAVE THIS *FUNNY* SAYING: *GUNS* DON'T KILL PEOPLE, *HATS* DO!
OF COURSE, YOU HAVE TO BE WEARING ONE OF MY *SPECIAL* HATS TO REALLY APPRECIATE THE *JOKE...*

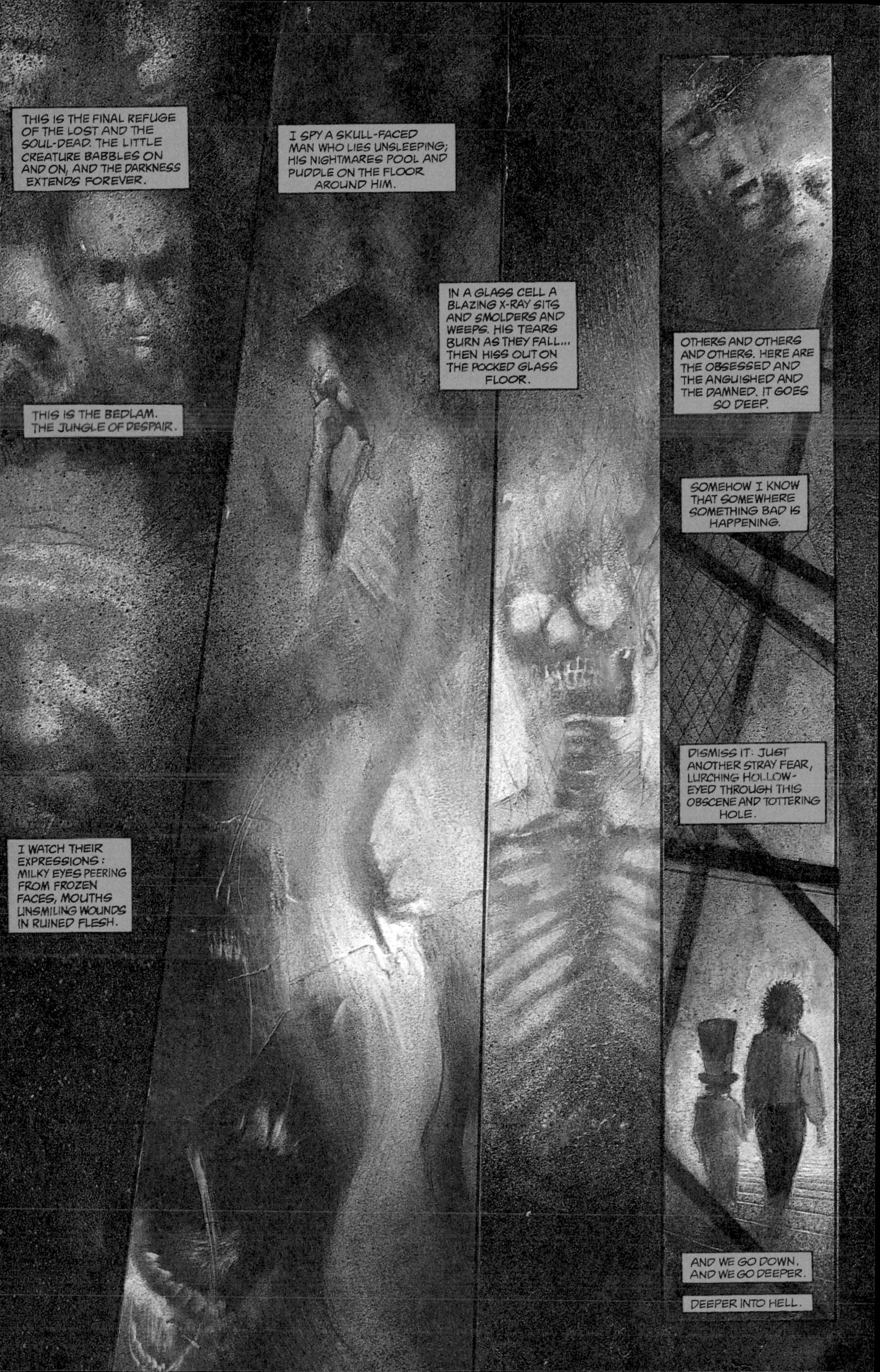
THIS IS THE FINAL REFUGE OF THE LOST AND THE SOUL-DEAD. THE LITTLE CREATURE BABBLES ON AND ON, AND THE DARKNESS EXTENDS FOREVER.
THIS IS THE BEDLAM. THE JUNGLE OF DESPAIR.
I WATCH THEIR EXPRESSIONS: MILKY EYES PEERING FROM FROZEN FACES, MOUTHS UNSMILING WOUNDS IN RUINED FLESH.
I SPY A SKULL-FACED MAN WHO LIES UNSLEEPING; HIS NIGHTMARES POOL AND PUDDLE ON THE FLOOR AROUND HIM.
IN A GLASS CELL A BLAZING X-RAY SITS AND SMOLDERS AND WEEPS. HIS TEARS BURN AS THEY FALL... THEN HISS OUT ON THE POCKED GLASS FLOOR.
OTHERS AND OTHERS AND OTHERS. HERE ARE THE OBSESSED AND THE ANGUISHED AND THE DAMNED. IT GOES SO DEEP.
SOMEHOW I KNOW THAT SOMEWHERE SOMETHING BAD IS HAPPENING.
DISMISS IT: JUST ANOTHER STRAY FEAR, LURCHING HOLLOW-EYED THROUGH THIS OBSCENE AND TOTTERING HOLE.
AND WE GO DOWN. AND WE GO DEEPER.
DEEPER INTO HELL.

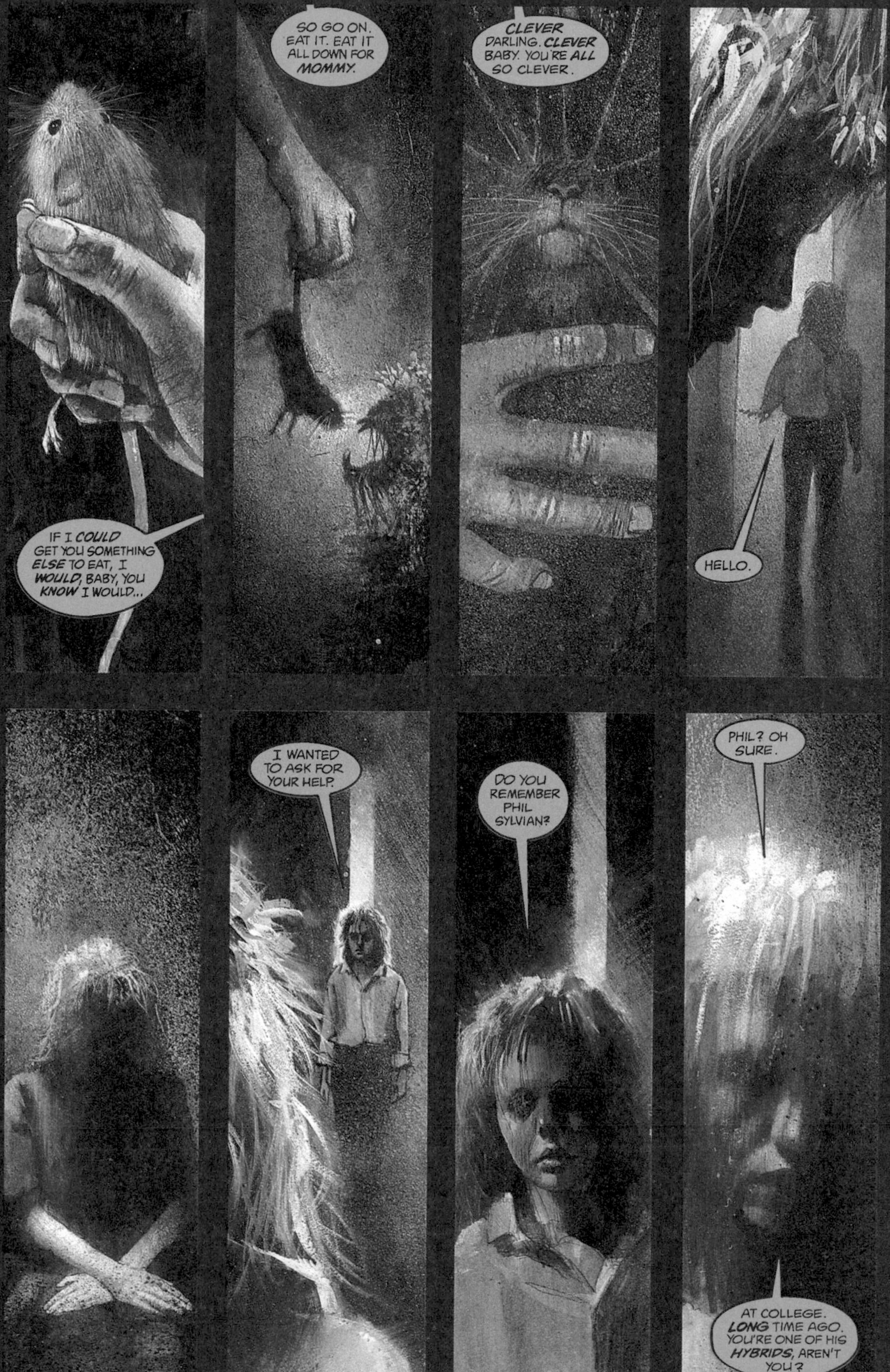

IF I COULD GET YOU SOMETHING ELSE TO EAT, I WOULD, BABY, YOU KNOW I WOULD...
SO GO ON. EAT IT. EAT IT ALL DOWN FOR MOMMY.
CLEVER DARLING. CLEVER BABY. YOU'RE ALL SO CLEVER.
HELLO.
I WANTED TO ASK FOR YOUR HELP.
DO YOU REMEMBER PHIL SYLVIAN?
PHIL? OH SURE.
AT COLLEGE. LONG TIME AGO. YOU'RE ONE OF HIS HYBRIDS, AREN'T YOU?

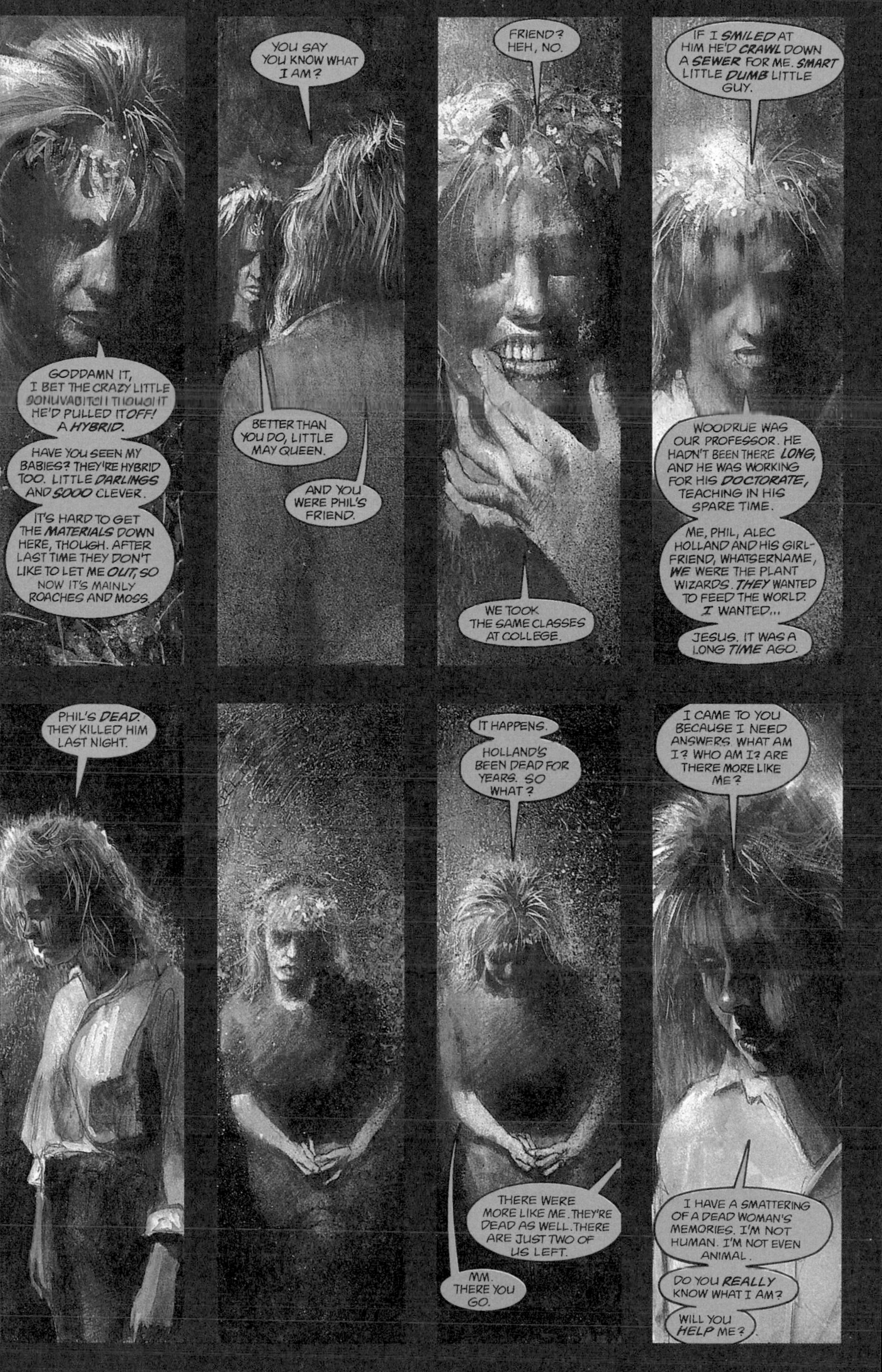
GODDAMN IT, I BET THE CRAZY LITTLE SONUVABITCH THOUGHT HE'D PULLED IT OFF! A HYBRID.
HAVE YOU SEEN MY BABIES? THEY'RE HYBRID TOO. LITTLE DARLINGS AND SOOO CLEVER.
IT'S HARD TO GET THE MATERIALS DOWN HERE, THOUGH. AFTER LAST TIME THEY DON'T LIKE TO LET ME OUT, SO NOW IT'S MAINLY ROACHES AND MOSS.
YOU SAY YOU KNOW WHAT I AM?
BETTER THAN YOU DO, LITTLE MAY QUEEN.
AND YOU WERE PHIL'S FRIEND.
FRIEND? HEH, NO.
WE TOOK THE SAME CLASSES AT COLLEGE.
IF I SMILED AT HIM HE'D CRAWL DOWN A SEWER FOR ME. SMART LITTLE DUMB LITTLE GUY.
WOODRUE WAS OUR PROFESSOR. HE HADN'T BEEN THERE LONG, AND HE WAS WORKING FOR HIS DOCTORATE, TEACHING IN HIS SPARE TIME.
ME, PHIL, ALEC HOLLAND AND HIS GIRL-FRIEND, WHATSERNAME, WE WERE THE PLANT WIZARDS. THEY WANTED TO FEED THE WORLD. I WANTED...
JESUS. IT WAS A LONG TIME AGO.
PHIL'S DEAD. THEY KILLED HIM LAST NIGHT.
IT HAPPENS.
HOLLAND'S BEEN DEAD FOR YEARS. SO WHAT?
THERE WERE MORE LIKE ME. THEY'RE DEAD AS WELL. THERE ARE JUST TWO OF US LEFT.
MM. THERE YOU GO.
I CAME TO YOU BECAUSE I NEED ANSWERS. WHAT AM I? WHO AM I? ARE THERE MORE LIKE ME?
I HAVE A SMATTERING OF A DEAD WOMAN'S MEMORIES. I'M NOT HUMAN. I'M NOT EVEN ANIMAL.
DO YOU REALLY KNOW WHAT I AM?
WILL YOU HELP ME?

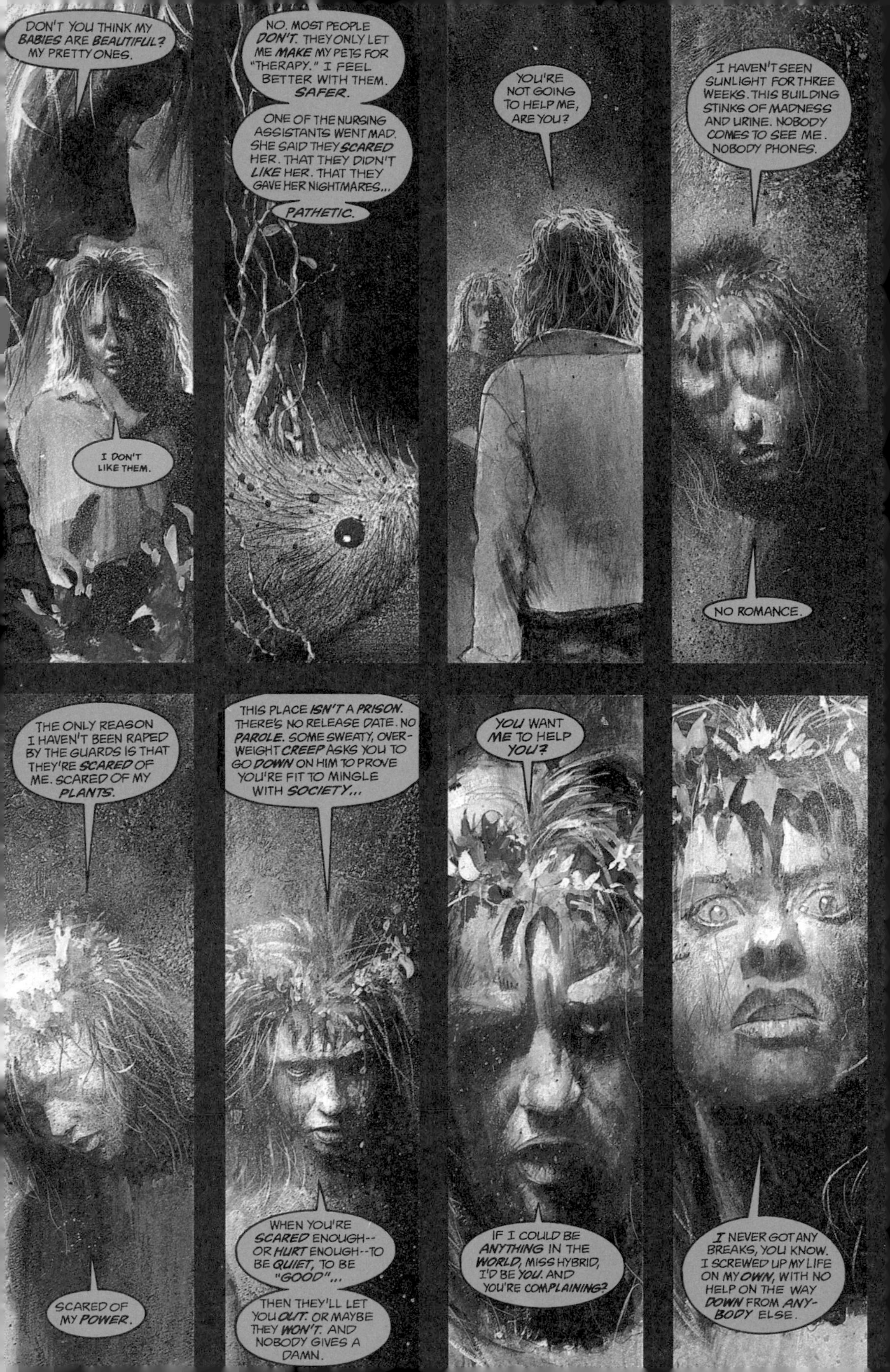
DON'T YOU THINK MY BABIES ARE BEAUTIFUL? MY PRETTY ONES.
I DON'T LIKE THEM.
NO. MOST PEOPLE DON'T. THEY ONLY LET ME MAKE MY PETS FOR "THERAPY." I FEEL BETTER WITH THEM. SAFER.
ONE OF THE NURSING ASSISTANTS WENT MAD. SHE SAID THEY SCARED HER. THAT THEY DIDN'T LIKE HER. THAT THEY GAVE HER NIGHTMARES...
PATHETIC.
YOU'RE NOT GOING TO HELP ME, ARE YOU?
I HAVEN'T SEEN SUNLIGHT FOR THREE WEEKS. THIS BUILDING STINKS OF MADNESS AND URINE. NOBODY COMES TO SEE ME. NOBODY PHONES.
NO ROMANCE.
THE ONLY REASON I HAVEN'T BEEN RAPED BY THE GUARDS IS THAT THEY'RE SCARED OF ME. SCARED OF MY PLANTS.
SCARED OF MY POWER.
THIS PLACE ISN'T A PRISON. THERE'S NO RELEASE DATE. NO PAROLE. SOME SWEATY, OVER-WEIGHT CREEP ASKS YOU TO GO DOWN ON HIM TO PROVE YOU'RE FIT TO MINGLE WITH SOCIETY...
WHEN YOU'RE SCARED ENOUGH-- OR HURT ENOUGH--TO BE QUIET, TO BE "GOOD"...
THEN THEY'LL LET YOU OUT. OR MAYBE THEY WON'T. AND NOBODY GIVES A DAMN.
YOU WANT ME TO HELP YOU?
IF I COULD BE ANYTHING IN THE WORLD, MISS HYBRID, I'D BE YOU. AND YOU'RE COMPLAINING?
I NEVER GOT ANY BREAKS, YOU KNOW. I SCREWED UP MY LIFE ON MY OWN, WITH NO HELP ON THE WAY DOWN FROM ANY-BODY ELSE.

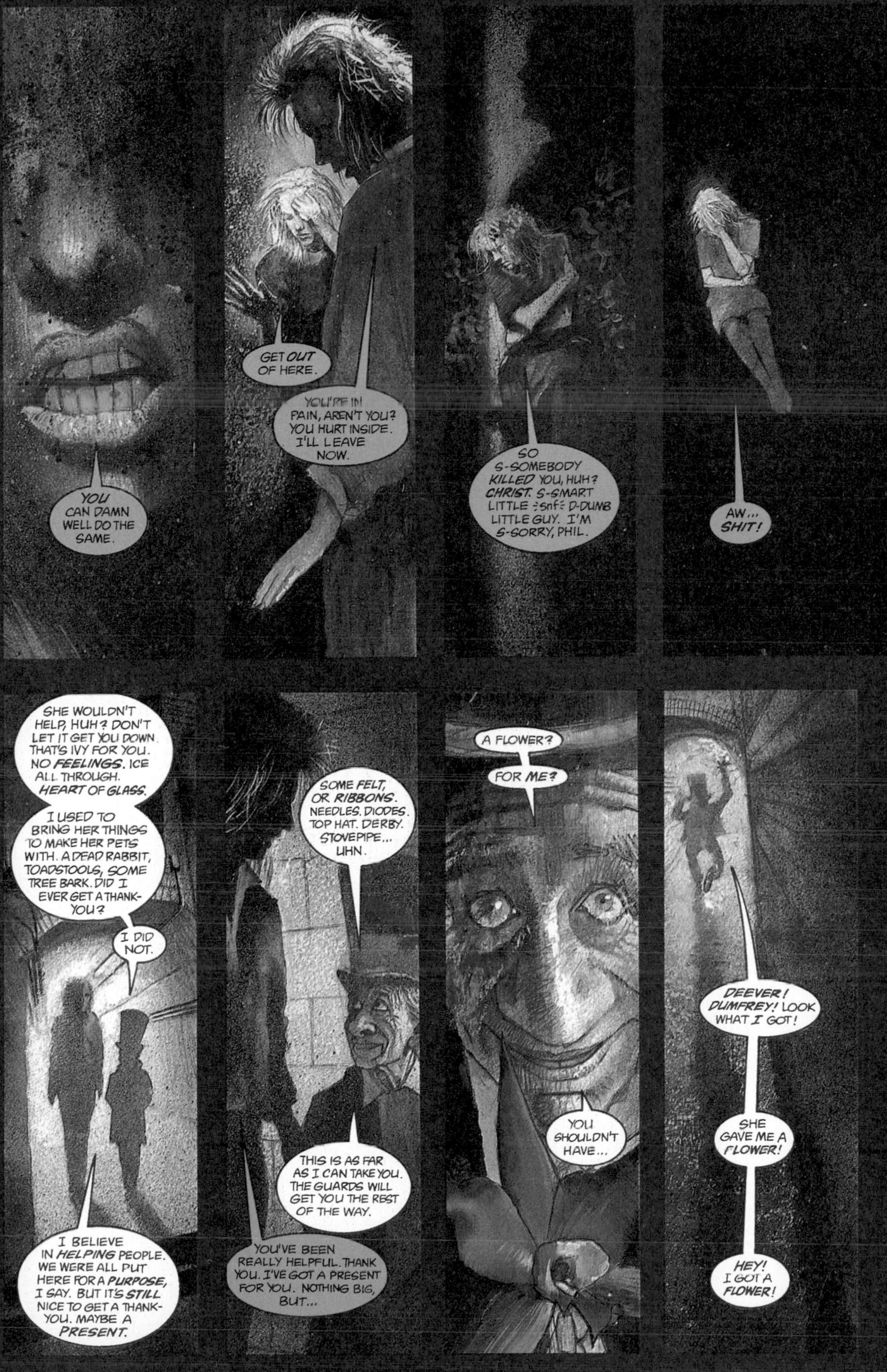
YOU CAN DAMN WELL DO THE SAME.
GET OUT OF HERE.
YOU'RE IN PAIN, AREN'T YOU? YOU HURT INSIDE. I'LL LEAVE NOW.
SO S-SOMEBODY KILLED YOU, HUH? CHRIST. S-SMART LITTLE ÷snf÷ D-DUMB LITTLE GUY. I'M S-SORRY, PHIL.
AW... SHIT!
SHE WOULDN'T HELP, HUH? DON'T LET IT GET YOU DOWN. THAT'S IVY FOR YOU. NO FEELINGS. ICE ALL THROUGH. HEART OF GLASS.
I USED TO BRING HER THINGS TO MAKE HER PETS WITH. A DEAD RABBIT, TOADSTOOLS, SOME TREE BARK. DID I EVER GET A THANK-YOU?
I DID NOT.
I BELIEVE IN HELPING PEOPLE. WE WERE ALL PUT HERE FOR A PURPOSE, I SAY. BUT IT'S STILL NICE TO GET A THANK-YOU. MAYBE A PRESENT.
SOME FELT, OR RIBBONS. NEEDLES. DIODES. TOP HAT. DERBY. STOVEPIPE... UHN.
THIS IS AS FAR AS I CAN TAKE YOU. THE GUARDS WILL GET YOU THE REST OF THE WAY.
YOU'VE BEEN REALLY HELPFUL. THANK YOU. I'VE GOT A PRESENT FOR YOU. NOTHING BIG, BUT...
A FLOWER?
FOR ME?
YOU SHOULDN'T HAVE...
DEEVER! DUMFREY! LOOK WHAT I GOT!
SHE GAVE ME A FLOWER!
HEY! I GOT A FLOWER!

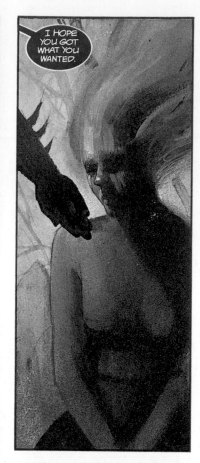

I HOPE YOU GOT WHAT YOU WANTED.

...ONE-EIGHTY -- ONE-NINETY -- TWO GRAND. ON THE NAIL.

THANK YOU, YOUNG FELLOW. IT'LL SURE GO DOWN WELL.

YEAH, YEAH, POPS. DON'T WAVE IT AROUND OR IT WON'T LAST LONG. NOW AMSCRAY.

HEY! JIMMY! MERCHANDISE ALL FASTENED DOWN?

SAFE AND SECURE, BOSS. LET'S TAKE OFF --

--WE GOT WHAT WE CAME FOR.

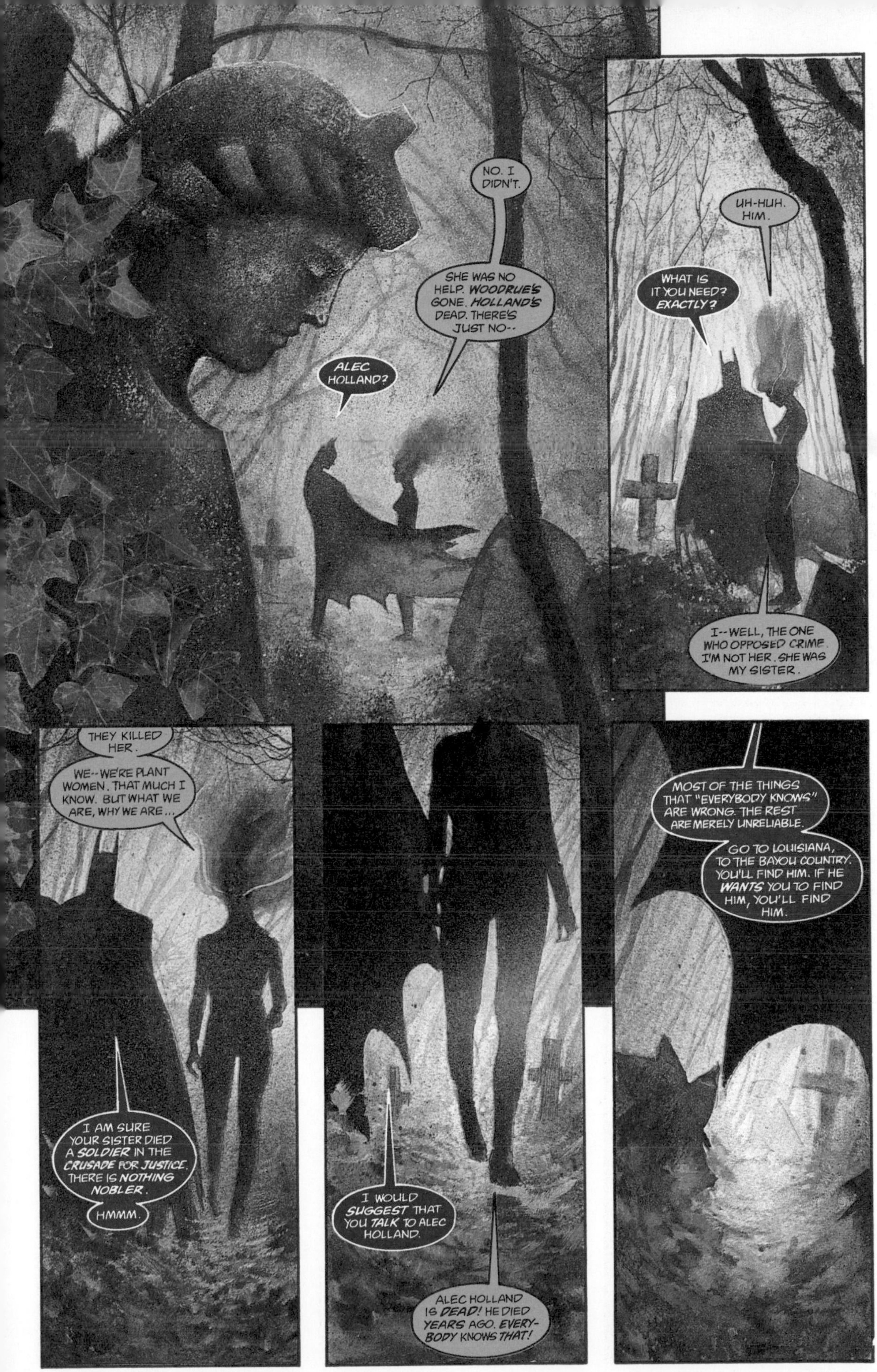

NO. I DIDN'T.
SHE WAS NO HELP. WOODRUE'S GONE. HOLLAND'S DEAD. THERE'S JUST NO--
ALEC HOLLAND?
UH-HUH. HIM.
WHAT IS IT YOU NEED? EXACTLY?
I--WELL, THE ONE WHO OPPOSED CRIME. I'M NOT HER. SHE WAS MY SISTER.
THEY KILLED HER.
WE--WE'RE PLANT WOMEN. THAT MUCH I KNOW. BUT WHAT WE ARE, WHY WE ARE...
I AM SURE YOUR SISTER DIED A SOLDIER IN THE CRUSADE FOR JUSTICE. THERE IS NOTHING NOBLER.
HMMM.
I WOULD SUGGEST THAT YOU TALK TO ALEC HOLLAND.
ALEC HOLLAND IS DEAD! HE DIED YEARS AGO. EVERYBODY KNOWS THAT!
MOST OF THE THINGS THAT "EVERYBODY KNOWS" ARE WRONG. THE REST ARE MERELY UNRELIABLE.
GO TO LOUISIANA, TO THE BAYOU COUNTRY. YOU'LL FIND HIM. IF HE WANTS YOU TO FIND HIM, YOU'LL FIND HIM.

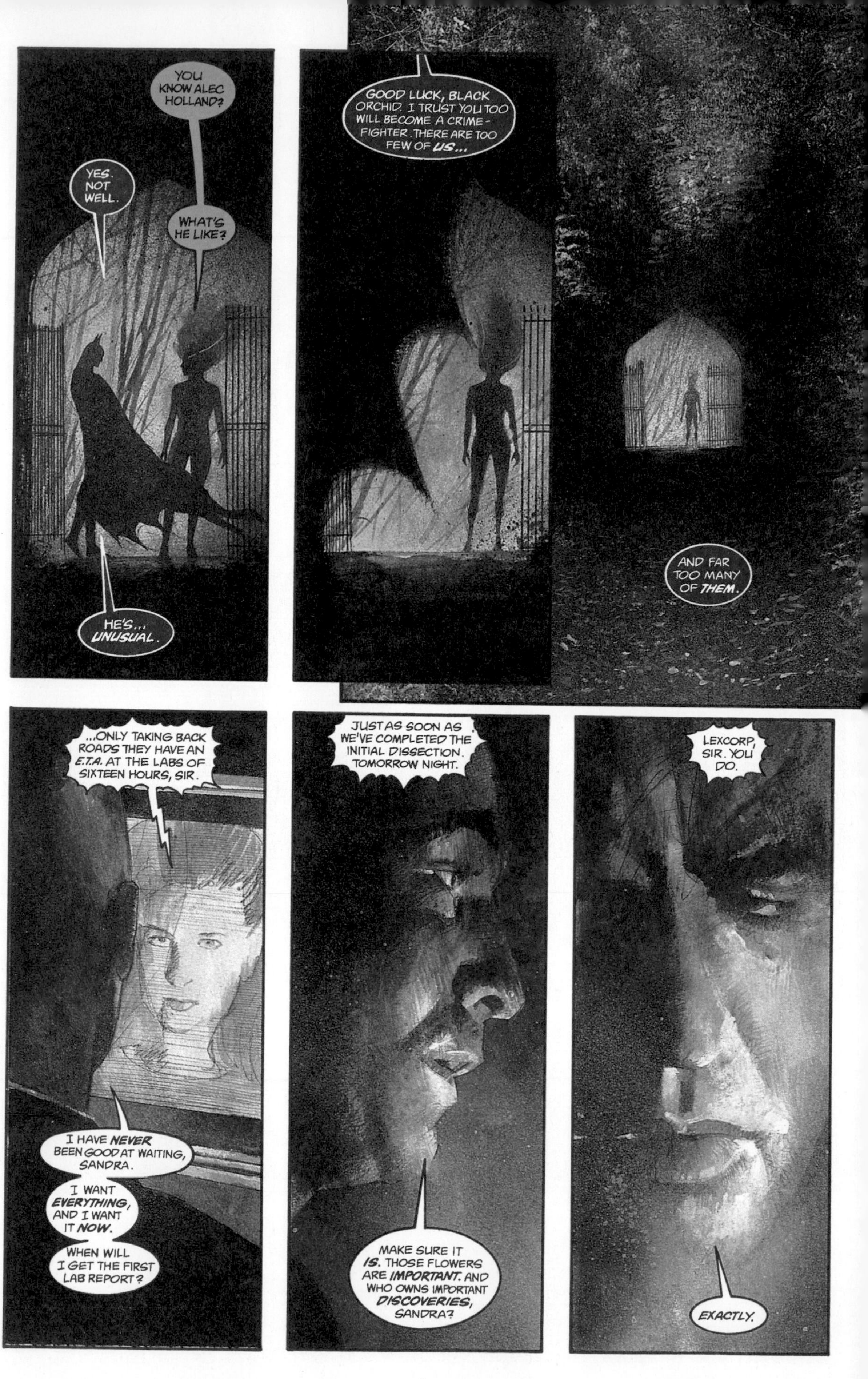
YOU KNOW ALEC HOLLAND?
YES. NOT WELL.
WHAT'S HE LIKE?
HE'S... UNUSUAL.
GOOD LUCK, BLACK ORCHID. I TRUST YOU TOO WILL BECOME A CRIME-FIGHTER. THERE ARE TOO FEW OF US...
AND FAR TOO MANY OF THEM.
...ONLY TAKING BACK ROADS THEY HAVE AN E.T.A. AT THE LABS OF SIXTEEN HOURS, SIR.
I HAVE NEVER BEEN GOOD AT WAITING, SANDRA.
I WANT EVERYTHING, AND I WANT IT NOW.
WHEN WILL I GET THE FIRST LAB REPORT?
JUST AS SOON AS WE'VE COMPLETED THE INITIAL DISSECTION. TOMORROW NIGHT.
MAKE SURE IT IS. THOSE FLOWERS ARE IMPORTANT. AND WHO OWNS IMPORTANT DISCOVERIES, SANDRA?
LEXCORP, SIR. YOU DO.
EXACTLY.

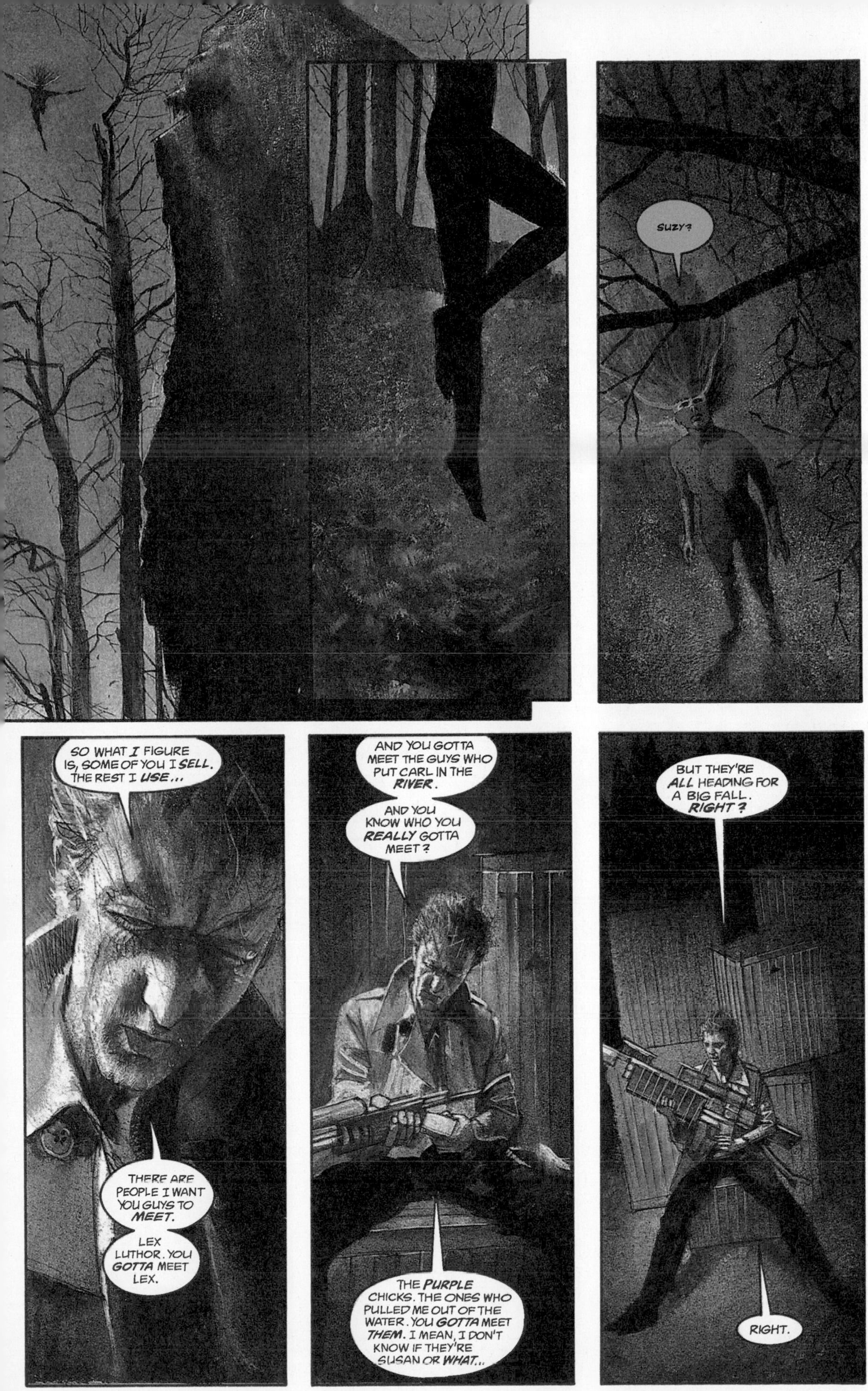
SUZY?
SO WHAT I FIGURE IS, SOME OF YOU I SELL. THE REST I USE...
THERE ARE PEOPLE I WANT YOU GUYS TO MEET.
LEX LUTHOR. YOU GOTTA MEET LEX.
AND YOU GOTTA MEET THE GUYS WHO PUT CARL IN THE RIVER.
AND YOU KNOW WHO YOU REALLY GOTTA MEET?
THE PURPLE CHICKS. THE ONES WHO PULLED ME OUT OF THE WATER. YOU GOTTA MEET THEM. I MEAN, I DON'T KNOW IF THEY'RE SUSAN OR WHAT...
BUT THEY'RE ALL HEADING FOR A BIG FALL. RIGHT?
RIGHT.

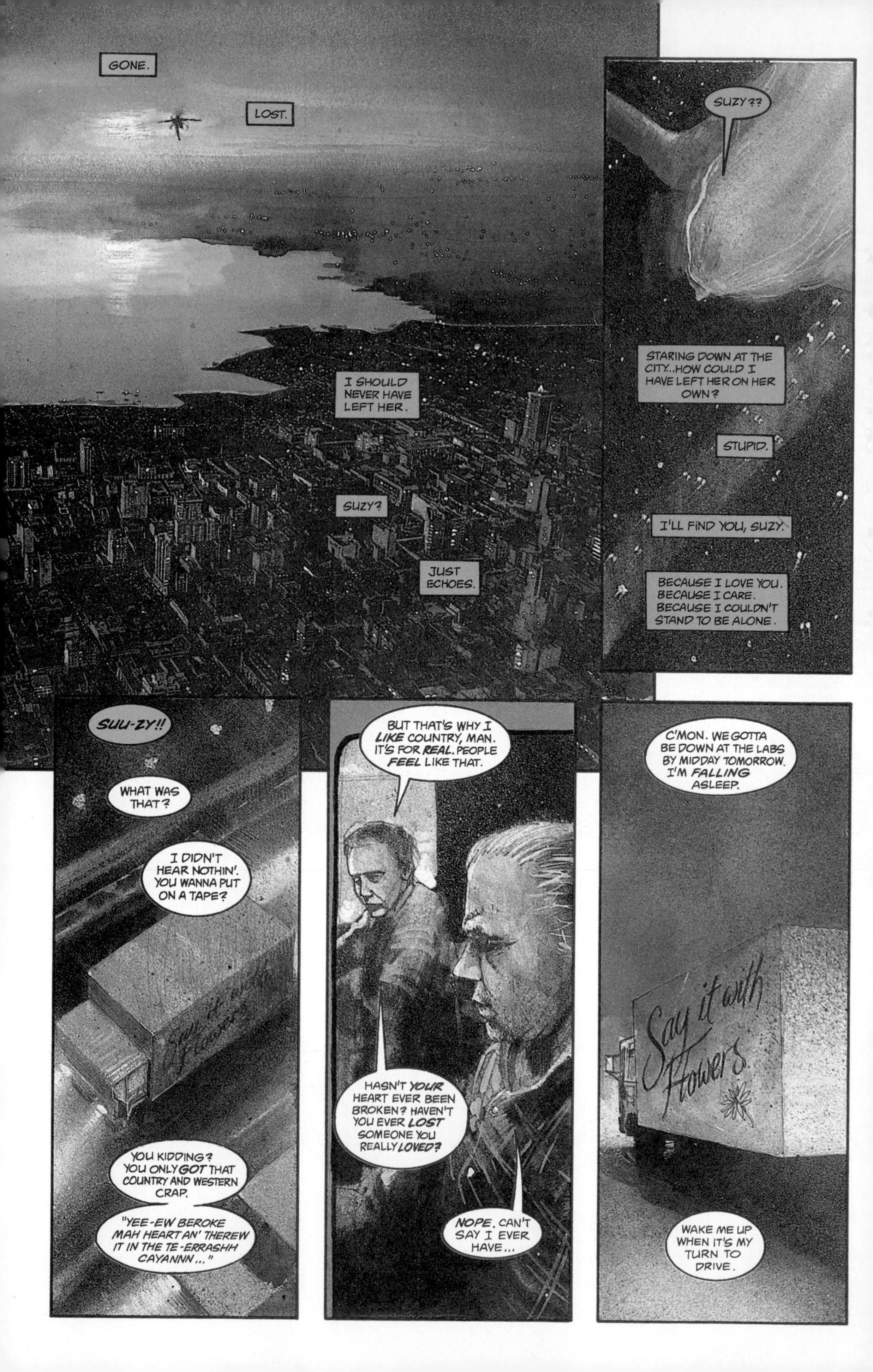
GONE.
LOST.
I SHOULD NEVER HAVE LEFT HER.
SUZY?
JUST ECHOES.
SUZY??
STARING DOWN AT THE CITY..HOW COULD I HAVE LEFT HER ON HER OWN?
STUPID.
I'LL FIND YOU, SUZY.
BECAUSE I LOVE YOU. BECAUSE I CARE. BECAUSE I COULDN'T STAND TO BE ALONE.
SUU-ZY!!
WHAT WAS THAT?
I DIDN'T HEAR NOTHIN'. YOU WANNA PUT ON A TAPE?
YOU KIDDING? YOU ONLY GOT THAT COUNTRY AND WESTERN CRAP.
"YEE-EW BEROKE MAH HEART AN' THEREW IT IN THE TE-ERRASHH CAYANNN..."
BUT THAT'S WHY I LIKE COUNTRY, MAN. IT'S FOR REAL. PEOPLE FEEL LIKE THAT.
HASN'T YOUR HEART EVER BEEN BROKEN? HAVEN'T YOU EVER LOST SOMEONE YOU REALLY LOVED?
NOPE. CAN'T SAY I EVER HAVE...
C'MON. WE GOTTA BE DOWN AT THE LABS BY MIDDAY TOMORROW. I'M FALLING ASLEEP.
Say it with Flowers
WAKE ME UP WHEN IT'S MY TURN TO DRIVE.

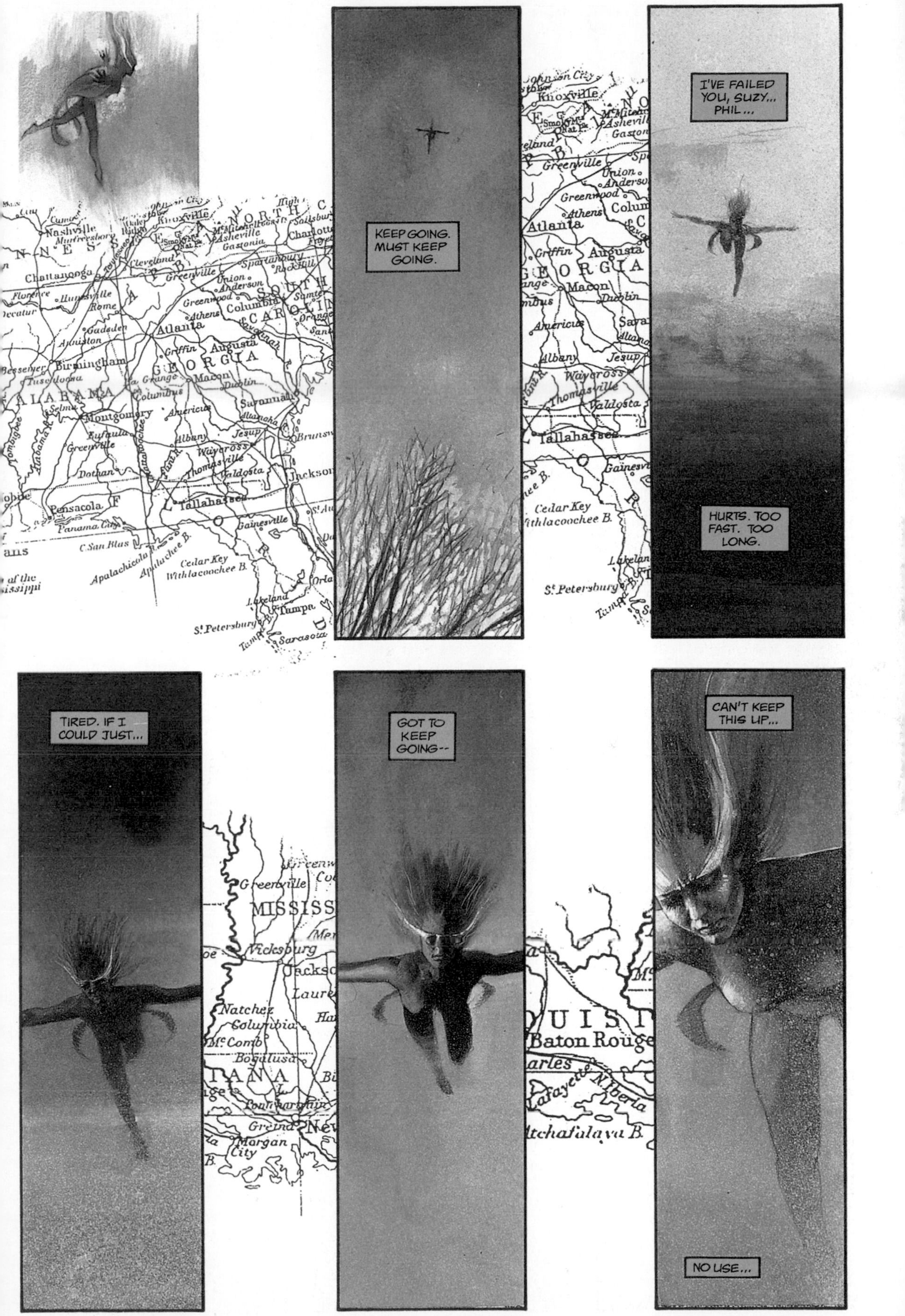
KEEP GOING. MUST KEEP GOING.
I'VE FAILED YOU, SUZY... PHIL...
HURTS. TOO FAST. TOO LONG.
TIRED. IF I COULD JUST...
GOT TO KEEP GOING--
CAN'T KEEP THIS UP...
NO USE...

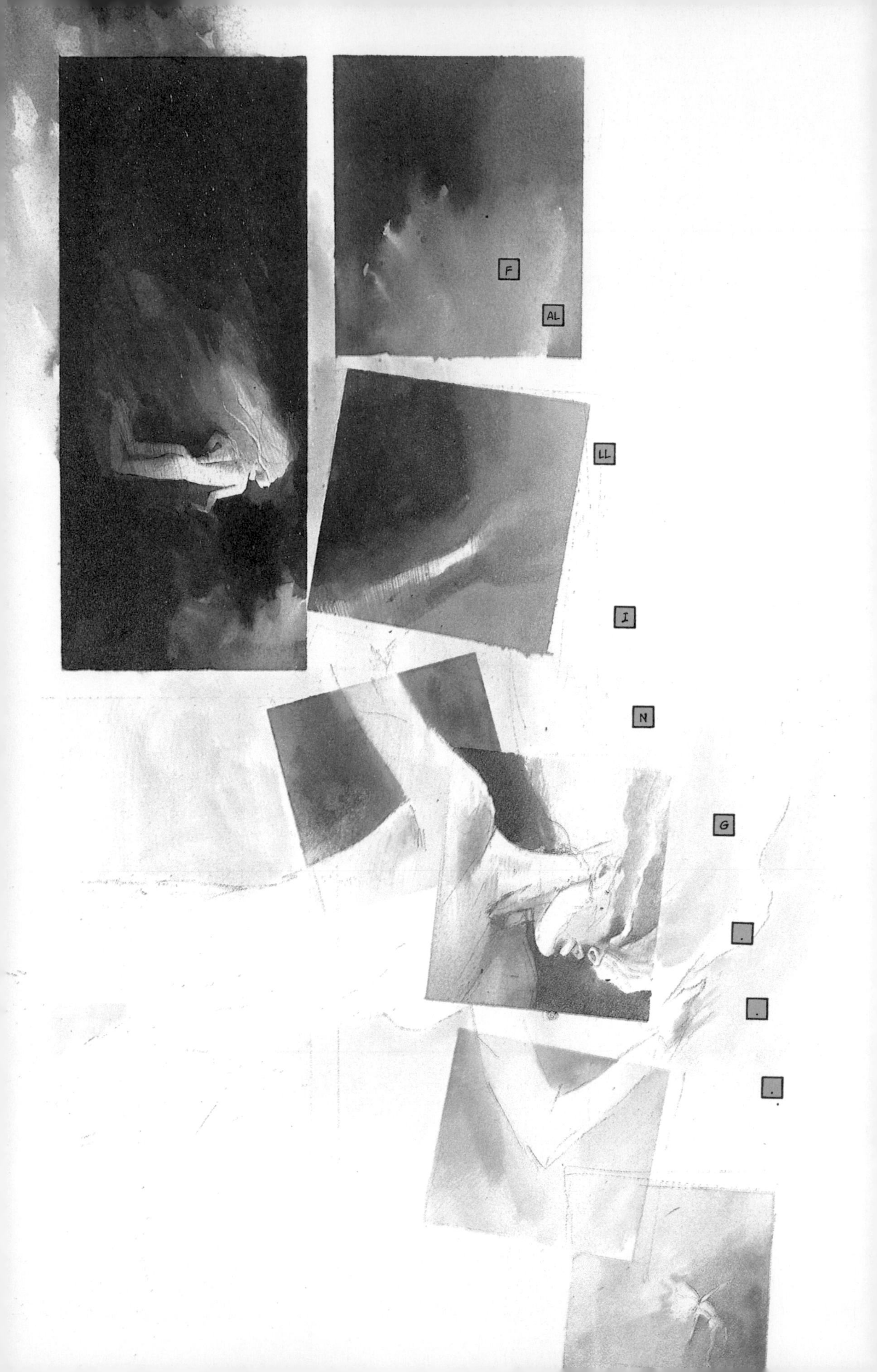
F
AL
LL
I
N
G
.
.
.

When you're in a dream and you think you've got
your problems all mapped out,

Pieces of the scheme seem to rattle up
and then to rattle down,

And when you start to fall and those footsteps
they start to beat...

Then you know you're going down,

Yes, you're falling on the ground,
And you know you're **going down**,
For the last time.

"Going Down" by Lou Reed

CHAPTER *3*

Yes...

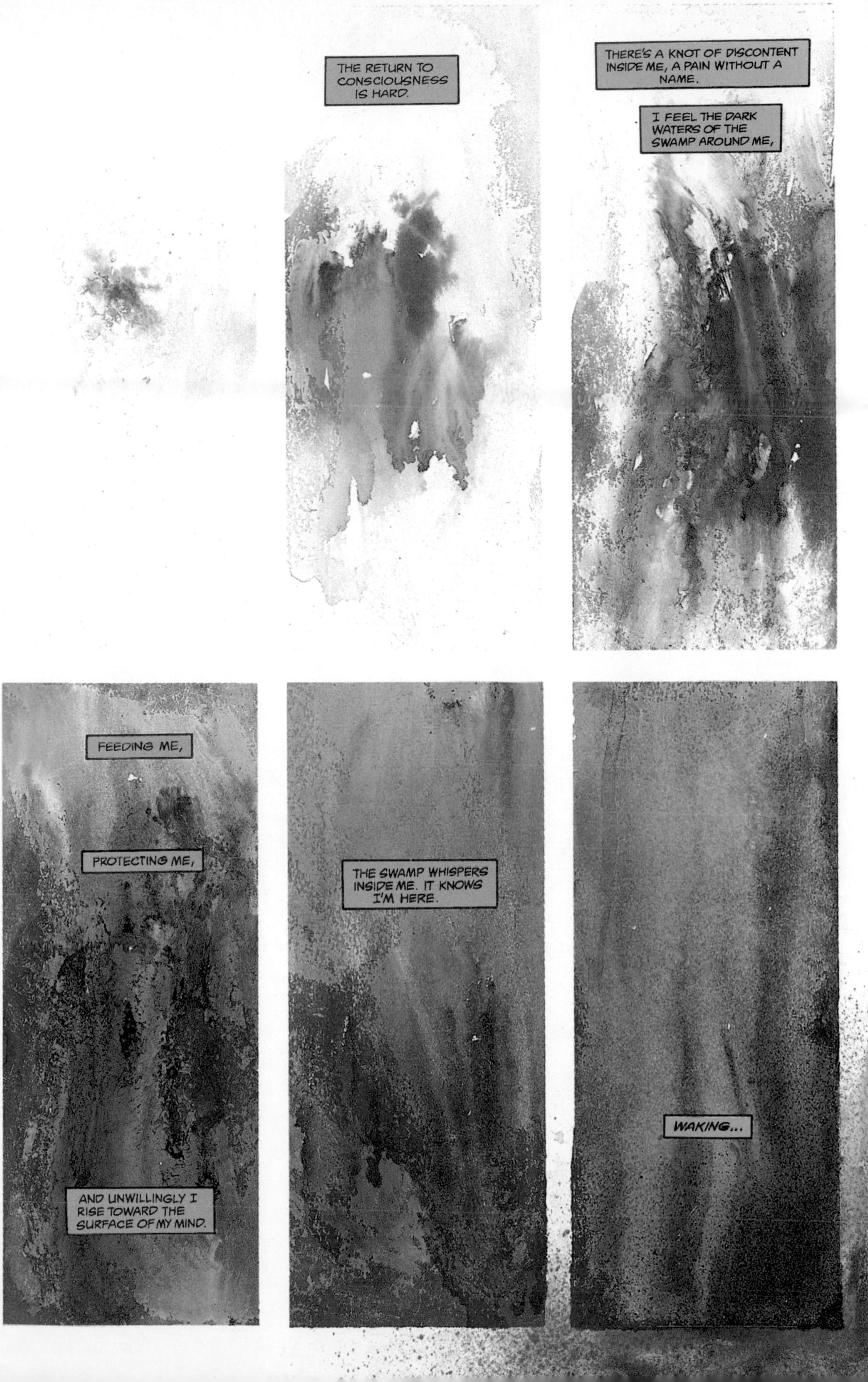
THE RETURN TO CONSCIOUSNESS IS HARD.
THERE'S A KNOT OF DISCONTENT INSIDE ME, A PAIN WITHOUT A NAME.
I FEEL THE DARK WATERS OF THE SWAMP AROUND ME,
FEEDING ME,
PROTECTING ME,
AND UNWILLINGLY I RISE TOWARD THE SURFACE OF MY MIND.
THE SWAMP WHISPERS INSIDE ME. IT KNOWS I'M HERE.
WAKING...

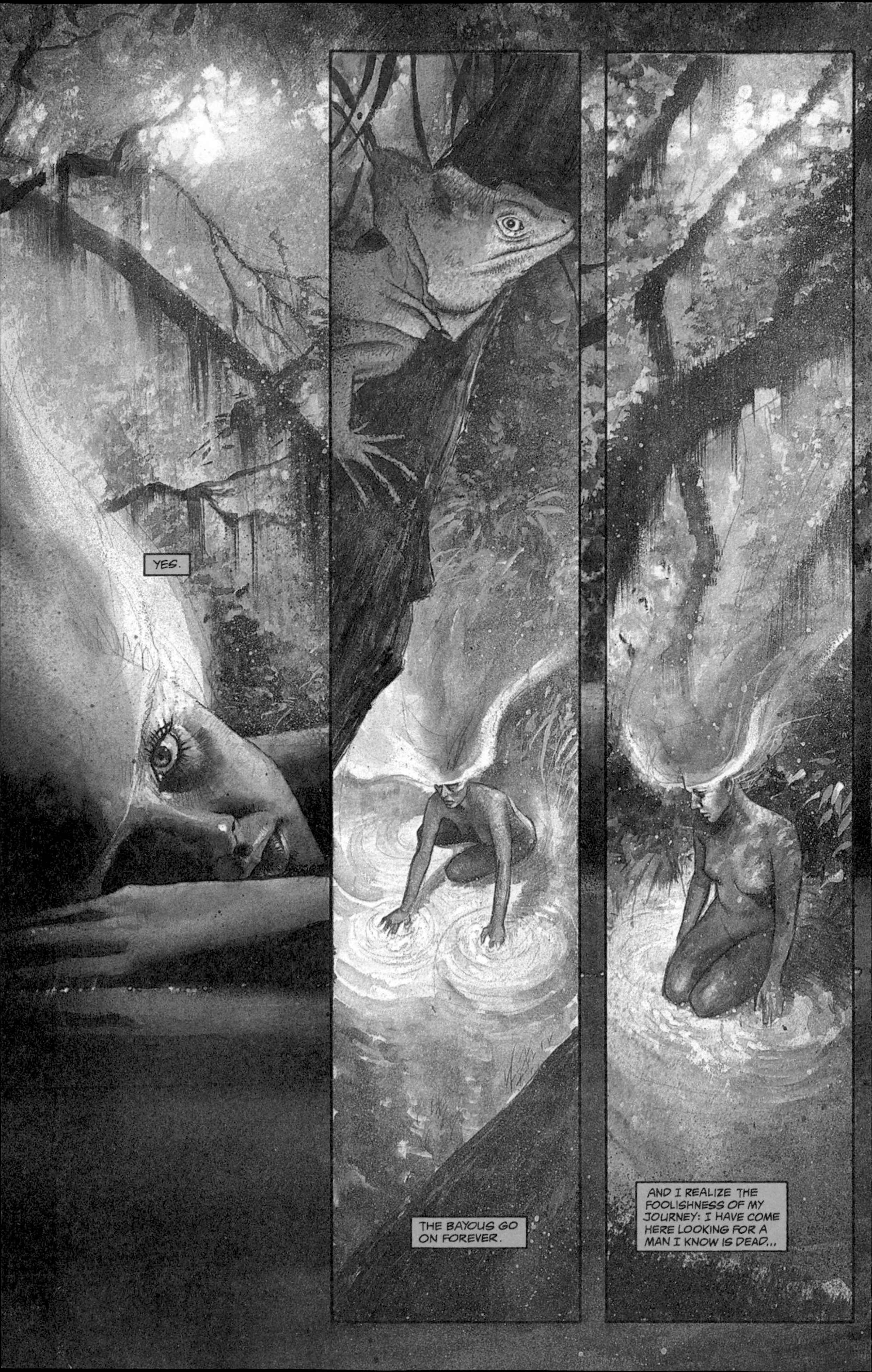
YES.
THE BAYOUS GO ON FOREVER.
AND I REALIZE THE FOOLISHNESS OF MY JOURNEY: I HAVE COME HERE LOOKING FOR A MAN I KNOW IS DEAD...

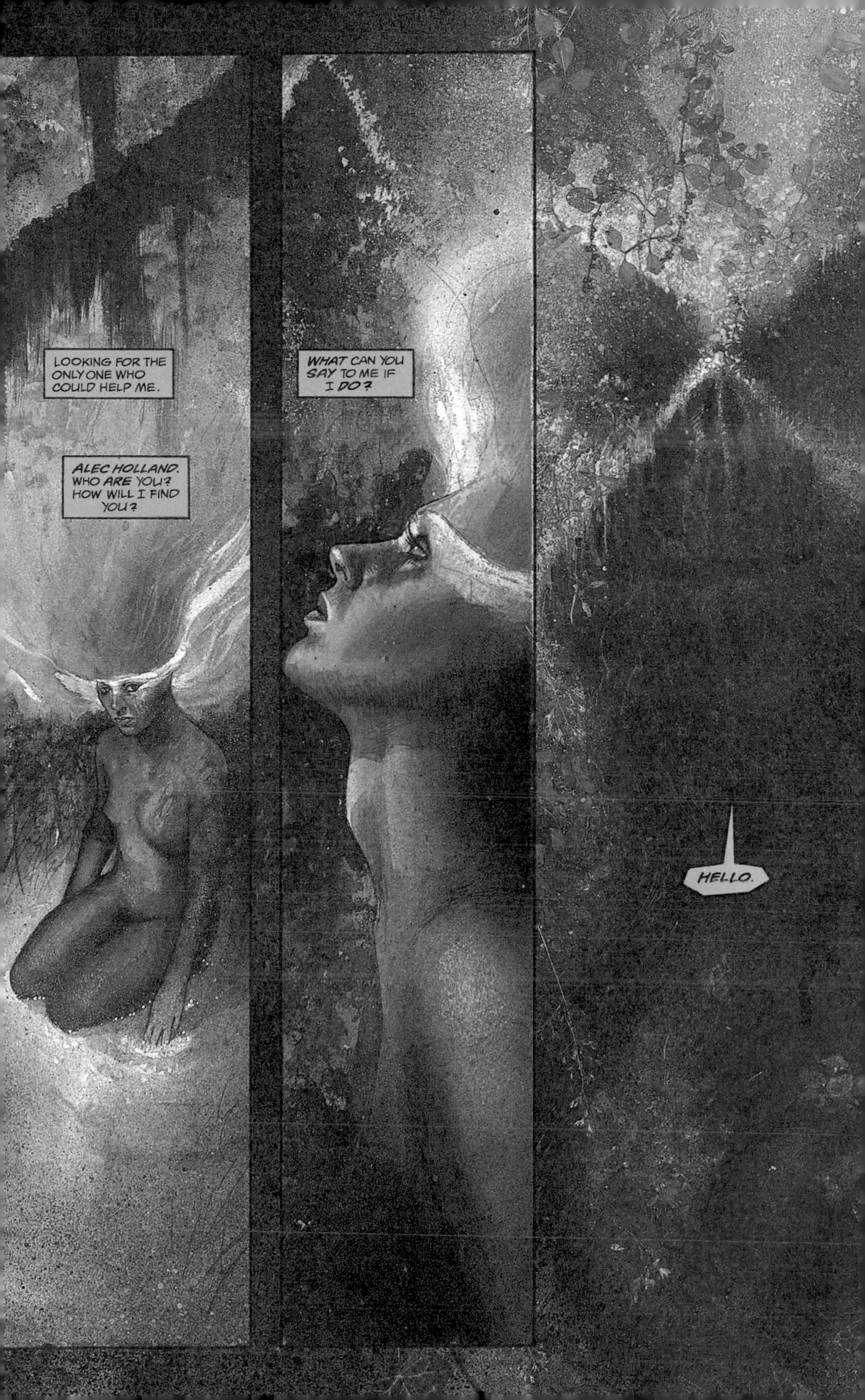
LOOKING FOR THE ONLY ONE WHO COULD HELP ME.
ALEC HOLLAND. WHO ARE YOU? HOW WILL I FIND YOU?
WHAT CAN YOU SAY TO ME IF I DO?
HELLO.

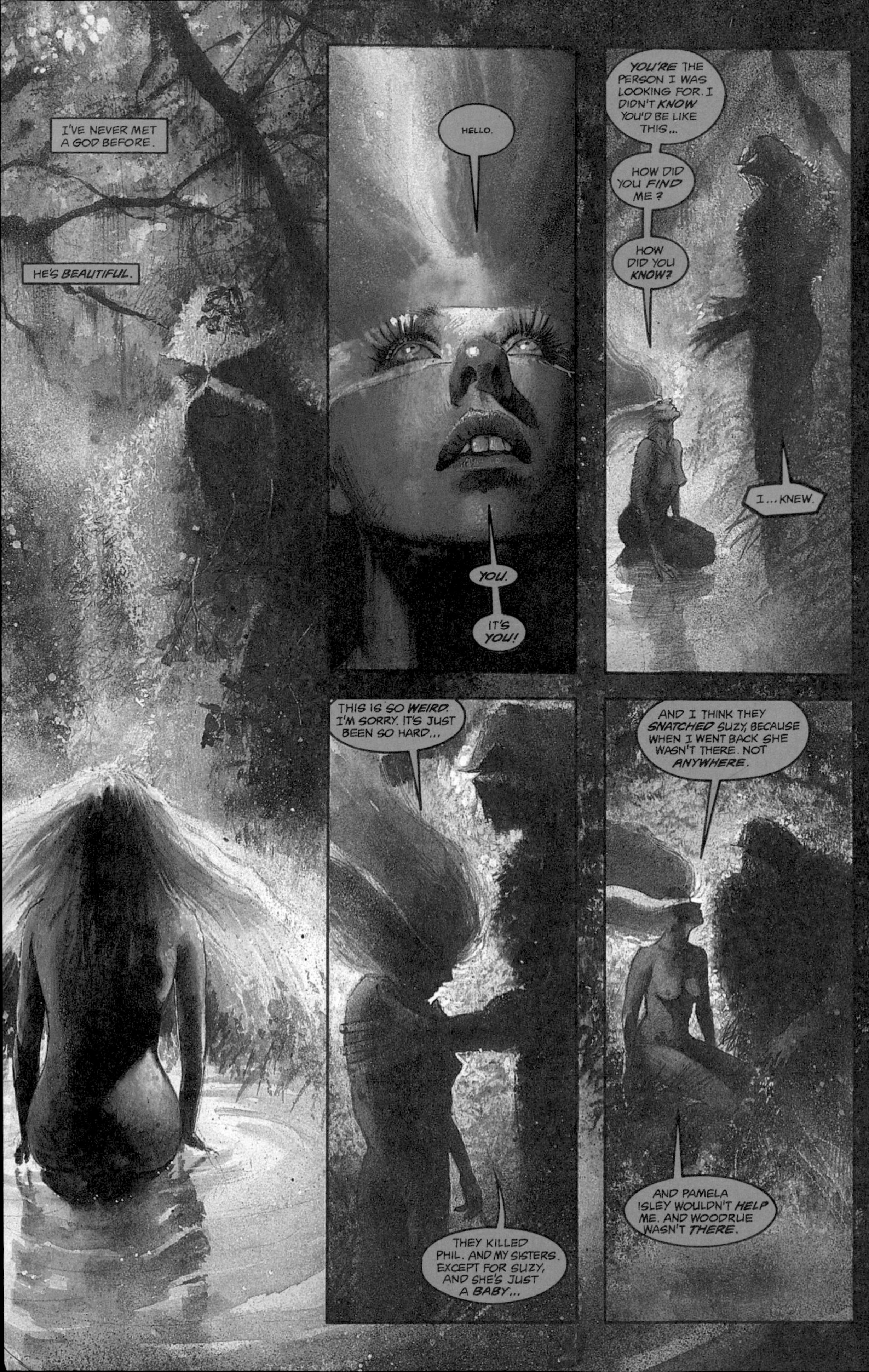
I'VE NEVER MET A GOD BEFORE.
HE'S BEAUTIFUL.
HELLO.
YOU.
IT'S YOU!
YOU'RE THE PERSON I WAS LOOKING FOR. I DIDN'T KNOW YOU'D BE LIKE THIS...
HOW DID YOU FIND ME?
HOW DID YOU KNOW?
I... KNEW.
THIS IS SO WEIRD. I'M SORRY. IT'S JUST BEEN SO HARD...
THEY KILLED PHIL. AND MY SISTERS. EXCEPT FOR SUZY, AND SHE'S JUST A BABY...
AND I THINK THEY SNATCHED SUZY, BECAUSE WHEN I WENT BACK SHE WASN'T THERE. NOT ANYWHERE.
AND PAMELA ISLEY WOULDN'T HELP ME. AND WOODRUE WASN'T THERE.

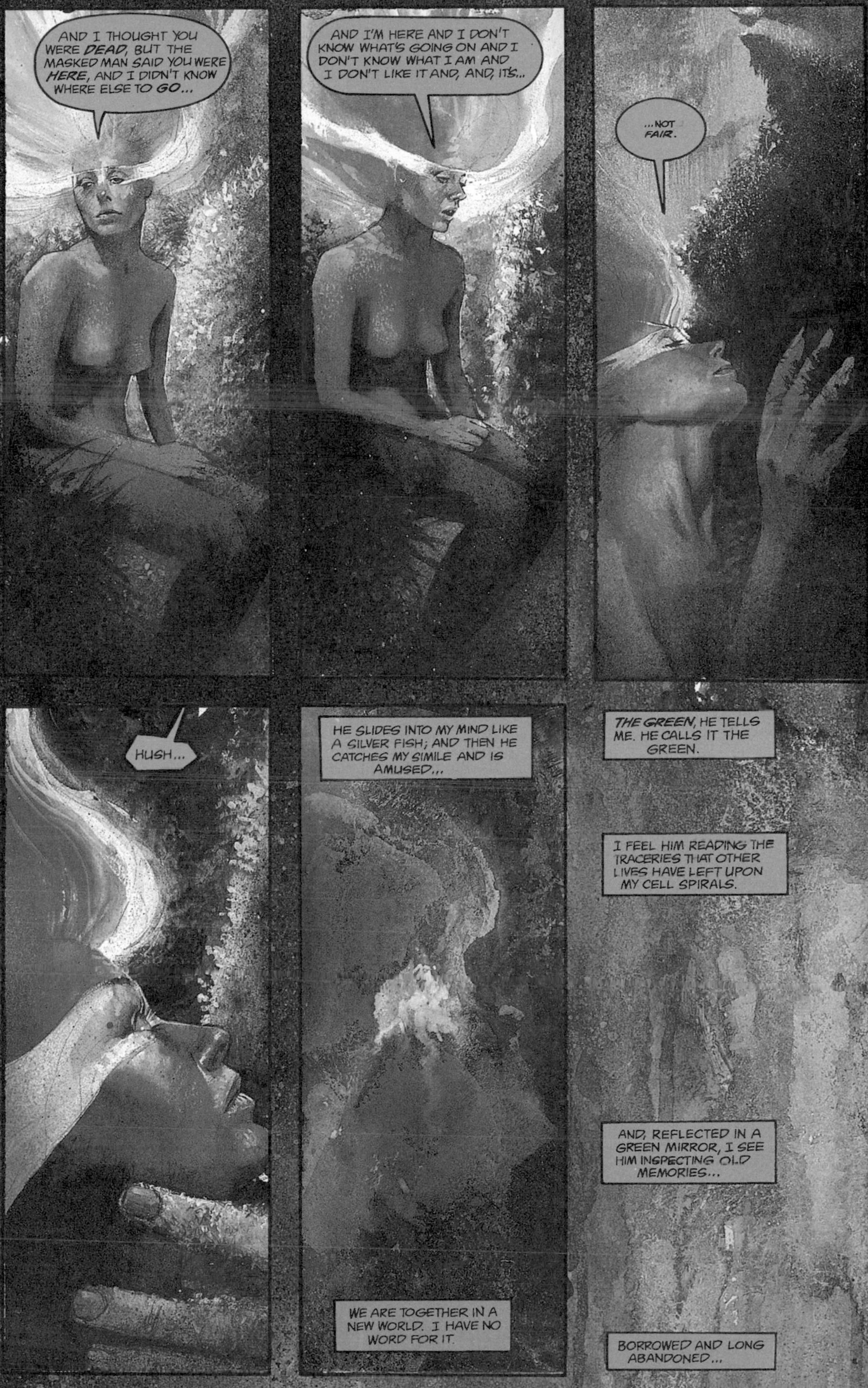
AND I THOUGHT YOU WERE DEAD, BUT THE MASKED MAN SAID YOU WERE HERE, AND I DIDN'T KNOW WHERE ELSE TO GO...
AND I'M HERE AND I DON'T KNOW WHAT'S GOING ON AND I DON'T KNOW WHAT I AM AND I DON'T LIKE IT AND, AND, IT'S...
...NOT FAIR.
HUSH...
HE SLIDES INTO MY MIND LIKE A SILVER FISH; AND THEN HE CATCHES MY SIMILE AND IS AMUSED...
WE ARE TOGETHER IN A NEW WORLD. I HAVE NO WORD FOR IT.
THE GREEN, HE TELLS ME. HE CALLS IT THE GREEN.
I FEEL HIM READING THE TRACERIES THAT OTHER LIVES HAVE LEFT UPON MY CELL SPIRALS.
AND, REFLECTED IN A GREEN MIRROR, I SEE HIM INSPECTING OLD MEMORIES...
BORROWED AND LONG ABANDONED...

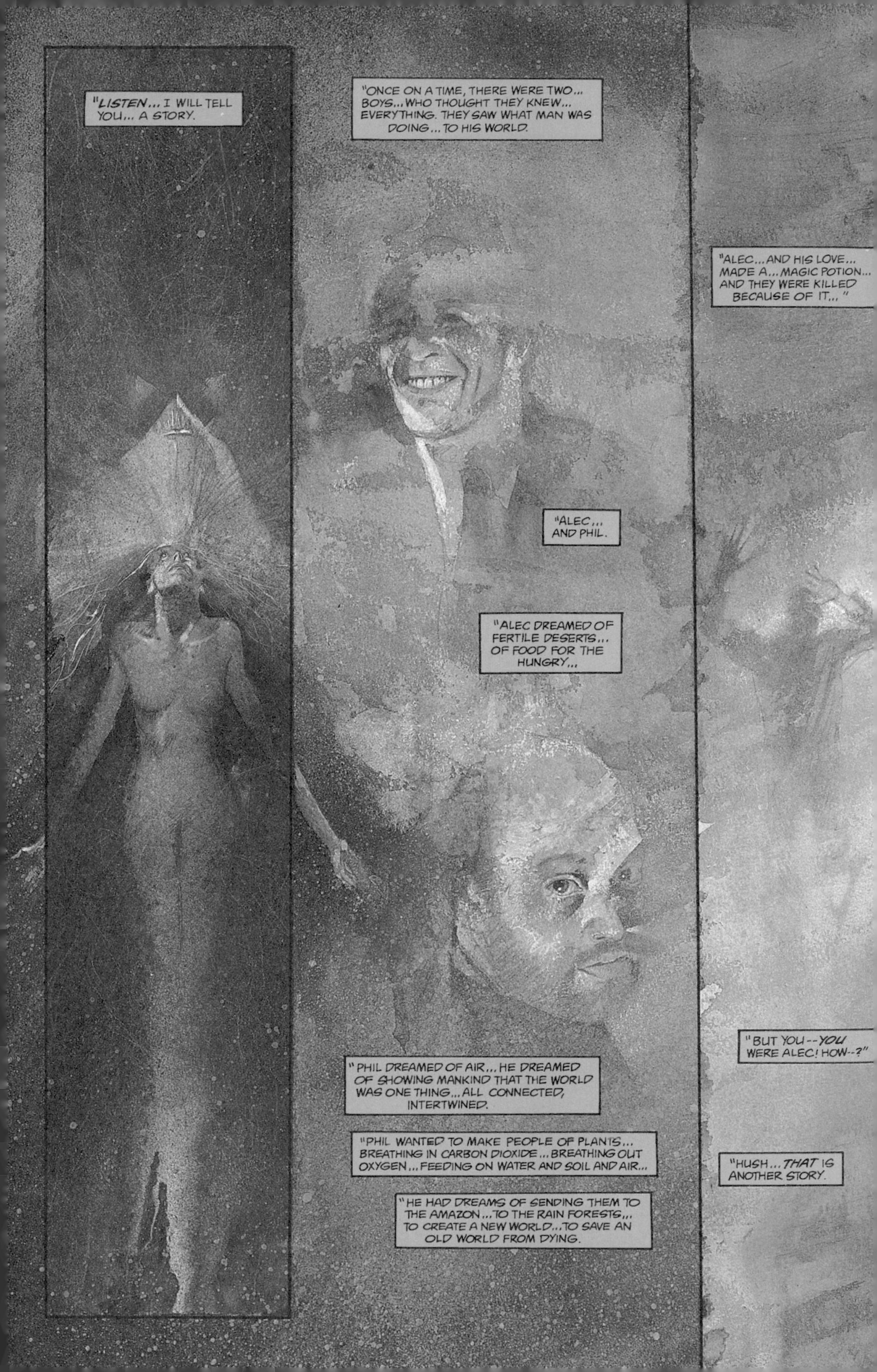
"LISTEN... I WILL TELL YOU... A STORY.
"ONCE ON A TIME, THERE WERE TWO... BOYS... WHO THOUGHT THEY KNEW... EVERYTHING. THEY SAW WHAT MAN WAS DOING... TO HIS WORLD.
"ALEC... AND PHIL.
"ALEC DREAMED OF FERTILE DESERTS... OF FOOD FOR THE HUNGRY...
"PHIL DREAMED OF AIR... HE DREAMED OF SHOWING MANKIND THAT THE WORLD WAS ONE THING... ALL CONNECTED, INTERTWINED.
"PHIL WANTED TO MAKE PEOPLE OF PLANTS... BREATHING IN CARBON DIOXIDE... BREATHING OUT OXYGEN... FEEDING ON WATER AND SOIL AND AIR...
"HE HAD DREAMS OF SENDING THEM TO THE AMAZON... TO THE RAIN FORESTS... TO CREATE A NEW WORLD... TO SAVE AN OLD WORLD FROM DYING.
"ALEC... AND HIS LOVE... MADE A... MAGIC POTION... AND THEY WERE KILLED BECAUSE OF IT... "
"BUT YOU--YOU WERE ALEC! HOW--?"
"HUSH... THAT IS ANOTHER STORY.

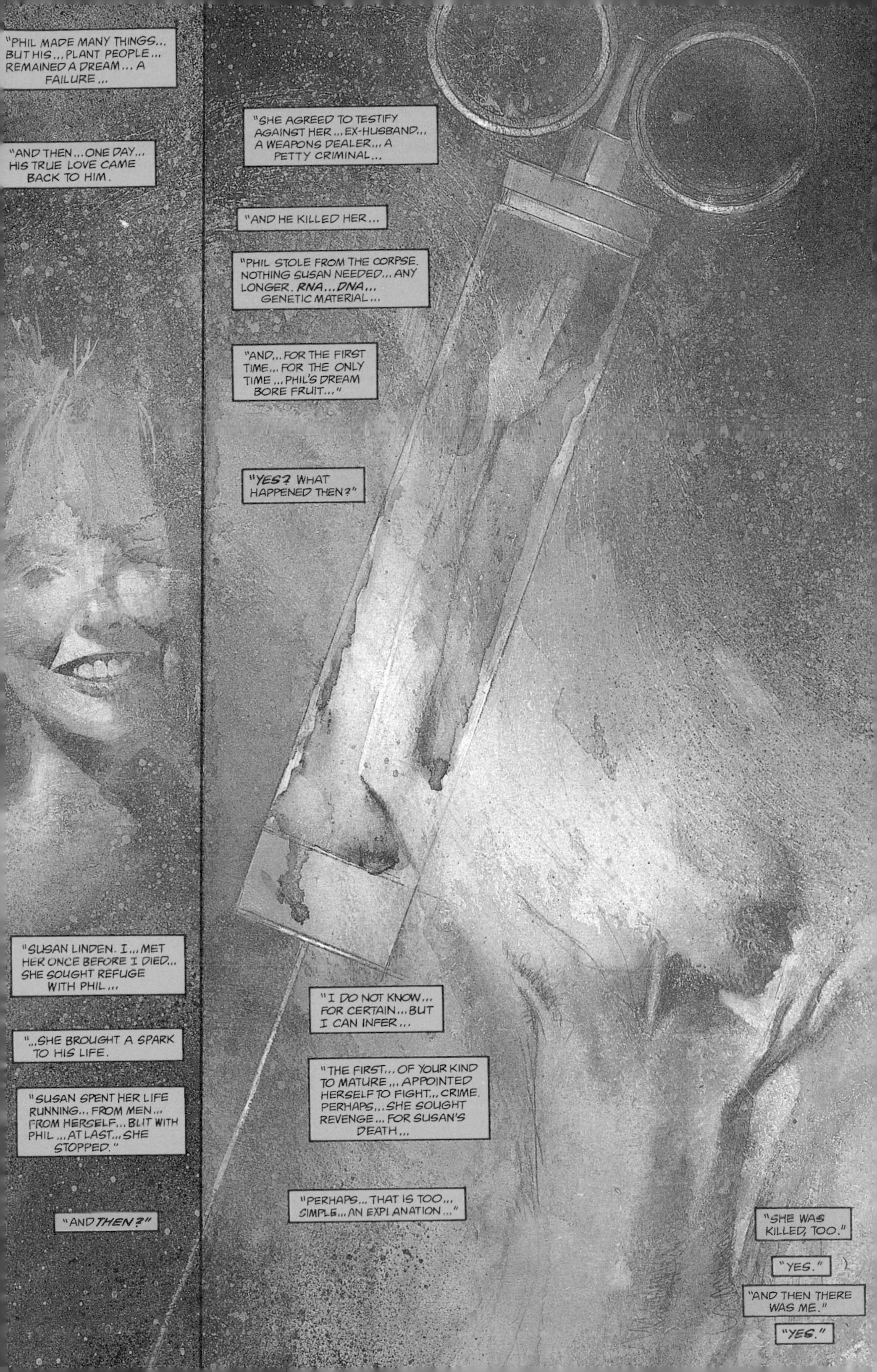
"PHIL MADE MANY THINGS... BUT HIS... PLANT PEOPLE... REMAINED A DREAM... A FAILURE...
"AND THEN... ONE DAY... HIS TRUE LOVE CAME BACK TO HIM.
"SUSAN LINDEN. I... MET HER ONCE BEFORE I DIED... SHE SOUGHT REFUGE WITH PHIL...
"...SHE BROUGHT A SPARK TO HIS LIFE.
"SUSAN SPENT HER LIFE RUNNING... FROM MEN... FROM HERSELF... BUT WITH PHIL... AT LAST... SHE STOPPED."
"AND THEN?"
"SHE AGREED TO TESTIFY AGAINST HER... EX-HUSBAND... A WEAPONS DEALER... A PETTY CRIMINAL...
"AND HE KILLED HER...
"PHIL STOLE FROM THE CORPSE. NOTHING SUSAN NEEDED... ANY LONGER. RNA... DNA... GENETIC MATERIAL...
"AND... FOR THE FIRST TIME... FOR THE ONLY TIME... PHIL'S DREAM BORE FRUIT..."
"YES? WHAT HAPPENED THEN?"
"I DO NOT KNOW... FOR CERTAIN... BUT I CAN INFER...
"THE FIRST... OF YOUR KIND TO MATURE... APPOINTED HERSELF TO FIGHT... CRIME. PERHAPS... SHE SOUGHT REVENGE... FOR SUSAN'S DEATH...
"PERHAPS... THAT IS TOO... SIMPLE... AN EXPLANATION..."
"SHE WAS KILLED, TOO."
"YES."
"AND THEN THERE WAS ME."
"YES."

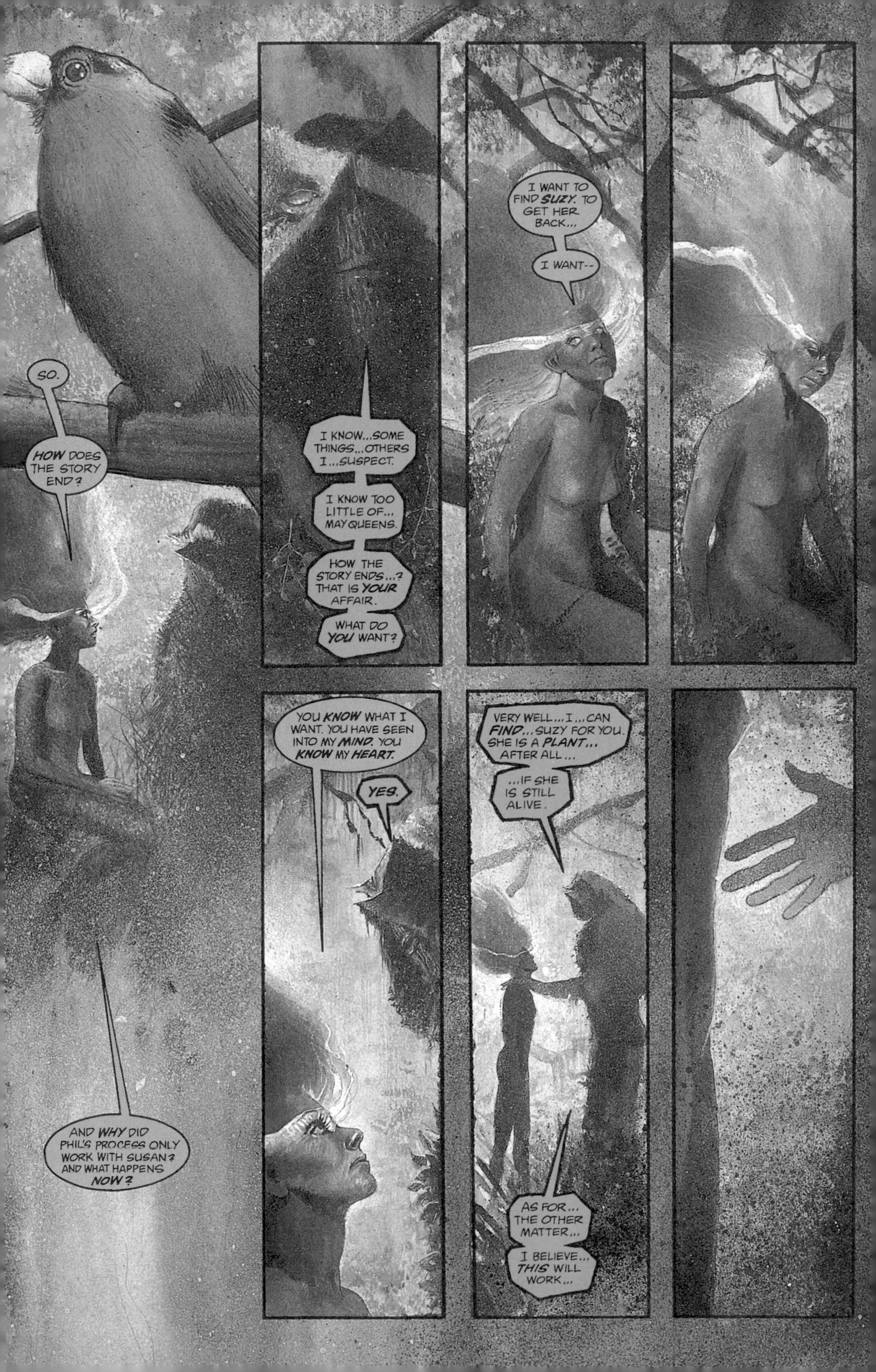
SO.
HOW DOES THE STORY END?
AND WHY DID PHIL'S PROCESS ONLY WORK WITH SUSAN? AND WHAT HAPPENS NOW?
I KNOW...SOME THINGS...OTHERS I...SUSPECT.
I KNOW TOO LITTLE OF... MAY QUEENS.
HOW THE STORY ENDS...? THAT IS YOUR AFFAIR.
WHAT DO YOU WANT?
I WANT TO FIND SUZY. TO GET HER BACK...
I WANT--
YOU KNOW WHAT I WANT. YOU HAVE SEEN INTO MY MIND. YOU KNOW MY HEART.
YES.
VERY WELL...I...CAN FIND...SUZY FOR YOU. SHE IS A PLANT... AFTER ALL...
...IF SHE IS STILL ALIVE.
AS FOR... THE OTHER MATTER...
I BELIEVE... THIS WILL WORK...

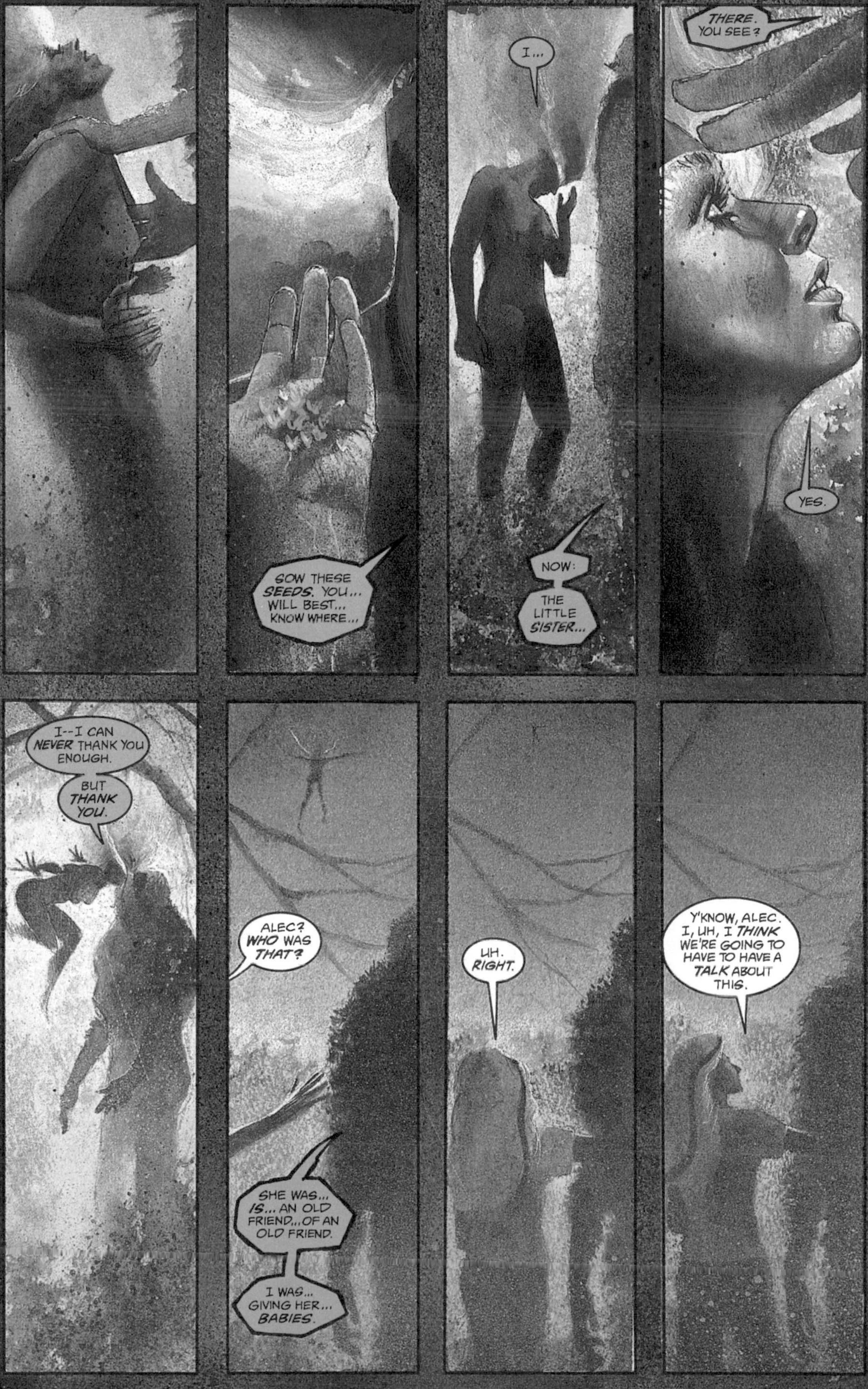
SOW THESE SEEDS. YOU... WILL BEST... KNOW WHERE...
I...
NOW:
THE LITTLE SISTER...
THERE. YOU SEE?
YES.
I--I CAN NEVER THANK YOU ENOUGH.
BUT THANK YOU.
ALEC? WHO WAS THAT?
SHE WAS... IS... AN OLD FRIEND... OF AN OLD FRIEND.
I WAS... GIVING HER... BABIES.
UH. RIGHT.
Y'KNOW, ALEC. I, UH, I THINK WE'RE GOING TO HAVE TO HAVE A TALK ABOUT THIS.

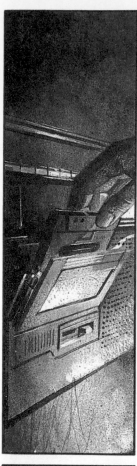

A CIGARETTE THAT BEARS A LIPSTICK TRACES...

AN AIRLINE TICKET TO ROMANTIC PLACES...

YEAH, I *KNOW* WHAT YOU'RE THINKING. YOU'RE THINKING I *HATE* YOU. RIGHT?

AUDIO TRANSMIT

WELL YOU'RE *WRONG.* I *DIDN'T* KILL YOU BECAUSE I *HATE* YOU.

I *LOVE* YOU.

WHAT DRIVES ME *CRAZY* IS THINKING ABOUT YOU. YOU WITH OTHER GUYS. YOU *LEAVING* ME.

THAT WAS WHY I *HAD* TA TAKE YOU OUT THE FIRST TIME.

...MY HEART HAS WINGS, THESE FOOLISH THINGS...

WHEN YOU WERE *GONE* I WAS HAPPY--UNLESS I THOUGHT ABOUT YOU.

YOU CAME, YOU SAW, YOU *CONQUERED* ME...

I GOTTA KEEP DOING IT. I GOTTA *FORGET* YOU, HONEY. THAT'S WHY THESE FLOWER BITCHES HAVE TO BE *TAKEN OUT* AS WELL.

BECAUSE I *LOVE* YOU AND IT'S GONNA DRIVE ME *NUTS.*

...OOOHHH HOW THE GHOST OF YOU CLINGS...

...THESE FOOLISH THINGS... REMIND ME OF YOU...

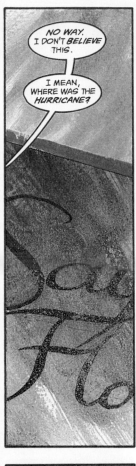

NO WAY. I DON'T BELIEVE THIS.

I MEAN, WHERE WAS THE HURRICANE?

LANDSLIDE, MAYBE?

YEAH, THAT'S WHAT I THOUGHT TOO. BUT IT LOOKED LIKE THEY JUST, I DUNNO, STARTED TO UPROOT...

"MOTHER?"

MAYBE IF I WALK BACK TO THE DINER, THEY GOT A CHAINSAW OR AN AX THEY COULD LOAN US...

YEAH. GOOD IDEA. YOU WANNA BRING BACK SOME COFFEE?

"YES."

HEY, I JUST HEARD SOMETHING. ARE THERE, UH MOUNTAIN LIONS 'ROUND HERE?

OH JEEZUS! LOOK!

SHOOT HER! FAGODSAKE! SHOOT HER!

WHAT DO YOU THINK I'M DOING?

I WAS SCARED. I WOKE UP IN THE DARK, AND I COULDN'T MOVE.

I'M SORRY. I WON'T LEAVE YOU AGAIN.

WHERE ARE WE GOING NOW?

SOUTH.

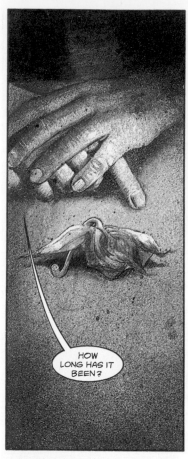

HOW LONG HAS IT BEEN?

TWO WEEKS, SIR.

EIGHTEEN DAYS, MISTER STERLING. *NOT* TWO WEEKS.

EIGHTEEN DAYS!

LOOK, I CAN'T SEE WHAT THE *PROBLEM* IS-- AFTER ALL--

QUIET!

I *WANT* THOSE WOMEN.

YOU KNOW THAT I ONLY ASK *ONE* THING OF PEOPLE WHO WORK FOR ME, STERLING.

WHAT AM I TALKING ABOUT?

RESULTS.

REEE*SULTS*. YES. SO.

FIND ME THESE SUPER-PURPLE-FLOWER-WOMEN. *ONE OR BOTH*. AND GET THEM TO THE *LABS* FOR EXAMINATION AND DISSECTION.

YES?

SIR, IT'S... NOT THAT *EASY*, I'M UP TO MY *NECK* WITH THE *ALBION* PROJECT, AND I'VE--

I OBVIOUSLY *HAVEN'T* MADE MYSELF CLEAR. YOU ARE *SUSPENDED* FROM YOUR POSITION.

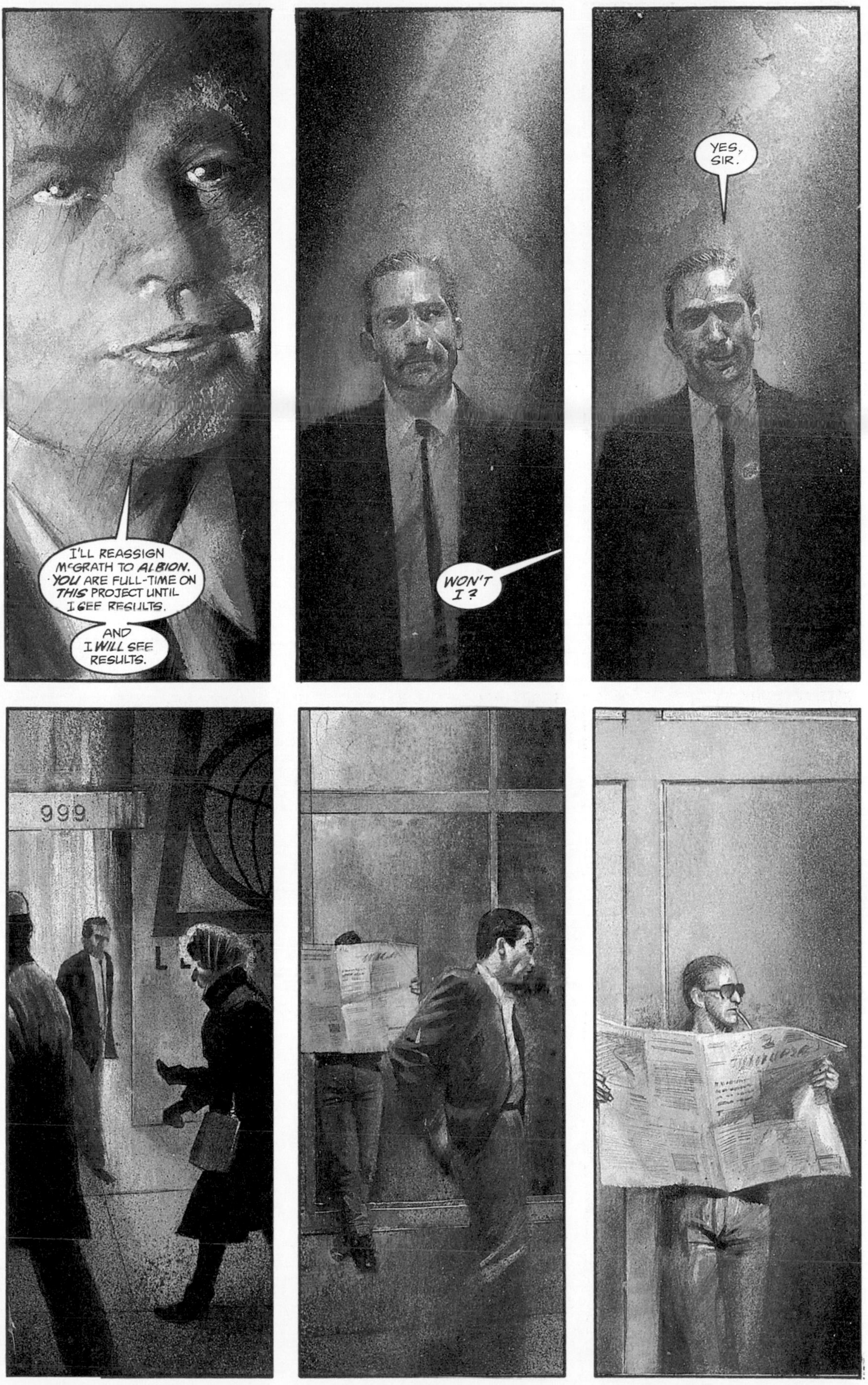
I'LL REASSIGN McGRATH TO ALBION. YOU ARE FULL-TIME ON THIS PROJECT UNTIL I SEE RESULTS.
AND I WILL SEE RESULTS.
WON'T I?
YES, SIR.
999

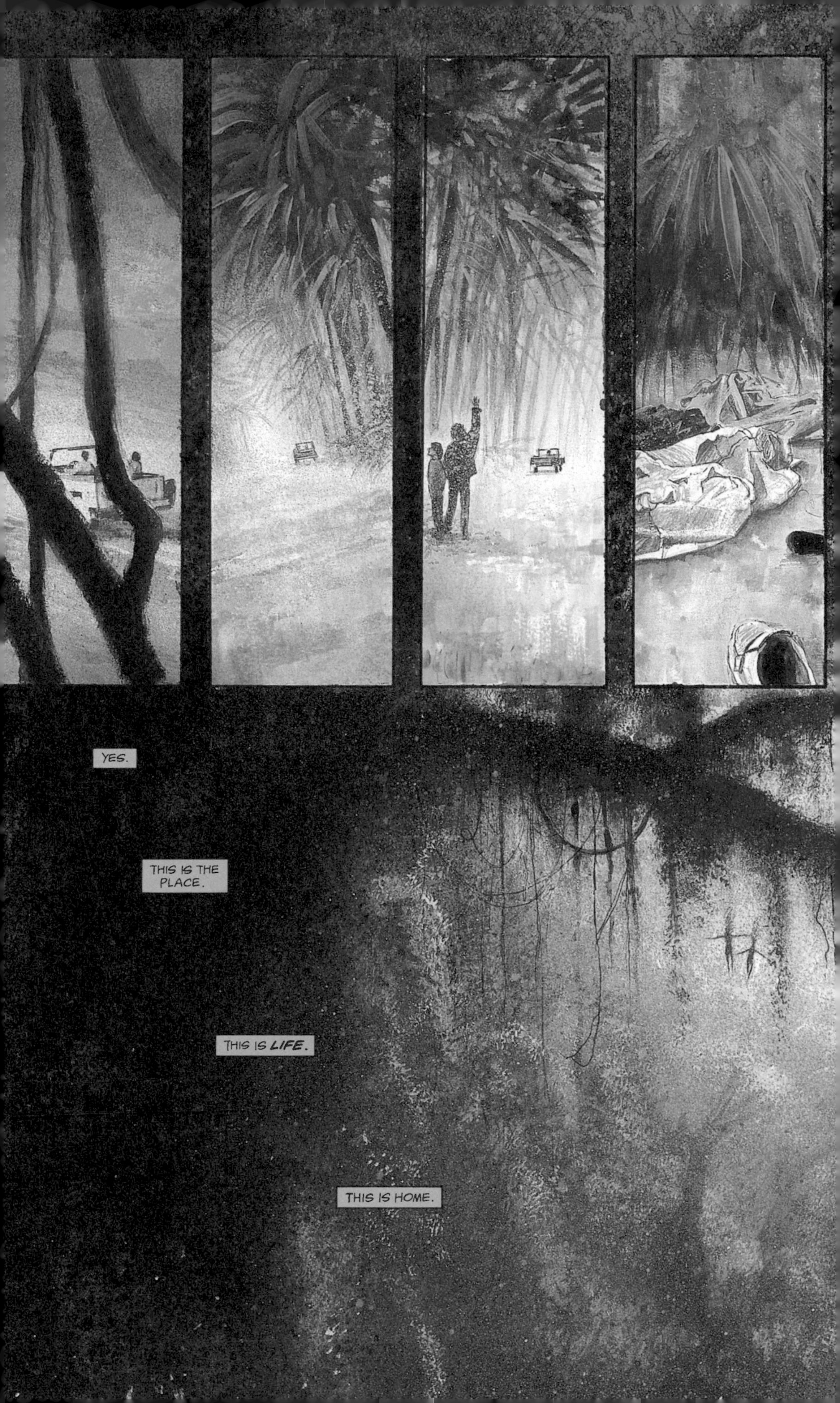
YES.
THIS IS THE PLACE.
THIS IS *LIFE*.
THIS IS HOME.

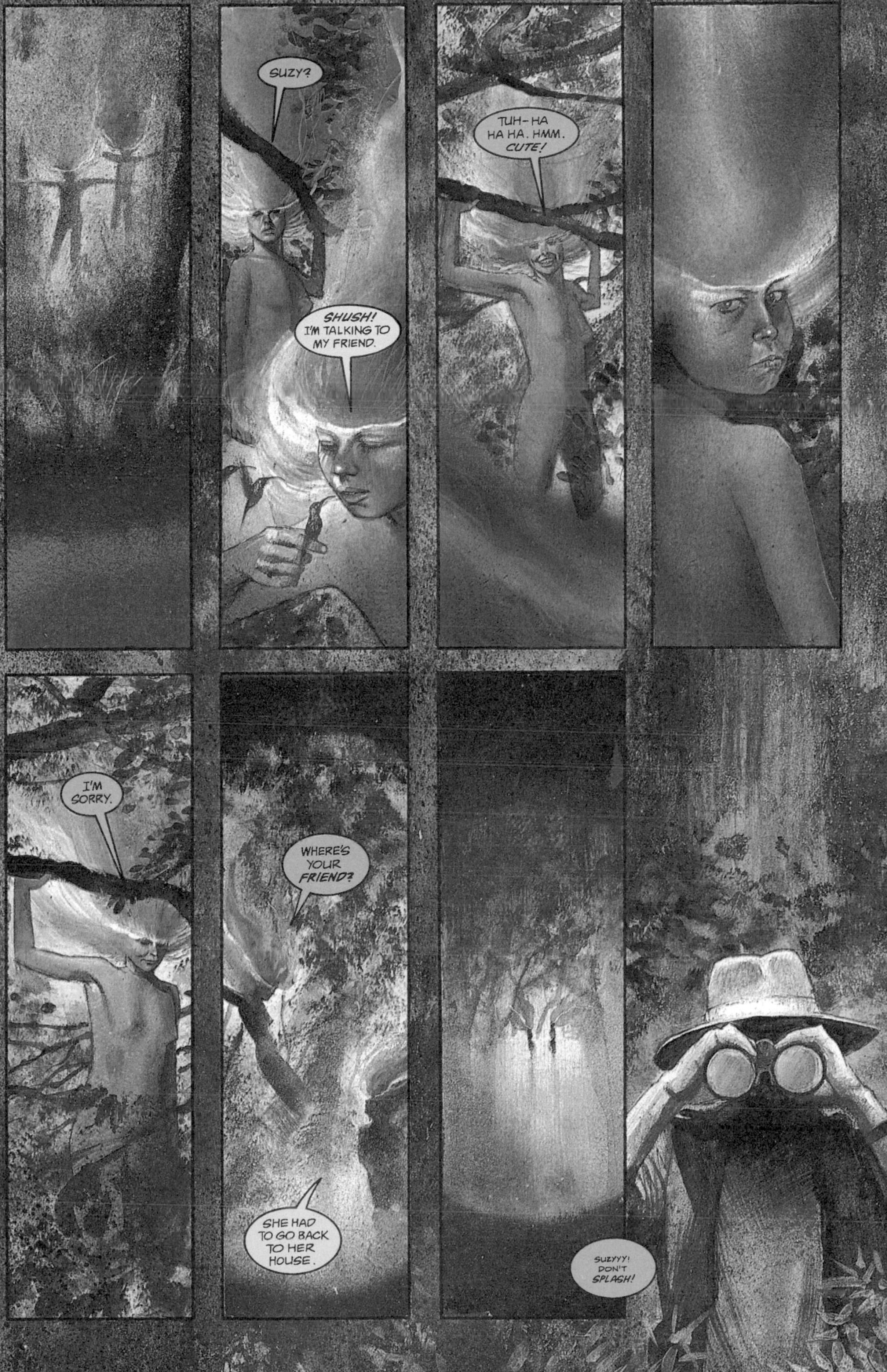
SUZY?
SHUSH! I'M TALKING TO MY FRIEND.
TUH-HA HA HA. HMM. CUTE!
I'M SORRY.
WHERE'S YOUR FRIEND?
SHE HAD TO GO BACK TO HER HOUSE.
SUZYYY! DON'T SPLASH!

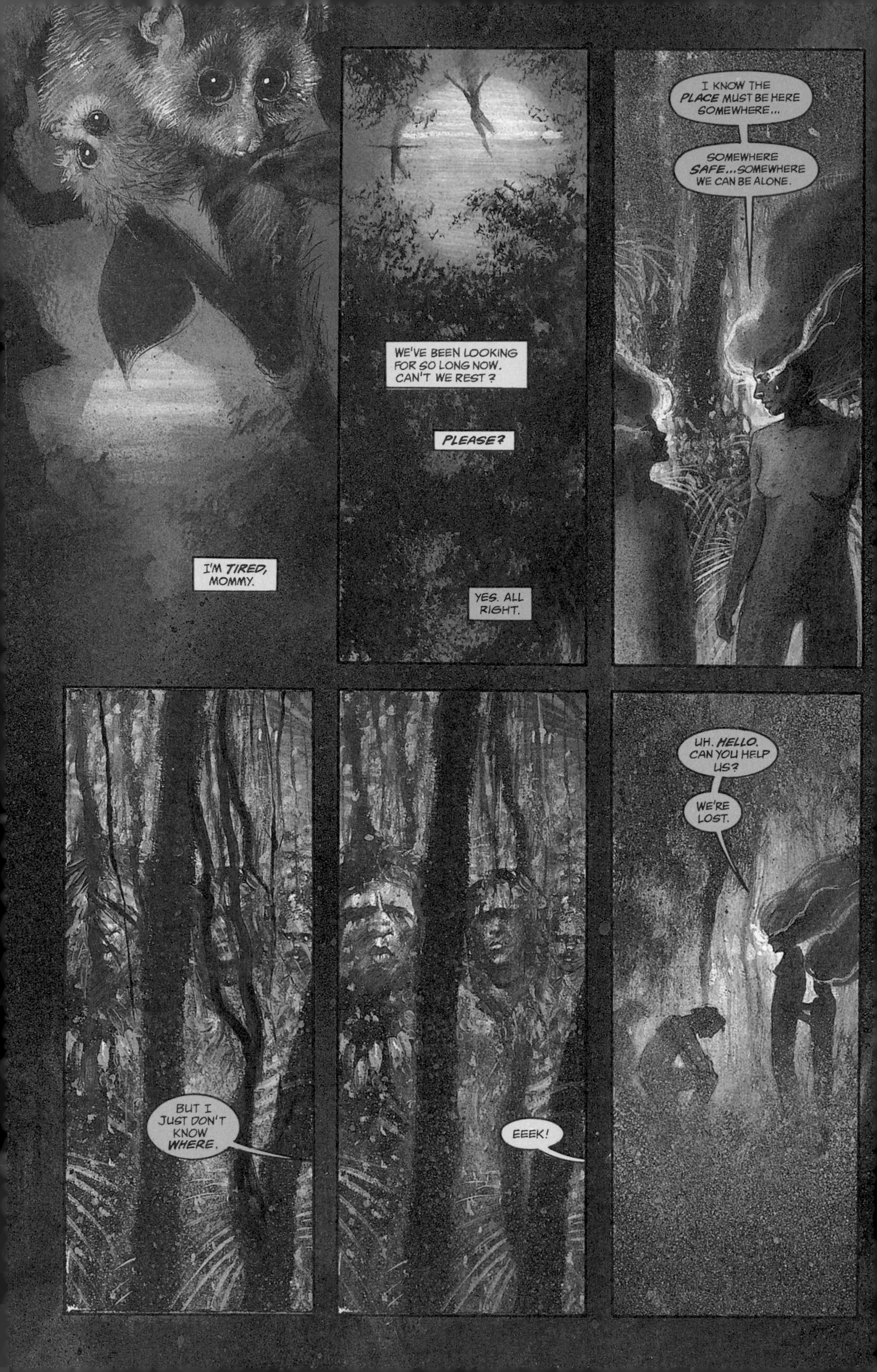
I'M TIRED, MOMMY.
WE'VE BEEN LOOKING FOR SO LONG NOW. CAN'T WE REST?
PLEASE?
YES. ALL RIGHT.
I KNOW THE PLACE MUST BE HERE SOMEWHERE...
SOMEWHERE SAFE...SOMEWHERE WE CAN BE ALONE.
BUT I JUST DON'T KNOW WHERE.
EEEK!
UH. HELLO. CAN YOU HELP US?
WE'RE LOST.

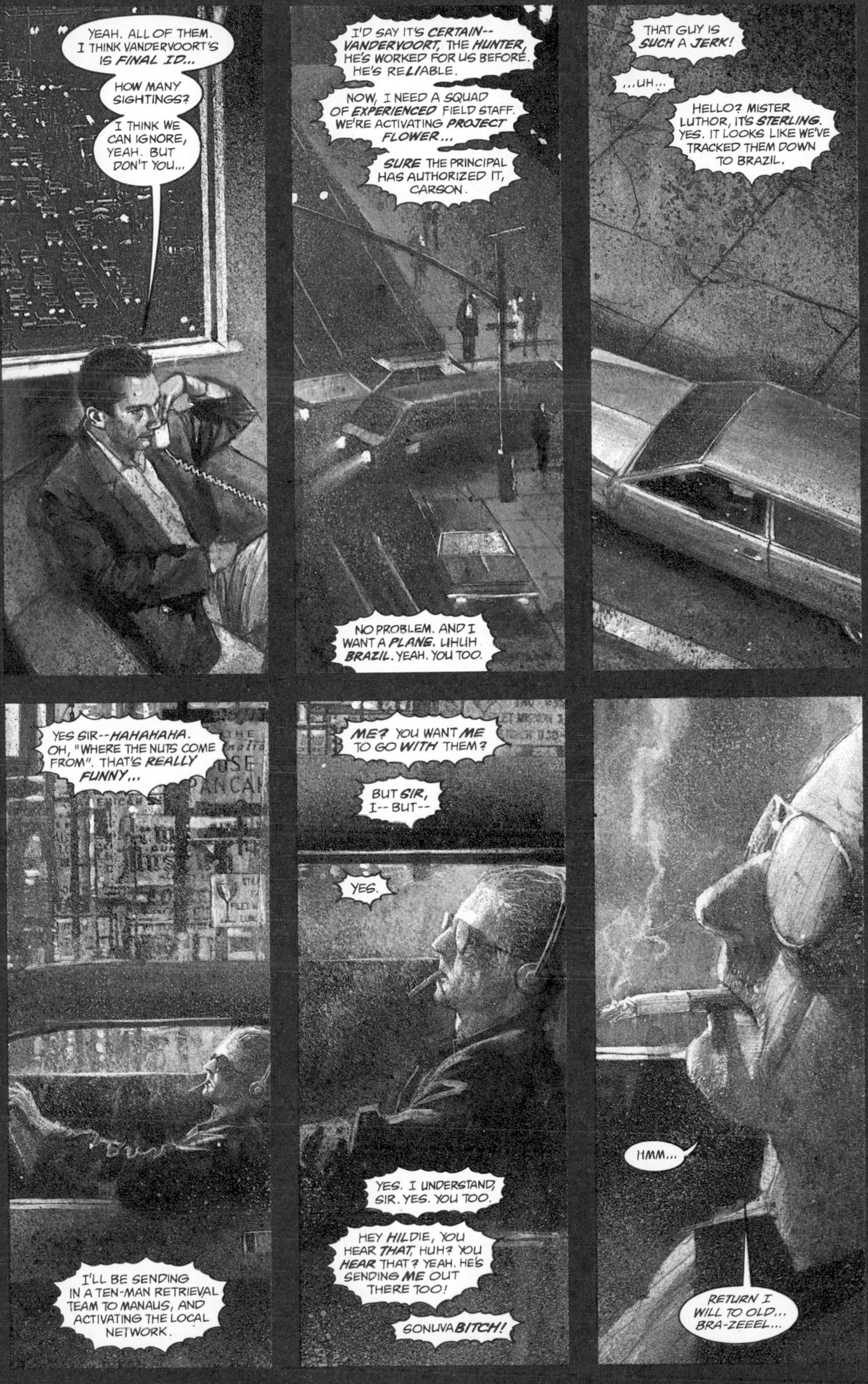
YEAH. ALL OF THEM. I THINK VANDERVOORT'S IS FINAL ID...
HOW MANY SIGHTINGS?
I THINK WE CAN IGNORE, YEAH. BUT DON'T YOU...
I'D SAY IT'S CERTAIN-- VANDERVOORT, THE HUNTER, HE'S WORKED FOR US BEFORE. HE'S RELIABLE.
NOW, I NEED A SQUAD OF EXPERIENCED FIELD STAFF. WE'RE ACTIVATING PROJECT FLOWER...
SURE THE PRINCIPAL HAS AUTHORIZED IT, CARSON.
NO PROBLEM. AND I WANT A PLANE. UHUH BRAZIL. YEAH. YOU TOO.
THAT GUY IS SUCH A JERK!
...UH...
HELLO? MISTER LUTHOR, IT'S STERLING. YES. IT LOOKS LIKE WE'VE TRACKED THEM DOWN TO BRAZIL.
YES SIR--HAHAHAHA. OH, "WHERE THE NUTS COME FROM". THAT'S REALLY FUNNY...
I'LL BE SENDING IN A TEN-MAN RETRIEVAL TEAM TO MANAUS, AND ACTIVATING THE LOCAL NETWORK.
ME? YOU WANT ME TO GO WITH THEM?
BUT SIR, I-- BUT--
YES.
YES. I UNDERSTAND, SIR. YES. YOU TOO.
HEY HILDIE, YOU HEAR THAT, HUH? YOU HEAR THAT? YEAH. HE'S SENDING ME OUT THERE TOO!
SONUVA BITCH!
HMM...
RETURN I WILL TO OLD... BRA-ZEEEL...

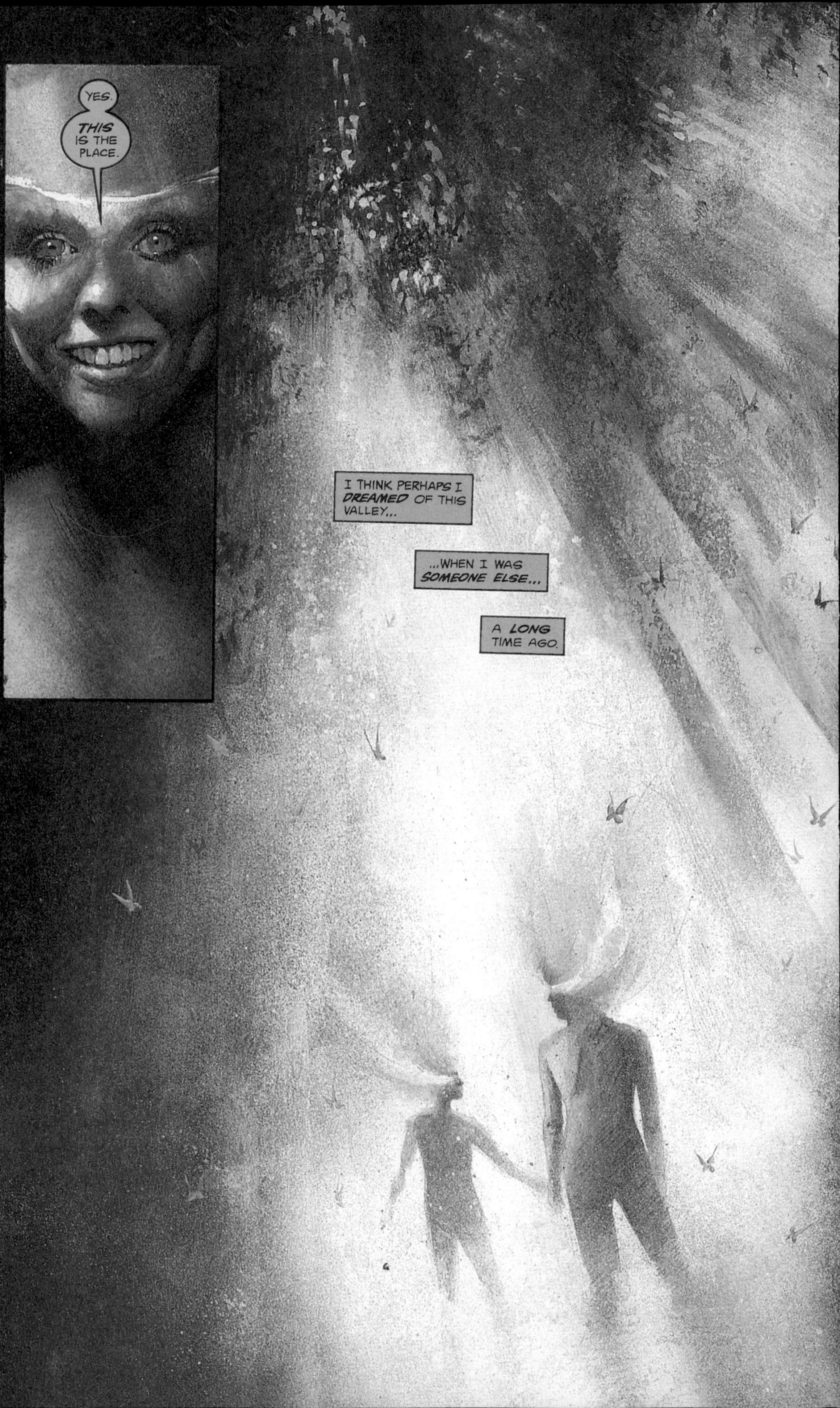
YES.
THIS IS THE PLACE.
I THINK PERHAPS I DREAMED OF THIS VALLEY...
...WHEN I WAS SOMEONE ELSE...
A LONG TIME AGO.

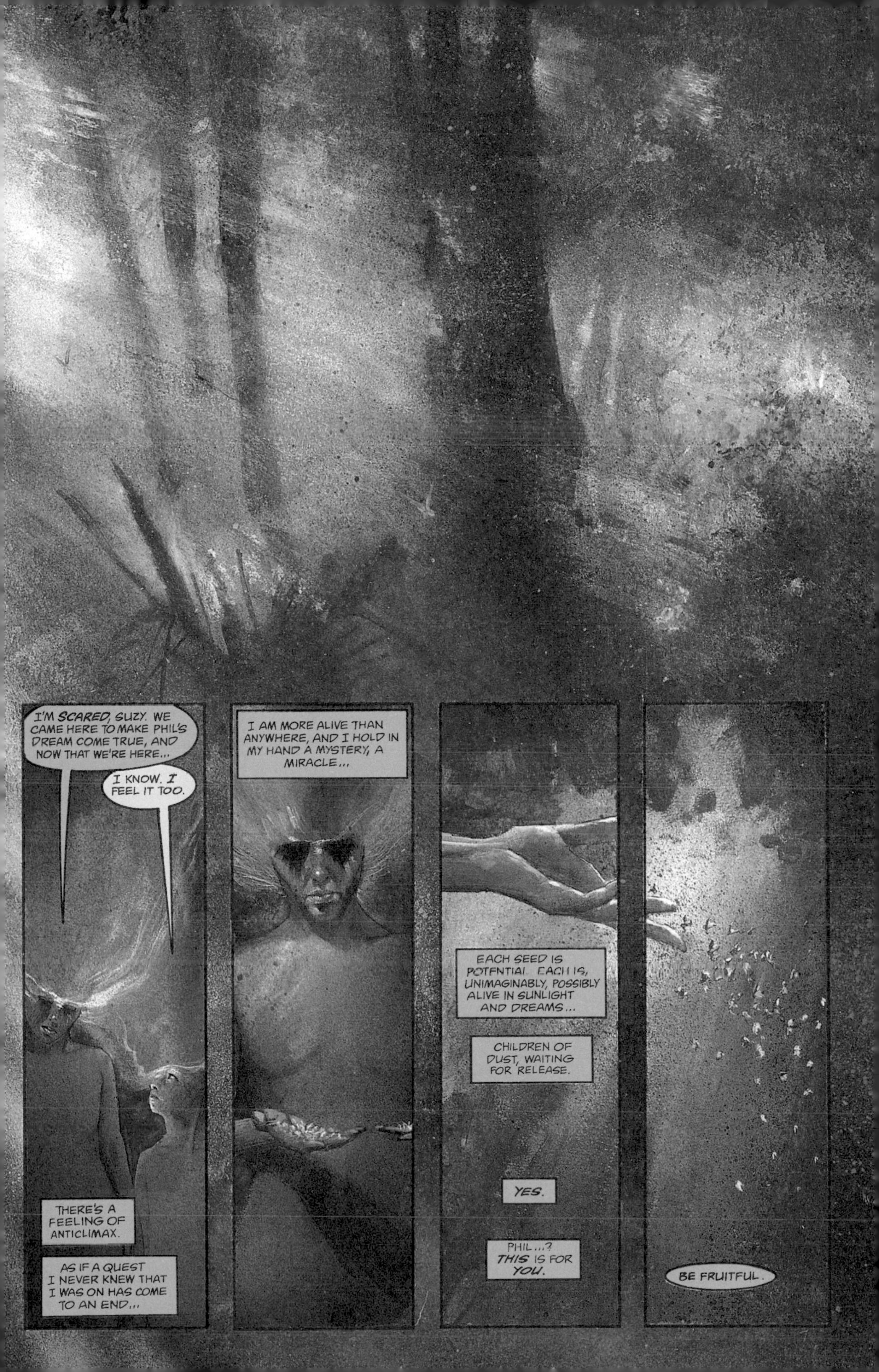
I'M SCARED, SUZY. WE CAME HERE TO MAKE PHIL'S DREAM COME TRUE, AND NOW THAT WE'RE HERE...
I KNOW. I FEEL IT TOO.
THERE'S A FEELING OF ANTICLIMAX.
AS IF A QUEST I NEVER KNEW THAT I WAS ON HAS COME TO AN END...
I AM MORE ALIVE THAN ANYWHERE, AND I HOLD IN MY HAND A MYSTERY, A MIRACLE...
EACH SEED IS POTENTIAL. EACH IS, UNIMAGINABLY, POSSIBLY ALIVE IN SUNLIGHT AND DREAMS...
CHILDREN OF DUST, WAITING FOR RELEASE.
YES.
PHIL...? THIS IS FOR YOU.
BE FRUITFUL.

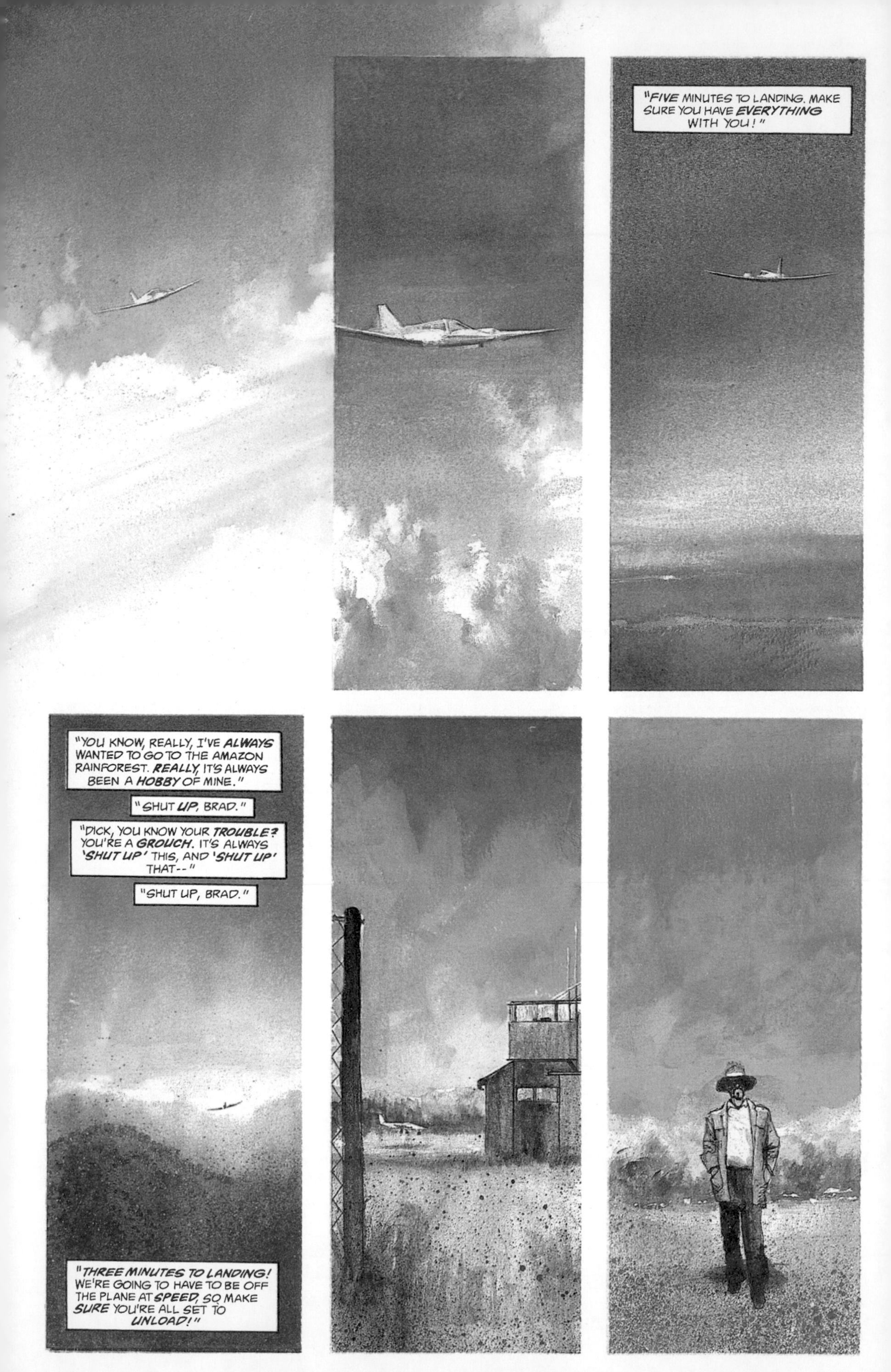
"FIVE MINUTES TO LANDING. MAKE SURE YOU HAVE EVERYTHING WITH YOU!"
"YOU KNOW, REALLY, I'VE ALWAYS WANTED TO GO TO THE AMAZON RAINFOREST. REALLY, IT'S ALWAYS BEEN A HOBBY OF MINE."
"SHUT UP, BRAD."
"DICK, YOU KNOW YOUR TROUBLE? YOU'RE A GROUCH. IT'S ALWAYS 'SHUT UP' THIS, AND 'SHUT UP' THAT--"
"SHUT UP, BRAD."
"THREE MINUTES TO LANDING! WE'RE GOING TO HAVE TO BE OFF THE PLANE AT SPEED, SO MAKE SURE YOU'RE ALL SET TO UNLOAD!"

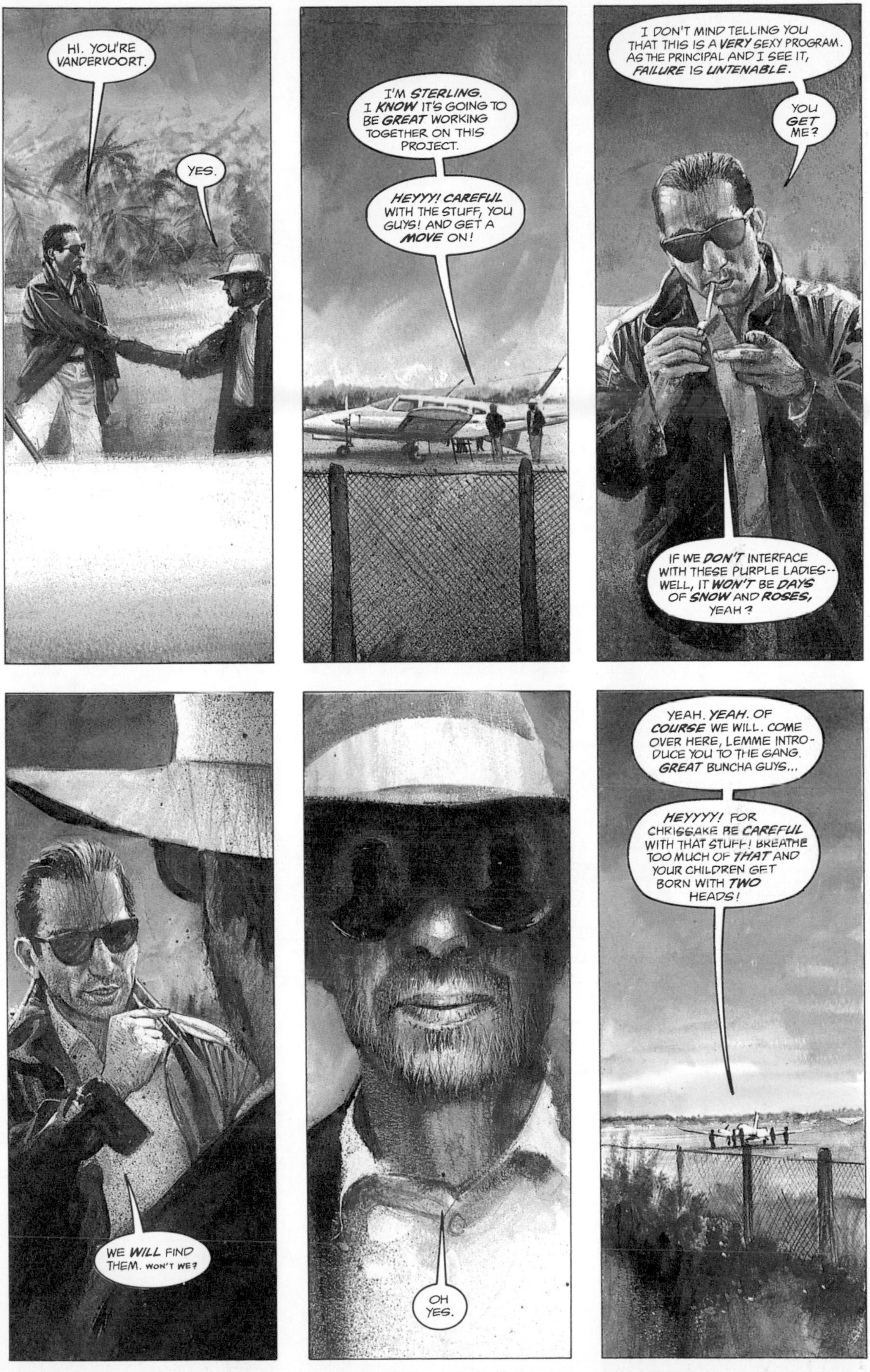

HI. YOU'RE VANDERVOORT.
YES.
I'M STERLING. I KNOW IT'S GOING TO BE GREAT WORKING TOGETHER ON THIS PROJECT.
HEYYY! CAREFUL WITH THE STUFF, YOU GUYS! AND GET A MOVE ON!
I DON'T MIND TELLING YOU THAT THIS IS A VERY SEXY PROGRAM. AS THE PRINCIPAL AND I SEE IT, FAILURE IS UNTENABLE.
YOU GET ME?
IF WE DON'T INTERFACE WITH THESE PURPLE LADIES-- WELL, IT WON'T BE DAYS OF SNOW AND ROSES, YEAH?
WE WILL FIND THEM. WON'T WE?
OH YES.
YEAH. YEAH. OF COURSE WE WILL. COME OVER HERE, LEMME INTRODUCE YOU TO THE GANG. GREAT BUNCHA GUYS...
HEYYYY! FOR CHRISSAKE BE CAREFUL WITH THAT STUFF! BREATHE TOO MUCH OF THAT AND YOUR CHILDREN GET BORN WITH TWO HEADS!

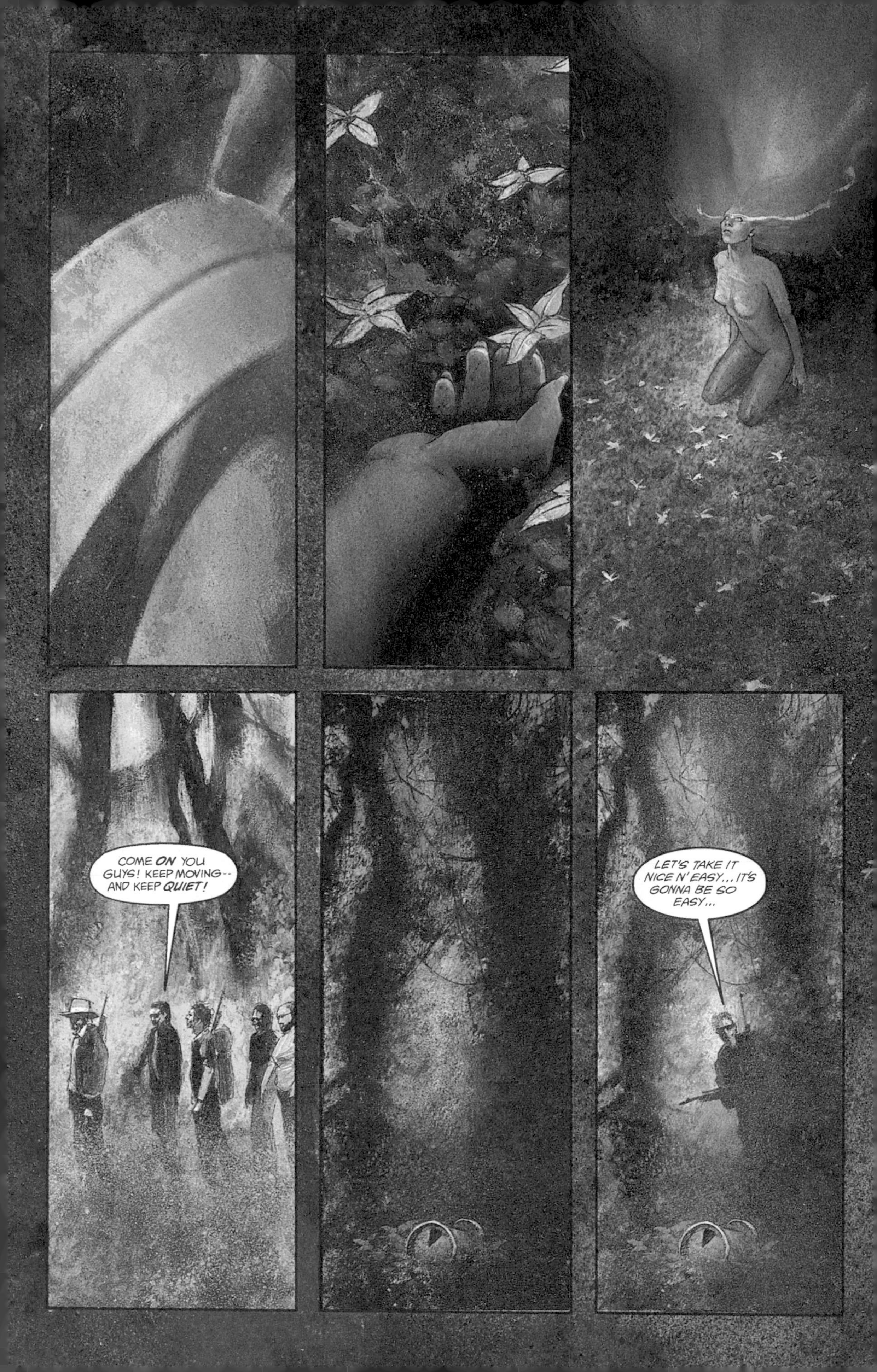
COME ON YOU GUYS! KEEP MOVING--AND KEEP QUIET!
LET'S TAKE IT NICE N' EASY... IT'S GONNA BE SO EASY...

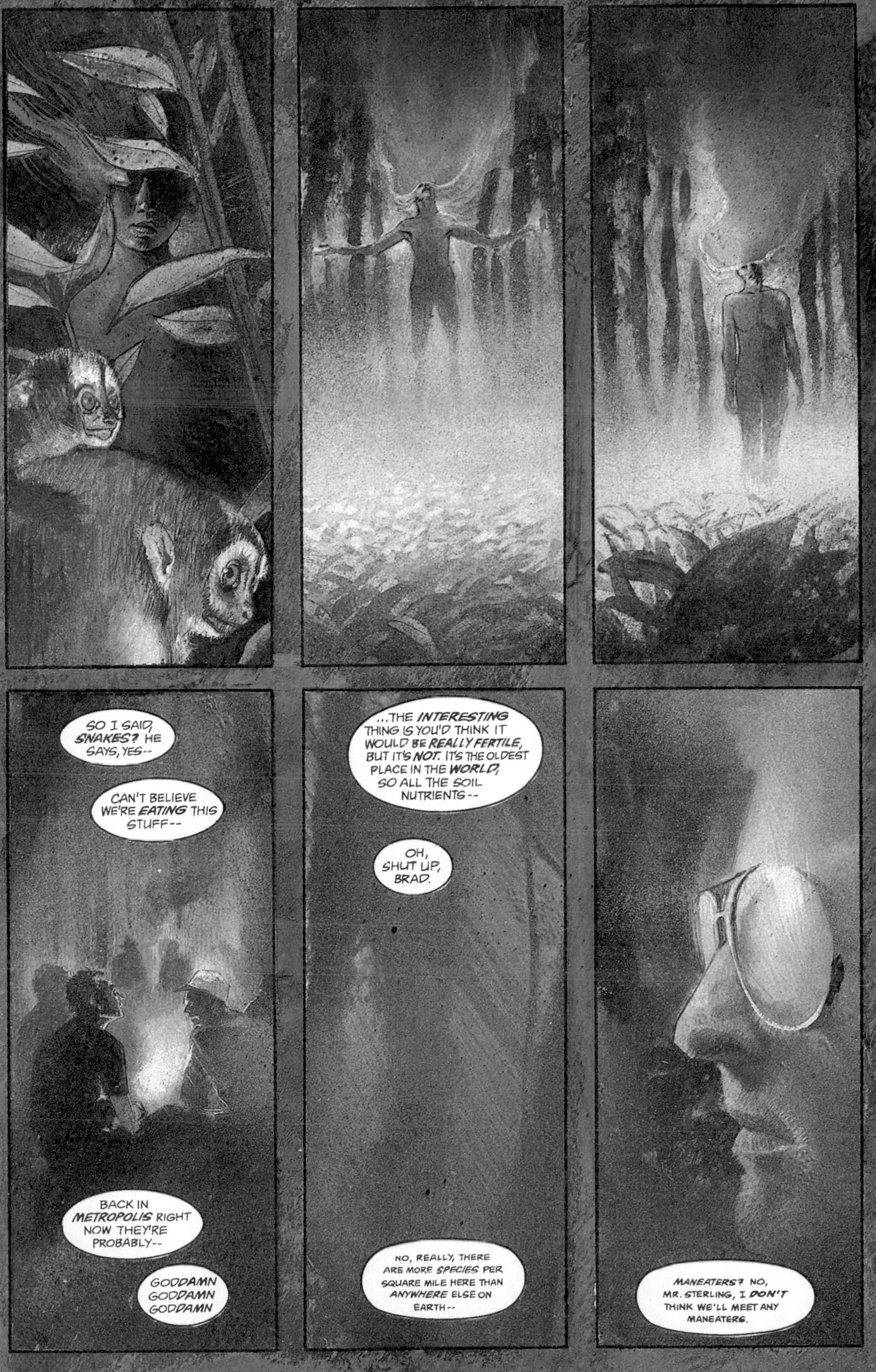
SO I SAID, SNAKES? HE SAYS, YES--
CAN'T BELIEVE WE'RE EATING THIS STUFF--
BACK IN METROPOLIS RIGHT NOW THEY'RE PROBABLY--
GODDAMN GODDAMN GODDAMN
...THE INTERESTING THING IS YOU'D THINK IT WOULD BE REALLY FERTILE, BUT IT'S NOT. IT'S THE OLDEST PLACE IN THE WORLD, SO ALL THE SOIL NUTRIENTS--
OH, SHUT UP, BRAD.
NO, REALLY, THERE ARE MORE SPECIES PER SQUARE MILE HERE THAN ANYWHERE ELSE ON EARTH--
MANEATERS? NO, MR. STERLING, I DON'T THINK WE'LL MEET ANY MANEATERS.

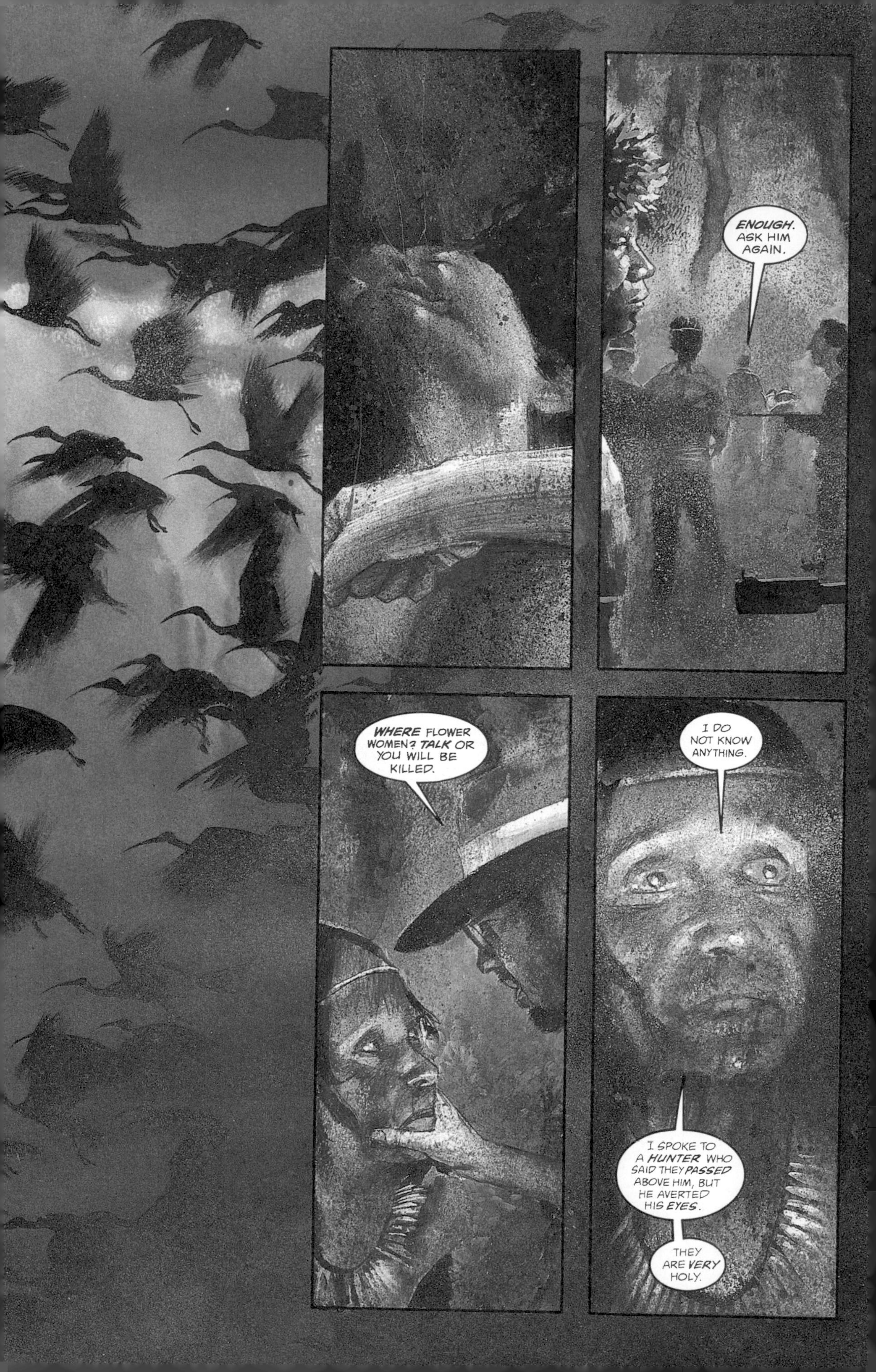
ENOUGH. ASK HIM AGAIN.
WHERE FLOWER WOMEN? TALK OR YOU WILL BE KILLED.
I DO NOT KNOW ANYTHING.
I SPOKE TO A HUNTER WHO SAID THEY PASSED ABOVE HIM, BUT HE AVERTED HIS EYES.
THEY ARE VERY HOLY.

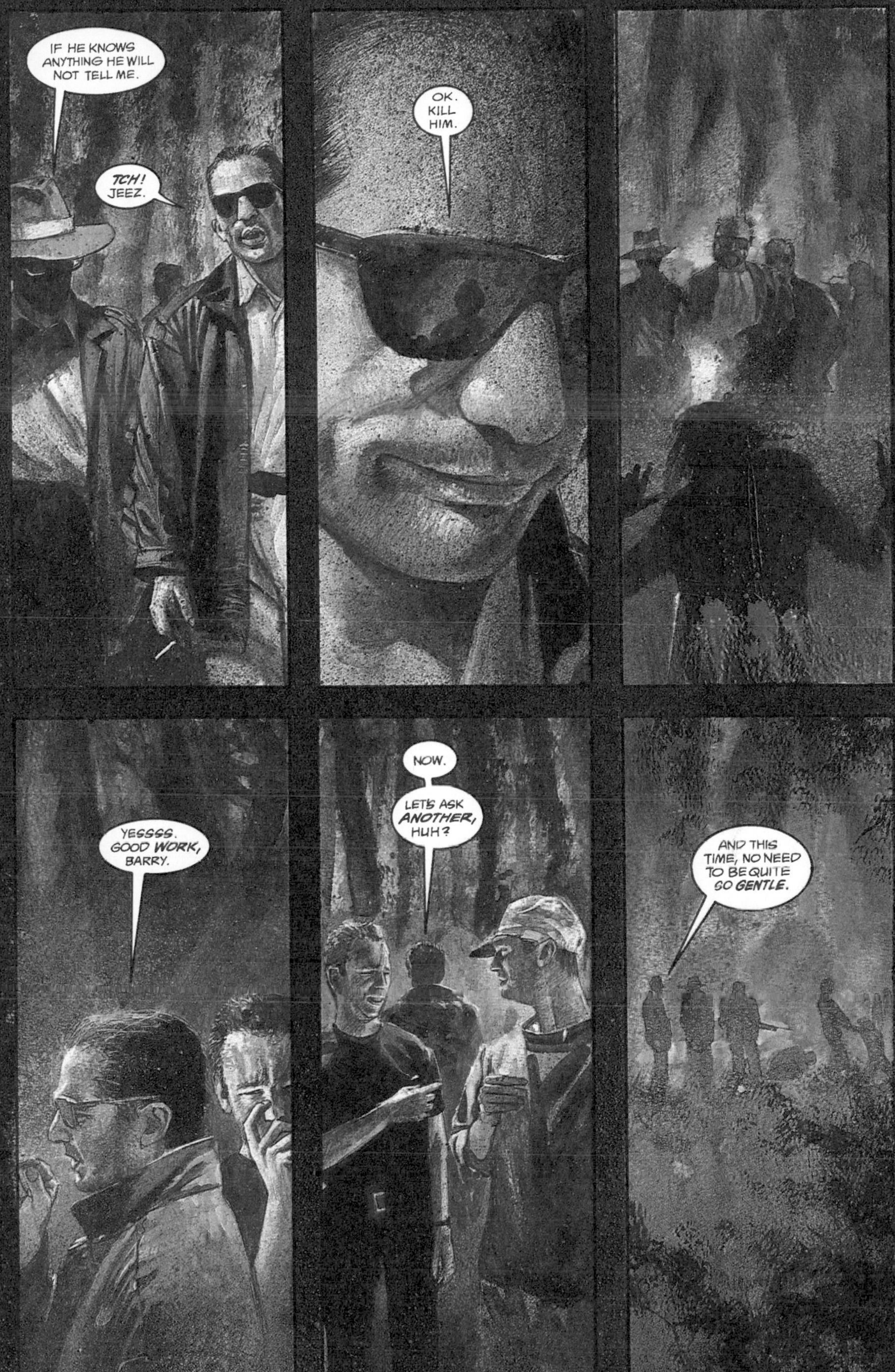
IF HE KNOWS ANYTHING HE WILL NOT TELL ME.
TCH! JEEZ.
OK. KILL HIM.
YESSSS. GOOD WORK, BARRY.
NOW.
LET'S ASK ANOTHER, HUH?
AND THIS TIME, NO NEED TO BE QUITE SO GENTLE.

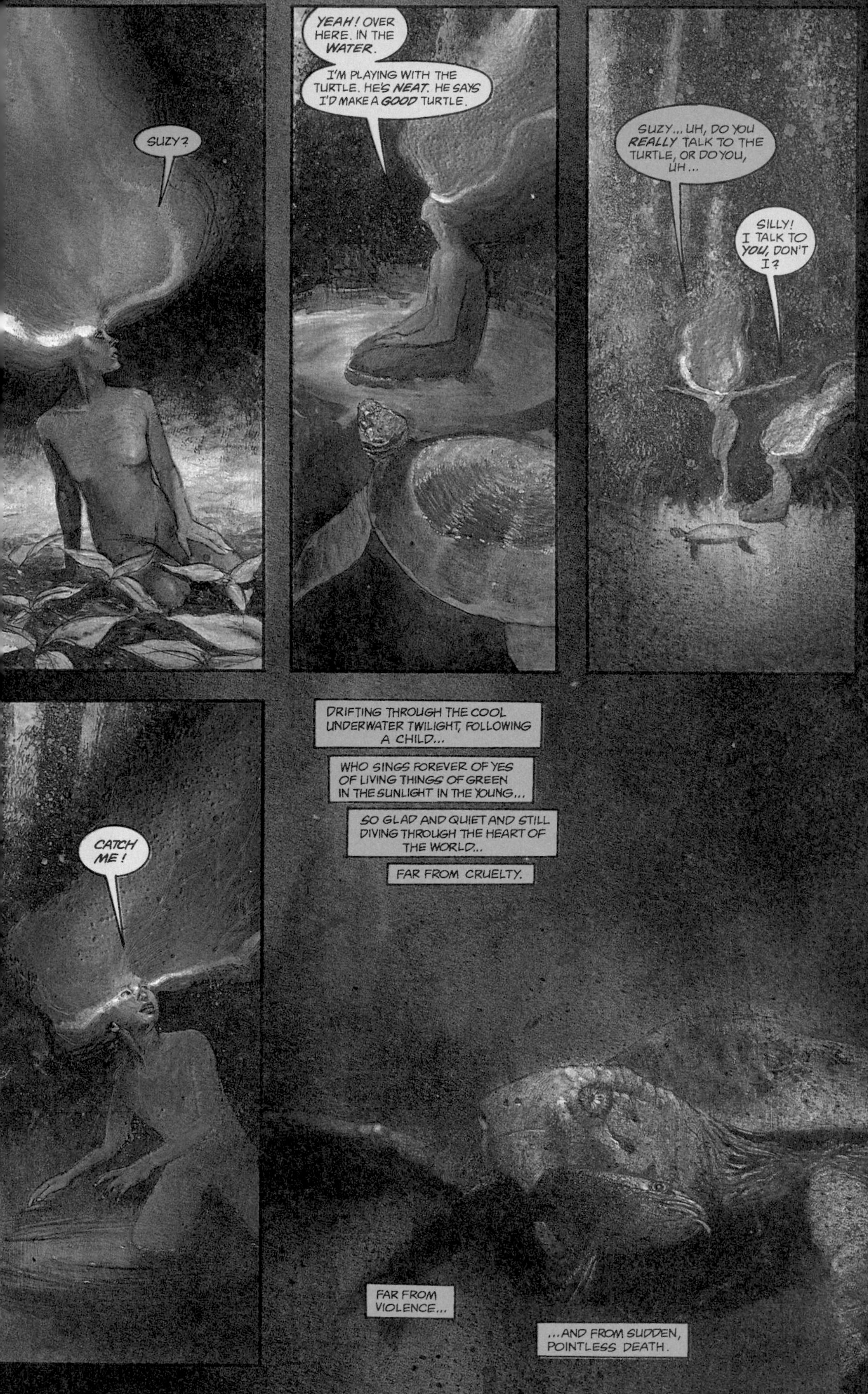
SUZY?
YEAH! OVER HERE. IN THE WATER.
I'M PLAYING WITH THE TURTLE. HE'S NEAT. HE SAYS I'D MAKE A GOOD TURTLE.
SUZY... UH, DO YOU REALLY TALK TO THE TURTLE, OR DO YOU, UH...
SILLY! I TALK TO YOU, DON'T I?
CATCH ME!
DRIFTING THROUGH THE COOL UNDERWATER TWILIGHT, FOLLOWING A CHILD...
WHO SINGS FOREVER OF YES OF LIVING THINGS OF GREEN IN THE SUNLIGHT IN THE YOUNG...
SO GLAD AND QUIET AND STILL DIVING THROUGH THE HEART OF THE WORLD...
FAR FROM CRUELTY.
FAR FROM VIOLENCE...
...AND FROM SUDDEN, POINTLESS DEATH.

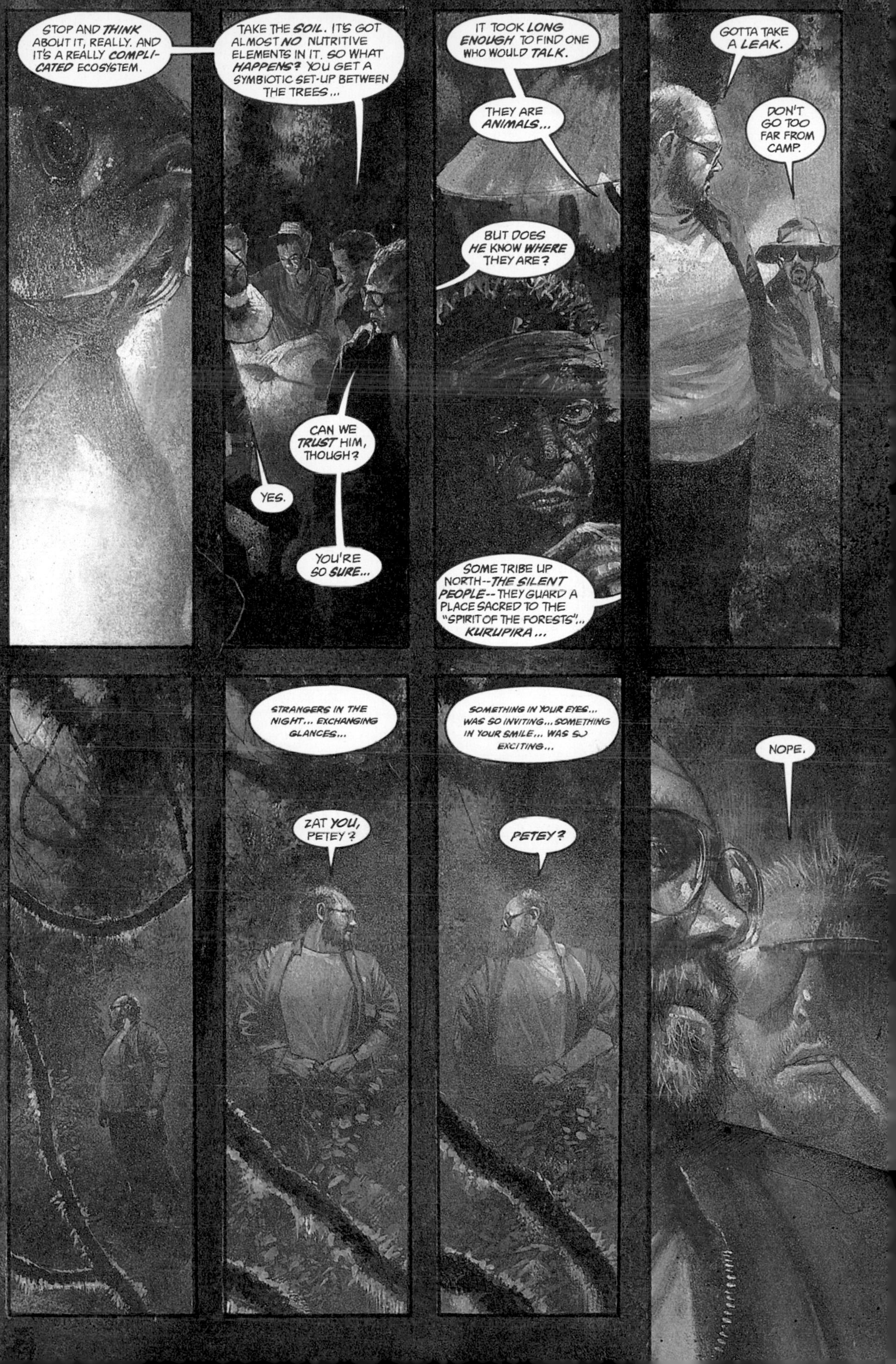
STOP AND THINK ABOUT IT, REALLY. AND IT'S A REALLY COMPLICATED ECOSYSTEM.
TAKE THE SOIL. IT'S GOT ALMOST NO NUTRITIVE ELEMENTS IN IT. SO WHAT HAPPENS? YOU GET A SYMBIOTIC SET-UP BETWEEN THE TREES...
CAN WE TRUST HIM, THOUGH?
YES.
YOU'RE SO SURE...
IT TOOK LONG ENOUGH TO FIND ONE WHO WOULD TALK.
THEY ARE ANIMALS...
BUT DOES HE KNOW WHERE THEY ARE?
SOME TRIBE UP NORTH--THE SILENT PEOPLE--THEY GUARD A PLACE SACRED TO THE "SPIRIT OF THE FORESTS"... KURUPIRA...
GOTTA TAKE A LEAK.
DON'T GO TOO FAR FROM CAMP.
STRANGERS IN THE NIGHT... EXCHANGING GLANCES...
ZAT YOU, PETEY?
SOMETHING IN YOUR EYES... WAS SO INVITING... SOMETHING IN YOUR SMILE... WAS SO EXCITING...
PETEY?
NOPE.

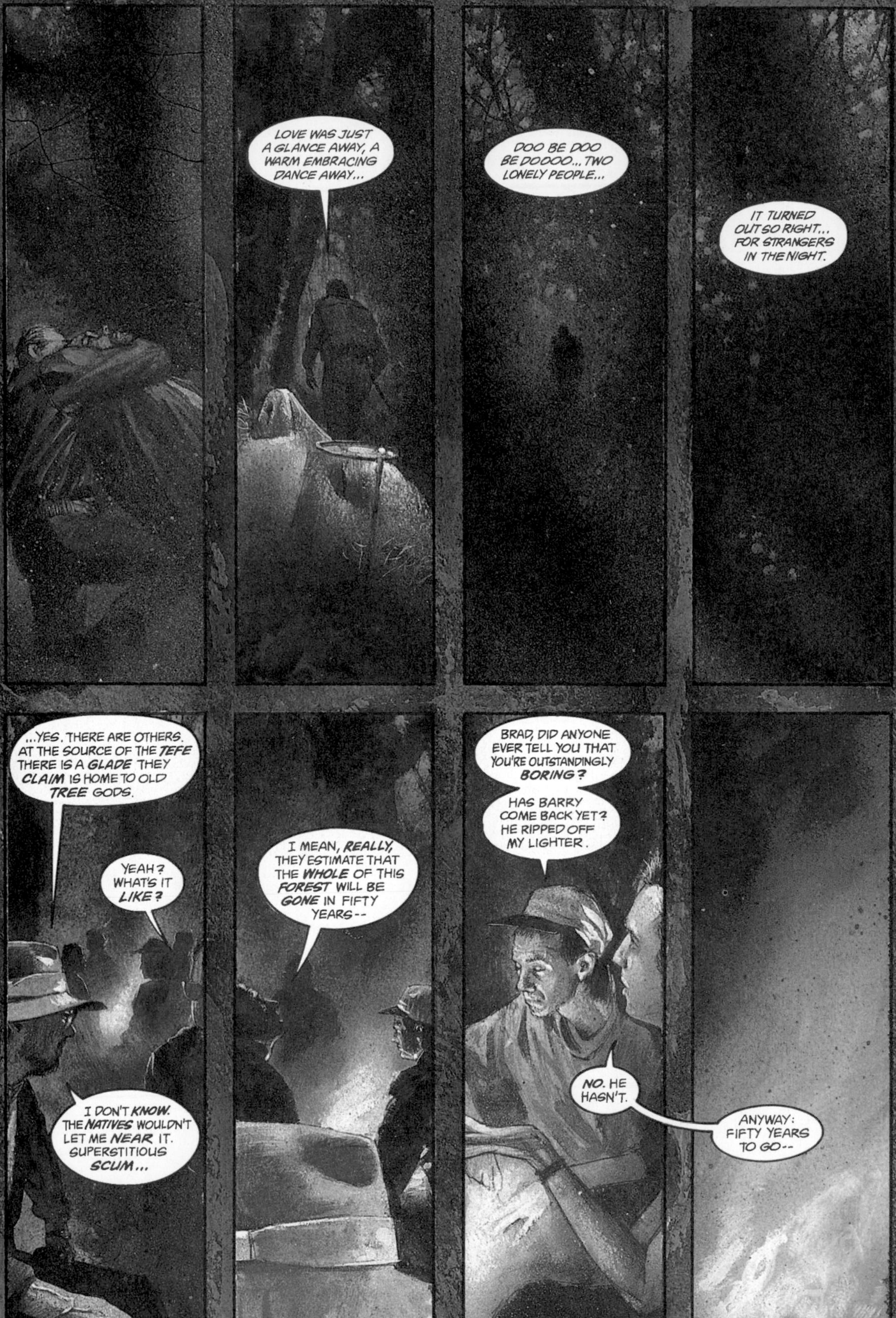
LOVE WAS JUST A GLANCE AWAY, A WARM EMBRACING DANCE AWAY...
DOO BE DOO BE DOOOO... TWO LONELY PEOPLE...
IT TURNED OUT SO RIGHT... FOR STRANGERS IN THE NIGHT.
...YES. THERE ARE OTHERS. AT THE SOURCE OF THE TEFE THERE IS A GLADE THEY CLAIM IS HOME TO OLD TREE GODS.
YEAH? WHAT'S IT LIKE?
I DON'T KNOW. THE NATIVES WOULDN'T LET ME NEAR IT. SUPERSTITIOUS SCUM...
I MEAN, REALLY, THEY ESTIMATE THAT THE WHOLE OF THIS FOREST WILL BE GONE IN FIFTY YEARS--
BRAD, DID ANYONE EVER TELL YOU THAT YOU'RE OUTSTANDINGLY BORING?
HAS BARRY COME BACK YET? HE RIPPED OFF MY LIGHTER.
NO. HE HASN'T.
ANYWAY: FIFTY YEARS TO GO--

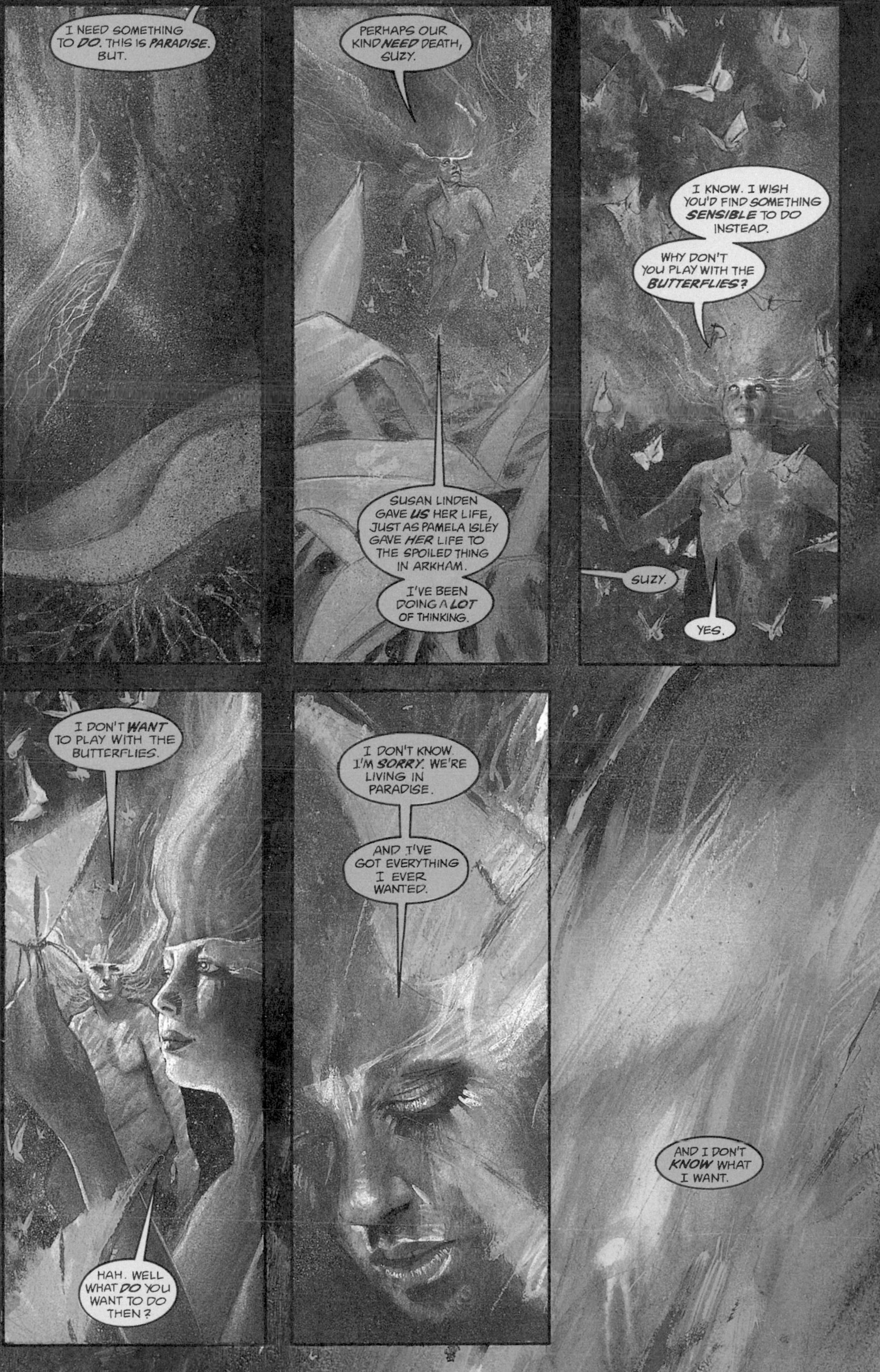

I NEED SOMETHING TO DO. THIS IS PARADISE. BUT.
PERHAPS OUR KIND NEED DEATH, SUZY.
SUSAN LINDEN GAVE US HER LIFE, JUST AS PAMELA ISLEY GAVE HER LIFE TO THE SPOILED THING IN ARKHAM.
I'VE BEEN DOING A LOT OF THINKING.
I KNOW. I WISH YOU'D FIND SOMETHING SENSIBLE TO DO INSTEAD.
WHY DON'T YOU PLAY WITH THE BUTTERFLIES?
SUZY.
YES.
I DON'T WANT TO PLAY WITH THE BUTTERFLIES.
HAH. WELL WHAT DO YOU WANT TO DO THEN?
I DON'T KNOW. I'M SORRY. WE'RE LIVING IN PARADISE.
AND I'VE GOT EVERYTHING I EVER WANTED.
AND I DON'T KNOW WHAT I WANT.

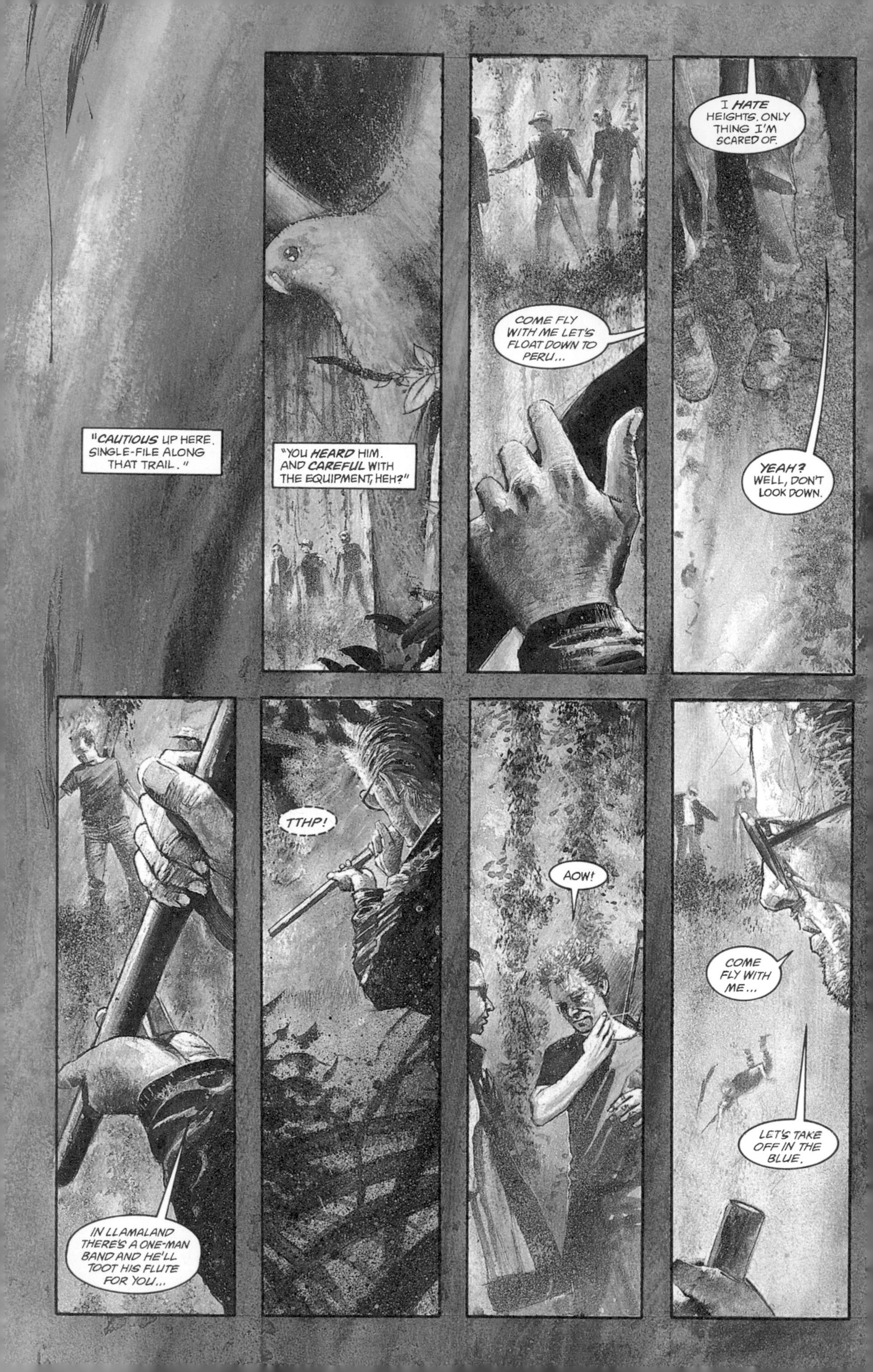
"CAUTIOUS UP HERE. SINGLE-FILE ALONG THAT TRAIL."
"YOU HEARD HIM. AND CAREFUL WITH THE EQUIPMENT, HEH?"
COME FLY WITH ME LET'S FLOAT DOWN TO PERU...
I HATE HEIGHTS. ONLY THING I'M SCARED OF.
YEAH? WELL, DON'T LOOK DOWN.
IN LLAMALAND THERE'S A ONE-MAN BAND AND HE'LL TOOT HIS FLUTE FOR YOU...
TTHP!
AOW!
COME FLY WITH ME...
LET'S TAKE OFF IN THE BLUE.

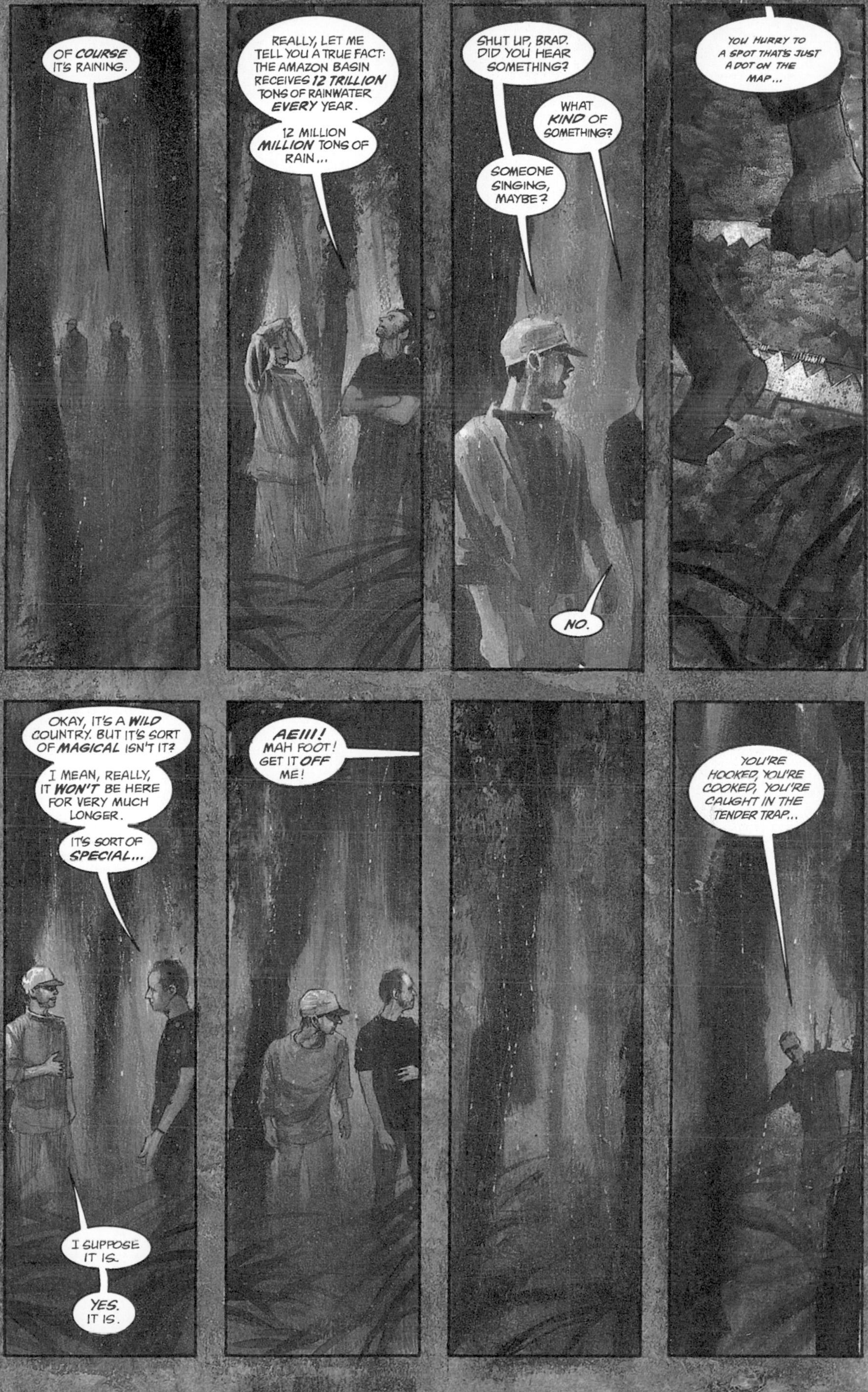
OF COURSE IT'S RAINING.
REALLY, LET ME TELL YOU A TRUE FACT: THE AMAZON BASIN RECEIVES 12 TRILLION TONS OF RAINWATER EVERY YEAR.
12 MILLION MILLION TONS OF RAIN...
SHUT UP, BRAD. DID YOU HEAR SOMETHING?
WHAT KIND OF SOMETHING?
SOMEONE SINGING, MAYBE?
NO.
YOU HURRY TO A SPOT THAT'S JUST A DOT ON THE MAP...
OKAY, IT'S A WILD COUNTRY. BUT IT'S SORT OF MAGICAL ISN'T IT?
I MEAN, REALLY, IT WON'T BE HERE FOR VERY MUCH LONGER.
IT'S SORT OF SPECIAL...
I SUPPOSE IT IS.
YES. IT IS.
AEIII! MAH FOOT! GET IT OFF ME!
YOU'RE HOOKED, YOU'RE COOKED, YOU'RE CAUGHT IN THE TENDER TRAP...

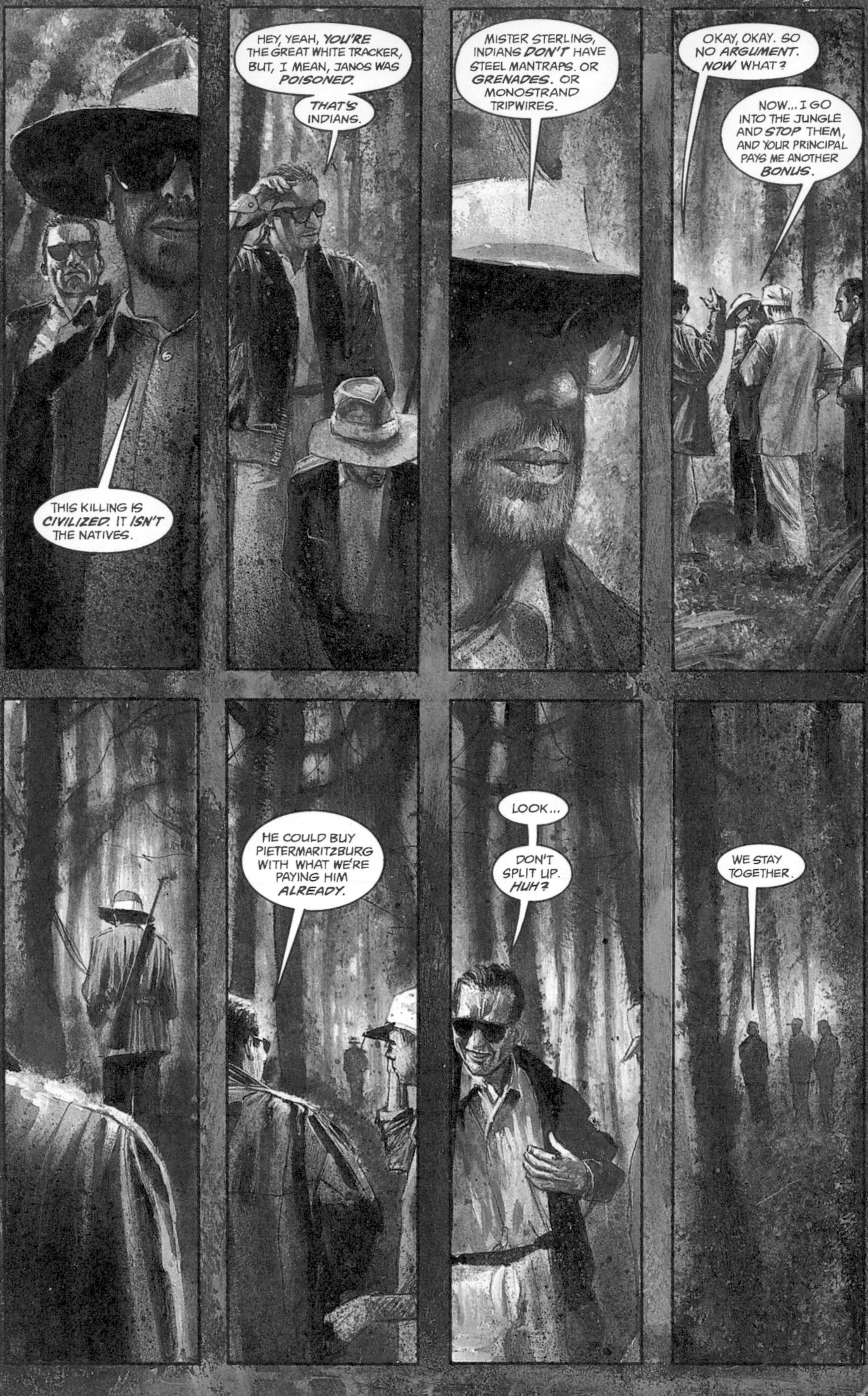

THIS KILLING IS CIVILIZED. IT ISN'T THE NATIVES.
HEY, YEAH, YOU'RE THE GREAT WHITE TRACKER, BUT, I MEAN, JANOS WAS POISONED.
THAT'S INDIANS.
MISTER STERLING, INDIANS DON'T HAVE STEEL MANTRAPS. OR GRENADES. OR MONOSTRAND TRIPWIRES.
OKAY, OKAY. SO NO ARGUMENT. NOW WHAT?
NOW... I GO INTO THE JUNGLE AND STOP THEM, AND YOUR PRINCIPAL PAYS ME ANOTHER BONUS.
HE COULD BUY PIETERMARITZBURG WITH WHAT WE'RE PAYING HIM ALREADY.
LOOK...
DON'T SPLIT UP. HUH?
WE STAY TOGETHER.

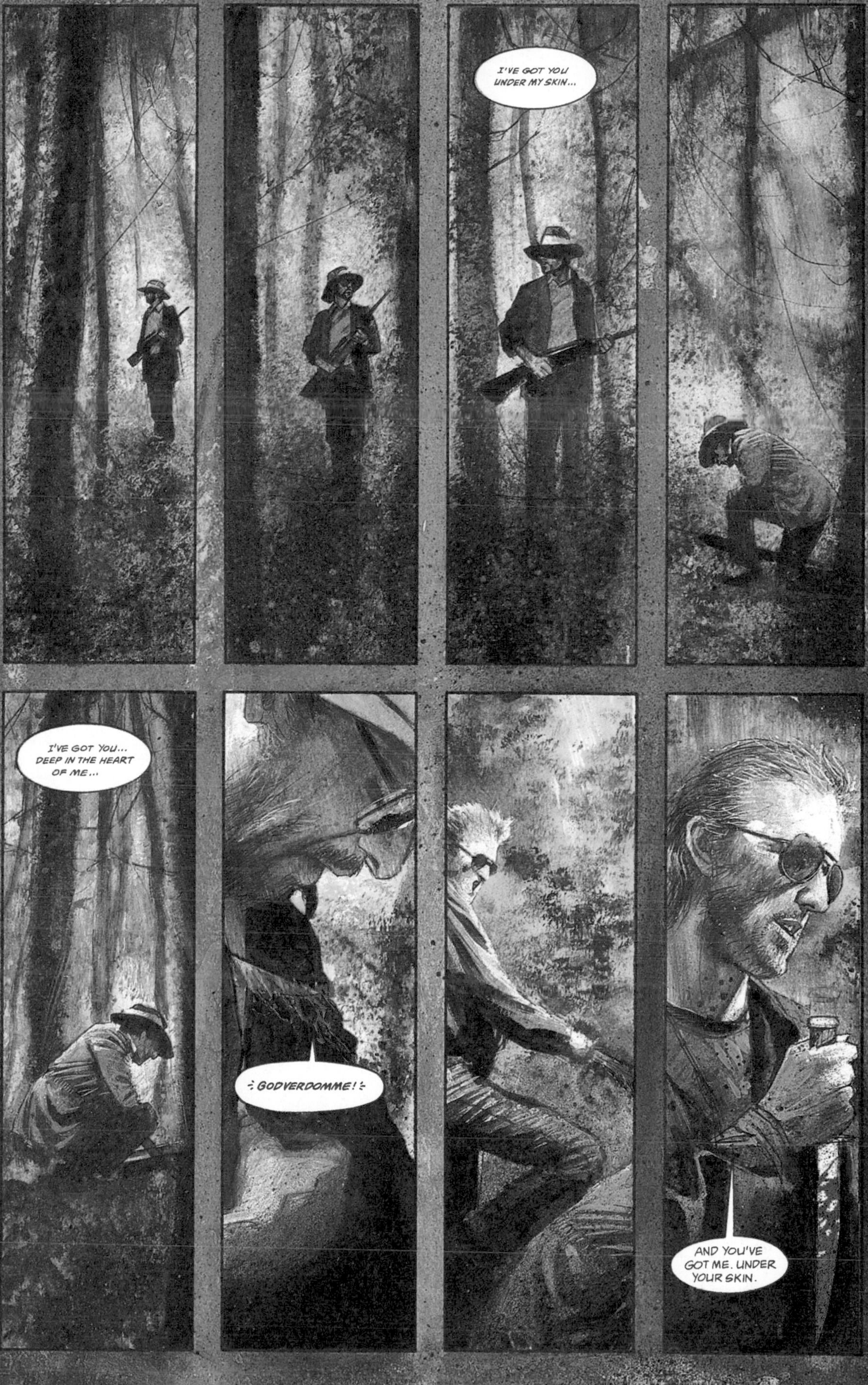
I'VE GOT YOU UNDER MY SKIN...
I'VE GOT YOU... DEEP IN THE HEART OF ME...
GODVERDOMME!
AND YOU'VE GOT ME. UNDER YOUR SKIN.

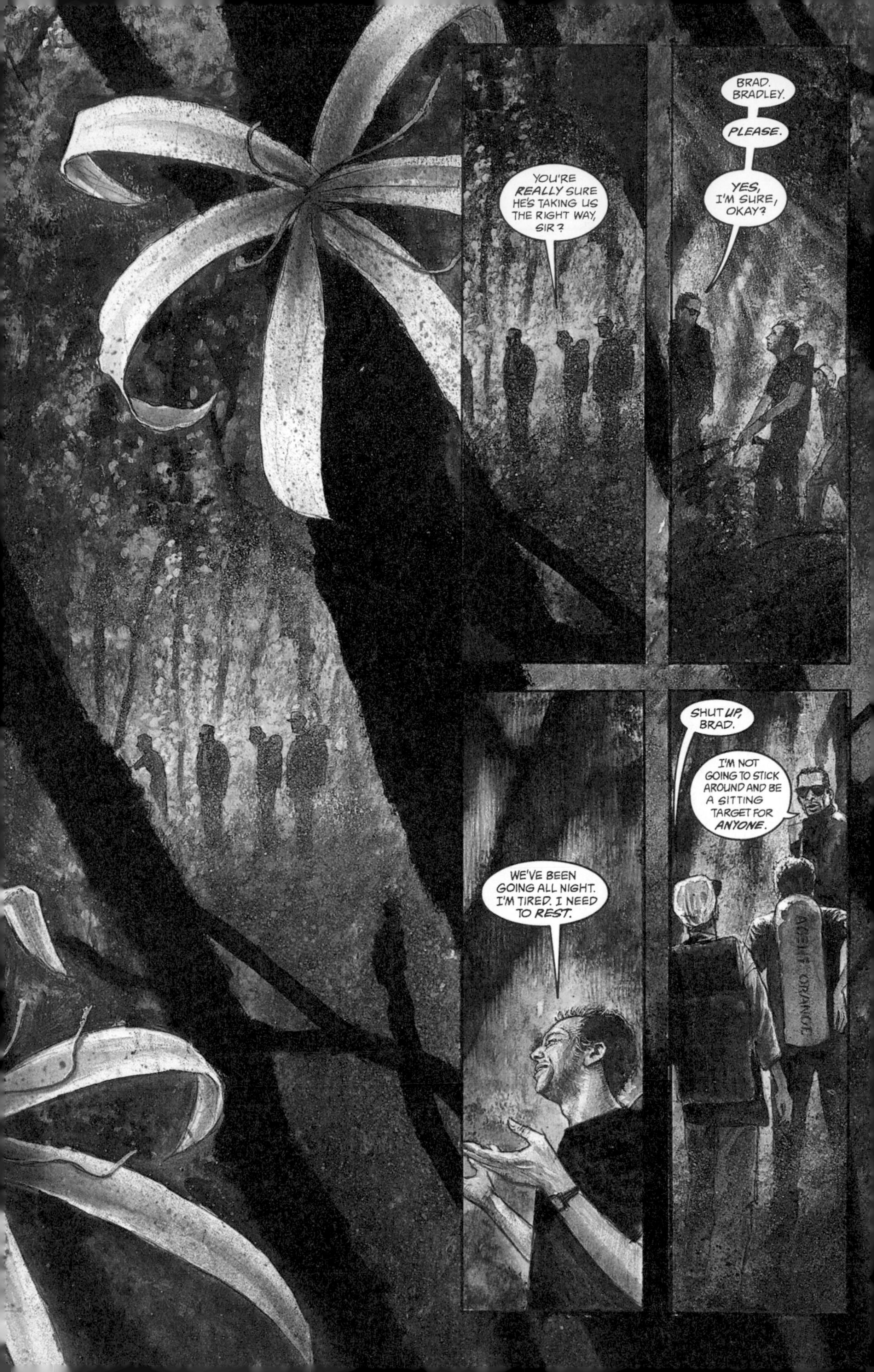
YOU'RE REALLY SURE HE'S TAKING US THE RIGHT WAY, SIR?
BRAD. BRADLEY.
PLEASE.
YES, I'M SURE, OKAY?
WE'VE BEEN GOING ALL NIGHT. I'M TIRED. I NEED TO REST.
SHUT UP, BRAD.
I'M NOT GOING TO STICK AROUND AND BE A SITTING TARGET FOR ANYONE.

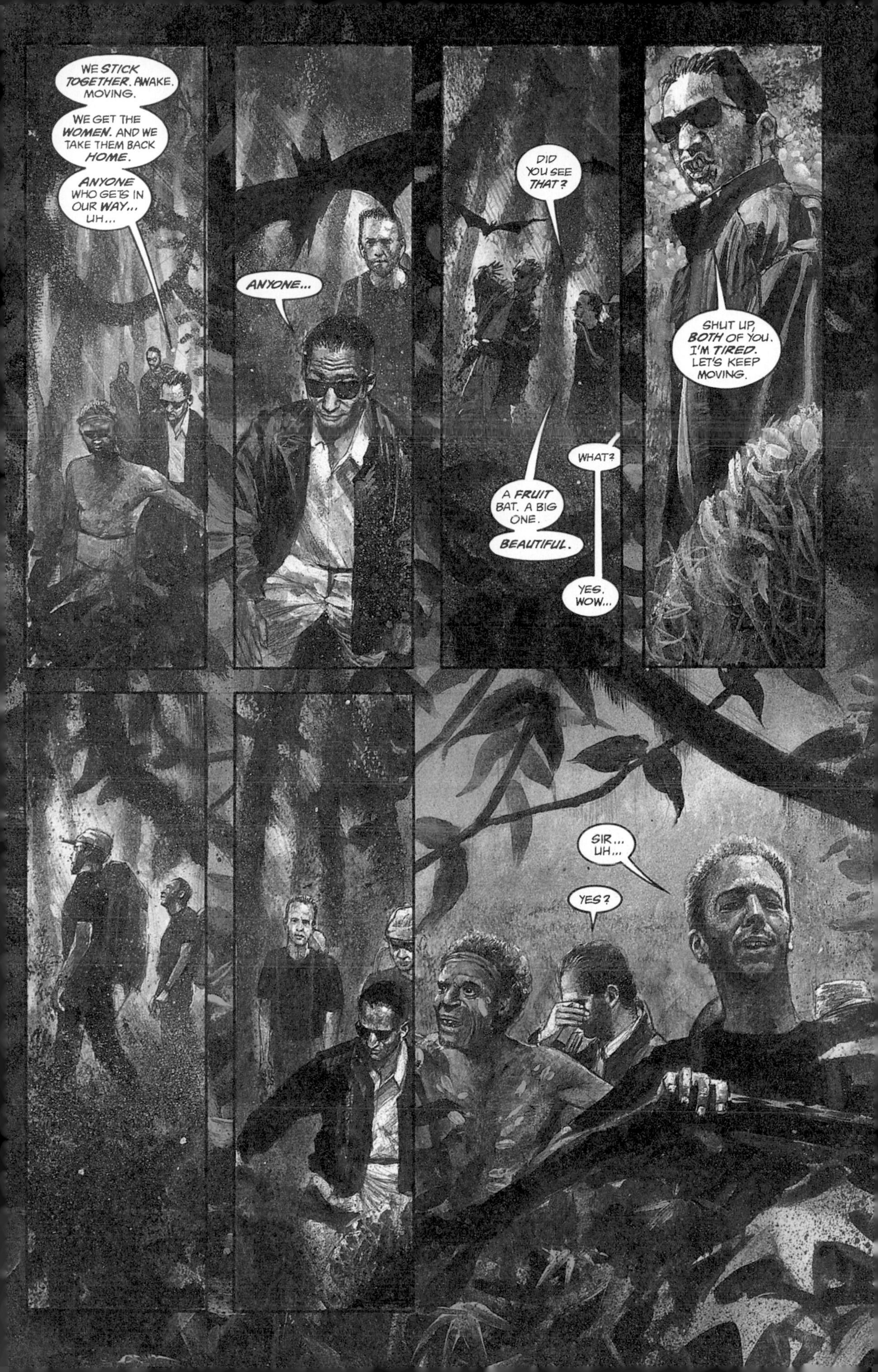
WE STICK TOGETHER. AWAKE. MOVING.
WE GET THE WOMEN. AND WE TAKE THEM BACK HOME.
ANYONE WHO GETS IN OUR WAY... UH...
ANYONE...
DID YOU SEE THAT?
WHAT?
A FRUIT BAT. A BIG ONE.
BEAUTIFUL.
YES. WOW...
SHUT UP, BOTH OF YOU. I'M TIRED. LET'S KEEP MOVING.
SIR... UH...
YES?

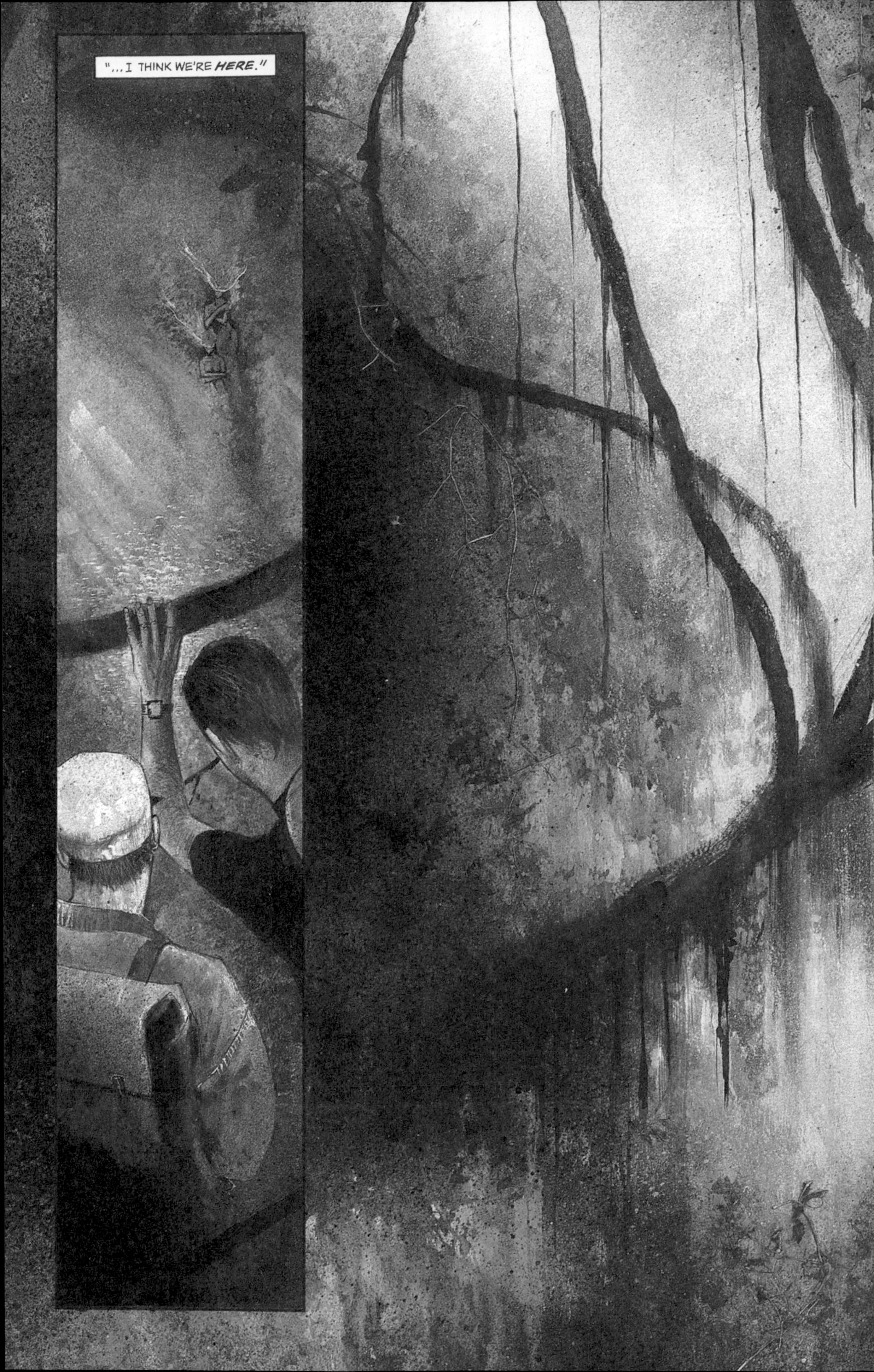
"...I THINK WE'RE HERE."

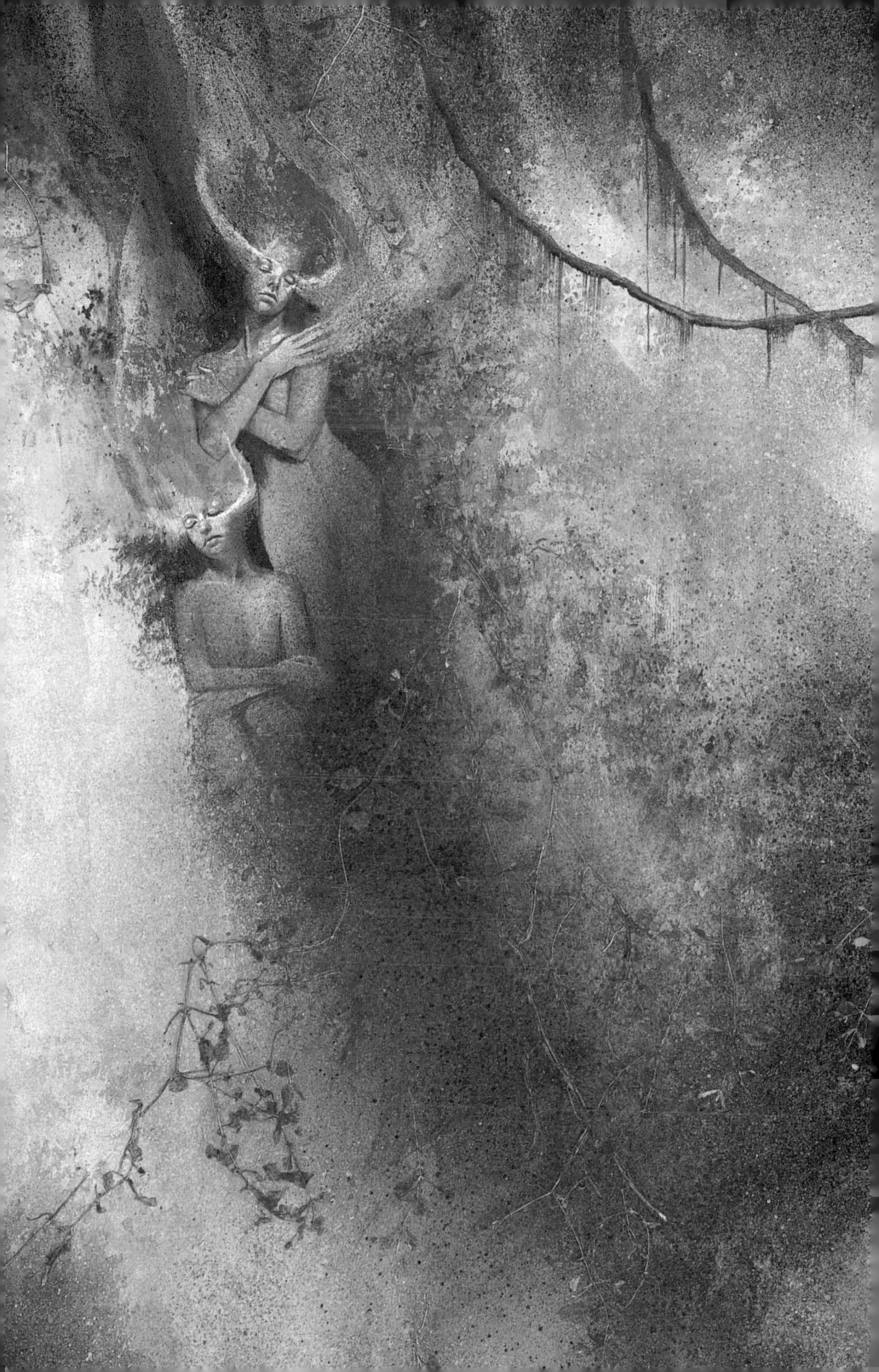

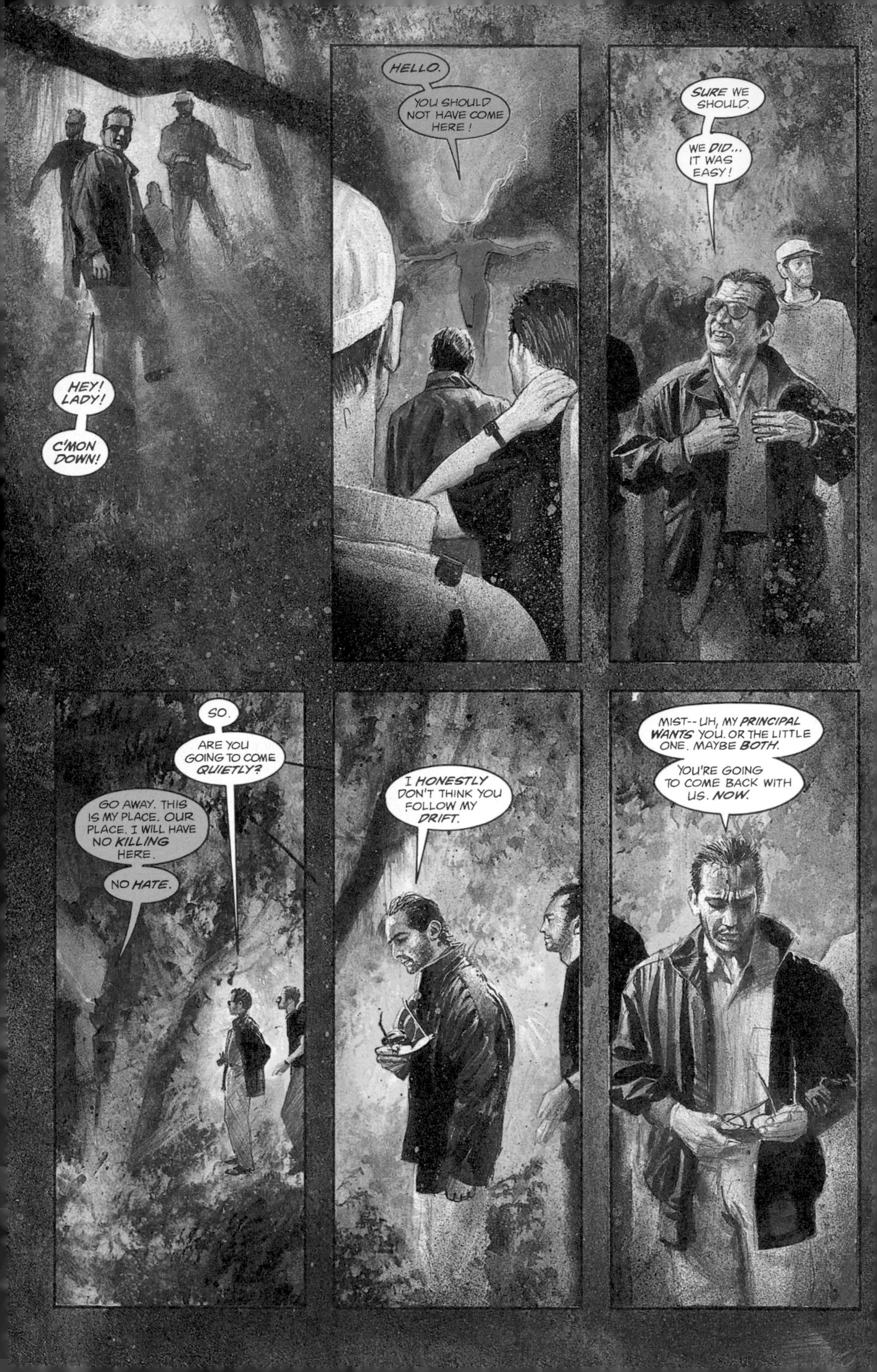
HEY! LADY!
C'MON DOWN!
HELLO.
YOU SHOULD NOT HAVE COME HERE!
SURE WE SHOULD.
WE DID... IT WAS EASY!
SO.
ARE YOU GOING TO COME QUIETLY?
GO AWAY. THIS IS MY PLACE. OUR PLACE. I WILL HAVE NO KILLING HERE.
NO HATE.
I HONESTLY DON'T THINK YOU FOLLOW MY DRIFT.
MIST-- UH, MY PRINCIPAL WANTS YOU. OR THE LITTLE ONE. MAYBE BOTH.
YOU'RE GOING TO COME BACK WITH US. NOW.

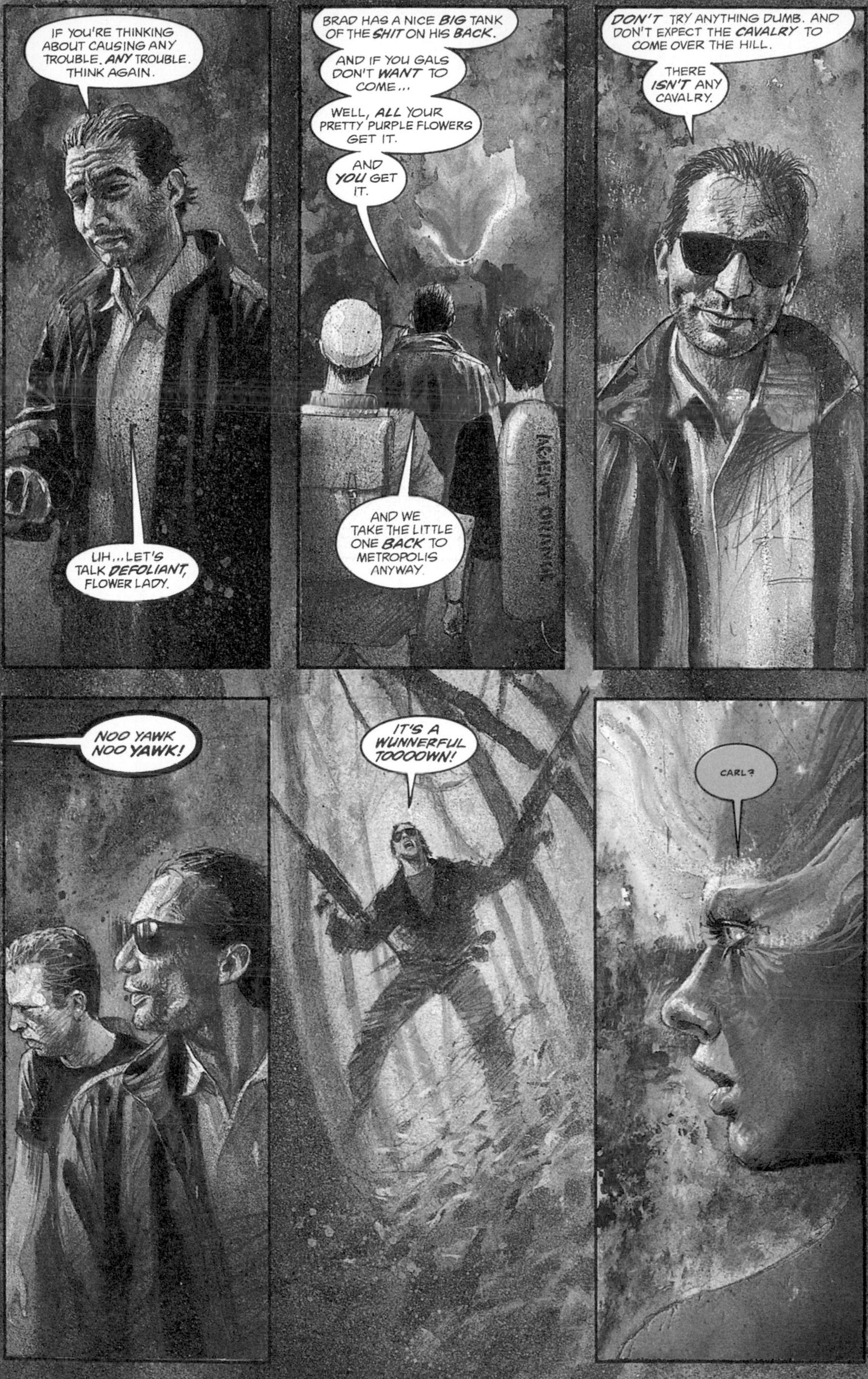
IF YOU'RE THINKING ABOUT CAUSING ANY TROUBLE. ANY TROUBLE. THINK AGAIN.
UH...LET'S TALK DEFOLIANT, FLOWER LADY.
BRAD HAS A NICE BIG TANK OF THE SHIT ON HIS BACK.
AND IF YOU GALS DON'T WANT TO COME...
WELL, ALL YOUR PRETTY PURPLE FLOWERS GET IT.
AND YOU GET IT.
AND WE TAKE THE LITTLE ONE BACK TO METROPOLIS ANYWAY.
AGENT ORANGE
DON'T TRY ANYTHING DUMB. AND DON'T EXPECT THE CAVALRY TO COME OVER THE HILL.
THERE ISN'T ANY CAVALRY.
NOO YAWK NOO YAWK!
IT'S A WUNNERFUL TOOOOWN!
CARL?

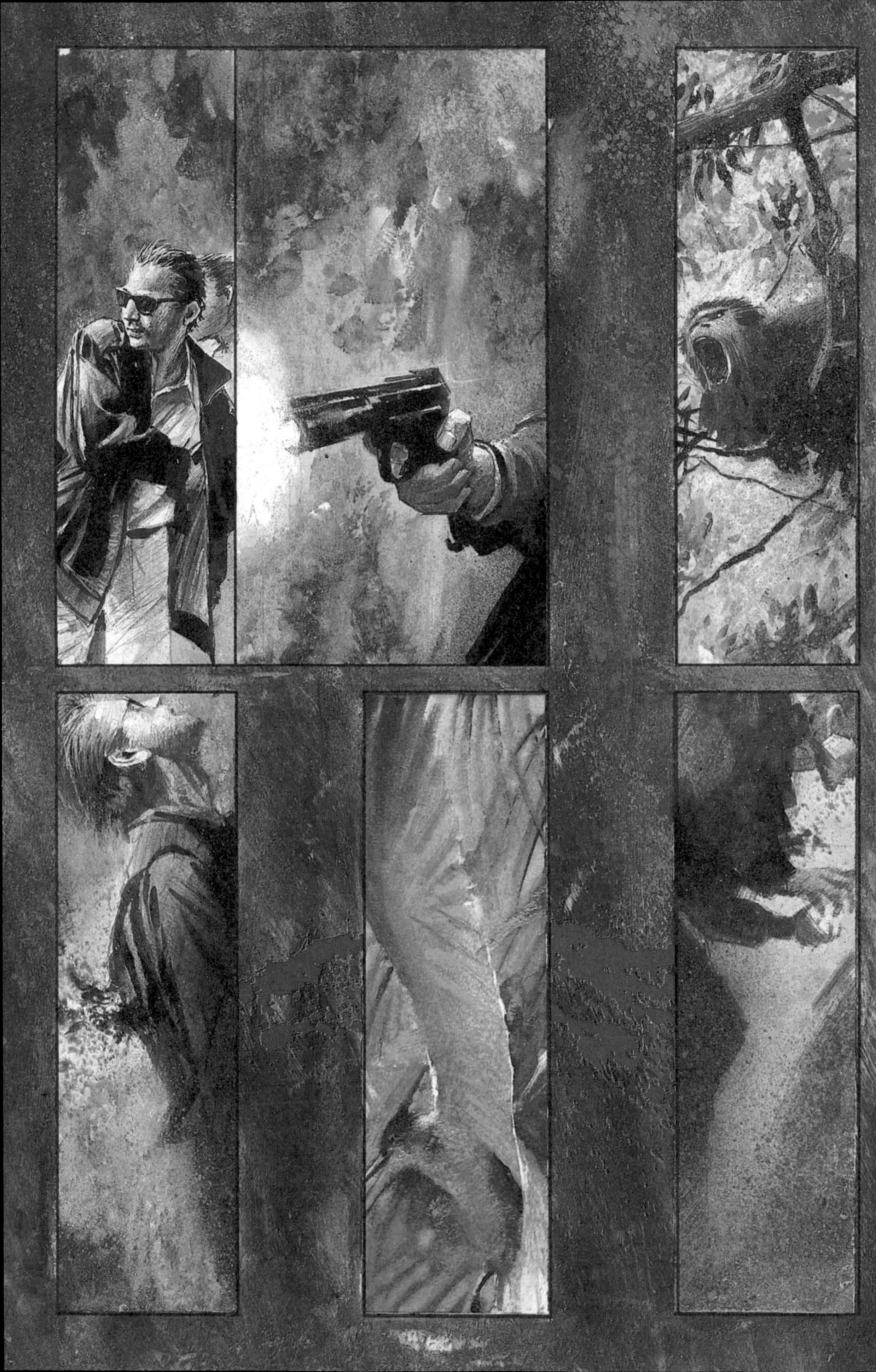

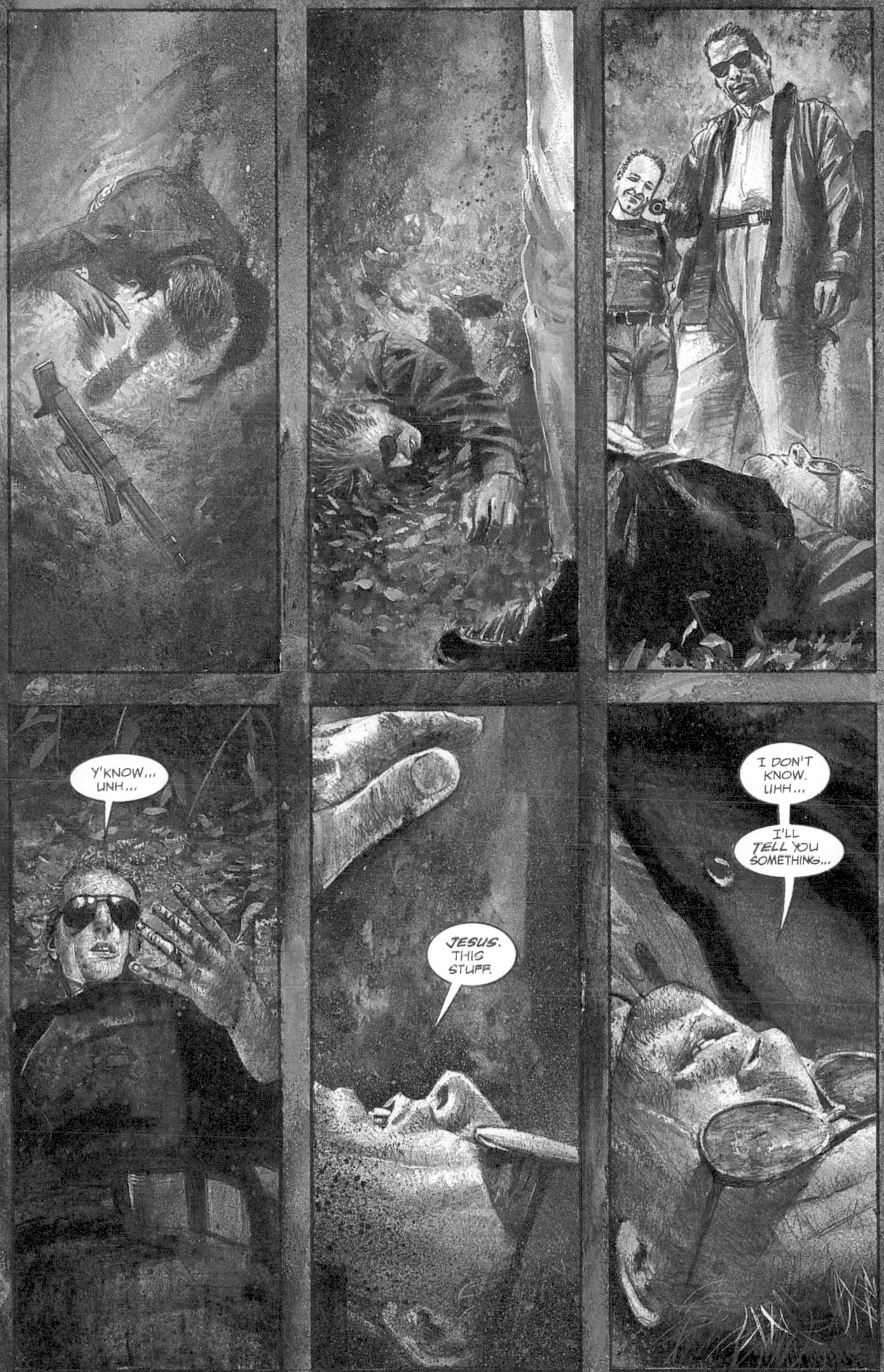
Y'KNOW... UNH...
JESUS. THIS STUFF.
I DON'T KNOW. UHH...
I'LL TELL YOU SOMETHING...

SHE ISN'T REAL. WE'VE BEEN RUNNING THROUGH THE JUNGLE AFTER A CRAZY DREAM...
NONE OF THIG STUFF...
NONE OF IT'S REAL...
SUSAN?
THERE'S NO SUCH THING AS... UH.
I'M GOING TO DIE. I'M REALLY GOING TO DIE. YOU BASTARDS KILLED ME.
HHHAHHH.
SAY G'BYE TO MISTER LUTHOR FOR ME.
YOU AREN'T SUSAN. YOU NEVER WERE.
YOU AREN'T ANYTHING...
AT LAST... THE END IS NEAR... AND I HAVE FACED...
THE FINAL...
UT.

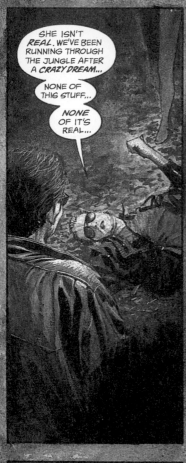

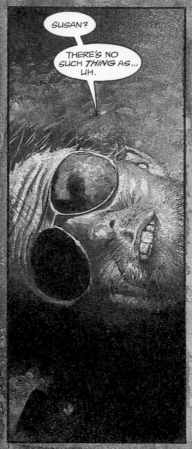

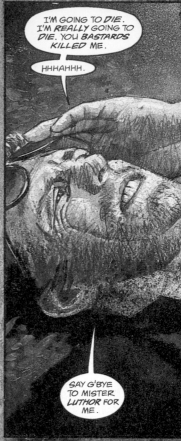

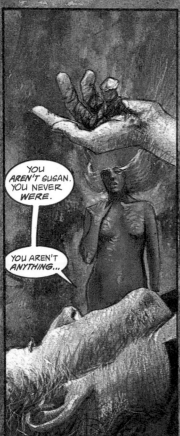

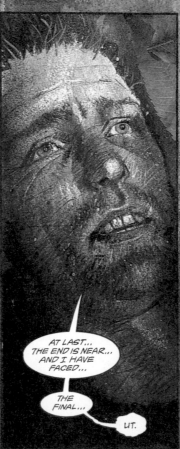

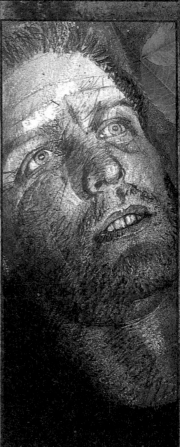

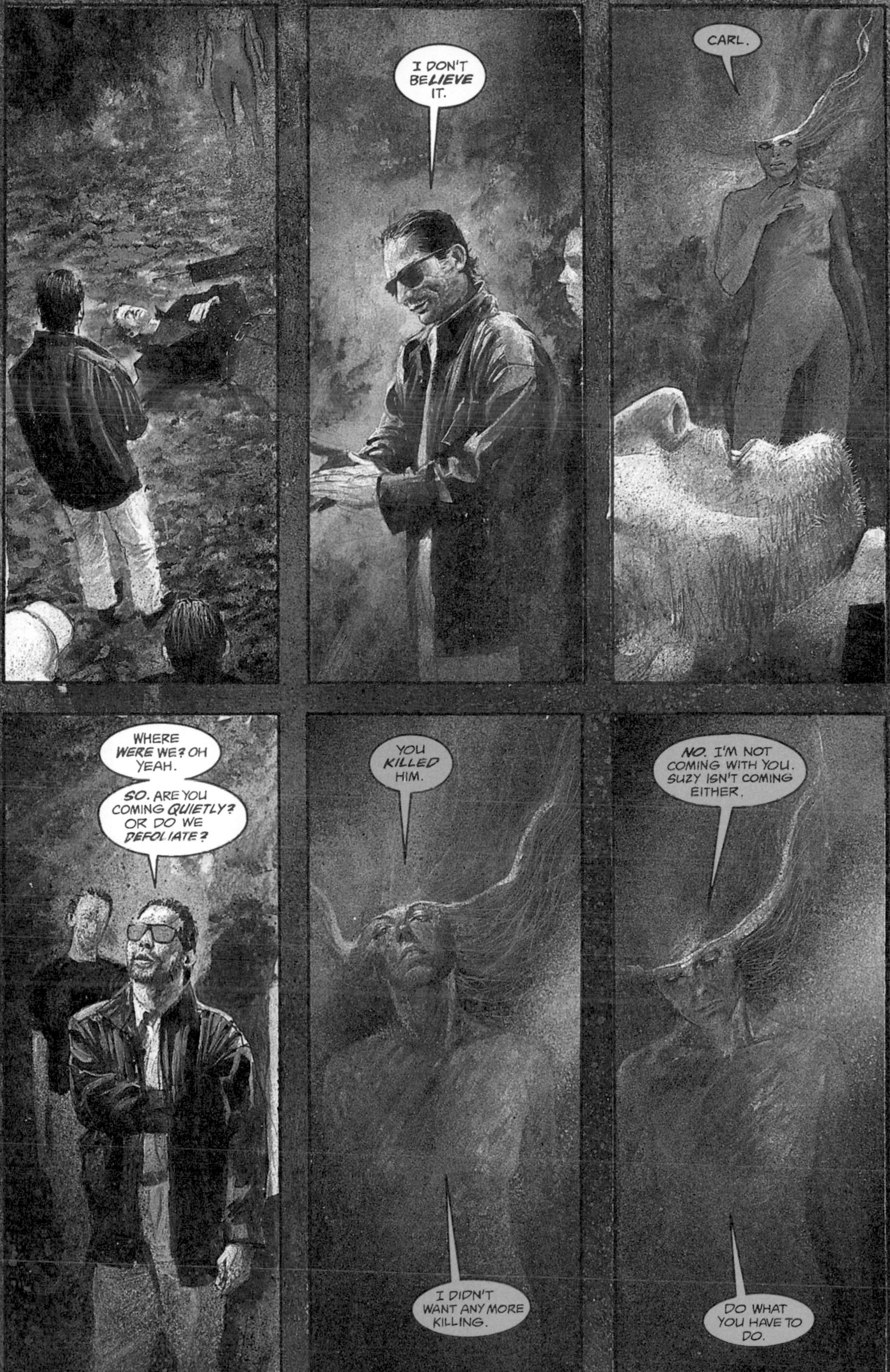
I DON'T BELIEVE IT.
CARL.
WHERE WERE WE? OH YEAH.
SO. ARE YOU COMING QUIETLY? OR DO WE DEFOLIATE?
YOU KILLED HIM.
I DIDN'T WANT ANY MORE KILLING.
NO. I'M NOT COMING WITH YOU. SUZY ISN'T COMING EITHER.
DO WHAT YOU HAVE TO DO.

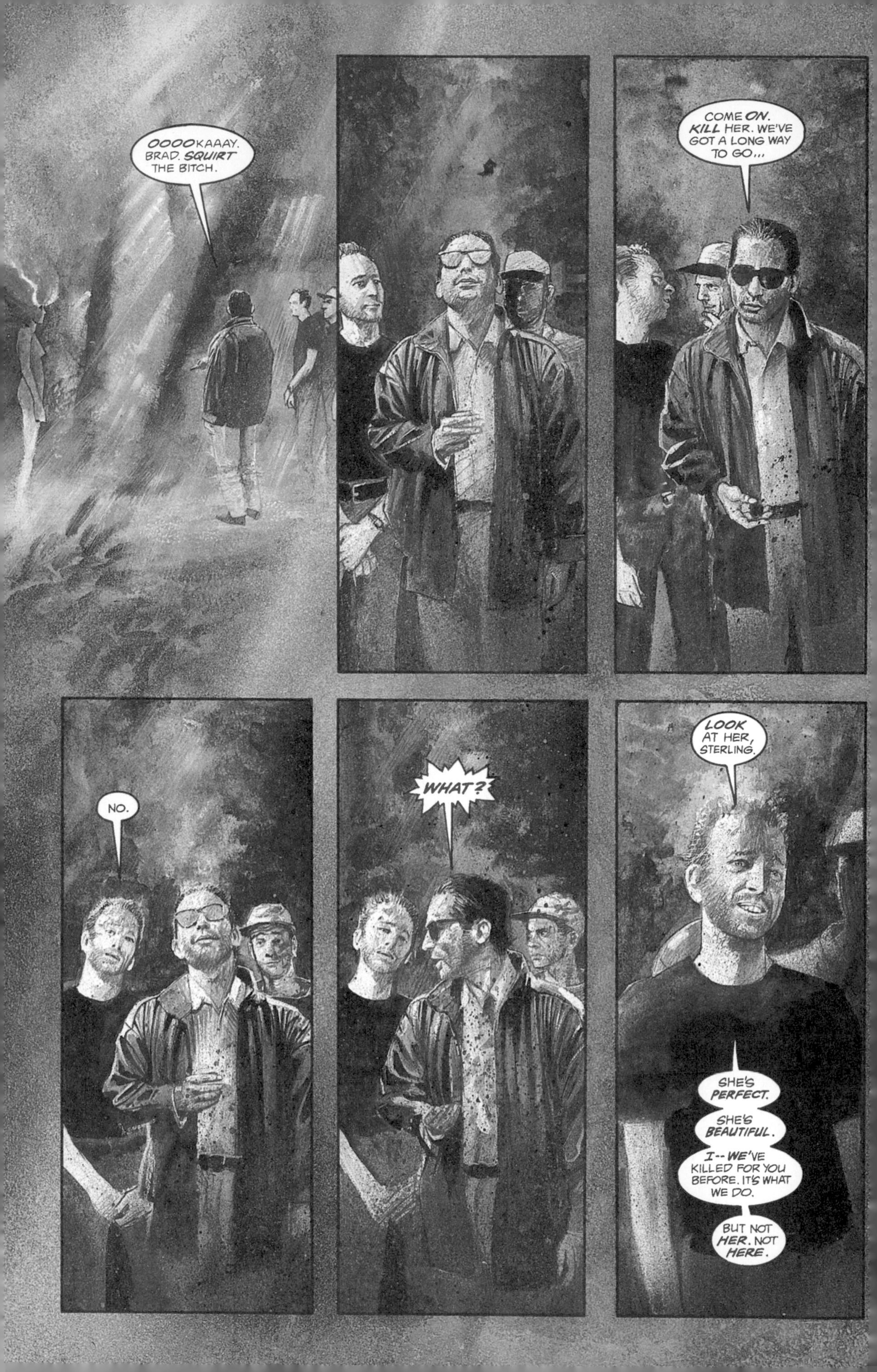
OOOOKAAAY. BRAD. SQUIRT THE BITCH.
COME ON. KILL HER. WE'VE GOT A LONG WAY TO GO...
NO.
WHAT?
LOOK AT HER, STERLING.
SHE'S PERFECT.
SHE'S BEAUTIFUL.
I--WE'VE KILLED FOR YOU BEFORE. IT'S WHAT WE DO.
BUT NOT HER. NOT HERE.

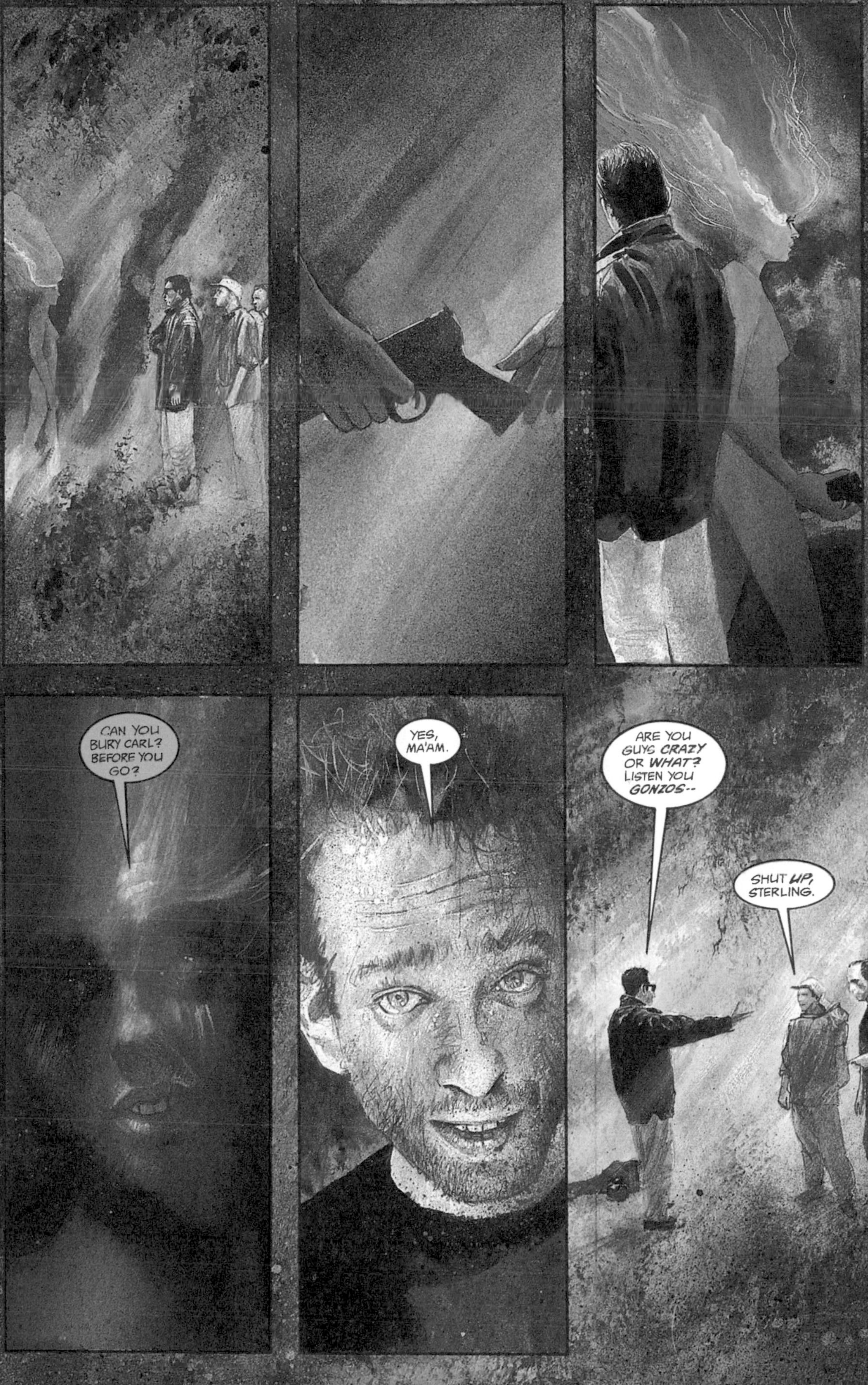
CAN YOU BURY CARL? BEFORE YOU GO?
YES, MA'AM.
ARE YOU GUYS CRAZY OR WHAT? LISTEN YOU GONZOS--
SHUT UP, STERLING.

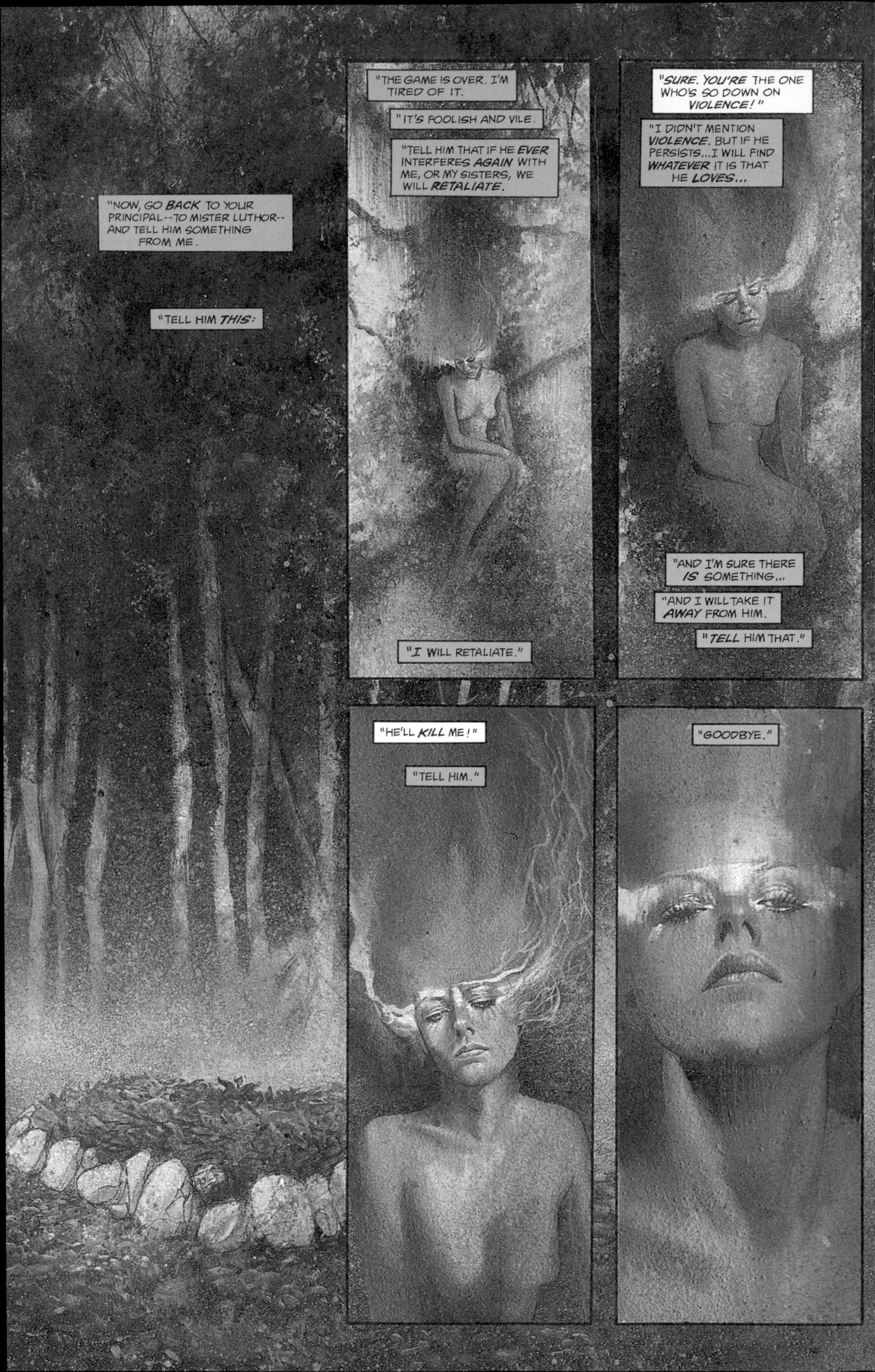

"NOW, GO *BACK* TO YOUR PRINCIPAL--TO MISTER LUTHOR-- AND TELL HIM SOMETHING FROM ME.

"TELL HIM *THIS*:

"THE GAME IS OVER. I'M TIRED OF IT.

"IT'S FOOLISH AND VILE.

"TELL HIM THAT IF HE *EVER* INTERFERES *AGAIN* WITH ME, OR MY SISTERS, WE WILL *RETALIATE*.

"*I* WILL RETALIATE."

"*SURE. YOU'RE* THE ONE WHO'S SO DOWN ON *VIOLENCE!*"

"I DIDN'T MENTION *VIOLENCE*. BUT IF HE PERSISTS...I WILL FIND *WHATEVER* IT IS THAT HE *LOVES*...

"AND I'M SURE THERE *IS* SOMETHING...

"AND I WILL TAKE IT *AWAY* FROM HIM.

"*TELL* HIM THAT."

"HE'LL *KILL* ME!"

"TELL HIM."

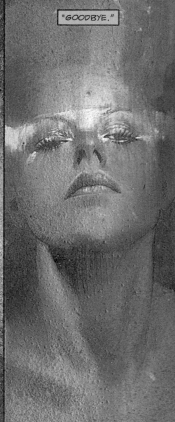

"GOODBYE."

MOM.

SUZY?

YOU AREN'T HAPPY HERE, ARE YOU? NOT ANY MORE.

THE SISTERS ARE GROWING FINE. IT'LL BE *YEARS* BEFORE THEY'RE PEOPLE.

I TALKED TO THE INDIANS.

YOU *TALKED*...?

IT'S EASY. THEY SAY THEY COULD LOOK AFTER THE VALLEY.

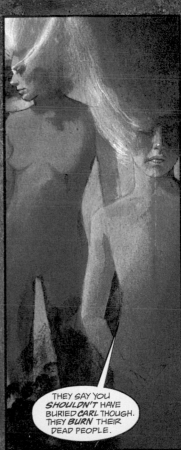

THEY SAY YOU *SHOULDN'T* HAVE BURIED *CARL* THOUGH. THEY *BURN* THEIR DEAD PEOPLE.

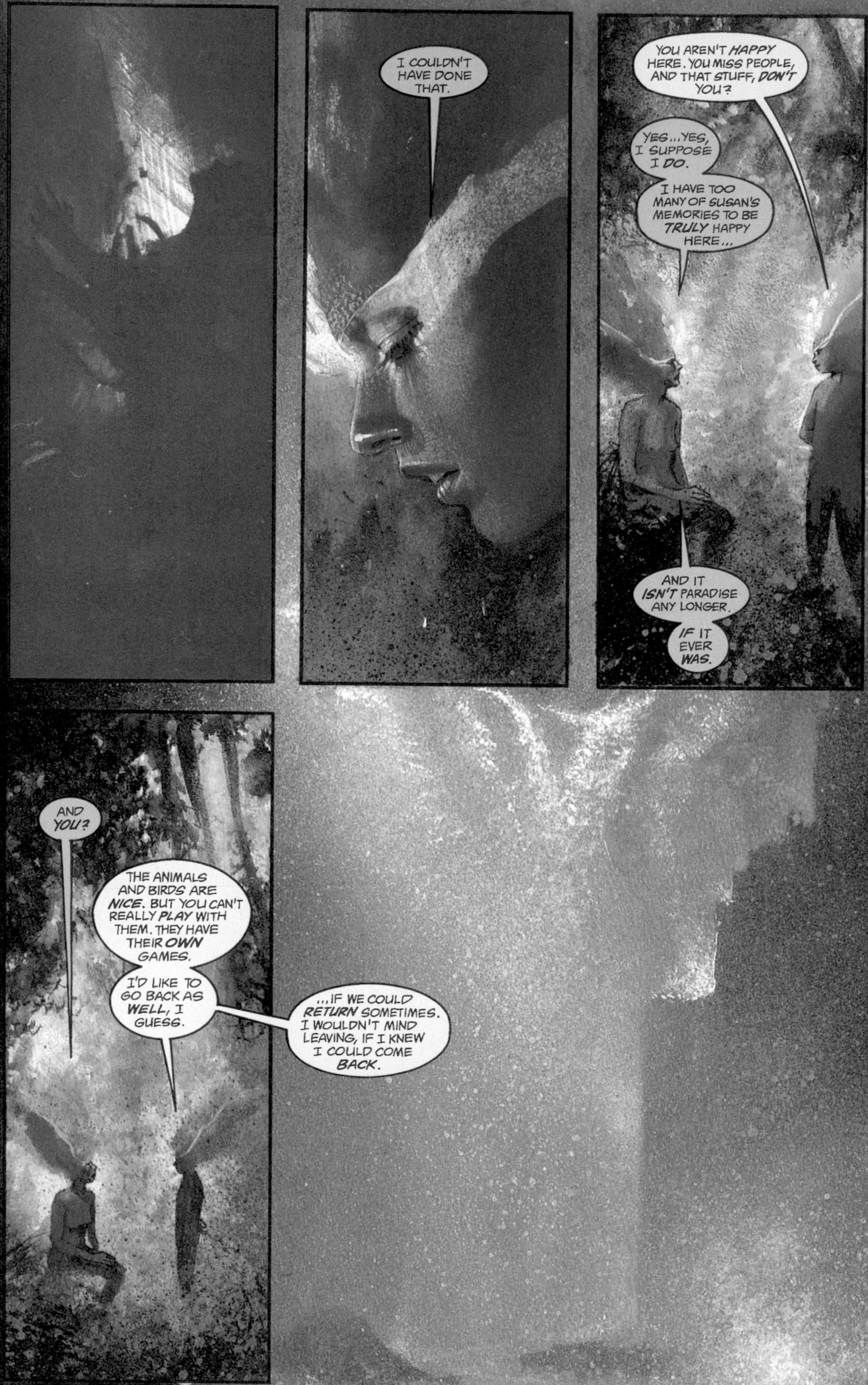
I COULDN'T HAVE DONE THAT.
YOU AREN'T HAPPY HERE. YOU MISS PEOPLE, AND THAT STUFF, DON'T YOU?
YES...YES, I SUPPOSE I DO.
I HAVE TOO MANY OF SUSAN'S MEMORIES TO BE TRULY HAPPY HERE...
AND IT ISN'T PARADISE ANY LONGER.
IF IT EVER WAS.
AND YOU?
THE ANIMALS AND BIRDS ARE NICE. BUT YOU CAN'T REALLY PLAY WITH THEM. THEY HAVE THEIR OWN GAMES.
I'D LIKE TO GO BACK AS WELL, I GUESS.
...IF WE COULD RETURN SOMETIMES. I WOULDN'T MIND LEAVING, IF I KNEW I COULD COME BACK.

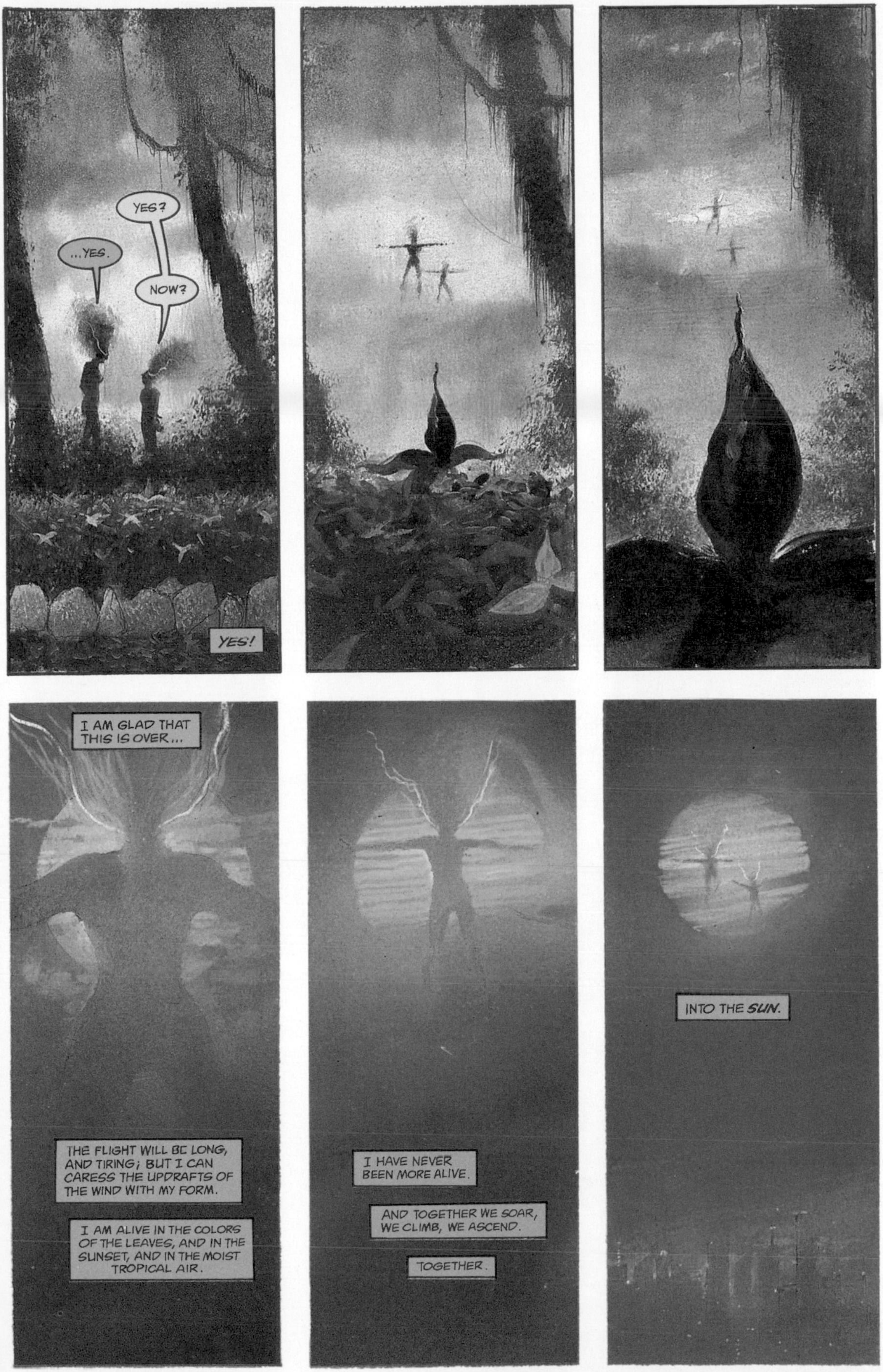
YES?
...YES.
NOW?
YES!
I AM GLAD THAT THIS IS OVER...
THE FLIGHT WILL BE LONG, AND TIRING; BUT I CAN CARESS THE UPDRAFTS OF THE WIND WITH MY FORM.
I AM ALIVE IN THE COLORS OF THE LEAVES, AND IN THE SUNSET, AND IN THE MOIST TROPICAL AIR.
I HAVE NEVER BEEN MORE ALIVE.
AND TOGETHER WE SOAR, WE CLIMB, WE ASCEND.
TOGETHER.
INTO THE SUN.

i thank You God for most this amazing
day: for the leaping greenly spirits of trees
and a blue true dream of sky; and for everything
which is natural which is infinite which is **yes**
(i who have died am alive again today,
and this is the sun's birthday; this is the birth
day of life and love and wings: and of the gay
great happening illimitably earth)

e. e. cummings

A C K N O W L E D G E M E N T S

No one is alone, nothing occurs in a vacuum. There are a number of people without whose work, artistry, inspiration or physical attributes this work would not exist.

Chief among them are Sheldon Mayer, Tony DeZuniga and Joe Orlando, who created the original Black Orchid to fly through our imaginations over fifteen years ago.

We owe thanks to Len Wein and Bernie Wrightson, Alan Moore, Steve Bissette, John Totleben and Rick Veitch for Swamp Thing; to Marv Wolfman for the new Luthor; to the many descendants of Bob Kane and Bill Finger for the protector and inhabitants of Gotham; to Denny O'Neil for Arkham.

Thanks to our stars: Gilda Lee Filsner, Neil Jones, Ed Wilson, Igor Goldkind, Leigh Baulch, Dick Jude, Dave ("the drunk in the bar") McKean, Jon Harrison, Rolie Green, Alan Mitchell, Aimee Horsting, Charlotte and Emma Carter, Clare Haythornthwaite, M. Brando, Helen Waring, Tony Stochmal, and the Cafe Munchen. Thanks to Splash of Paint Design, and to Garry Leach, Win Wiacek and Dave Elliott.

And special thanks to Bill Sienkiewicz, for his amoral support.

Neil Gaiman
Dave McKean
1991

Cuttings

Notes, sketches and excerpts from Neil Gaiman.

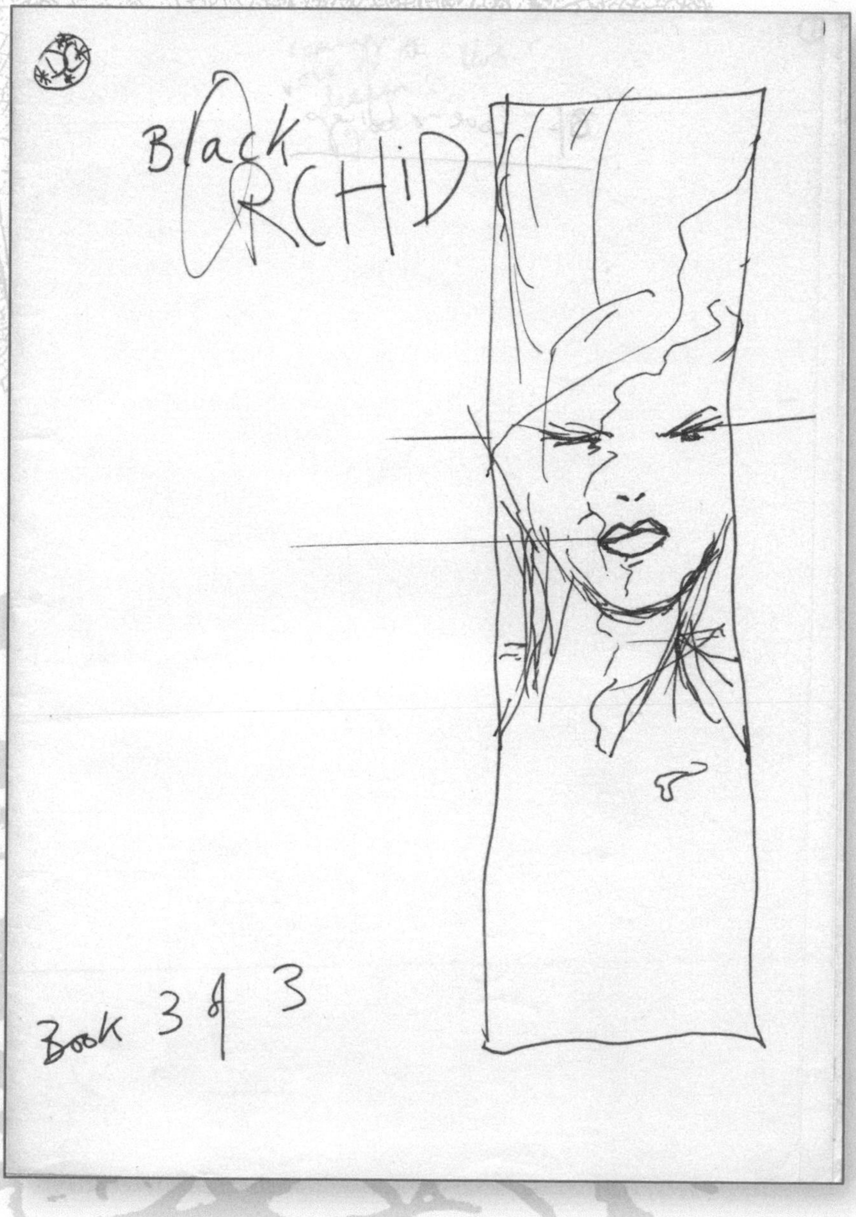
Black
ORCHID
Book 3 of 3

A thumbnail sketch for the cover to issue #3.

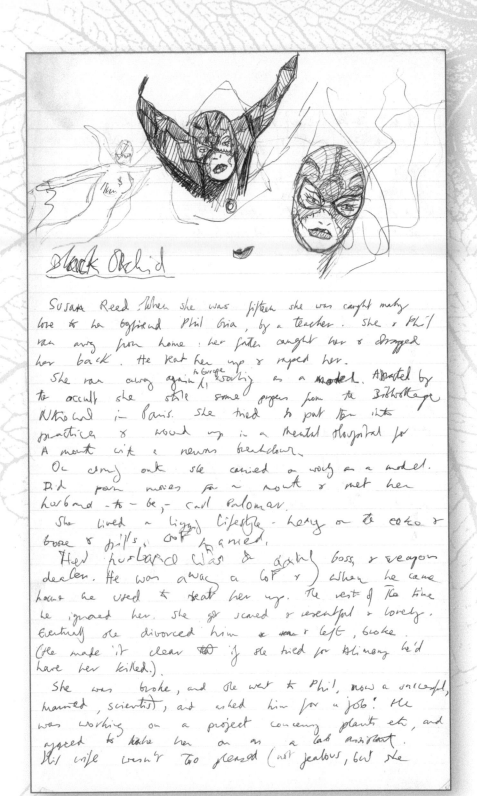

Black Orchid

Susan Reed. When she was fifteen she was caught making love to her boyfriend Phil Gria, by a teacher. She & Phil ran away from home : her father caught her & dragged her back. He beat her up & raped her.

She ran away again to Europe, working as a model. Attracted by the occult she stole some papers from the Bibliothèque Nationale in Paris. She tried to put them into practice & wound up in a mental hospital for a month with a nervous breakdown.

On coming out she carried on working as a model. Did porn movies for a month & met her husband-to-be,— Carl Paloman.

She lived a [illegible] lifestyle - heavy on the coke & booze & pills, got married.

Her husband was a drug boss, & weapons dealer. He was away a lot &) when he came home he used to beat her up. The rest of the time he ignored her. She got scared & resentful & lonely. Eventually she divorced him & left, broke. (He made it clear that if she tried for alimony he'd have her killed.)

She was broke, and she went to Phil, now a successful, married, scientist, and asked him for a job. He was working on a project concerning plants etc, and agreed to take her on as a lab assistant. His wife wasn't too pleased (not jealous, but she

Early brainstorming for the story from Gaiman's notebook.

didn't like Sue much, cos she danced & smoked too much & played loud Rock & Roll).

Phil was tempted by the potential destruction of the Amazon rain forest & is (works) a genetic bio-engineer: it occurs to him that if he can create vegetable people they would & happen — they could breathe CO_2 ...

(It is to be presumed that he corresponded with Dr Jason Woodrue at this time)

Then Sue was subpoena'd to testify against her ex-husband. Rather than run the risk, Carl had her executed.

Phil extracted RNA/DNA from the still warm body & bio-engineered it with plant cells. He planted it in the greenhouse:

A year later he had a fully grown Black Orchid. She possessed some — not all — of her Sue's memories, but was a great deal less screwed up. She could also fly, extrude latex masks, and grew orchids. Her costume (petals) were almost impenetrable & her strength amazing. She was a vegetable / animal hybrid, and she wanted her own back on her husband & the Syndicators.

[Black Canary — Adventure 428—430) etc.]

part 3
— rose & Thorn?

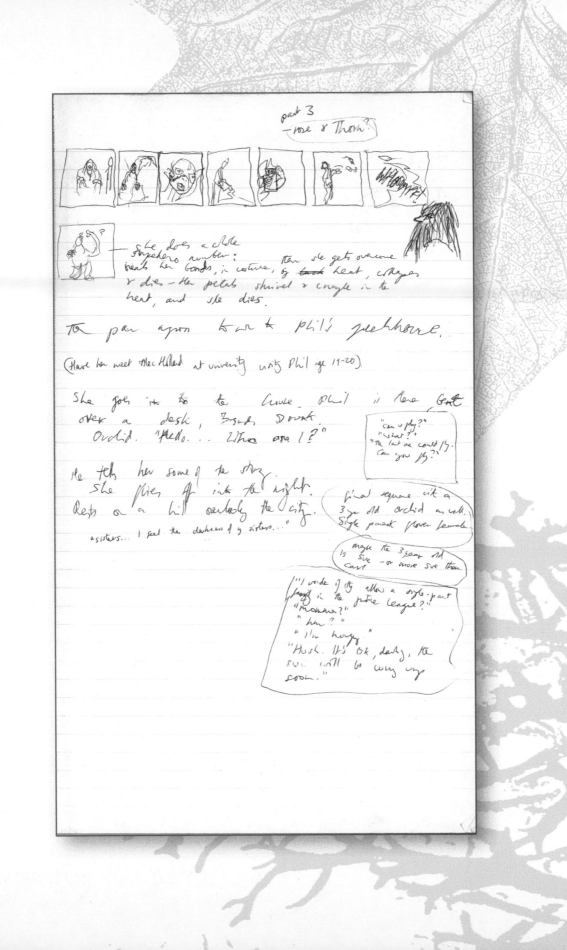

She does a little
superhero number:
breaks her bonds, in costume, then she gets overcome
by too much heat, collapses
& dies — her petals shrivel & crumple in the
heat, and she dies.

The pan again to we to Phil's greenhouse.

(Have her meet Alec Holland at university until Phil age 17-20).

She goes into to the house. Phil is there bent
over a desk, fighting Drunk
Orchid. "Hello... Who am I?"

"Can u fly?"
"What?"
"The last one could fly.
Can you fly?"

He tells her some of the story.
She flies off into the night.
Rests on a hill overlooking the city.

"sisters... I feel the darkness of my sisters..."

final sequence with a
3 yr old orchid as well.
Single parent flower female.

maybe the 3 year old
is Sue
cast — or more Sue than

"I wonder if they allow a single-parent
[   ] in the Justice League?"
"momma?"
"hm?"
" I'm hungry."
"Hush. It's OK, darling, the
sun will be coming very very
soon."

DC COMICS INC.
666 Fifth Avenue
New York, New York 10103
(212) 484-2847

Karen Berger/Editor

3/26/87

Dear Neil,

   Hi! My apologies again for the delay in getting this letter
out. Things seemed to get the better of me around here the
last week or so, but life is back on track and less overwhelming.
Okay, now on to the Black Orchid --

   As I mentioned to you on the phone last week, I really like
the concept you've developed for the character and the series.
I do think, though, that a bit of streamlining and simplifying
needs to be done on some of the more complicated elements, as
well as a harder push on the stronger, dramatic elements. Greg
Weisman, who's assisting me on the British material, and I
had a long lunch about the series and together we came up with
a bunch of questions, possible solutions, and story directions.
I'd like to stress that these are all suggestions and not meant
to weigh you down. We both got really excited about the series
and got a little carried away. I'll try to be as brief and
succinct as possible.

   First, I admire your desire to tie everything ever established
about the character into your story. But, to my mind, some things
seem a little weird now, and don't make much sense, considering
the dual human/vegetable nature--like the latex mask. Since she
① is very much a flower, she can alter her cosmetic appearance
in a more natural and organic fashion by blooming(or unblooming),
and thus, she still remains a master of disguise. The mask just
doesn't work with her new "natural" being, personality.

   The powers of the new (2nd) Black Orchid should also evolve
from her nature. Just like Swamp Thing can control his form,
② she should be able to as well, but in a different and limited
way. She might be able to control her density--at high density,
she could have super-strength; at low density, she'd be light enough

A Warner Communications Company

Comments from editor Karen Berger.

to fly, with butterfly-like petals. Maybe a color change when
she changes density, too. The idea of her growing a special
calling-card orchid is real good.

Onto Susan (the original) --

③ 　First, you might want to change her name because of the similarity
to Susan and Reed Richards from the Fantastic Four. I'm sure you
could come up with some other great metaphor.

④ 　Second, it might be good if we really play up Susan's victimization
to make her more realistic. If she was an abused child, she would
likely seek out an abusive relationship where she should would still
remain the victim, like with Carl Thorne. Emotionally, Carl is
sick, he gets drunk, and beats his wife, maybe even to death. The
thug thing is indirect. Phil could testify at Carl's trial, and Carl
⑤ is sent to prison on voluntary manslaughter. This gives the 2 guys
a real reason to hate each other.

　Third, the college brain trust is a great idea. Maybe we can add
⑥ a couple of others who "grew up" in the DC Universe like Jenette
Klyburn of STAR Labs, for example.

　Getting back to Carl-- in his own way, he probably loved Susan.
⑦ It might be good to set up a destructive cycle where when Susan
crashes with Phil after being beaten, Carl comes back apologetic,
with candy and flowers. Phil would watch sadly as she went back to Carl.

BLACK ORCHID #1--

⑧ 　It's a good idea to remain vague about her, but I'd strongly
advise against her retaining an "intellectual" memory of Susan's
experiences. It would be more effective if she retained just an
emotional memory, (the same for Black Orchid #2, more on that later).
Since Carl was in prison during her existence, Phil could have
a very positive influence on her. She's crime fighter, but we need
a good reason for her to have chosen this life. Again, maybe
Phil's influence or maybe something that happens to her when she's
first "born."(I'd need to know more on Susan's technological know-how.
⑨ Did her life afford her the time for intense studying? Maybe, as
a complete and utter diversionary life-saver from her messed-up life
at home?) The first Black Orchid could have really had the opportunity ⑩

enhance that training.

⑩ I'd also suggest that in your first scene here, the "death by
fire" is a little too close to Swamp Thing's. Maybe just a shotgun
to the back of her head.

NEW BLACK ORCHID -- OUR HERO

Like her predecessor, she has an emotional memory of Susan's life.
She's pretty confused, because Carl is out of prison, and she has
strange feelings of love and fear for this violent man.
⑪ * Instead of stopping the story here to have Phil reveal her origin,
perhaps the series can be structured as a mystery that reveals pieces
of the puzzle, so that by the end of the series, the reader and
Black Orchid knows the full secret origin behind the original Black
Orchard, and Susan. Phil, of course, would be extremely important
here, but a) maybe he doesn't want to reveal the secret story.
Crushed by Susan's death, he hopes to recreate her, perhaps, in
addition to furthering his scientific theories. b) Phil should
get killed, ~~possibly~~ probably by Carl, so then Black Orchid would be truly
alone in deciphering these strange feelings and mixed memories
⑫ that haunt her. Swamp Thing could be used as a key person in
giving her clues to her identity. There's also the irony that Swampy
for a long time thought he was in a sense what Black Orchid is.
We'd have to stay away from the Floronic Man, though, because he's
already spoken for in another major series, that will end up
⑬ altering him a lot. Maybe Poison Ivy?

⑭ Last but, not least, is the Black Orchid baby. I love the little
kid, but let's make him a little older, maybe 5 or 6. It'll make
situations more plausible. There's also a lot that could be done
⑮ with the single parent idea. It would also be great to create more
of a personal life for ~~our hero,~~ Black Orchid, and to give her little quirks
that relate to her half-flower essence. Something with bees, honey,
water, perfume, tea... Not to rip off anything from Swampy's seasonal
"attire"-- but, maybe she's stronger in the spring or summer?...

Anyway, I've said enough for now.   I know how quickly you rushed
out your "pre-proposal"-- and considering all that, you came up
with a lot of good stuff. I'd suggest the next step is to tighten

up the plot, and breakdown the story into 5 or how many parts you
need. At this point, I'd think about 27 page format. If we do
get a "Prestige" format book out of this, we could adjust.

Thanks again for your patience, Neil. I hope I didn't ramble too
much. Give me a call after you've received this.

Take Care--

Best,

BLACK ORCHID.

We are at a meeting of a large crime syndicate. It's an executive boardroom conference, with representatives from most of the underworld there - ten men and one woman. Business is just being wrapped up when the Chairman presses a button, the door opens, and four large thugs, armed with everything short of thermo-nuclear weaponry, come in, and take up positions around the woman. Steel restraints come out of the chair, imprisoning her arms, legs and torso.

The Chairman reaches over and pulls her face-mask off. Underneath is the familiar purple mask of the Black Orchid.

"I thought it was you," the Chairman tells her.

He's seen the movies and read the comics. Rather than imprison her, or unmask her, or even stop and gloat over her they're going to kill her. Now. And he knows her costume is bulletproof, so...

He signals to his henchmen. They start pouring gasoline on the floor. The various gang bosses and henchmen make an orderly exit. The Chairman flicks his zippo lighter and tosses it into the centre of the room.

The room is ablaze.

Black Orchid has a few seconds to go before the flames reach her. With a superhuman display of strength she breaks the left-hand manacle. Then the right-hand manacle. Then the bars across her chest and feet. She starts to fly upwards and --

WHOOMPF!

The flames reach the gas tanks on the side of the room, and explode. The Black Orchid's trailing wings start to crumple and burn; her costume is burning; her face is burning. She falls to the floor on fire.

We pull away from the burning building as it collapses, and pull back into the night. We move across the city and out to the outskirts of town, until we reach a huge old country house, with a greenhouse (glasshouse) in the garden.

Moving in through the glasshouse doors we see a profusion of black orchids near the door. Further back into the darkened glasshouse the blooms get larger and stranger. Here are flowers a foot long, two feet long, or larger.

At the farthest end of the glasshouse is a bloom over six feet long. As we look at it the petals begin to tremble, then unfold to reveal themselves as the petals/wings of another Black Orchid. And she is screaming...

The opening page from the original series proposal.

To Art Young & Bob Wayne, DC Comics.

<u>Black Orchid Promo</u> -- version #2.

<u>SOME PEOPLE HAVE SECRET IDENTITIES...</u>
<u>SOME JUST HAVE SECRETS.</u>

She's a mystery. A strange, secretive, purple-clad flying woman
who fights crime -- quietly. She calls herself after a flower
that doesn't exist. There is, remember, no such thing as a black
orchid.

<u>Black Orchid</u> is a journey into secrets.

Along the way you'll meet some familiar faces. You'll meet some
new ones. Like Black Orchid -- you've never seen <u>her</u> before.

You'll travel from the grey of the city to a glade in the heart
of a vanishing wilderness. You'll pass some dark places on the
way -- places you might not want to go back to alone.

It's a journey through love and darkness and madness and horror,
from death to redemption. There's hope in there too, I hope.
And there are flowers.

We will show you strange beauty. Dave McKean's stunning painted
artwork in <u>Black Orchid</u> is like nothing you have <u>ever</u> seen
before.

For that matter, neither is Black Orchid.

It's her journey as well. The story of her haunted past and her
hunted present. And it's a journey that treads a new path
through the DC universe, tracing connections that were always
there, but never followed back. Until now.

It starts with an orchid and a bud against a sunset sky.

And secrets...

Neil Gaiman

Promotional text supplied by Gaiman for use in advertising and marketing.

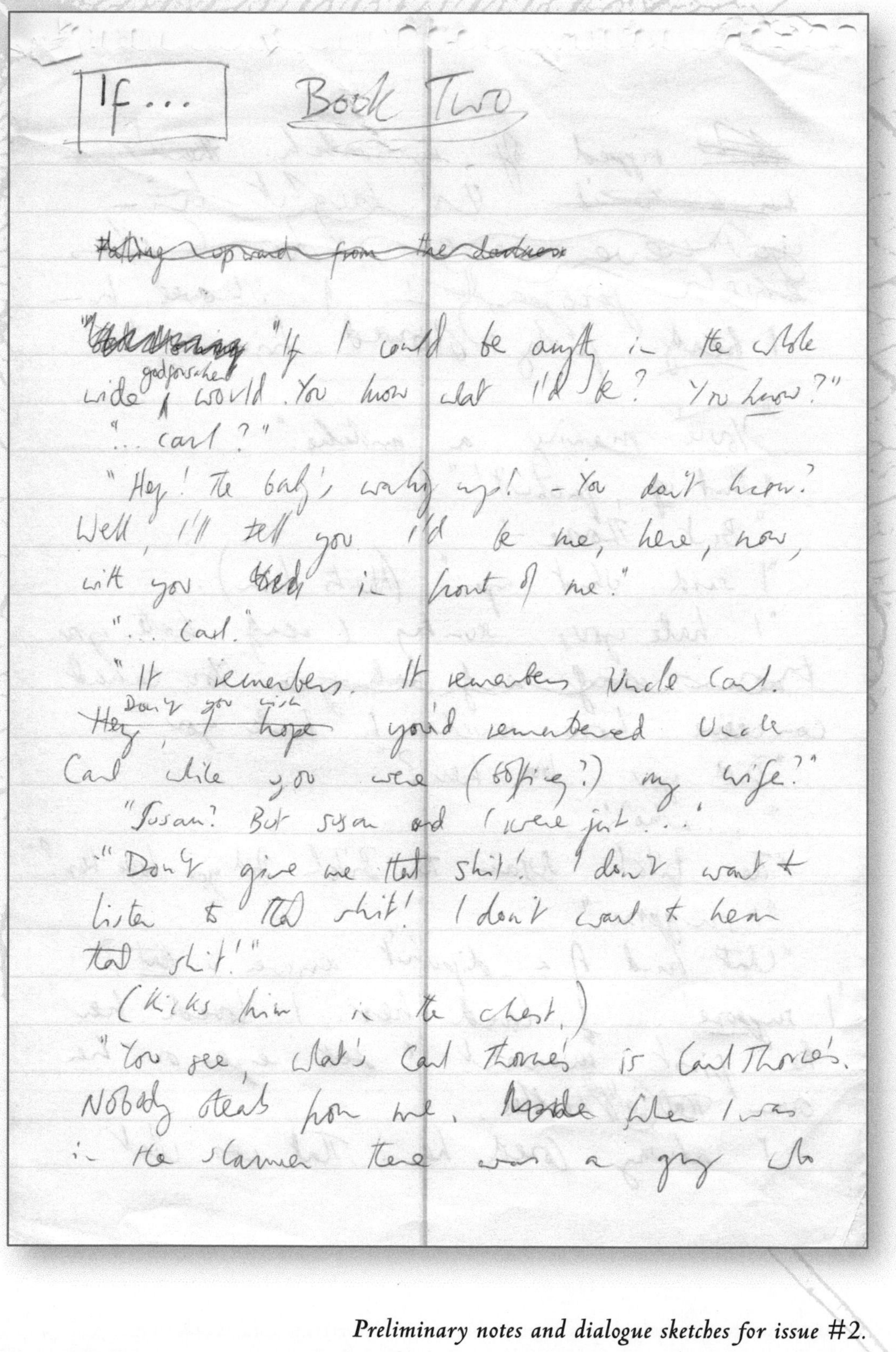
If... Book Two

~~Falling upward from the darkness~~

"If I could be anything in the whole godforsaken wide world. You know what I'd be? You know?"

"... Carl?"

"Hey! The baby's waking up! – You don't know? Well, I'll tell you. I'd be me, here, now, with you ~~tied~~ in front of me."

"... Carl."

"It remembers. It remembers Uncle Carl. ~~Hey, I hope~~ Don't you wish you'd remembered Uncle Carl while you were (boffing?) my wife?"

"Susan? But Susan and I were just..."

"Don't give me that shit! I don't want to listen to that shit! I don't want to hear that shit!"

(Kicks him in the chest.)

"You see, what's Carl Thorne's is Carl Thorne's. Nobody steals from me. ~~Inside~~ When I was in the slammer there was a guy who

Preliminary notes and dialogue sketches for issue #2.

~~She~~ ripped off my watch. ~~There's no touch to it~~ I taught him — ~~you never ever touch other people's property~~ I showed him. I ~~Really~~ fucking showed him."

"You're making a mistake."

"Shut up, fuckwit!"

"But Thorne—"

"I said shut up." (Hurts him).

"I hate you, scumbag. I really hate you. ~~I really really hate you.~~ You cannot conceive how much I hate you."

"Did you love her?"

"... who?"

"The Bitch. Susan the Bitch. Did you love her?"

"I suppose."

"What kind of a dipshit answer is <u>that</u>? 'I <u>suppose</u>'. I loved her. I loved her the first moment I set eyes on her over that (blackjack) table.

I always loved her. That was what

made it all so hard.

"When she left me, that hurt. When I
found she was here with you, that hurt
too. And when the Bitch testified against
me,

...that really hurt me. That hurt bad.

"I wanted to kill you, back then.
I said to Lex, I want to off the creep.
He vetoed it..."

"Damned if I can remember why, Hazel.
"Damned if I can remember why.

"So you loved her. Susan. The most beautiful,
the most... you with your stupid little body!
I'm surprised you didn't wanna marry her."

"I...did..."

"Huh?"

"I did... But I never touched her. But the
night she was...killed... I asked her, in
the taxi... to...marry me. And then —"

"Then they damped you guys out. Yeah
I remember it. Like it was yesterday

1. Falling leaf.
2. Carl Rant
3. Carl Rant
4. Carl Ranting and breaking up the Lab
5. Carl breaking up things and going outside
6. Greenhouse
7. Greenhouse
8. Greenhouse/baby Orchid
9. Baby in the tree
10. Carl phones Luthor
11. Baby Orchid found by Black Orchid. (Abstract.)
12. Orchid and Baby Waiting in tree ?.
13. Carl waiting inside.?
14. Luthor arrives
15. His men survey the house and report back.
16. Luthor tells Calr he's useless. Has him bundled into car,
17. Orchid finds Phil in house.
18. Car drives followed by Orchid.
19. Luthor's helicopter takes off.
20. Carl is thrown off the pier.
21. Carl is drowning. A purple blur moves into the water.
22. Carl is rescued.
23. Orchid and Baby fly home.
24. Train station.
25. Train travel. (Reflections in window.)
26. First Arkham sequence. travel to Arkham, refused admittance.
27. Arkham cont. Ends on a crow.
28. Begins on Seagull with Carl staggering round.
29. Carl wandering through the city, sort of crazy.
30. Carl wandering. talking to himself. (Meets Dave?)
31. carl gets into warehouse. I'd like to go from some actual
missiles to...
32. Trees of gotham central park. Orchid leaves the child there.
33. Orchid goes into bars.
34. Batman encounter in alley.
35. Long first panel shot of Batman swooping off. Orchid child
and little old man.
36. Arkham: Romper room.
37. Walking through Arkham.
38. Ivy
39. Ivy
40. ivy
41. arkham
42. She leaves Arkham. We see the baby being knocked out and
placed in a truck.
43. Batman and her walk in the grounds of Arkham.
44. Batman and her take their leave. // Luthor being reported
back to.
45. Orchid searching central park.// carl in his warehouse.
46. Orchid flying// see truck heading out of gotham.
47. Orchid flies south.
48. Orchid falls.

Gaiman's page breakdown for issue #2.

Black Orchid Book II

Draft Script

"If I could..."

OK. Well, writing the first part was easy; I have a suspicion
that this is going to be a lot harder. Now, I've decided to make
no concessions to the fact that people may not have read Book 1.
I thought about recapitulating the plot, or whatever, but I feel
that since this is a prestige format book one would hope that we
are bringing our readers with us from book one, and that it's
probably still on the shelves. So this continues where Book 1
ended.

Cover:

As with book 1, a granite background, with a flower outlined on
the left. A long strip down the right contains a painting of
Black Orchid. We are closer to her than we were on the first
cover, and the colour scheme is very heavily green, to distingush
it at a glance from the covers of I and III.

The Text Reads:
Black Orchid. Book Two of Three. By Neil Gaiman and Dave McKean.

Inside Front Cover:
Indicia and a like grey orchid -- the same as the first book.
Above the indicia is the title.
Title: "If I Could..."

Scene 1.

We are in the laboratory in Phil Sylvian's house, although this
is not immediately apparent. The lab was seen briefly in Book One
when Orchid walked through it. Now, however, all the lights are
on, and we will get to see most of it: around the room there are
high tables, loaded with fragile and expensive looking equipment:
retorts, distillation paraphernalia, and other scientific
(botanical and biological) fixtures. These shouldn't be pseudo-
scientific, or examples of superscience -- it's the kind of stuff
you really would see in this kind of situation. There are a few
flowers and plants in various states of dissection and experimen-
tation around the laboratory as well. In one corner is a small
computer screen. Also there's a glass canister full of gas.

After knocking him out, smashing a bottle over his head, at the
end of part one, Carl dragged Phil into the Lab. He's waiting for
Phil to wake up.

An excerpt from the draft script for issue #2.

As the story starts, on the first page of the comic, Phil is coming round. We are looking from his viewpoint at a falling leaf -- part of his dream. Behind the leaf, solidifying slowly is a grey, insubtantial figure. This is Carl Thorne.

Phil:

Captions:

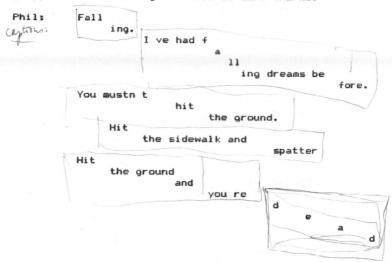

Fall
        ing.

I ve had f
            a
              ll
                ing dreams be
                                fore.

You mustn t
            hit
                the ground.

Hit
    the sidewalk and
                      spatter

Hit
    the ground
              and
                  you re

d
    e
        a
            d

Carl: If I could be anything in the whole wide
        world -- anything! -- I'd be me.

        Here. Now.

        With you.

        'N what do you think of that, then?

By this time we've seen or are about to see Phil. He's lying at Carl's feet. He looks terrible. The bottle was broken over the right side of his head. It broke the skin, and has also caused fairly massive bruising and swelling. Blood has poured (this is a head injury and they're messy things) down one side of his head, soaking and matting his hair, and drying to a reddish brown, in which the wetter or fresher areas are blood coloured.

Phil: Who...are you? Wh-why...?

Carl moves closer.

Carl: You don't recognise me? Aw, c'mon. You came
        to my wedding...

(Between panels, a sepia picture of a radiant Susan introducing Carl and Phil. Carl's shaking Phil's hand and grinning. They all look ten years younger and they all look pretty good. Susan's in a wedding dress, holding her bouquet in one hand. Carl, in a suit, is holding a champagne glass.)

Phil: You're... Carl Thorne. Susan's ex-husb--

Carl: Yeah.

            You remember that much, huh?

            You shoulda remembered that while you were
            messing around with my <u>wife!</u>

Phil: But I didn't --

Carl's smile is gone. Up until now he's seemed sort of nice. Suddenly he's crazy. Carl kicks Phil, hard, in the chest. (He's not holding anything back, here. This is violent and unpleasant.)

Phil: <u>Unng!</u>

Carl's smile is back.

Carl: Don't tell <u>me</u> that stuff, geek. I <u>know</u> **what**
            men do to women. I <u>know</u> what that <u>slut</u> was
            like.

            Susan.

Phil: Thorne. Uh, <u>Carl, listen,</u> we're both reasona-
            ble men, we can work this out. Why don't you
            let me <u>up</u> and I'll, uh, we can, uh, <u>talk</u>
            about this, uh...

Carl has turned away. Is asking a rhetorical question to the room.

Carl: She coulda had <u>me!</u> Dammit she <u>did</u> have <u>me!</u>
            And she <u>went</u> to <u>you?</u>

            Just the <u>thought</u> is enough to make me sick to
            my goddam <u>stomach.</u> It is to <u>puke,</u> jerk.

(Carl is crying. It's maudlin, drunk, sorry for-himself crying, not genuine grief.)

            I mean, I <u>loved</u> her, y'know? I really <u>did.</u>
            Snf.

            <u>I</u> (Kicks Phil hard in the ribs)
            <u>LOVED</u> (Kicks Phil again)

                    Her... (Kicks Phil -- about the face this
                    time.)

Phil looks a mess. The cuts have opened up on the side of his
head, and fresh blood is flowing.

Phil: Unh. Stop. Please stop if you - unh - for
            god's sake, just...

He wipes the blood from his face with his hand.

            She's dead, Carl. This won't bring her back.

Carl: Of course she's dead, geek.

(Between the panels, a sepia image of Susan's death. While the
other panels of Carl (masked) shooting her while Phil looks on
have always been impressionistic/dream related, this one is for
real. Susan is being machine gunned.)

Carl: Who the hell did you think it was that killed
            her?

Phil: ...You?

(Another sepia between-panel. Phil is bent over Susan's dead
body, extracting blood with a syringe.)

Carl leans back against one of the benches. Finishes the last of
the bottle he's holding. Grins.

Carl: I think I'm gonna give you a lesson from my
            hard-won experience. Say 'Thank you, teache-
            r.'

Phil: Oh god, this is --

Carl kicks him.

Carl: Say it!

Phil: Thank you...teacher...

Carl: You see, one thing I've learned is that
            there's two kinds of people. There's the
            wolves, and there's the sheep.

            Now the Wolves --

            That's me --

            We go out and we fight for what we want. We
            take what we want. We goddam kill for what we
            want.

BIOGRAPHIES

Neil Gaiman is the creator and writer of the internationally acclaimed comics masterpiece THE SANDMAN, which was the first comic book to receive mainstream literary recognition when issue #19 ("A Midsummer Night's Dream") won the World Fantasy Award for Short Fiction in 1991. His most recent installment in the series, THE SANDMAN: OVERTURE, won the Hugo Award for Best Graphic Fiction in 2016.

He is also a *New York Times* best-selling author of books, short stories, films, and graphic novels for all ages. Some of his most notable titles include *American Gods*, for which he received the Hugo, Nebula, Bram Stoker, and Locus awards; *The Graveyard Book*, which was the first book to ever win both the Newbery and Carnegie medals; and *The Ocean at the End of the Lane*, which was named Book of the Year in 2013 by the UK's National Book Awards. His most recent title, *Norse Mythology*, is a retelling of the stories of the Norse gods and giants from the *Prose and Poetic Eddas*, and he recently adapted *Good Omens*, the novel he co-wrote with Sir Terry Pratchett, into a six-part television series with the BBC and Amazon Studios.

In addition to his work on the page and screen, Gaiman is a professor in the arts at Bard College. He has four children and is married to the writer and performer Amanda Palmer.

Dave McKean has illustrated over 80 books and graphic novels, including *Signal to Noise, The Wolves in the Walls, Coraline* and *The Graveyard Book*, all written by Neil Gaiman, *The Magic of Reality* by Richard Dawkins, *The Fat Duck Cookbook* by Heston Blumenthal, and *What's Welsh for Zen* by John Cale. He has written and illustrated the multi-award-winning *Cages, Pictures That Tick 1* and *2*, and *Black Dog: The Dreams of Paul Nash*. He has also directed several short films and three features: *MirrorMask, The Gospel of Us* with Michael Sheen, and *Luna*, which premiered at the Toronto International Film Festival in 2014. He lives on the Isle of Oxney in Kent, UK.

One of the industry's most versatile and accomplished letterers, **Todd Klein** has been lettering comics since 1977 and has won numerous Eisner and Harvey awards for his work. A highlight of his career has been working with Neil Gaiman on nearly all the original issues of THE SANDMAN, as well as BLACK ORCHID, DEATH: THE HIGH COST OF LIVING, DEATH: THE TIME OF YOUR LIFE, and THE BOOKS OF MAGIC.